DAVID FINCHER
MIND GAMES

Adam Nayman

Little White Lies

DAVID FINCHER
MIND GAMES

Adam Nayman

Foreword by Bong Joon-ho

Abrams, New York

CONTENTS

FOREWORD: BONG JOON-HO

때로는 영화들을 두 가지 부류로 나눠 볼 때가 있다.
'곡선의 영화'와 '직선의 영화'

그렇다. 지극히 개인적이고 주관적인, 심지어 폭력적인
구분이다.

하지만 지금 내가 필름코멘트 또는 카이에 뒤 씨네마에 이
글을 쓰고 있는 것은 아니니까,
읽는 분들도 너그럽게 이해해주시기 바란다.

어쨌든, 영화를 보다보면
인물과 카메라의 움직임, 화면의 조형과 심지어 음악에
이르기까지 …

곡선과 원의 느낌으로 물결치는 영화가 있다.
'곡선의 영화'다

반대로 직선과 직각의 날카로움이 러닝타임을 지배하는
영화들도 있다.
'직선의 영화'다.

내게 펠리니, 쿠스트리차의 영화들은 대표적인 곡선
영화다.
반면, 대표적인 직선영화는 큐브릭 그리고 데이빗 핀쳐의
영화들이다.

특히 핀쳐의 영화는, 그냥 직선이 아니라 면도날로 베어낸
듯한 직선의 영화다.
보는이의 눈과 가슴이 쓰라릴만큼, 예리하게
베어내버리는 영화.

그렇기 때문에, 그의 영화를 보고 나면,
언제나 마음의 한구석에서 붉은 피가 흘러내리는 느낌을
받는다.

그의 정확하고 아름다운 카메라 무브먼트가 남기는
잔상들.

오로지 그 앵글, 그 사이즈 여야만 하는, 확고하고
대체불가능한 프레이밍의 쾌감.

자로 잰듯 냉정하게 평행선을 유지하며, 결코 무의미하게
요동치지 않는 카메라와 피사체의 거리

이 모든 것에서 오는 순수한 영화적 흥분이, 흘린 피에
대한 보상으로 주어진다.

조디악 살인마의 먹잇감이 될 노란택시가 수직의 머리
위에 떠있는 허공의 카메라와 함께
(실은 full vfx 쇼트이긴 하지만 어쨌든) 싱크로나이즈 된
움직임으로 직각의 우회전을 하는 …
그런 '극단적인' 쇼트를 예로 들고 싶지는 않다.

경이로운 뮤직비디오를 찍을 때부터, 초창기의 〈에어리언
3〉〈세븐〉〈파이트 클럽〉등을 만들었을때부터,
그는 이미 우리시대 최고의 스타일리스트이자 테크니션의
자리에 있었으니까.

오히려 가장 무색무취하게 찍혀진 조디악 막바지의 그 장면.
제이크 질란할이 마침내 그 가게를 찾아가 존 캐롤 린치의
얼굴을 바라볼 때.

또는

제시 아이젠버그가 (결코 오지않을) 루니 마라의 응답을
기다리며
멍하게 랩탑컴퓨터를 바라볼 때,

그 순간 우리는 조용하고 깊은 '영화적 출혈'을 느낀다.

가장 고전적이고 덤덤하게 (또는 덤덤한 척) 찍혀있는
그 쇼트들에서,
우리의 무의식은 뒤흔들리고, 마음의 한복판이 날카롭게
베어져 나가는 것이다.

그것은 오로지 데이빗 핀쳐만이 만들어 낼 수 있는, 길고
섬세한 일직선의 핏자국이자,
무척이나 아름다운 영화적 흉터이다.

2021.03.16
봉준호

I tend to classify the films I watch into two types: the "linear" type and the "curvilinear" type. It's a highly subjective method of classification, and the division I impose is severe, perhaps even violent.

But I'm not an expert critic writing for *Film Comment* or *Cahiers du Cinéma* so I hope readers will forgive the crudeness of my method.

Some films abound with curves. From the characters to the movement of camera to the mise en scène and music, we are enveloped by waves and circular motions. These are the curvilinear films.

Some films are strongly dominated by sharp lines and angles throughout their running time. These are the linear.

For me, Fellini and Kusturica exemplify curvilinear filmmaking while Stanley Kubrick and David Fincher are masters of the linear.

Fincher, especially, pushes beyond the linear and cuts us with such razor-sharp precision that it almost hurts our eyes and hearts to watch.

In fact, whenever I finish watching one of his films, I feel like my heart is bleeding from its corner.

His exactingly beautiful camera movements leave haunting, lasting impressions while the fiercely self-assured composition—where no other angle or framing is even imaginable—gives you complete satisfaction. The camera and subject always move in parallel, maintaining the perfectly measured distance, never engaging in a needless tug of war.

The purity of cinematic excitement derived from these moments more than compensates for the figurative blood that is shed.

I do not wish to talk about 'extreme' examples like the stunning overhead shot of the yellow cab in *Zodiac* (actually a VFX shot), where the camera makes a seamless 90-degree turn with the car, the target of the serial killer, in perfect synchrony.

Since the days of his awe-inducing music videos and early features like *Alien 3*, *Se7en*, and *Fight Club*, David Fincher has unquestionably been the greatest stylist and technician.

But I'd rather talk about the much more plain, unflamboyant shot of Jake Gyllenhaal staring at John Carroll Lynch in the hardware store near the end of the film.

Or when Jesse Eisenberg blankly stares at his laptop waiting for a reply from Rooney Mara in *The Social Network*. A response that never comes.

These are the moments that quietly deliver the deepest cuts, causing us to bleed helplessly.

In those classic and (seemingly) ordinary shots, our unconscious is violently shaken and our hearts sharply pierced in the middle.

It's a long, straight, precise cut that only David Fincher can administer, and we are left with a beautiful cinematic scar.

March 16, 2021
Bong Joon-ho

AN INTRODUCTION

1. THE MOST DANGEROUS GAME

Robert Graysmith: "Man is the most dangerous animal of all . . . I knew I'd heard that somewhere. *The Most Dangerous Game*! It's a movie about a guy who hunts people for sport. People! The most dangerous game!"
Paul Avery: "Who's that guy there?"
Robert Graysmith: "That's Count Zaroff."
Paul Avery: "Zaroff? With a 'Z?'"

Early on in David Fincher's *Zodiac* (2007), newspaper cartoonist Robert Graysmith connects the cryptic, coded messages and astrological pseudonym of an elusive serial killer to the villain of the 1932 horror classic *The Most Dangerous Game*, about an aristocratic psychopath who conceives of leisure time as a matter of life or death.

The films of David Fincher are filled with dangerous games and apex predators: Think of Kevin Spacey's John Doe in *Se7en* (1995), God's Lonely Man meting out Biblical punishments until a real rain comes to wash the scum off the streets; or *Gone Girl*'s Amy Dunne (2014), marionetting the people around her in a live-action Punch-and-Judy show. Sinister conspiracies proliferate in *The Game* (1998) and *Fight Club* (1999), paranoid thrillers whose protagonists come to wonder who's been jerking them around, and why. Elsewhere, the director's protagonists bristle with exceptional, rebellious intelligence: what connects *Fight Club*'s insurgent Tyler Durden to *The Social Network*'s (2010) squirmy Mark Zuckerburg to the deadpan heroine of *The Girl with the Dragon Tattoo* (2011) is a skepticism about the status quo and a desire to disrupt it, whether by building systems, penetrating them or crashing them to the ground.

Few directors are as fascinated by the idea of high-level, top-down control—from the panopticonal prisons of *Alien 3* (1992) and *Panic Room* (2002) to the power-gaming political machinations of *House of Cards* (2013–2018)—and few are as equipped to exercise it. Over the past thirty years, Fincher has cultivated and maintained a reputation that precedes him of formal rigor and technocratic exactitude, of moviemaking as a game of inches. In 1939, surveying the backlot at RKO, Orson Welles said that "the cinema was the biggest electric train set any boy ever had"; the most succinct way of defining the cinema of David Fincher might be to say that, on his watch, the trains run on time.

2. THE EYES OF ORSON WELLES

In 1943, the popular CBS radio program *Suspense* aired an audio-play adaptation of *The Most Dangerous Game* starring Orson Welles as Count Zaroff—a superb piece of casting drawing on the star's fame as Lamont Cranton in *The Shadow*, the phantasmic vigilante claiming to know the evil that lurked in the hearts of men. A few years earlier, in 1940, Welles had been planning a film version for RKO of Joseph Conrad's novel *Heart of Darkness*, also about a mad exile presiding over an isolated kingdom; in 1942, after decamping to Brazil to shoot the ultimately unfinished Pan-American odyssey *It's All True*, Welles had become perceived as an American Kurtz, an idealistic iconoclast playing dangerous games with studio money.

Few filmmakers have ever been as magnetic, onscreen or off, as Welles, which is why he has been impersonated in so many period pieces and biopics over the years. There exists an entire subgenre of what might be called Welles-centric cinema, with Fincher's 2020 drama *Mank* as the latest and most contentious contemporary addition. In it, Welles is played by the British actor Tom Burke and stares out at the world with a lazy, half-lidded confidence in his own supremacy. Until he's challenged, at which point his dark pupils blaze and dilate, combining with his close-cropped Caesar haircut and goatee to give a man referred to in the film by his collaborators as a "dog-faced prodigy" a devilish aspect. This Welles is glimpsed mostly in swift interstitials which gesture towards his yearning to play Kurtz, as well as his incarnations in *The Shadow* and *The Stranger* (1946), and the hard-driving tyro of *Citizen Kane* (1941)— the film whose genesis serves

as *Mank*'s backdrop. But his appearance suggests another filmmaker as well. As *Rolling Stone*'s K. Austin Collins observes, "the Orson Welles of *Mank* bears a humorously cutting physical resemblance not only to the real Welles but to one David Fincher."

If the visual equation of Burke-as-Welles-as-Fincher in *Mank* is indeed intentional—a big if—it's probably better characterized as a throwaway joke rather than a serious attempt at directorial self-portraiture. Where Welles was apt to stand at the center of his movies as an ever-mutable emblem of his own authorship—with later, gone-to-seed incarnations in *Touch of Evil* (1958) and *Chimes at Midnight* (1966) plumbing tender, aching depths of self-deprecation—Fincher imposes his presence through the actions and psychologies of thinly veiled proxies: Clockmakers and safecrackers; hackers and terrorists; detectives and serial killers.

3. REPEAT OFFENDER

It is serial killers that provide the clearest throughline for Fincher's filmography to date. *Se7en*, *Zodiac*, and the Netflix original series *Mindhunter* (2016–2019) form an unofficial trilogy preoccupied with procedure and predation; taken together, they suggest that to know what evil lurks in the hearts of men is also to look inside oneself. No American filmmaker of the era—or probably ever—has become so identified with serial-killing as Fincher, a fact he acknowledges and plays for self-deprecating comedy. "I know that if a script has a serial killer—or any kind of killer—in it, I have to be sent it," he told *Playboy* in 2014. "I don't have any choice." Cue Peter Lorre's anguished comments at the end of *M* (1931) about the terror of being ruled by unconscious compulsions, and the metronomically consistent output of *M*'s director Fritz Lang provides one possible measuring stick for Fincher's own obsessive, geometrically precise cinema. "Lang's vision of the world is profoundly expressed by his visual forms," wrote Andrew Sarris in 1968, and there are uncanny echoes of the German master's iconography throughout Fincher's movies. The two directors share a love of maps, mazes and underground chambers; both are fascinated by systems and structures, crime and punishment, and especially, puppet-masters and patterns. In *M* Lang used Edvard Grieg's insinuating "In the Hall of the Mountain King," to herald the appearances of his villain; in *The Social Network*, Fincher repurposed the composition as comically contrapuntal accompaniment for a rowing regatta.

"I am profoundly fascinated by cruelty, fear, horror and death," Lang once said, and the idea of auteur-as-serial killer is not as objectionable or absurd as it may seem. Both are practices ruled by repetition-compulsion, of clues left, consciously or not, for investigators to pore over. The most distinctive filmmakers—the ones whose surnames get transformed into adjectives synechodizing their sensibility—are recidivists: repeat offenders tempting critics and audiences into the roles of psychological profilers. To say a film is Fincherian—Fincher-esque, Fincher-ish, whatever—is to note that it is preoccupied on some level with process, minutiae, and the accumulation of details, a task that drives his characters and directs us on how to watch along with them, often over their shoulders in set-ups that enmesh us in investigations and interrogations. "We're collecting all the evidence," explains Morgan Freeman's detective of his lonely, observational vocation in *Se7en*. "Taking all the pictures and samples, writing everything down, noting the times things happen . . . putting everything into neat little piles and filing it away on the off chance it will ever be needed in the courtroom."

The case against David Fincher as an auteur actually begins with Fincher himself. In the introduction to the 2014 anthology *David Fincher: Interviews* Laurence Knapp writes that his subject "hates being defined as an auteur," but that [Fincher's] "need for absolute control . . . compels him, begrudgingly, to take ownership of his work." This double vision of the director as a reluctant figurehead and a control freak converges in *Gone Girl* in the scene where a high-priced trial lawyer coaches a client to sharpen his posture, delivery and affect for an upcoming television show appearance. Placed near the midpoint of a thriller spring-loaded with Hitchockian tropes (alternate title: *The Lady Vanishes*), the lawyer's hectoring rhetoric and Pavlovian methodology—"I will drill you"—serves doubly as a Hichcockian-cameo-by proxy and a poke at Fincher's own persona—an ethos best summed up by his oft-quoted observation that, "people will say that there are a million ways to shoot a scene, but I don't think so . . . I think there are two, maybe, and the other way is wrong."

Gone Girl dramatizes this strident, my-way-or-the-highway ultimatum through a plotline that's explicitly about wresting and maintaining control, whether in a marriage, a media narrative, or over the perception of reality itself. *Gone Girl* also fulfills Fincher's other motto about being interested in "films that scar" (the subtitle of Mark Browning's 2010 critical study on the filmmaker), a comment dating back to 1996, when Fincher was promoting *Se7en*. That film's equation of torture with a lacerating, Old Testament morality was meant to be taken with a grain of salt (all the better for rubbing in open wounds), but its motif of mutilation extends forward through *Fight Club*—whose would-be insurgent burns his hand with lye as a mark of committment to the cause—to *The Girl with the Dragon Tattoo*—with its avenging-angel heroine carving scarlet letters into the chest of her rapist—to *Gone Girl*—which obliges its Hitchcock blonde to wield a boxcutter against an enemy—and slots alongside the other provocations that give Fincher's films their sense of morbid showmanship.

In his 1968 auteur study *The American Cinema*, Sarris placed prospective candidates for the pantheon into alliterative categories: "Lightly Likeable"; "Expressive Esoterica"; "Strained Seriousness." Fincher's chapter, then, could plausibly be called "Saleable Sadism," or maybe "Cool Cruelty."

Cruelty is, above all, lucid, and it is a virtuoso, disconcerting lucidity—a stark tactility of objects, environments and behaviours topped off by a floating sense of being somehow above it all—that has served as the hallmark of Fincher's style. His films operate primarily inside established genre structures yet manifest as frictionless slipstreams of smooth camera movement, swift cutting, and a mesmerizing shallow-focus *mise-en-scène* that guides the viewer's attention like a stage hypnotist's bauble. While not conventionally "dreamy," the resultant sense of hyper-focus—all those details, details, details—induces a trippy, almost subliminal feeling of incipience, of being caught (or wired into) a developing situation It's a cinema not of eyes wide shut, but a bleary, paranoid doomscrolling—literally so in the extremely online trilogy of *The Social Network*, *The Girl with the Dragon Tattoo*, and *Gone Girl*. "I'm interested in just presenting something and letting people decide for themselves what they want to look at," Fincher has said, limning the contradiction between his grueling, and-the-other-way-is-wrong process and the hovering omniscience of the final product—an all-seeing, all-knowing and seductively all-powerful perspective akin to Lang and his "vision of the world" but with an element of Spielbergian kineticism and Kubrick's sardonic, master-shot malevolence.

In November of 2020, prior to the release of *Mank*, the *New York Times Magazine* published an admiring profile of the director entitled "David Fincher's Impossible Eye." In it, staff writer Jonah Weiner duly rehearsed the obsessive aspects of Fincher's directorial persona—his neo-Apollonian precision; his Sisyphyian penchant for multiple takes; his Darwinian approach to on-set and post-production problem-solving—while also providing him a platform with which to bemoan the resulting (yet, as the author implies, fully accurate) perception of himself as a "dictatorially fussy artiste." "I get it, 'he's a perfectionist,'" Fincher said, speaking in the third person, and as ever, protesting a bit too much. "No, there's just a difference between mediocre and acceptable."

That the difference between mediocre and acceptance is sometimes imperceptible to the naked eye—or to the actors dishing to interviewers about Fincher's dictatorial fussiness—scarcely matters: shoot it all, and let God sort it out in the editing room. The more pressing difference, for critics, is between exterior excellence and Sarris's long-standing auteurist criteria of "interior meaning"—the ephemeral "substance" laying latent and hypothetically hardening in the crevices and fissures of a filmmaker's style, holding it together and rendering it inhabitable for the long haul. "I want to build a house with my films," said Rainer Werner Fassbinder (who might have added that his desired super-structure was, undoubtedly a flop house). One argument against Fincher might be that he makes condos: Sleek, steely, luxurious and interchangeable. *Fight Club* is catalyzed by the sabotage of just such a dwelling, by a character whose distaste for mass-production (and the people swallowed up in its operations) belies the fanatical efficiency of his own domestic terror campaign. It is in the split between Tyler Durden and his lucid-dreaming host—the drone who yearns for a Devil to sit on his shoulder and direct his hand—that we see one of best arguments if not for than about Fincher: Whether it's possible for a genuine artist to emerge out of—or transcend—the world of advertising, or if perusing this particular Gen-X-era filmography is just like flipping through a Sharper Image catalog.

What in another director's work could be taken for a signature in Fincher's sometimes resembles a barcode, or a logo or a quality-control warranty. He made his name in commercials and he has not left them behind; in February of 2021, he oversaw a Super Bowl ad for Anheuser-Busch whose climactic black-and-white passages employed the same greyscale cinematographic values as *Mank* (and some of the same off-brand sentimentality as well). Fincher is not the only auteur who's made ads—David Lynch does it all the time—but Lynch's spots somehow belong solely to him while Fincher's commercials, like his music videos, created blueprints for other leaders in the field. The commercials Fincher devised in the 1980s and '90 for Levis, Nike, and Coca-Cola helped to redefine the visual style of television advertising in the US; this is usually the point in the deposition where somebody notes that the production company Fincher helped to build as an off-Hollywood talent incubator was called Propaganda Films.

4. STORY OF THE EYE

How David Fincher got ahead in advertising had everything to do with the particular "look" of his TV spots, a mix of gloss and grit typically more seductive than the products they were hawking. A 1988 ad for Colt 45 strings together a set of vivid, inexplicable signifiers—moving statues; snapping rottweilers; Billy Dee Williams; a beer can superimposed on a modernist office tower in the same style as the opening titles of *Panic Room*—and locates poetry in the sheer incongruity of elements. The ends-justify-the-means tagline—"it works every time"—becomes a joke that's also a statement of purpose. The same confidence propels the music videos that Fincher made for superstars like Madonna, Aerosmith and the Rolling Stones, all previously adept in the field of

image management but willing to submit fully to the director's vision—transformatively so for Madonna and George Michael, who along with the less-dynamic Don Henley featured in three clips nominated side-by-side-by-side for "Video of the Year" at the 1990 MTV Video Music Awards. It's a record for a single director that will probably never be broken, and indicates just how successful and influential Fincher had become in the videodeome by his mid-twenties. Even more than Michael Bay, Spike Jonze or Hype Williams—or any of his fellow Propagandists—Fincher's trajectory exemplifies the migration and refinement of what scholar Marco Calavita defines as "MTV aesthetics" into American feature filmmaking, which in turn explains some of the wariness around his work from old-guard cinephiles. If Fincher's career is the story of an eye, the case could and has been made that his exquisitely visualized features are ultimately, to paraphrase another one of Sarris's catchy chapter categories, less than that which meets it.

In a way, the case for and against Fincher is very much the same: He's a skilled technician with a basic instinct for what will startle or unnerve the mainstream audience that his movies—especially the unlikely blockbuster that was *Se7en*—have done their part to help shock-train. The always polarized reception of his films was never more evident than in the discourse around *Mank*, a tonal outlier in his filmography and a niche project that likely would not have been greenlit at a $25 million dollar budget for any other currently working US filmmaker—and certainly not by any studio other than Netflix, a company unconcerned with selling tickets or filling seats (and which had done its part for Welles's legacy by helping to subsidize, reconstruct and distribute his unfinished film *The Other Side of the Wind*). *Mank* is a movie produced, distributed and

analyzed under the auspices of auteurism even as it dramatizes Fincher's ambivalence about auteurism as theory, practice and mythology, whether applied to himself or anybody else—Orson Welles included. "I think anybody who knows anything, knows trying to get the troops to all face the same direction is f*****g hard," Fincher told *Collider*'s Nev Pierce in 2021. "And the notion that you're going to be able to beautifully articulate for all of these different interests, educational backgrounds, generations, this entire group that's separated by all these different personal experiences, and simply impart to them how you'd like to see it happen then sit back in your chair and watch it unfold." Or, as Fincher put it succinctly in 2012 to *The Playlist*: "The reality of moviemaking is, y'know, it's a rat fuck."

Working from this philosophical position, *Mank* whittles away termite-style at the myth of the Total Filmmaker, with Welles as foil for its actual protagonist, Herman K. Mankewicz, a lowly wordslinger—and self-styled rat fucker—who takes center stage in a behind-the-scenes melodrama whose details are derived in part from Pauline Kael's 1971 essay "Raising Kane." Kael's dubious and debunked piece of scholarship-cum-gossip used Welles as a strawman to air its author's grievances about Sarris and his auteurist acolytes, and *Mank*'s release became an occasion for its relitigation, as well as to re-enumerate the list of grievances between Mankewicz and Welles that culminated in the older man's comment after learning the pair were to share the Best Original Screenplay Academy Award for *Citizen Kane*: "I am very happy to accept this award in Mr. Welles's absence, because the script was written in Mr. Welles's absence."

5. F FOR FAKE

Mank uses this morning-after crack as a final punchline. Suffice to say that a sizable contingent of critics and scholars forgot to laugh. "[David] Fincher is not worthy of carrying [Orson] Welles's viewfinder," wrote Joseph McBride on the website Wellesnet, an image belittling its target's vaunted compositional abilities as well as the symbolic superimposition encoded, however incidentally, into *Mank*'s Welles-as-Fincher sight gag. McBride's withering essay "*Mank* and the Ghost of Christmas Past" served as a rallying point for online detractors on social media platforms like Letterboxd and Twitter even as *Mank* was received happily in mainstream critical outlets as a proverbial "love letter to the movies"—the same designation applied to *The Artist* (2011), which won the Oscars *Mank* seemed to be angling for. "*Mank* and the Ghost of Christmas Past" comes from its own place of movie love, and it's as persuasive and authoritative as you'd expect from a scholar who literally wrote the book on Welles (in fact, three of them), and is motivated to take the movie and its creator to task—or maybe, as per *Gone Girl*, to the woodshed—for myriad historical inaccuracies and a lack of supplication to a true visionary.

It did not help Fincher's case with the keepers of Welles's flame (or his own ready-and-eager haters) that, during *Mank*'s European press tour, he evoked the tongue-in-cheek assessment offered by his predecessor about his career at the opening of 1971's *F for Fake*, that he "started at the top and [had] been working his way down ever since." Uncharitably categorizing Welles a "showman and a juggler"—a theatricalized persona that *F for Fake* wields with purpose, like a magic wand—Fincher referred also to the "delusional hubris" and "filthy immaturity" that he believed derailed Welles's prospects post–*Citizen Kane*. As McBride implies, there is potentially some projection at work in this simplistic and unsympathetic assessment; while there is no plausible equivalency between *Citizen Kane* and *Alien 3*, it's worth remembering that, in 1991, presiding in England over a $60 million franchise sequel coming apart at the seams, the twenty-nine-year-old Fincher was characterized in the entertainment press (and in the boardrooms at 20th Century Fox) as delusional and hubristic himself—a neo-Wellesian intruder in Hollywood by way of MTV rather than the Mercury Theater, flailing away hopelessly on his first studio assignment.

After licking his wounds in the aftermath of *Alien 3*—a movie re-edited by the studio and that he continues to disavow to this day, which would make it something more like his *The Magnificent Ambersons* (1942)—Fincher ended up inflicting some damage of his own with *Se7en*, a smaller and freer movie with a larger reach and a longer shadow. In terms of form and execution, *Se7en* remains probably the most perfect movie by an inveterate perfectionist—perfect, maybe, to a fault—and its success, achieved not in spite of its violent extremity but as a direct result of it, rerouted Fincher's reputation from failed caretaker of a profitable intellectual property into a valuable studio asset in his own right. It was a reversal of fortune that allowed Fincher to go back to Fox in 1999 with serious cachet and set the terms for making *Fight Club*, a wild, palpably imperfect-to-a-fault movie that inspired the kind of obsessive devotion from fans (and contempt from the establishment) that transforms a filmmaker from a promising pro into a cult hero—and, later, into a commodity, regardless of his films' views on commodification. (*Fight Club*, for the record, is against it.)

From there, Fincher's progression from pulp (*The Game* [1997]) to prestige (*The Social Network* [2010]) to prestige pulp (*The Girl with the Dragon Tattoo* and *Gone Girl*) is well-documented, but originally Fincher had planned to follow up his debut with *Mank*, which would have not only delayed or cancelled *Se7en* outright but jump-started the unflattering critical comparisons between himself and Welles decades in advance. *Mank*'s script was written by the director's father, Jack, a reporter for *Life* who gravitated towards Kael's account of Mankewicz as a knight-of-the-Algonquin-roundtable swashbuckler—an image materialized by the script's multiple quotations of Don Quixote. For Fincher, Jr., though, the first draft of the *Mank* script went too far in vilifying Welles—who never finished his own version of Quixote—as a "showboating megalomaniac." As Fincher told *Vulture* in 2020: "Once I had gone to Pinewood for two years and had been through a situation where I was a hired gun to make a library title for a multinational, vertically integrated media conglomerate, I had a different view of how writers and directors needed to work . . . I kind of resented [the script's] anti-auteurist take. I felt that what [it] really needed to talk about was the notion of enforced collaboration: You may not like the fact that you're going to be beholden to so many different disciplines and skill sets in the making of a movie, but if you're not acknowledging it, you're missing the side of the barn."

6. MIND GAMES

"If you get into it," Welles once said of Hollywood, "you have no right to be bitter. You're the one who sat down and joined the game." It would seem that since the chaotic experience of *Alien 3*, Fincher has managed to have it both ways, holding onto and honing his bitterness (never more biliously than in *Mank*, which climaxes with its hero regurgitating his dinner at his host) while demonstrating a prodigious ability and willingness to play a game at which he proved a quick study. Games and gamesmanship figure centrally in Fincher's films, with their atmosphere of choking claustrophobia and clearly delineated boundaries—most notably in *Alien 3* and *Panic Room*, which reconfigure their enclosed settings as three-dimensional chess boards—and shared emphasis on rules and regulations: "Figuring out the object of the game is the object of the game"; "The first rule of fight club is you do not talk about fight club." His procedurals are organized conceptually around clues and codes; the common denominator between the murderers and murderesses of *Se7en*, *Zodiac*, and *Gone Girl* is a tendency to mediate their messages through

cryptic communiques. In *Panic Room*, a mother and daughter holed up in the midst of a home invasion try to get the attention of their neighbor by improvising a morse code signal with a flashlight; in *The Girl with the Dragon Tattoo*, a gone girl sends a family member pressed flowers annually on her birthday, a gesture meant to comfort him in her absence but which has the effect of nearly driving the old man mad.

This playfulness finds its most menacing and unsettling expression in *Zodiac*, which centers on a pair of characters mutually addicted to and adept at mind games: movie buff Robert Graysmith, who "likes puzzles," and the Zodiac-with-a-Z, who likes making them. But it's also present in the pranks of the Space Monkeys in *Fight Club*, singing a Nirvana-style smiley face ten stories high into the facade of an office building, or the pungent whiff of teen spirit wafting off of *The Social Network*, whose accidental billionaires exploit a hot-or-not video game algorithm to hook users throughout Harvard's student body. The Kaelian hypothesis of *Mank* is that Mankewicz intended the script for *Citizen Kane* as a between-the-lines attack on William Randolph Hearst, but in Fincher's strategically fictionalized retelling of the myth, the rules of the game get twisted; *Mank*'s sense of melancholy—and uncommonly direct political valence—emanates from its namesake watching helplessly as an offhand remark about cinema's powers of suggestion inspires his bosses to subsidize a series of newsreels dismantling the progressive California gubernatorial candidacy of Upton Sinclair. Here, the suspended disbelief that Arliss Howard's Louis B. Mayer cynically refers to as the "magic of the movies" mutates into Fake News, and a truth-teller unwittingly enables the creation of Propaganda Films.

It is in the dilemma of a man who prides himself as being sand rather than oil in the gears of the Hollywood moloch recognizing his own culpability as a cog where *Mank* begins to make sense both as drama and as a fragmented self-portrait of the artist, with Fincher caught somewhere between Welles and Mankewicz and, in a way, sympathetic to both. The rigidly regimented attitude towards the division of creative labor that has led the director to rule out the possibility of ever writing his own scripts—insisting in interviews that he's too busy doing his job to attempt anybody else's—is, paradoxically, at the heart of what some saw as *Mank*'s vexing veneration of a behind-the-scenes scribe at the expense of a multi-hyphenate. Hence the claims by Fincher's champions that his is a throwback, genuinely old-school auteurism, closer in spirit and execution to Hitchcock—who always sent out for his screenplays, and who imposed his personality and obsessions through the sheer force and singularity of his technique—than to Welles, or even generational peers like Paul Thomas Anderson or Quentin Tarantino, who inhabit the more protean writer-director mold and are perhaps easier to advocate for as a result. That, and they tend to lead with an eccentric, ecumenical cinephilia miles broader than Fincher's valorization of the New Hollywood: Asked to list his favourite movies of all time, Fincher produced a list with no films earlier than *Citizen Kane* and none later

than *The Terminator* (1984), and with '70s touchstones like *All The President's Men* (1975), *Chinatown* (1974), and *Taxi Driver* (1976) crowded near the top.

Laurence Knapp has written that Jack Fincher's advice to David on the eve of entering the film business was "learn your craft—it will never stop you from being a genius." By selecting, personalizing, and (depending on one's mileage) elevating either original or literary adaptations, Fincher cuts a Langian figure of craftsman-as-genius—or, to paraphrase Thomas Schatz, of a genius in but not necessarily of the system. For detractors, it is this same comfortable, prolific ensconcement in Hollywood—and lately Silicon Valley, as exemplified by the exclusive deal with Netflix that subsidized *House of Cards* and *Mindhunter* as well as *Mank*—that renders suspect Fincher's verdict on Welles' lack of "discipline" and gives the lie to his own multinational, vertically integrated output, especially when his "uncompromising" attitude is measured against genuinely Wellesian rebelliousness. *Fight Club* is probably Fincher's most contentious movie and, apart from *Alien 3*, the one that caused its financiers the most grief; it imagines and even celebrates the collapse of the global financial order. But its subversion—like its sadism—is saleable; all those dorm rooms plastered with the smirking images of Brad Pitt and Edward Norton as movie-star Che Guevaras had to be paid for, after all.

"Fincher is I suppose what you would call an anti-authoritarian filmmaker, with certain conspiracy-minded tendencies, [and] I wonder if he ever wonders why these positions have cost him so little, personally and professionally," writes Nick Pinkerton, who on several occasions has taken it upon himself to be a Witness for the Prosecution against the idea of Fincher as the new Otto Preminger—a half-step down from Lang, but more prestigious than being the new Alan J. Pakula. These uncharitable sentiments are echoed by Kelly Dong, who measured the gap between Welles and Fincher in her scathing review of *Mank* by sarcastically noting that "in each trailer [for the film], the word "Netflix" appears above a parodied replica of RKO's radio tower logo." In *Cinema Scope*, Andrew Tracy picks up Dong's rhetorical thread and jabs it where it hurts most: Directly through Fincher's Impossible Eye. "[*Mank*'s] fetishism," Tracy writes, "is bereft of

the intense focus and attention to detail that real fetishism feeds off of . . . the film's aesthetic texture not only makes a distorted claim about how movies looked Back Then, but also enrols Kane itself into this distortion."

Distortion is a loaded word, but the fact of *Mank*'s digital production and alignment with a global streaming giant—and Fincher's own revealing, putatively sarcastic appraisal in the *New York Times* of his work for Netflix as "medium-priced challenging content"—fits the profile of the director as anodyne usurper against a venerable photochemical tradition—in other words, as a faker.

Where the even-more-vertically integrated Christopher Nolan and the more plausibly Wellesian PTA—who, getting ahead of the anti-Fincher curve, wished testicular cancer on the director in response to *Fight Club*'s survivor-group satire—advocate for the artistry and ontology of the analogue image (and as a result probably won't ever end up working for Netflix), Fincher has embraced digital on both a practical and ideological level, and also as a fetchingly retro disguise. As A. S. Hamrah writes, "[Fincher] insists that digital technology has special powers that allow him to praise film without using it. Since permanently making the switch away from celluloid, Fincher has alternated between a gleaming immediacy and the retro, faux-cellulois fetishism of *Zodiac*, *The Curious Case of Benjamin Button* (2008), and *Mank*.

In the same way that his movies tingle with a feeling of convergence—of gliding towards some serenely sinister vanishing point—Fincher's beta-test process keeps pushing irrevocably forward. He has adopted and refined a state-of-the-art approach somewhere between reinventing the wheel and optimizing its rotation. With this in mind, the tenderest of Fincher's onscreen surrogates is the mournful watchmaker M. Gateaux in *The Curious Case of Benjamin Button*, a craftsman-genius bound and determined to reverse time's flow and resurrect the past through the novel application of technology; through this lens, Fincher's

most atypical feature is transformed, warmly, into an allegory of itself.

Befitting his affinity for Kubrick—himself the owner of an impossible eye, and who thought nothing of soliciting NASA for deep-space lenses to capture candlelight dinners in *Barry Lyndon* (1975) and pioneered the use of the Steadicam for *The Shining* (1980)—Fincher swears by the process of shot stabilization, which provides him and his cinematographers a buffer of excess visual information that allows them, as per the *New York Times*, to "correct the slightest trembles, lurches and late starts in any given frame." In "David Fincher's Impossible Eye," Weiner finds Fincher guilty on charges of perfectionism and calls as a character witness Steven Soderbergh, himself an avowed gearhead who marvels at his contemporary's human-viewfinder acuity ("Oh my God, to see like that? All the time? Everywhere?") as well as Brad Pitt, who duly reminisces about "doing a shot, and there would be the slightest imperceptible wiggle from the camera and you could see Finch literally tense up—like, it physically hurts him."

Mitigating such pains (the better to inflict them on others) is at the core of Fincher's project, including the integration of subtle-to-invisible computer generated imagery at every level of his *mise-en-scène*. The director began his career as a matte illustrator and camera operator for George Lucas's Industrial Light and Magic, and was obliged for his debut to use an animatronic monster as a major character. *Alien 3*'s creature is a vivid creation—faster and more agile than its antecedents, despite the hobbled, funereal pace of the movie around it—yet it's telling that in the thirty years since Fincher has moved steadily away from such explicitly fantastical imagery (although he was at different points attached to *Spider-Man* and a remake of *20,000 Leagues Under the Sea*). Like Robert Zemeckis, whose *Forrest Gump*

(1994) is like an evil older twin to *The Curious Case of Benjamin Button*—and which was, before *Mank*, our director's clearest stab at Oscar glory—Fincher is a problem solver, but he doesn't flaunt or immerse in artificiality. Instead, he employs CGI to either subtly augment or convincingly re-create everyday reality—as in the period backdrops of *Zodiac*, *The Curious Case of Benjamin Button*, and *Mank*—or else to create a reality that feels enchanted around the edges, as with Brad Pitt's synthetic Benjamin or the villainous, mirror-image Winklevosses in *The Social Network*, heroes and villains straddling both sides of the uncanny valley. Where Alfred Hitchcock notoriously used Hershey's chocolate syrup for *Psycho*'s shower sequence, the crime-scene splatter patterns and arterial spray in *The Girl with the Dragon Tattoo* and *Gone Girl* are entirely CGI—as good a metaphor as any for how these later paperback adaptations can somehow feel prurient and bloodless at the same time, like pulp pureed in a high-end blender.

7. THE MAN BEHIND THE CURTAIN

Fincher's ILM heritage as, in his words, a "special effects lettuce picker," places his career suggestively in the shadow of *Star Wars* (1977). George Lucas's movie marks the dividing line between the New Hollywood and the New New Hollywood—between geniuses flowering in the system and being either weeded out or humbled by corporate John Does for sins of idiosyncratic excess. These film-historical tensions are enfolded into Fincher's biography, with its two-best known bits of trivia: That the director, who was born in Denver, Colorado, in 1962, grew up living down the street from Lucas in San Anselmo, California (the same idyllic suburban stretch prowled in the early '70s by the Zodiac), and that he was inspired to make movies by a behind-the-scenes documentary about the production of *Butch Cassidy and the Sundance Kid* (1969)—an endearingly deconstructive variation on directorial origin myths about wide-eyed kids mesmerized by the "magic of the movies." David Lynch, as we all know, grew up obsessed with *The Wizard of Oz* (1939); even at the age of eight, Fincher was paying attention to the men behind the curtain. "It never occurred to me that movies didn't take place in real time," he told the Canadian website *Art of the Title* in 2012. "I knew that they were fake, I knew that the people were acting, but it had never occurred to me that it could take, good God, four months to make a movie."

Forty years later, Fincher's own exhaustive methodology has been chronicled in numerous behind-the-scenes featurettes and documentaries, as well as a set of director commentaries as candid, informative and hilarious as any ever recorded. If it's possible to be imperiously personable, that's how Fincher presents himself in making-of materials, which is in truth preferable to the lofty proclamations or evasions of filmmakers more eager to spend their tracks talking about themes. Whether narrating alone or in a group—the *Fight Club* commentary with the director, Pitt and

Norton functioning almost as well as a boys-club one-liner generator as the movie it's attached to—Fincher is funny, candid and unapologetic. "Carrie Coon learned the hard way that the last thing you want to do in one of my movies is eat . . . she probably sucked down at least five-and-a-half pounds of french fries," says Fincher on the commentary for *Gone Girl*, painting the actress as a victim of his need to shoot even the most basic set-ups over and over again; his anecdote about doing an end run around the Writer's Guild of America on *The Game* by inserting three minor characters in the film named "Detective Andrews," "Detective Kevin," and "Detective Walker" to honour the (uncredited) punch-up by his friend Andrew Kevin Walker recasts the taskmaster as a prankster.

Because he's spoken so frequently on the record about how he makes movies and why—piling on takes not to demoralize or denigrate actors but to create the conditions for spontaneous variations of performance and more editing-room options—Fincher doesn't come off as much of an enigma. If *L'affaire Mank* indicates anything, it's that he's become increasingly unfiltered over the years, although an Indiewire story in February of 2021 that the director had denied Marc Maron permission to release their two-and-a-half-hour episode of the comedian's podcast *WTF with Marc Maron* (a freewheeling chat show whose slovenly lack of structure is the source of its appeal) is surely destined for the Fincher Files, along with the leaked 2014 email from producer Scott Rudin to Angelina Jolie and Amy Pascal comparing him (jokingly, but still) to Adolf Hitler, and Robert Downey Jr's jibe that he "was a perfect person to work for [Fincher]," because "I understand gulags." Honorable mention goes to Jodie Foster recalling the making of *Panic Room*: "It would be take eighty-five, I'd be standing behind him and he'd say, 'which one is better?' and I'd say 'honestly, you're a very sick man, there is nothing different between those last three takes.'"

Claims that Fincher is press shy are contradicted by the existence of Knapp's invaluable interview anthology, which only goes up to 2011 and would be twice as long if it compiled all the profiles and features that have proliferated in the decade since. The description refers more accurately to the director's private life, which while hardly mysterious, is rarely a topic of conversation and bereft of Wellesian extra-curriculars (although in 2020, the Canadian music video critic Sydney Urbanek went semi-viral on Twitter for a Substack essay speculating on Fincher's personal relationship with Madonna in the early '90s). In 1996, Fincher married producer Ceán Chaffin, a Los Angeles native whose credits include every one of her husband's movies since *The Game*, and is the closest (though not quite-longest serving) in a group of constant collaborators whose steadfast loyalty and dedication complicate the image of the director as tyrant. The corollary to Fincher's motto that "the other way is wrong" is that he's always willing to argue his position; in several of the interviews that follow in this book, one recurring scenario is the director ceding on set or in the editing room to somebody with a better idea and the temerity to fight for it. While Fincher is undoubtedly fixated on power, he is equally driven by responsibility, both towards the movies themselves and the very auteurist fallacy he rails against with clockwork regularity. "My name's going to be on [a movie]" he told *Esquire* in 2007. "It's a different thing when your name is on it, when you have to wear it for the rest of your life, when it's on a DVD and it's hung around your neck. . . . It's your albatross."

8. THE RULES OF THE GAME

This book organizes David Fincher's feature films together into five major sections, punctuated by interviews with a number of important technical collaborators and bookended by a consideration of his music videos and commercials and an extended postscript about *Mank*, which was nominated for ten Academy Awards and won two. Although it's meant as a detailed critical overview of Fincher's work to date, this book also has a number of omissions, foremost among them *House of Cards*. The series deserves a place in Fincher's oeuvre as his first foray into streaming—and also the larger history of "Prestige TV" as one of the original "Netflix Originals"—but the extent of his work didn't ultimately provide enough inspiration (or enough material) to warrant its own chapter. The show's evocation of Clinton-era Washington rot—exemplified by Kevin Spacey's sneeringly Shakespearean White House fixer Frank Underwood, a complicitous manipulator dishing *sotto voice* asides to the camera—feels closer to the work of Fincher's *Social Network* writer Araon Sorkin than any of Fincher's own features; his direction of the first two episodes is slick and effective without evincing the same interest or commitment as the pilot for *Mindhunter*, for which he helmed another nine episodes and served as a runner during its superlative second season.

As mentioned above, *Mindhunter* exists as a complement-slash-extension of *Se7en* and *Zodiac*, both in its law-enforcement milieu (more realistically sketched than in *Se7en*'s) and dramatic focus on the moments where professional curiosity mutates inscrutably into personal obsession (the transformation that gives *Zodiac* its heart of darkness). The multifaceted relationship between Fincher's procedurals for film and TV is the subject of Chapter One, "Crime Scenes." Chapter Two, "Maximum Security," examines images and themes of incarceration and surveillance in *Alien 3* and *Panic Room*, leveraging their shared status as genre films—a sci-fi sequel and a home invasion thriller—against the backstories of their similarly troubled productions. In both films, there is a feeling of a director trying to find his way into—and out of—the material, with varying degrees of success and freedom.

Chapter Three, "Reality Bites," contrasts two consecutive movies from Fincher's '90s period awash in sensations of paranoia and helplessness, whether as the result of an externally orchestrated conspiracy or an extended schizophrenic episode. Each film can be also seen as an allegory of Fincher's filmmaking process, and way cinema creates and sustain alternate realities; the "experiential book of the month club" peddled by

Consumer Recreation Services in *The Game* and the X-rated "reel changes" spliced into family matinees by Tyler Durden in *Fight Club* kid and critique ideas of creativity and consumption.

Chapter Four, "Uncanny Valleys," covers the first two Fincher films deliberately positioned by their distributors (and their director) as awards-season competitors: *The Curious Case of Benjamin Button* and *The Social Network*. These prestige pictures also intersect in their use of sophisticated digital special effects and underlying literary textures, one a Fitzgeraldian tale of the Jazz Age finessed into a meditation on time and mortality, the other a twenty-first st century status update about the mores and manners of a similarly aristocratic class clicking anxiously into the void.

Inevitably, Chapter Five, "His and Hers," pairs *The Girl with the Dragon Tattoo* and *Gone Girl*, dual bad romances and paperback adaptations that also serve as commentaries on cultures of omnipresent misogyny in America and abroad. Eyes down, guard up and fingers perpetually poised at her keyboard, the pierced and battered Lisbeth Salander holds her own in a world of Men Who Hate Women; her late excursion into glamorous, blondes-have-more-fun cosplay anticipates the reverse masquerade of "Amazing" Amy Dunne, an urban(e) overachiever who tries to slum it on the run as a country girl and gets taken by a pair of locals with nothing to hide before reasserting her mastery of image management for the unblinking (and uncomprehending) gaze of the TV Eye.

The question of what to do with *Mank* is trickier. It's impossible to take the long view on what is at the time of writing a brand new movie whose discourse is still forming (and which, on the eve of our going to press, won two Academy Awards for Best Production

Design and Best Cinematography). It's also clear that for all its ambivalence about "the magic of the movies"—explicated as late-capitalist sleight-of-hand in which "what [the moviegoer] bought belongs to the man who sold it"—it's a film imbued as much by sentiment as cynicism (as thickly interlaced as art and commerce), and while by no means an endpoint in Fincher's story (his next project, the assassination-themed drama *The Killer*, has already been announced), it does serve as a reasonable late-career prompt to begin considering his legacy.

With its focus on life and art—and the criss-crossing ways they imitate each other—*Mank* is very much a movie about legacies: Those of Mankiewicz and Welles, certainly, but also Jack Fincher, who prophesied the ratio of craftsmanship and genius that has come to define his son's directorial legend, and instilled the (frankly Wellesian) fascination for games that plays out in so many of his films. "At one point in his life, [Jack] wanted to create a board game," Fincher told *Little Whites Lies* in 2020. "He disappeared down a well for about a month trying to make this card game work. And then, at one point, someone showed him a magic trick that he became obsessed with, and he worked his way all around it, trying to figure out how this thing was done."

For those of us consistently fascinated by his films, figuring out how David Fincher does the things he does—which is to say the hard way, or the way where the other way is always wrong—is actually the easy part: The evidence is out there, on the record and ready to be put in neat little piles and trotted out on the occasion of each new movie. What's more difficult—and maddening, and addictive, and exhilarating—is trying to make the case for what it all means, if anything; in trying to reconcile how a director so drawn to disruption exudes such smoothness; whether it's possible to truly rage against the machine while working inside it; how an adman transitions into an artist (or if he ever really transforms at all); and how movies that feel so airtight can also be so spacious, whether plunging us into hidden depths like Michael Douglas toppling towards his destiny at the end of *The Game*, or else unwinding as labyrinths where the monster in the middle of the maze waits patiently to meet our gaze.

Fincher has called *Zodiac* "a movie about a cartoonist and a murderer who never got caught." At its climax, Robert Graysmith locks eyes with a man who may or not be the most dangerous animal of all, and the way Fincher directs the scene, he can't be sure of what he sees, and neither can we. It's there, in the space between focus and understanding—between metaphysical mystery and high-definition clarity, between control and its limits—that David Fincher invites us to play mind games.

HARD-SELL: MUSIC VIDEOS AND COMMERCIALS

"It's a celebration of cop-out," wrote Pauline Kael of *2001: A Space Odyssey* (1968). Where the final shot of Stanley Kubrick's film seemed intelligently designed by its maker as a Rorschach Test—equally legible as an emblem of alien intervention, thermonuclear detente or a secularized Christ—Kael saw its floating Starchild as the mascot for a nihilistic sales pitch. "There's an intelligence out there in space controlling your destiny from ape to angel, so just follow the slab. Drop up."

This diss comes near the end of Kael's 1969 essay "Trash, Art and the Movies," which limns the pernicious influence of hard-sell advertising techniques on cinema in a transformational decade. "Movies," Kael said, "are now often made in terms of what television viewers have learned to settle for [. . .] the 'visuals' of TV commercials are a disguise for static material, expressive of nothing so much as the need to keep you from getting bored and leaving."

For Kael, patient zero in this contagion was the British director Richard Lester, a formalist with a faster, zippier style than Kubrick (as showcased in the same year's kaleidoscopic *Petulia*, shot by Nicolas Roeg) and who proved easier to imitate as well. A few years earlier, Lester had been handpicked by the Beatles to direct *A Hard Day's Night* (1964); the group was attracted to the spontaneous, black-out sketch irreverence of Lester's television commercials and short films. The genius of a *Hard Day's Night* lay in the way it revealed its seams as a promotional showcase—a nifty trick that Kael felt was fated to backfire. "The Beatles," she wrote, "were thought to be anti-Establishment, but with astonishing speed, the advertising establishment has incorporated rebellion [. . .] anarchism becomes just another teenage fad, another pitch."

In time, *A Hard Day's Night* and the movies made in its wake—the Dave Clark Five's *Catch Us If You Can* (1965); Gerry and the Pacemakers's *Ferry Cross the Mersey* (1965); the Monkees' *Head* (1968)—would come to be acknowledged as direct progenitors of MTV. (Lester once reputedly received a vellum scroll citing him as the "father" of music videos; he responded with Lennon-esque drollery by asking for a paternity test.) On August 1, 1981, MTV launched its network in the US with a video by by a band basing their name on the Beatles and their glam aesthetic on "Starman"-era David Bowie: the Buggles' "Video Killed the Radio Star," is staged by director Russell Mulcahy as an oblique, playful exploration of the song's paradigm-shifting subtext. A young girl listening to the radio is transported suddenly into a silvery, jump-suited future, a one-way ticket to ride: "We can't rewind, we've gone too far."

MTV cofounder Bob Pittman described Mulcahy's video as an "aspirational statement," although what it aspired to—and augured for both the format and realms of commerce and culture beyond it—was more complicated. The new channel's motto, "I Want My MTV," spoke a dialect of radical subjectivity and also conspicuous, addictive consumption requiring a steadily digestible stream of product. What was at stake now for pop musicians (and their managers, publicists and record labels) was adaptation and innovation in a medium that would swiftly weed out weaklings while helping others to thrive. If the correlation between image-making and album sales was not absolute, the chart dominance of music-video adepts like Prince, Cyndi Lauper and Michael Jackson—whose "Billie Jean" offered a sinister update of *A Hard Day's Night*—hinted that whichever radio stars video didn't kill, it could only make stronger.

One secondary byproduct of MTV's launch was its role in propagating "the second British invasion," with English New Wave acts like the Buggles, Def Leppard, Adam Ant, and Eurythmics using witty and ingenious videos to shore up their American popularity. "A revolution in sound and style—lying somewhere between artful ingenuity and pure pop fun—has taken root in this country over the past year and a half," wrote Park Puterbargh in *Rolling Stone* in 1984. "Much like the first great explosion of pop culture upon mass consciousness, which commenced with the Beatles' arrival in America in February 1964, the primary impetus for all this has been emanating from the far side of the Atlantic."

But there was also a third, parallel British invasion, as movies by UK filmmakers like Adrian Lyne, Alan Parker, Hugh Hudson and Ridley and Tony Scott—all, like Lester, ad-world adepts with their sharp eyes trained on Hollywood—channeled some of the same anxieties once flagged by Kael. Not only was Lyne's *Flashdance* (1983) edited to the same swift rhythms as the pop promos airing around the clock on MTV, its musical numbers were actually staged as self-contained vignettes that could be excerpted by the network for heavy rotation. In *Body Double* (1984), Brian De Palma mocked this development by having his hapless hero stumble into the shoot for a Frankie Goes to Hollywood video; one reason that the director could absorb that film's commercial flop was the cash he pocketed the same year shooting Bruce Springsteen's "Dancing in the Dark." Such moonlight was a sign that the MTV-Hollywood relationship was a two-way street—not just a training ground for newcomers like live drama and

advertising had been in the 1950s and '60s, but a means for veterans to support themselves in a turbulent industry (a condition replicated in the present tense by the auteur exodus towards Netflix).

In the early 1980s, movies—be they trash, art, or whatever else—were becoming invaded by music-video aesthetics (a trend allegorized by Paul Thomas Anderson in *Boogie Nights* [1997] which uses shot-on-celluloid porn as a corollary to a fading New Hollywood). As prophesied by Kael, cinema was being increasingly instrumentalized as a tool for ancillary promotion, with prevalent production placement and a proliferation of non-human characters who could be easily reproduced for merchandising purposes.

It was into this fraught ecosystem that the twenty-three-year-old David Fincher broke with Industrial Light and Magic to make his first commercial: A thirty second PSA commissioned for $7000 by the American Cancer Society called "Smoking Fetus."[1] It remains the primal scene of his work: Creepy, funny, visionary, and above all subversive; in the space of just thirty seconds, the spot weaponizes special effects, product placement and even postmodernism itself, settling on the eerie, perversely hilarious image of a baby smoking a cigarette in utero. It's a *tableaux* modelled visually on the last shot of *2001*, here connoting the dangers for women of smoking while pregnant. In his 1979 ad for Chanel No. 5, Ridley Scott, the most successful of the British invaders, had invited viewers to "share the fantasy"; working with a fraction of the budget, Fincher proved determined to shock his audience into awareness. In the parlance of the high-concept, hard-sell mid-80s, the message of "Smoking Fetus" amounted, basically, to "Just Don't Do It."

"I didn't want to be the guy who's loading the magazines for the guy who was shooting the scene for the guy who had the whole thing in his head," said Fincher of his exodus from ILM. "I wanted to be the guy who had the whole thing in his head." The bad-seed imagery of "Smoking Fetus," which was whipped up by the director and a group of fellow technicians on off-hours from their studio gigs, served nicely as a calling-card for Fincher's own prodigal-punk posture. By being deemed "too graphic for broadcast" on several networks, it marked its director as an *enfant terrible*: a new style Starchild. (In this analogy, the similarly up-and-coming Michael Bay, waiting his turn in line after Tony Scott to man the Jerry Bruckheimer-Don Simpson action movie assembly line, was the Antichrist.)

After moving to Los Angeles, Fincher was contacted by a number of music video producers and performers seeking edgy treatments, including the Australian rocker Rick Springfield, who liked the director's idea to make a *Star Wars*–style video for his single "Bop 'Til You Drop."[16] The clip, which premiered on MTV in 1984, casts Springfield as a lanky savior figure in a post-apocalyptic landscape presided over by a monster whose skeletal, tech-noir physiognomy evokes H.R. Geiger. The storyline of an enslaved population rising up and out of chains, meanwhile, was straight out of Fritz Lang's *Metropolis* (1927), albeit with production design closer to *Mad Max* (1979) and *The Road Warrior* (1981).

The debt that "Bop 'Til You Drop" owes to *Alien* (1979) is obvious enough, and "Smoking Fetus," with its merciless uterine anxiety, owes one too. It's through comparison to Scott's contemporaneous "1984" Super Bowl commercial for Apple, however, that Fincher's mix of invention and irreverence comes into focus. Commissioned in the wake of *Blade Runner* (1982)— Scott's third consecutive foray into Kubrickian cosplay after *The Duellists* (1977) and *Alien*—the Orwellian allusions of "1984" were hyped as a landmark in the intersection of "cinematic" aesthetics and commercial short-form, but the ad's core (and unexamined) irony lay in its attempt to portray a nascent tech giant as a populist underdog, with the Macintosh reconfigured as a slingshot in the unblinking eye of IBM's Goliath. "Bop 'Til You Drop" also peddles a science-fictional image of rebellion, albeit one closer to a genuinely Lucasian

17.

B-movie, with Springfield liberating a colony of pale-faced worker drones through the sheer, insurrectionist power of slick, synthesized dance pop. (It's a good song, though it's no "Jessie's Girl" as *Boogie Nights* can attest). The difference lies in Fincher's recognition of his sci-fi mash-up's inherent ridiculousness, which kids processes of pop-cultural mythification without stripping them of their potency (a quality linking him to Roger Corman's stable of trash-artisans-turned-easy riders.)

What's immediately apparent in "Bop 'Til You Drop" and "Dance This World Away"[2]—another Springfield clip incorporating a surreal "Mr. Rogers" motif—is Fincher's instinct to metamorphize pop stars into larger-than-life icons—an idea literalized ten years later in his clip for the Rolling Stones' "Love is Strong"[5] (1994). That video would give Mick, Keith et al. their due as ninety-foot-tall Godzillas stomping through the downtown core while also insinuating that the former sixties bad boys had matured into dinosaurs: Mythification and mockery in one flashy package.

The progression from Rick Springfield to the Rolling Stones—from Top 40 to the rock-star pantheon—structures the first phase of Fincher's career as a music video specialist, a run culminating in the making, release and aftermath of *Alien 3* (certain sequences of which clearly had their roots in "Bop 'Til You Drop") and punctuated in the middle with the formation of Propaganda Films in 1986. For those worried that commercials were going to destroy the movies, Propaganda identified itself as an incursions home base; *Adweek*'s Richard Linnett described the company and its "provocative, socialist-constructivist logo" as new-style disruptors, "giving the bird to the

Cold War mindset." He might have added that that middle finger was attached to an outstretched hand. Most of the directors hired on at Propaganda ended up moving into features; in Fincher, who was one of the group's first recruits (and credited along with Greg Gold, Steve Golin and Joni Sighvatsson in 1987 as a co-founder) the group had hit upon a viable prototype. Fincher had put in time in the studio trenches and possessed an uncommon technical fluency to go with his behind-the-scenes experience; more importantly, he was uninterested in working outside the system like the Spikes-Mikes-Slackers-and-Dykes chronicled in John Pierson's indie-cinema *bildungsroman*. His impetus was different, and in the spirit of "Smoking Fetus" body-horror imagery, perhaps more Cronenbergian: He came from within.

In a 2010 interview for the *Believer* with fellow director Mark Romanek—who got his start at Propaganda's subsidiary division Satellite in the early 1990s—Fincher described what he saw as the similarities between the start-up operation depicted in *The Social Network* and the early days of Propaganda, particularly in terms of wanting to succeed on the industry's terms while also resetting them:

"You can understand how these people, these creative, hardworking dreamers, all come under one roof and try to change the way people think. I certainly saw your work as emblematic of a generation of filmmakers that was trying to say, hey, music videos don't have to be the redheaded stepchild of television commercials or films. They can be their own thing. If there had been a mission statement for Propaganda at that time, not to equate those two things, but it was the notion of all these kids in jeans with their laptops and their backpacks and their scooters, all coming to work at this place to tear a new asshole in this paradigm."

In *The Sundance Kids: How the Mavericks Took Back Hollywood*, James Mottram describes Propaganda's upstart vibe as "part Bauhaus, part frat house," and quotes Fincher's crack about the company functioning as a factory for potential clients: "You don't know what the fuck goes on there, but you put your money in one end and your cassette goes out the other." If anything, Fincher's description of this highly transactional exchange evokes a jukebox, and in his first few years at Propaganda the director shuffled indiscriminately through acts in different musical genres: UK and Canadian imports like the Outfield, Johnny Hates Jazz and Loverboy; American pop stars like Eddie Money, Patty Smyth, and Jody Watley. The recurring images, techniques and ideas in these early clips—high-contrast black and white photography (sometimes streaked or interspersed with hard, primary colors); sculptural lighting; forced perspectives; gliding camerawork; industrial backdrops; a self-reflexive focus on construction and assembly—evince a mix of control, adaptability and expressiveness, but not necessarily a distinctive artistic personality: In all cases, the musicians are front-and-center.

In 1988, Fincher worked with his first true superstars: Sting—filmed walking thoughtfully through a high-contrast Manhattan in the rather literal clip for "An Englishman in New York";[4] Steve Winwood—featured in a beer-soaked, sepia-tinged barroom performance for "Roll With It"[6]—and Paula Abdul, whose "It's Just the Way You Love Me"[3] plays smartly with the idea of commodification. The song is built around Abdul's claim to her lover that she's "not impressed with [his] material things," a shameless paraphrase of Madonna's earlier hit "Material Girl"; the video opens with a close-up of a CD slipping into a stereo and headphones being plugged into a jack, flashes of high-end, electronic product, echoing Fincher's Propaganda-as-pipeline analogy and also eroticizing the exchange between performer and consumer.

What Abdul's lively, athletic persona brought out in Fincher was admiration for her physical precision; to watch "It's Just The Way You Love Me" is to see a star and a director moving in sync. "I have no idea whether David Fincher thinks Paul Abdul can sing," wrote the *Ringer*'s Chris Ryan in 2020, "but I guarantee you he thinks she's an incredible choreographer and dancer . . . in this period of time he's fascinated with the human body and how it moves, and I think so is she."

Choreography dominates Fincher's videos for Abdul's 1988 album *Forever Your Girl*, which exalt the singer's physicality in different ways: the up-tempo calisthenics of "Straight Up"[7], which bisects the screen into black and white zones with Abdul moving freely between them, as if balancing the mise-en-scène with her body; the gentle mentorship narrative of "Forever Your Girl," which shows her modelling dance moves for a set of wholesome pre-teen apprentices (and anticipates her later maternal persona on *American Idol*); and, most enjoyably of all, the uninhibited vamping of "Cold Hearted,"[9] which expands from a jokey *Flashdance* parody (an audition at a prestigious dance academy) into a lubricious ensemble number with Abdul surrounded by writhing, gyrating hard-bodied male dancers—a configuration that Fincher repeated to more spectacular effect in the 1989 Madonna video "Express Yourself."[17]

In Mary Lambert's 1984 video for "Material Girl," Madonna flawlessly evoked the Marilyn Monroe of *Gentlemen Prefer Blondes* (1954) while flipping the Beatles' insistence that "money can't buy me love" into an anthem of Me Decade acquisitiveness. Actually, she chirped, yes it can, and thank you for offering. The key to Madonna's MTV success circa "Material Girl" was a mutability that didn't cancel out her personality but came to stand in for it; like David Bowie, Madonna was a shape-shifter, always different yet always herself. And, like Bowie—and the Beatles, Elvis, Prince, and even Rick Springfield in the forgotten *Hard to Hold* (1984)—she'd tried to transfer these chameleonic qualities to cinema, first in offbeat independent films like *Desperately Seeking Susan* (1984) and later as a full-fledged movie star in *Dick Tracy* (1990), which gave her a chance to play a femme fatale opposite a straight-arrow (and boring) Warren Beatty.

In 2020, the Toronto-based critic Sydney Urbanek's resurrected a 1993 interview Madonna did for the French television program *Le Journal du Cinéma* in which the singer expressed her affinity for the Austrian director Josef von Sternberg, and implied that Fincher had been the von Sternberg to her Dietrich on a quartet of videos that—more than any of his previous clips—made their director seriously famous and prompted speculation about the pair's personal relationship. (A *Vanity Fair* article published in 1991 seemed to confirm that they had been an item during some of their working relationship.) "We work on everything together, and we probably will do a movie someday," Madonna told Isabelle Giordano. "But I feel like the relationship I have with him is the one that she had with him, that Marlene had with von Sternberg . . . it's just almost like a silent language. It's with eyes, you know, when you know someone so well. And it also has to do with love. I think the director kind of has to be in love with the actress, and only want the best for her."

The Dietrich connection is made explicit in "Express Yourself," which at one point finds Madonna styled like the actress in von Sternberg's 1932 film *Blonde Venus*, and "Vogue"[8] (1990), which name-checks Dietrich during a mid-song, monotone inventory of twentieth century pop-culture icons alongside Rita Hayworth, Joan Crawford and Bette Davis. For "Express Yourself," working on his biggest-ever scale and with his biggest-ever star, Fincher crafted a video coursing with equal measures of confidence and confusion, revising "Bop 'Til You Drop"'s story of dystopia and liberation with Madonna cycling between guises as a siren, guru, CEO and submissive object of desire.

"Express Yourself" was released on Madonna's 1989 "divorce album" *Like A Prayer*, but the video makes the personal political, if not demagogic. Fincher places the singer at the top level of a stratified, post-industrial setting divided between a ruling class and well-muscled laborers toiling away sweatily in the trenches. The debt to *Metropolis* is even more apparent than in "Bop 'Til You Drop," largely drained of sci-fi elements but with a greater emphasis on class difference and a murkier notion of liberation. In this surreally hierarchical landscape, it's difficult to tell which of Madonna's ensembles— evening gown; negligee; power-suit; S&M cat-collar— are meant to be "real" and which are the fantasy projections, or whether the fantasies in question belong to the filmmaker, the singer, the characters, or the audience; coherence takes a back seat to provocation.

"I think I have a dick in my brain," Madonna wrote in the introduction to her 1992 book *Sex*; for critic B.L. Panther, Fincher's video for "Express Yourself" channels this "spiritual masculinity" to the point of dulling its star's feminist edge, using her as a vessel to express and inhabit patriarchal concepts of power, subjugation and "unbridled consumption." In other words, the video's confusion is counter-revolutionary, showcasing not a libertine, but the same old Material Girl. One year later, Fincher's video for George Michael's "Freedom! '90"[10] would get at gender-bending performativity from different angle, gathering together five of the world's leading supermodels— Naomi Campbell, Linda Evangelista, Christy Turlington, Cindy Crawford and Tatjana Patitz—at Merton Studios in London to lip-synch a song that could have just as easily been titled "Express Yourself."

In the lyrics to "Freedom '90," Michael professes a sincere, disarming ambivalence about his celebrity, success, and sexual orientation. Around the time of the song's release, he had vowed to not make another music video, and he sings dismissively of the "the brand-new face for the boys on MTV" he had flashed in the 1980s as part of the channel's telegenic all-star roster. Part of the appeal of the concept for "Freedom! '90" was that it would literally set Michael's forced, outdated image ablaze. Fincher's interest in deconstruction and reinvention takes an incendiary turn here;during the song's chorus, we watch as a Wurlitzer jukebox, electric guitar and vintage leather jacket—three items figuring into the the famous 1987 clip for "Faith"—burst spontaneously and gloriously into flame.

By appending the number "90" to the title of "Freedom!," Michael made it clear that he was entering a new decade and new phase. Fincher's video added five brand-new faces for the boys on MTV, kidding the increasing glamourization of pop stars (or else) by employing runway icons as delivery devices for a hit they had no part in recording. As sensual as any of Fincher's clips for Madonna but less preoccupied with power and its discontents, "Freedom! '90" unapologetically revels in the beauty of its silhouetted and semi-nude

18.

female headliners. But the emphasis—as in "Express Yourself"—is on models' collective pantomime of pleasure, inspiration and fulfillment, as well as the complex ways in which Michael's frustration with his own self-branding ("posing for another picture/ everybody's got to sell") gets filtered through the prism of the lip-synchers' own burgeoning celebrity.

Just as "Bop 'Til You Drop" and "Express Yourself" anticipate aspects of *Alien 3*, "Freedom! '90" contains images that Fincher would reprise later on in his career: The symbolic leather jacket and cleansing fire return in the title sequence of *The Girl with the Dragon Tattoo*, while the opening push-in on Linda Evangelista—framed through an open-backed chair and a percolating coffee-pot—rehearses the disembodied camerawork in *Panic Room*. It's tempting to comb through Fincher's music videos to draw parallels with his features, and sometimes, the calculus adds up: The crime-scene narrative of "Janie's Got a Gun,"[11] matches an uncharacteristically serious Aerosmith single about incest and murder to grim, floridly backlit glimpses of murder, crime scenes, and post-mortem forensics, like a police procedural in miniature; Madonna's black-and-white "Oh Father,"[12] (another paternal pathos play) opens with a visual quote of *Citizen Kane* and contains a *Se7en*-ish close-up of a corpse with her lips stitched shut that got cut by MTV for tapping the same vein of body horror as "Smoking Fetus."

The connections are even stronger, though, when you revisit Fincher's commercials, which are starker, cooler and more graphically spectacular, like Levi's "Rivet,"[13] which features a punky kid punctured through his nose with a golden bolt—consumerism as a combination fashion statement and hazing ritual. (He even looks a little bit like Lisbeth Salanader.) There are clear foreshocks of *Fight Club*'s anti-materialist recruiting pitches in Fincher's two sports-themed campaigns for Nike, each of which used pop-cultural iconoclasts in knowingly playful ways. "Barkley on Broadway" (1992) reinforced the stocky power forward's mantra about not being a role model (or a commodity) by having him rap his grievances within an anachronistic black-and-white Busby Berkeley pastiche, surrounded by chorines and eventually headbutting a paparazzo. The 1994 "Referee" series starred Dennis Hopper in village-crazy mode as an unhinged NFL official whose paranoid rants undermined his aura of uniformed authority; the perversity of using a countercultural hero like Hopper to promote a conservative, rules-obsessed league spokesman was beautifully counterintuitive.

Budweiser's "Classic" series from 1993 featured hipster pals debating trivial pop culture either-ors (Deep Purple or Foreigner; Ginger or Mary-Anne) as warm-ups for *Fight Club*'s walk-and-talks about which historical figures the antiheroes would opt to box. 2005's "Beer Run"—made on the other side of Fincher's Hollywood breakthrough—casts Brad Pitt as himself, pursued by photographers on his way to the corner store for a Heineken. The allusion to the band-on-the-run opening of *A Hard Day's Night* is unmistakable, and in "Beer Run"—as well as the 2013 double shot of Justin Timberlake's "Suit and Tie"[14] (for which Fincher came out of music-video "retirement") and Rooney Mara's Calvin Klein spot "Downtown"—the director's satirical impulses clash with a desire to present lifestyles-of-the-rich-and-famous as reverently and glossily as possible. "Downtown" shoots Mara as fetishistically as "Vogue"-era Madonna, depicting a promotional tour whose behind-the-scenes glimpses of the star reading, napping, and (presumably) reflecting on her own blindingly bright celebrity are just as posed, artificial and art-directed as the photo shoots and press conferences that make up her itinerary. Mara's malleability in Fincher's features—especially *The Girl with the Dragon Tattoo*—makes her Madonna's spiritual inheritor, and "Downtown" could be a sanitized, airbrushed variation on *Truth or Dare* (1991), set in an alternate, high-definition reality where even what happens behind-the-scenes is unblemished and camera-ready.

In 2014, Fincher worked with his semi-regular cinematographer Jeff Cronenweth on a series for the Gap called "Dress Normal"[15.] A series of cryptic vignettes introduce characters *in media res*, as if excerpted from a larger mood piece. Each spot came outfitted with its own enigmatic slogan, one of which—"the uniform of rebellion and conformity"—offers a succinct a precis about

the 1:1 ratio of salesmanship and subversion that runs through and defines most of Fincher's work since the primal scene of "Smoking Fetus." The 2021 Budweiser Super Bowl ad "Let's Grab a Beer"[18] (which was technically directed by Adam Hashemi under Fincher's supervision as a Creative Director/Executive Producer) introduces a new and curious tone of sentimentality; on a series of short vignettes lasting no more than ten seconds each—the same swift-yet-distended rhythm as in "Downtown"—characters in variable states of boredom, euphoria and distress (a couple surveying a downpour at their outdoor wedding; passengers waiting out a flight delay; strangers on either side of a fender bender) opt to laugh and drown their sorrows together. The beer itself is unimportant: As usual in Fincher's commercials, it feels less like product placement than signifying the kind of person—informed, status-conscious, with available disposable income—who would choose certain brands over others.

What's being really being sold here (as in "Classic") is intimacy and fellow-feeling, with more attempted gravitas than usual; for critic Steve MacFarlane, "Let's Grab a Beer" "shows a world of relationships tested, battered, tarnished [and] necessarily imperfect"; as well as a "feeling that something is not right somewhere outside the frame." MacFarlane is referring to the contradiction of a commercial about camaraderie being produced under socially distanced conditions in the midst of a global pandemic, a structuring absence that "Let's Grab a Beer" milks for all it's worth. The creative brief by Fincher and Hashemi for Wieden+Kennedy suggested that the spot "should capture the spirit of this country, and the role that beer plays in our national psyche and social cohesion"; in other words: they'd like to teach the world to sing in perfect harmony.

The absence of adversarial bravado here can't be solely attributable to the ad's commissioning entities, featured product or global context, nor is it simply an inevitably middle-aged mellowing on Fincher's—not when *Gone Girl*'s small-town setting contains a bar called "The Bar" and the film as a whole equates rapacious consumerism with psychopathology. In *Gone Girl*'s self-aware universe, the line about "The Bar" being "very meta" becomes a joke on either the proprietor's ironic detachment or his lack of imagination. The calculated humanism of "Let's Grab a Beer"—whose specific-yet-archetypal imbibers all look and sound like they'd be ready patrons at *Gone Girl*'s it-is-what-is establishment—suggests that one may be a symptom of the other, and also perhaps that Fincher has arrived at a point of automatic, brand-name mastery where the "uniform of rebellion and conformity" is no longer a disguise but fits him like a suit and tie.

CRIME SCENES

< Shot specially by Harris
  Savides, *Se7en's* opening
  titles are designed to
  put the audience inside
  the head of a psychopath
  and his meticulous process
  of assembly—the first
  of several allusions
  to John Doe as an artist-
  director figure.

1.1
SE7EN

1995

"Wanting people to listen," says John Doe (Kevin Spacey) to Detectives Somerset (Morgan Freeman) and Mills (Brad Pitt), "you can't just tap them on the shoulder anymore. You have to hit them with a sledgehammer. And then you'll notice you've got their strict attention."

The very idea of a movie directed with a sledgehammer does conjure up a bludgeoning clumsiness, or maybe some form of accidental expressionism. Observing the Jackson Pollock-like splatter of another senseless murder at the beginning of *Se7en*, William Somerset sighs, "Look at all that passion all over the wall," but from there, the film unfolds via a series of precise strokes, its pace is as finely calibrated as the metronome in Somserset's study, its shocks as carefully curated as a museum retrospective. In this gallery analogy, there is a didactic aspect to an artist using excess as a tool of communication, and a real-world precedent for such pummelling innovations as the ones used by John Doe. In 1971, the American artist Chris Burden, whose oeuvre included shutting himself inside a locker for five days and crucifying himself to the hood of a Volkswagen Beetle, arranged for a friend to fire a bullet from a small-caliber rifle into his arm as part of a performance piece titled *Shoot*. "In this instant," Burden reflected later, "I was a sculpture."

Ever the vanguard *artiste*, John Doe adapts Burden's gambit while interrogating its mixture of self-aggrandizement and self-endangerment-the frisson that occurs when

1-2.	The essentially
	dialectical
	relationship between
	Mills and Somerset
	is expressed through
	glimpses of their
	domestic life; even
	as David draws
	strength from his
	relationship with
	Tracy, his love for her
	makes him vulnerable,
	while William begins—
	and ends—the film with
	nothing to lose.

3.	"All these books,
	a world of knowledge
	at your fingertips."
	The library becomes
	a refuge from the
	city's darkness.

4.	Predatory perspectives
	abound in *Se7en*,
	which visualizes its
	villain's elevated
	sense of superiority
	through bird's-eye
	views; the top-down
	angles also evoke
	the city-as-labyrinth
	as imagined in its
	spiritual progenitor *M*.

art is remodeled into a life or death venture. Burden made his mark without resorting to full-on martyrdom; as a self-styled *fin-de-siècle* aesthete jointly projecting his superiority and self-loathing onto the world around him, John Doe goes further. He has to, because he's on the margins of a marketplace oversaturated with morbid images and ideas. In order to make an impact, he must swing for the fences.

Se7en embodies and interrogates such blunt-force strategies, enfolding a meditation on—and enactment of—avant-garde artistry in genre-movie packaging. The film's outer shape is that of a thriller, specifically the kind of gritty, big-city police procedural patented in the sweltering Seventies by Sidney Lumet: preparing for his first day on the job, John Mills (Brad Pitt) jokingly tells his wife Tracy (Gwyneth Paltrow), "Serpico's got to go to work." ("You might want to get rid of this little crusty in your eye, Serpico," she responds sleepily.) More significantly, *Se7en* erects itself as a landmark in the history of serial-killer movies. The genre began in earnest in 1931 with Fritz Lang's *M*, whose guilt-wracked pederast is played by Peter Lorre as a mewling victim of his own insatiable compulsions, as well as a broken byproduct of early twentieth-century modernity. Playing a man whose need to harm others reflects his own sense of victimization ("who knows what it's like to be me?") the actor is unforgettable, but the film's other star is the steel and glass labyrinth of Weimar-era Berlin, which provides Lorre's squirrelly Hans Beckert with an endless array of hiding places from cop and fellow criminal alike.

Lorre's anguish at the end of *M* would be revisited and deepened by Anthony Perkins in Alfred Hitchcock's *Psycho* (1960) and Carl Boehm in Michael Powell's *Peeping Tom* (1960), twin masterpieces which, in their respective ways—elliptically in Hitchcock; allegorically in Powell—equated murderous psychosis with voyeurism, if not cinephilia itself. *Psycho*'s staccato editing rhythms slashed, viscerally and subliminally, through both the fraying barriers of Hays Code censorship and spectatorial defense mechanisms, presaging a healthy cycle of serial killer films in the 1970—an era in which the popularization of psychopathology became a multi-platform growth industry encompassing both "true crime" fiction and grindhouse cinema. The eerie proximity to Hollywood of Charles Manson and the thinly veiled depiction of San Francisco's Zodiac Killer in Don Siegel's *Dirty Harry* (1971)—which picked up Lang's vision of the city-as-labyrinth and ran with it through

1.

2.

3.

4.

winding streets—were key markers in this development. So too were faux-naturalistic shockers like Wes Craven's Mansonian *The Last House on the Left* (1973) and the best-selling novels of Thomas Harris, whose 1981 *Red Dragon* filtered authentic Quantico protocol through allusions to William Blake and Guignol grander than *The Texas Chainsaw Massacre*.

Taking off from Harris's Gothic potboiler formula while blending in phantasmagorical social satire, Bret Easton Ellis's controversial 1991 novel, *American Psycho*, about a Wall Street power broker nursing a secret identity as a serial killer, brought the genre to a bleeding edge; that same year, Jonathan Demme's film *The Silence of The Lambs*, a Harris adaption featuring Anthony Hopkins on irresistible form as Hannibal Lecter—in whose immaculate personage Norman Bates and his exposition-dispensing psychiatrist were humorously and horrifyingly combined—won five Academy Awards. Both of these pop-cultural conversation pieces fed indirectly into the creation of *Se7en*, a risky $30 million bet by the ever-hip production outfit New Line Cinema (known as "The House That Freddy Built" thanks to *A Nightmare on Elm Street* [1984]) against serial-killer fatigue. The film opened in the fall of 1995 with a cryptic ad campaign and minimal hype and grossed $300 million worldwide, emerging as an oddly paradoxical crowd-pleaser: the sort of movie your friends urged you to see and warned you against in the same breath.

As with *American Psycho* and *The Silence of the Lambs*, *Se7en* draws its strength from a set of well-established conventions while also distancing itself from them. It does this mostly via the toxic potency of its visual style, which strips the rust off the script's cop movie tropes and exposes their gleaming bones. Meanwhile, the serial-killer material, which is so self-consciously lurid as to threaten unintentional comedy,

is elevated, if not consecrated, by the story's central gimmick: a suite of murders inspired by the seven deadly sins, carried out consecutively by John Doe as a sermon wherein Old Testament messaging is etched on the bodies of his victims and conveyed to the masses by a sensation-hungry media establishment playing into his game.

As high concepts go, *Se7en's* is dizzyingly vertiginous—which is to say pretentious, a quality the film owns straight-up. It's a conceit most poetically expressed by the set-piece in the silent, church-like library whose cavernous expanse is illuminated by a set of golden-hued desk lamps—a place of refuge and literary worship containing the wisdom of the ages. "All these books," Detective Somserset sighs admiringly to the security guards while wandering the stacks to the strains of *Bach's Suite No. 3 in D Major.* "A world of knowledge at your fingertips . . . and you play cards." Just as *Se7en's* gore attempts to outstrip its predecessors, the film's omnipresent intellectualism exceeds the po-faced Freudian slippage of *Psycho* or the Lacanian quid pro quo of *The Silence of the Lambs*; the film is pure pulp, but its gristle comes fully marinated in a thick stew of scriptural and liturgical references.

Anachronisms and artifacts are embedded in *Se7en's* aesthetic. One potentially illuminating way to look at the film is as a kind of contemporary "cabinet of curiosities," or *wunderkammer*, a Medieval invention housing a set of disparate, exotic objects like a miniaturized museum. *Se7en's* first *wunderkammer* moment comes during its opening credit sequence, conceived by designer Kyle Cooper as a hallucinatory collage (shot specially by Harris Savides) conveying John Doe's abject worldview and artisanal process through shots of scribbled prose and stitched-together notebooks. The unsettling bits of handwritten text and truly grotesque medical-textbook-style photographs get hammered into place by the industrial beats of Nine Inch Nails, whose 1994 album *The Downward Spiral* anticipated and heralded *Se7en*'s extremity (in the same year, Pearl Jam styled the liner notes of their their hit record *Vitalogy* as a faux and grotesque medical textbook cataloguing a set of human abnormalities.)

Se7en's *wunderkammer* motif is literalized later on during a tracking shot along a shelf in John Doe's apartment that displays trophies from his victims. Beyond serving as a concise recap of the film's storyline thus far, the shot links motifs of obsessive sadism, eccentric collectorship and outsider artistry. A row of symmetrically arranged tomato sauce cans nods comically towards Andy Warhol, but also, more generally, the mix of conceptual rigor and corporeal horror suggests an atrocity exhibition co-signed by Ed Gein and Damien Hirst, in whose distinctive disciplines and artistic traditions *Se7en*'s bad guy could be said to operate. As a result, John Doe's sledgehammer analogy, including that cloying acknowledgement of feeling the need to be heard—dial *M* for murder—scan as a weaponized *sotto voce* aside on behalf of its director, halfway between a brag and an ironic plea for clemency. Whatever else you can say about *Se7en*, it is not a tap on the shoulder; whatever ambivalences or contradictions David Fincher cultivates in his second feature, he gets, and keeps, our strict attention.

#

"A Sickening Catalogue of Sins, Every One of Them Deadly," screamed the header to Janet Maslin's review of *Se7en* in the *New York Times*, evoking the lurid tabloid covers strewn throughout Fincher's film—grotty dispatches chronicling a killing spree in a large, unnamed American city. "Why here— why *this place*?" queries Somerset of his new partner Mills upon their first meeting; Freeman places such an emphasis of disgust on those final two words that they gesture at some larger, collective understanding of hell-on-earth. Maslin's description of *Se7en*'s "grim urban environment" understates the extent to which Arthur Max's borderline-dystopian production design sets and maintains the film's tone, while her ultimate appraisal of the film as "boring" intersects interestingly and contrastingly with John Doe's wink-nudge explanation of his (and Fincher's) shock-to-the-system methodology. "Not even bags of body parts, a bitten-off tongue or a man being forced to cut off a pound of his own flesh (think 'The Merchant of Venice')," writes Maslin, "keep

[*Se7en*] from being dull." Her inventory is a few corpses short: the critic might have added to her list an obese shut-in fatally force-fed spaghetti; a woman penetrated with a weaponized leather-shop strap-on; myriad self-inflicted disfigurements; and a decapitated scion of Hollywood royalty— a sleight-of-head magic trick that serves as *Se7en*'s missing *pièce de résistance*.

Most of the initial dissent against *Se7en*—Maslin's review included—was rooted in the old shibboleth of style over substance. What the film's supporters saw, though, was an act of transubstantiation in which one became the other. "What I've done is going to be puzzled over, studied, and followed," promises the diabolical John Doe to his pursuers, and indeed, time has conferred a mostly rapturous critical consensus on *Se7en* highlighted by Richard Dyer's 2008 BFI Classics monograph, which distributes its author's analysis under a septet of alliterative chapter headings encompassing "sin," "story," "structure," "seriality," "sound," "sight" and "salvation." Dyer takes *Se7en* seriously while still allowing for its gallows humor, and it *is* a funny movie, especially the running joke of Mills feeling double-teamed by Somerset's high-minded condescension and John Doe's intellectual preening while he struggles through Cliff's Notes. "Fucker's got a library card, doesn't make him Yoda," the cop snarls, consolidating his anti-intellectualism under the sign of *Star Wars*. His quip also points at *Se7en*'s most provocative and problematic aspect: the veneration of its serial killer figure as a modern guru with something to say about society. That this potential sticking point is completely indivisible from the things that make *Se7en* powerful is a good place to begin considering the question of Fincher's transformative directorial presence.

#

After his experience helming *Alien 3* for 20th Century Fox, Fincher claimed that he'd rather "die of colon cancer than make another movie." This oft-quoted, grandly self-pitying proclamation clarifies *Alien 3*'s themes of noble martyrdom, with Ellen Ripley dying by her own hand for her corporate overseers' sins. It also establishes the morbid mindset necessary to embrace a property like *Se7en*, which came to Fincher after being rejected by its original director and subjected to studio demands for a more

5.

5.   John Doe's trick of posing as a journalist aligns with his overall media savvy as he mobilizes the local tabloid press into messengers for his moralistic warnings.

6-9. "I want you to look and I want you to listen"; the red-ringed eyes in the photograph at the "Greed" murder teach us how to scrutinize *Se7en*'s carefully detailed frames (6); Shakespeare's *The Merchant of Venice* is evoked through the proverbial pound of flesh; (7) the wages of sin are spelled out in blood for the perpetrator (8), and then reflected back at the investigator (and the audience).(9)

6.

7.

8.

9.

SE7EN

palatable rewrite—i.e., one that didn't end with a head in a box. The draft with the head in the box, as Fincher is fond of pointing out, was the one that he preferred.

The details of Se7en's genesis as an edgy industry outlier speak to a mid-90s moment where mini-major studios like New Line were all aiming to make their own versions of *The Silence of the Lambs*, which in addition to its awards haul was a tantalizing case study in return on investment. New Line's hunger for an R-rated hit connected with Fincher's yearning for genuine directorial control—a lust that's legible not only in Se7en's laboriously worked-over and bleach-bypassed frames, but also at the core of its story, with its shifting power dynamics and ever-deepening ambiguity about who's pursuing whom. In interviews, Fincher admitted that he was bored by the ritualistic police-procedural aspects of Se7en's script; what kept him hooked was the creeping, insidious sense of purpose encoded in John Doe's project, and the vise-like tension therein between surprise and inevitability. "I found myself getting more and more trapped in this kind of evil," he told *Empire* in 1996. "And even though I felt uncomfortable about being there, I had to keep going."

Walker's screenplay is notably bereft of detours or digressions, forging relentlessly ahead and littering its dialogue with suggestions of momentum. These begin following Somerset's admonition to his partner to "look" and "listen" in a city whose baseline threshold for brutality is above and beyond. (Walker wrote Se7en as an anti-love letter to New York after an unhappy stint living there in the 1980s.) "I've worked homicide for five years," Mills protests, before Somerset chides him, sharply: "Not here." Mills nods grudgingly, and his partner continues: "Over the next seven days, Detective, you'll do me the favor of remembering that."

Instantly, a pre-ordained time frame is established: "the next seven days," initially identified as the length of time prior to Somerset's announced retirement date, and repurposed predictively as the span of John Doe's rampage. As Se7en continues, the characters' conversations keep alluding to that same numerologically determined vanishing point, as well as a more general sense of impending doom. "You can expect five more of these," says Somerset to his superior (R. Lee Ermey) after the discovery of the second body. "This isn't going to have a happy ending," he tells Mills later on, setting up the final act. "I feel like saying more, but I don't want to ruin the surprise,"

smirks John Doe over the phone, taunting his pursuers and the viewer simultaneously with the knowledge of his eventual *coup de grâce*.

Of course, the unhappy ending prophesied by Detective Somerset is the surprise alluded to by John Doe. While there has been much documentation about the different incarnations of Walker's script and, in particular, the events of its climax, the central idea—seven murders for seven sins in seven days—was always present. It's a conceptual framework so tight that it could potentially paralyze any director who took it on, but for Fincher, the script's rigid boundaries and smaller scale were in sync with a resolve to downsize his process after *Alien 3*'s gigantism. "I thought I was making a tiny genre movie," the director told *Sight and Sound* in 1996. "I tried not to have a hundred fucking trucks, but every time you take the camera out of the box, it gets complicated." The same fastidiousness that had seen Fincher branded as a control freak was now perfectly suited to a parable of perfectionism—one deceptively less invested in its archetypal crime-solvers and their occasional, all-too-human sloppiness than the ways in which they're instrumentalized

10. One of Se7en's sickest jokes is the double entendre of "Help Me," ostensibly a plea for clemency that's actually an invitation to assist the killer.

11. Arriving at the police station literally red-handed two murders ahead of schedule John Doe has the upper hand even when he's being restrained face down.

by their quarry as victims and, sometimes, even accidental perpetrators.

In terms of point of view, Se7en is recognizably aligned with the two cops, who are dichotomized by a set of Platonic binaries: not only veteran and rookie—a contrast smartly informed by the casting of ace character actor Freeman and emerging heartthrob Pitt—but also Black and white (which tapped into the racialized "wisdom" associated with Freeman's famous roles in *Driving Miss Daisy* [1989] and *The Shawshank Redemption* [1994]); bachelor and husband (the two only start to bond after Tracy arranges a group dinner date); cerebral and impulsive (Somerset's physical and linguistic delicacy are offset by Mills's thick syllables and two-fisted posturing); and, most crucially, pragmatism and idealism.

On this point, William Somerset is a nicely layered character, at once principled and evasive, familiar and yet oddly remote as an entry point into the story. Freeman projects his usual intelligence, but also a flinty reticence that's not always sympathetic—or convincing. Somerset's capitulation via early retirement to the ambient helplessness of his surroundings is no less misanthropic for being cloaked in the language of home truths ("apathy is a solution," he sighs). Meanwhile, Mills's belief in the eternal verities of justice and retribution (and dishing them out) is only partially compromised by his hotheadedness: his joke about wanting to be Frank Serpico comes from a place of real longing for heroism. As much as Somerset tries to suggest that this attitude is misplaced, Pitt's pumped-up yet emotionally translucent performance—sandwiched in between Freeman's relaxed mastery and Spacey's implosive pyrotechnics—never loses sight of his character's essential righteousness.

Se7en cultivates plenty of pleasing odd-couple comedy from the detectives' contrasting manner and slow creep towards friendship, an arc derived from racially coded buddy-cop movies like Norman Jewison's *In the Heat of the Night* (1967) and Richard Donner's *Lethal Weapon* (1987), although lessons about racial solidarity are not on the film's agenda. The pair's warring viewpoints ultimately converge, however perversely, in the work and words of John Doe, which frighteningly and suggestively synthesizes Somerset's nihilism—his contention that people are beyond saving—with Mills's impulsive idealism, while superseding both on an aesthetic level. Because the world in which Se7en takes place—*this place*, as Somerset calls it; *this city*, as later echoed by Tracy—is tailor-made, without exception, to John Doe's (and Fincher's) judgmental specifications, the detectives' attempts to foil him can only be futile. When Somerset cries at a moment of truth that, "John Doe has the upper hand," it's less startling than reassuring: the actor's delivery generates the feeling of jagged, metallic pieces locking seamlessly into place.

Se7en's most serrated point—its amoral, and thoroughly auteurist, organizing principle—is that Somerset and Mills's double act embodies not law-and-order, but an existential threat to the satisfaction promised by what its auteur-as-killer calls, "the whole complete act." Which is to say: the satisfaction, for us in the audience, of perceiving the complete and fully realized work of art that Se7en at once narrativizes and stands in for a wryly self-allegorizing fashion.

#

To return to the idea of auteurism as repetition-compulsion and criticism as a form of psychological profiling, the tricky part is establishing a newcomer as a subject for further surveillance. "[David] Fincher is like a Baudelarian aesthete in reverse," wrote Amy Taubin in a 1995 review of Se7en in Sight and Sound, staking an investigative claim. Like Maslin, Taubin saw Se7en's script as pretentious, and also "as right-wing as Newt Gingrich's natterings about New York . . . cities are cesspools of contagion, spreading sin faster than TB." And yet through the reactionary haze, Taubin

10.

glimpsed a promising young director with "a stunning control over the rhythm and pace of individual scenes." Citing the eroticism latent in the film's rising and falling action, her piece deems Se7en "as lush and lyrical a film as has ever come out of Hollywood."

Taubin's invocation of Charles Baudelaire, a poet anticipating early-twentieth-century modernity who believed less in the philosophy of "beautification" than the possibility that blight itself might be sublime, makes wonderful sense in the context of Se7en's putrefied mise-en-scène.

Although the author's 1857 opus Les Fleurs du Mal (The Flowers of Evil) is not one of the texts corralled into the screenplay's pasture of literary sacred cows, Baudelaire's strategic blasphemy, invoking Satan as a supreme aesthete and outcast hero à la Milton's Lucifer in Paradise Lost, is echoed in John Doe's stated rationale. If Se7en is beautiful, it's beautiful in a Baudelarian way, in the same grandly desiccated fashion as Nicholas Roeg's Don't Look Now (1973), another saga including a doomed detective and a serial killer stitched together via jump cuts and

bathed in—to paraphrase Taubin—"the allure of decay."

Ever-perceptive about the film's use of point of view, Taubin writes about the ways in which Fincher "controls the viewer's eye," including the use of shallow focus, which finely etches faces and objects into our consciousness against swimming, indistinct backdrops: do look now. The style turns nearly everything in the film's cluttered foreground into quasi-hypnotic fixation points; Se7en's trance-like fascination is generated by Fincher's uncanny compositional sense—all jutting, unexpected angles and sculptural blocking that subdivides offices and crimes scenes into tense, contested territory—and by the high-contrast lighting set-ups of cinematographer Darius Khonji, which manifest, in the best noir tradition, not as artifice but rather a stylized realism. The darkness swallowing up the characters in various locations is fully diegetic, as are the stray beams of light that keep cutting through via handheld pen-lights and torches, Spielbergian flourishes tinged not with wonderment but dread. "Long is the way and hard that out of Hell leads up into light," says Somerset, repeating John Doe's quotation of Paradise Lost and neatly summarizing the games that Se7en is playing with visibility. The film's palette gradually modulates from inky blacks and mundane greys to a blinding, jaundiced, white-hot brightness. "There's sure as shit no ambush out here," attests a helicopter pilot hovering over a cloudless desert horizon with no

11.

12. This split-screen composition ominously doubles Detective Mills with the suspect in the "Lust" murder, anticipating his own impending manipulation by John Doe into becoming "Wrath."

analog outside Manhattan, or anywhere in New York State.

"I want you to look, and I want you to listen": *Se7en* is a movie that teaches us how to watch it as it goes along (and also how to rewatch it later on). The grotesquely retouched black-and-white photograph of Mrs. Gould (Julie Araskog), left by John Doe on her shylock husband's desk as a witness to his lethal self-bloodletting, piques Mills's interest and unlocks further clues, all of which are tied to the idea of *seeing*. Mrs. Gould's red-ringed eyes in the photo are actually pointed at a modernist painting in the dead lawyer's office which has been tauntingly hung upside down, and whose abstract swirl recalls Somerset's comments about "all that passion all over the wall." What it conceals is a set of handprints that are themselves only fully visible under the black light supplied by a print technician. Fully unveiled, these smudges spell out a plea borrowed directly from *The Exorcist* (1973) that continues the motif of fingertips and authorship developed in the opening-credit scenes, with its images of razor blades painfully slivering away traditional loci of identification and also doubling as a retrospectively devastating message from the killer to the "law enforcement agents" he so teasingly professes to respect: "HELP ME."

That Somerset and especially Mills actually do end up "helping" their enemy—on his terms, not theirs, and irreversibly so—is a bitter irony that *Se7en* plays for inverted Greek tragedy. In lieu of a *deus ex machina* in which a higher power saves the day, the cops' investigation only helps to grind the gears of John Doe's industriousness. Fincher is undeniably compelled by the details of police investigation, a fascination that will find full flower later on in his career; here, though, the emphasis is on the intricacy of the puzzles being laid out for the detectives rather than their investigative acumen. Even the hard-won discovery of John Doe's downtown lair, accomplished through some highly unethical, pre-Patriot Act surveillance, manifests at best as a "minor setback" for the killer, who is out buying groceries when they arrive (a rare example of his basic, everyday humanity).

If cop movies are by their nature reliant on clichés, *Se7en*'s mid-film foot chase, which begins with its equivalent of a starter's pistol when John Doe fires on his callers from the end of his apartment hallway, is the dustiest old trope of them all. But Fincher's direction redeems the creaking of the plot machinery, personified by an agile handheld camera whose movement clashes excitingly with the smooth, mobile tracking and locked-off master shots utilized throughout the rest of the film. The overriding impression, as David pursues John Doe through hallways, out of windows and down fire escapes, is of jostling chaos, and yet the editing by Richard Francis Bruce is never less than precise, matching movement to action in a way that delineates rather than fractures space and emphasizes the killer's silhouetted, surprisingly athletic elusiveness against the solid, panicked physicality of the bystanders.

13.

"To handle language skillfully is to practice a kind of evocative sorcery," wrote Baudelaire by way of praising Edgar Allan Poe's 1840 short story "The Man of the Crowd," whose nameless narrator surveils an elderly cipher through the streets of London, compelled by a curiosity about his nature and motivations. *Se7en*'s detective narrative is less existential than Poe's, but Fincher's use of film language during the chase scene—skillful bordering on sorcery—conjures up the same sinister modernist subtext of Poe's fable, of a fruitless pursuit through a winding, indifferent cityscape. A cunning play with height and levels abounds: in one spectacularly choreographed edit, we see Mills sliding down an aluminum roof through a dingy, cracked window, training his lens through it—and at us—before a fleet cut to the reverse-shot reveals John Doe vaulting from a balcony down to the ground, his trenchcoat flared out behind him like a superhero. In an online essay at *Cinephilia and Beyond*, critic Ryan Lambie points out that a later shot of a beaten, ambushed Mills kneeling in the rain with John Doe's pistol pressed against his temple echoes Ellen Ripley's close encounter in *Alien 3*. It also anticipates a reversal of positions later on, neatly reconciling the adrenalized freneticism of the chase with the film's larger, more tableaux-based image system.

The raid on John Doe's apartment briefly permits *Se7en* to adopt the kinetic pleasures of an action movie, but it's a blip within a more processional, funereal structure. The heroes' intervention permits a glimpse at their suspect's inner life: a series of notebooks

13.   Shaving their chests together at the police station, Mills and Somerset cap their partnership with a final moment of tender, faux-macho intimacy.

respect for John Doe's intelligence and curiosity about his rationale places him somewhere between sounding board and acolyte—or maybe a respectable mirror image—is transformed by circumstance into a reverse Pandora, duty-bound to open a box containing not the evils of the world but a severed memento of its innocence.

Any discussion of Fincher's ongoing—and increasingly complicated and convoluted—relationship to/enactment of misogyny has to begin with *Se7en*'s ending, and the ruthless ways that the movie uses Tracy: first to humanize/domesticate Mills against Somerset (and our) first impression of him as a punchy lummox; to moan to Somerset (whom she tenderly calls "William") about her general unhappiness and unplanned, secret pregnancy (which will add ballast to the shock of her death); and finally to reappear after an extended absence from the narrative as one last, unseen, but still indelible/*objet d'art* in John Doe's arsenal. It is one of the trickier ploys in Walker's script that he uses the thriller genre's general disinterest and sidelining of its female characters against the audience; after John Doe shows up at the police station, we assume that the important questions of figuring out what he's done, and to whom, and why—and also whether a movie marked largely by posthumous discoveries will erupt into real-time violence—will proceed exclusively via the male characters (Serpico's got to go to work, after all, while his wife stays home). In truth, *Se7en* plays fair with this twist, sprinkling in little references to Tracy to throw us off the scent ("Your wife called, get yourself an answering machine," Mills is informed as he walks into the precinct) but the way in which the whole movie turns on the spectacle of

filled with Poe-like maunderings about the city and its inhabitants (descriptions of frailty and ugliness right out of "The Man of the Crowd") but it doesn't really upend anything. Their efforts are still within the guidelines of John Doe's plan, which, predicated as it is on the pretense of "turning the sin against the sinner," requires Mills to act as his Red Right Hand. David murders John Doe in police custody after learning that he'd earlier killed Tracy as a symbol of his own "envy." Inflamed beyond the point of no return, Mills is transformed into an avatar of "wrath," completing the numerical sequence.

There are multiple levels on which John Doe (and Walker's) logic is faulty here: if people are being killed in *Se7en* for flouting social conventions—for being vain, slothful, gluttonous, etc.—then Tracy, a flawless blonde *naif*, defined by kindness is collateral damage rather than a complicit casualty, unless one takes her unwillingness to inform her partner about her pregnancy as an ethical breach. (Somerset's suggestion to Tracy to quietly terminate the pregnancy if necessary manifests as pro-choice rhetoric in an otherwise apolitical film, but it's also an echo of his own decision, many years earlier, to push his partner toward an abortion.) Showmanship is an argument in and of itself, and the home stretch of *Se7en* proves spectacularly effective in filling out

the film's cabinet of curiosities (one prize item among many: Richard Schiff as the killer's lawyer, a Charles Addams caricature in an expensively ill-fitting suit). From the moment that John Doe turns himself in at the police station—his dripping, reddened fingertips testifying both to his self-mutilating method of evading detection and the more-than-metaphorical idea that he has "blood on his hands"—through the delivery of the fateful parcel that concludes his labors and confirms Somerset's worst fears (while finally shaking his desensitized complacency) *Se7en* peaks as a showcase in directorial control.

If you extend the idea of John Doe as a luxuriously (self-)subsidized artist—a fleshy, crypto-populist semiotician—wrangling a cast of players (living and dead) through a series of locations in the service of a story with a predetermined payoff, he could just as easily be pegged as a film director. His victory is one of staging, of manipulating his twin leading men just so. Detective Mills, who John Doe rightly suspects would enjoy "time alone with [him] in a room without windows," fulfills both his own volubility and his captive's combination transcendence-bid-slash-death-wish, collapsing the distance between director/author and his dearly departed "collaborators" with a series of close-range shots. Somerset, whose wary

14-15. Shooting Mills and John Doe's argument through the wire bars of the police cruiser, Fincher presents both cop and killer as being enmeshed within their respective perspectives, adding visual dynamism to what would otherwise be expository back-and-forth dialogue.

starlet as sacrificial lamb bypasses standard-issue exploitation.

Except that it's not quite a spectacle: Fincher's juvenile drive to direct a script that ends with a head in a box is harnessed to a restraint that precludes him actually showing it. The final image of Tracy in *Se7en* is a near subliminal, single-frame insert that represents the film's only truly subjective, hallucinatory view—the camera is on Mills as he agonizes over the decision to avenge her death but the flash of her face is unmistakably from his point of view.

As outlined on *Se7en*'s special-edition DVD, Fincher rejected a rewrite that saw Somerset step in to break up John Doe's fatal homage to Chris Burden and shoot him in Mills's stead, complete with a Schwarzenegger-style one-liner ("I'm retired") to punctuate his selfless act of heroism. His plan was to cut to black on the shot of John Doe toppling over in a cloud of blood, forgoing any sense of aftermath in a sly reversal of the film's pre-established pattern: John Doe and Tracy's deaths would be the only ones not descended upon post-mortem. But the director couldn't convince New Line to sign off on a completely abrupt ending, and *Se7en*'s coda yields mixed results. In it, William, composure regained, assures his colleagues that he'll be "around," forgoing retirement for the purgatory of continued service—an extended sojourn as The Man of the Crowd. The character's fate is fair enough, especially given Freeman's ability to project world-weariness as a state of grace, but his closing voice-over, which adds Hemingway to the film's literary syllabus, sounds a bum note. "The world is a fine place, and worth fighting for," William says, before adding: "I agree with the second part"—an aside that lands like a sledgehammer.

Obviously, the world in *Se7en* is not a "fine place." Fincher's main achievement lies in how consistently and vividly it reminds us of this fact. The notion that said world contains anything "worth fighting for," however, is at best a sentimental abstraction. As adept as Paltrow is at inhabiting Tracy's kindness, the character is never more than a decorous prop. She can't be, because for *Se7en*'s grand design to work, the characters can never exceed their assigned function, including John Doe, who is finally just a mouthpiece for his creator's pride in a job well done—a blossoming auteur's wickedly idealized surrogate.

To attempt to determine who is "correct" in the Socratic squad-car throwdown between Mills and John Doe, which provides *Se7en* with its most quotable moments ("When a person is insane, as you clearly

16.

17.

18.

19.

20.

21.

22.

23.

16-23. The sudden insert of Tracey's face during Mills's standoff with John Doe has a subliminal quality—it stands in, grimly and ingeniously, for the shot of her head in a box that Fincher refuses to provide (and yet which some audience members swore to seeing after exiting the theater).

are, do you know you're insane?") may not be beside the point, but it scarcely matters when what we're looking at renders what we're listening to moot. Fincher's decision to shoot both parties through the wire mesh separating the front and back seats frames Mills and John Doe as equally entrapped by their own respective viewpoints, while the asexual, deadpan affect of Spacey's acting—his slow, droning oratory—catalyzes Pitt's agitation while strangely anaesthetizing our own responses. He's as coolly implacable as the movie itself, because the movie has been made in his image.

That Mills convincingly ripostes said image as the guise of a false prophet ("you're no messiah") could perhaps be taken as a cutting autocritique of a shallow masterpiece's hyper-articulated juvenalia—the peanut gallery calling bullshit. "You're a movie of the week . . . a fucking T-shirt, at best," Mills adds, as if filing his New York Times review in real time. He does not get the last laugh. In the context of its underlying numbers game, Se7en undoubtedly adds up, although exactly to what is less certain. Among other things, it sets up expectations of style and sensibility

that Fincher's follow-ups would variably fulfill and repudiate—both at once in Zodiac, which offers up an immersion in the ontological uncertainty that the engineering of Se7en sutures fully shut. As a cinematic wunderkammer, Se7en is singularly vivid and impeccably curated, while Zodiac is even more precisely catalogued while remaining as open and terrifying as reality itself.

Psycho, Alfred Hitchcock, 1960

The innovation of Alfred Hitchcock's legendary thriller was to implicate the audience in acts of voyeurism and violence, at once popularizing and weaponizing the subject of serial murder in cinema.

Fig B. *Silence of The Lambs*, **Jonathan Demme, 1991**

Anthony Hopkins's performance as erudite psychiatrist Hannibal Lecter anticipates the meek menace of Kevin Spacey's acting as John Doe; Both illustrations of the serial killer as intellectual guru.

Fig C. *Campbell's Soup Cans*, Andy Warhol, 1962

The soup cans stacked in John Doe's apartment nod to Andy Warhol's famed piece of branded Pop Art.

Shoot, **Chris Burden, 1971**

Chris Burden's 1971 performance piece-slash-provocation saw the artist being used as target practice in a gallery setting; John Doe's gambit at the end of *Se7en* plays out as an act of artistic homage.

Fig G. **Charles Baudelaire, 1821-1867**

Critic Amy Taubin tagged Fincher as cinematic heir to the French poet who wrote *The Flowers of Evil*, proposing an involuted hierarchy of beauty in which decay itself could be beautiful.

Fig H. *The Man of the Crowd*, **Edgar Allan Poe, 1840; illustrated here by Harry Clarke, 1923**

Poe's short story describes one man tailing another through crowded city streets, providing a literary model for *Se7en*'s frenetic mid-film foot chase.

Fig D. *Wunderkammer*

These Medieval cabinets of curiosity typically housed items testifying to the eccentricity of their collector; the rows of trophies in John Doe's apartment suggest a similar sensibility.

Fig E. *M*, **Fritz Lang, 1931**

Fritz Lang's parable of a city under siege by a child murderer has been proposed as *Se7en*'s stylistic and spiritual progenitor.

Fig I. *American Psycho*, **Bret Easton Ellis, 1991 [Novel]**

The Reagan Eighties were mercilessly dissected in Bret Easton Ellis's controversial best-seller about a Wall Street power broker who moonlights as a chainsaw-wielding maniac.

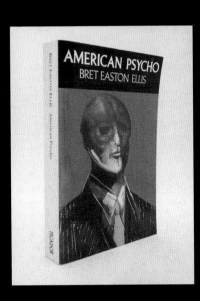

Fig J. *The Physical Impossibility of Death in the Mind of Someone Living*, **Damien Hirst, 1991**

Hirst's 1991 exhibition of a tiger shark preserved in formaldehyde was hailed as a vanguard artwork on the subject of death.

INFLUENCES

WRITER Andrew Kevin Walker
CINEMATOGRAPHER Darius Kohndji
EDITOR Richard Francis-Brucae

BUDGET $33 million
BOX OFFICE $327.3 million
LENGTH 127 min

1.2

TITLE SEQUENCE
EMMA KING-LEWIS

< *Zodiac*'s credits slyly identify and intercut between the film's two major characters: Robert Graysmith, revealed swiftly as a lover of codes and doodles, and the killer, who is not seen but embodied as the envelope being delivered to the offices of the *San Francisco Chronicle*.

1.2
ZODIAC

The American modernist composer Charles Ives referred to his 1906 work "The Unanswered Question" as a "cosmic drama," a metaphysical debate conducted through musical dialogue. The piece begins with a string arrangement that is repeatedly punctured by bursts of solo trumpet; its anxious, probing notes poke through the ethereal melody. In the program notes for the piece's first performance in 1946, Ives wrote that the trumpet's intrusion voiced, "the perennial question of existence," while the agitated whirl of woodwinds following in its wake—the third instrumental element in a tripartite structure—embodied some futile attempt at a reply.

In terms of compositional technique, Ives's collage imagined a bold collision of tonal and atonal style; in terms of its outlook, however, "The Unanswered Question" vibrates with humility. The three instrumental perspectives represented by the strings, horns, and woodwinds never quite harmonize; the silence that greets the final trumpet figure marks the piece's loudest moment. It's the aural equivalent of a hard cut to black, the flourish of an artist motivated to say that in the final analysis he doesn't really know anything at all.

That same lonely trumpet finds its way into *Zodiac*, soundtracking San Francisco Police Department detective David Toschi's (Mark Ruffalo) arrival at a

crime scene in Presidio Heights, where a taxi driver has been gunned down by a fare who witnesses have reason to believe may also be the Zodiac killer. The interpolation of Ives's piece is a subtle masterstroke of David Shire's musical score; stepping out of his car into the vast of night, Ruffalo's rumpled investigator is met by a plaintive brass tone. "The moment conveys something mysterious and unexpected . . ." writes Kent Jones in *Cinema Scope*. "It's as if [Toschi] has had a premonition that years will be spent tracking down the perpetrator of this split-second event, only half an hour old but already as distant in time as the birth of the universe."

Jones's analysis of *Zodiac* echoes Ives's reference to "cosmic drama"; if Fincher's sixth feature fits this metaphysical definition, it's because it works simultaneously on both macro and micro levels. The film's fact-based depiction of the hunt for one of the most mysterious American serial killers of the twentieth century switches assiduously between intimacy and omniscience; while focusing intently on the literally microscopic details of police forensics, it remains attuned to fluid, wide-scale gradations of fashion, technology, politics and pop culture over a quarter-century span from 1969 to 1991. Its timeline is restlessly annotated in to-the-minute increments, with some vignettes separated only by a matter of hours; here, historical sweep is a game of inches. Reviewing *Zodiac* for the *Village Voice*, Nathan Lee labelled it as an "orgy of empiricism" and sardonically quoted a friend's appraisal that watching the film was "like being locked in a filing cabinet for three hours." The friend, Lee explains, was complaining; the critic took his description as a compliment.

#

By the time of *Zodiac*'s theatrical release in March of 2007, ahead of its international bow Out of Competition in Cannes, David Fincher's reputation as a scrupulous blueprinter was already well-established. What *Zodiac* represented was an attempt to redirect those skills in the service of authenticity. Whatever the merits of carefully plotted thrillers like *The Game* and *Panic Room*, a sense of history was not among them; *Zodiac*'s subject matter demanded a balance between virtuosity and veracity. "There are no car chases in [the film,]" Fincher told *Entertainment Weekly*, framing Paramount's $70 million investment as a calculated gamble. "People talk a lot in it . . . it's about a cartoonist and a murderer

who never got caught. So, yeah, the studio is nervous."

Screenwriter James Vanderbilt was not known for realism either, having previously written standard-issue genre fare like the Rock vehicle *The Rundown* (2003). *Zodiac*'s script represented a definite levelling up, deftly adapting and combining two nonfiction books by Robert Graysmith, the former San Francisco Chronicle cartoonist who maintained his own inquiry into the Zodiac's identity for decades after the case's formal expiration date. Published in 1986, the same year as *Manhunter* (Michael Mann's movie adaptation of *Red Dragon*), Graysmith's *Zodiac* is the definitive study of a killer whose victims included five individuals slain in Benicia, Napa Valley, Vallejo, and San Francisco between December 1968 and 1969, and who garnered additional notoriety for a set of incriminating cryptograms sent to Bay Area press. These messages alternated between self-aggrandizing confessions, oddly phrased and spelled non sequiturs and unfulfilled promises of further, large-scale carnage; taken in tandem with certain macabre consistencies in the killings themselves (the use of a specific calibre handgun; the proximity of the assaults to water) a profile emerged of an elusive yet exhibitionistic sociopath. Even after the killings stopped in the early 1970s, the letters continued; while the Zodiac's official body count remains at five dead (and two severely injured survivors), in his correspondence he claimed responsibility for thirty-seven murders.

Where a prose stylist like Truman Capote made poetry out of his reportage in 1965's fact-based homicide yarn *In Cold Blood*—which ushered in a vogue among readers and publishers for true-crime fiction—Graysmith is a dogged plodder, inventorying atrocities with a minimum of theatrical grimness. What gradually penetrates the book's veneer of polished objectivity is a sense of intellectual and ethical impasse, the paralysis of a man unwilling and unable to jump to conclusions and so staying rooted to the spot. Graysmith marks the differences between the efforts of state and local officials and his own amateur sleuthing, but he also emphasizes their forlorn common denominator: "If there is one key word for the entire story of the Zodiac mystery," he writes, "it is *obsession* . . . as over 2,500 suspects were scanned, people were swept away by a tide of mystery, tragedy and loss."

Coming after the claustrophobic cat-and-mouse manoeuvres of *Panic Room*, *Zodiac*'s scale presented an ambitious set

of logistical challenges: period-re-creation; location shooting; the representation of real-life figures. The project's sprawl was beyond anything that Fincher had previously attempted, including a copious research component: during preproduction, the director joined Vanderbilt and producer Bradley J. Fischer in reinterviewing numerous people involved with the case, including surviving victims, witnesses, and investigators. "Even when we did our own interviews, we would talk to two people," wrote Fincher in *Zodiac*'s production notes. "One would confirm some aspects of it and another would deny it. Plus, so much time had passed, memories are affected and the different telling of the stories would change perception." In this way, *Zodiac*'s methodical, lived-in dramatization of the investigative process reflects the conditions of its own creation, while Fincher's observation of the contradictions inherent in even the most scrupulous research reflects Graysmith's cautionary point about the helpless nature of obsession.

Zodiac was also a movie undertaken with a higher-than-usual degree of artistic self-consciousness. "David wants to make the film that ends the serial killer genre," Vanderbilt said in 2005, alluding indirectly but unmistakably to the legacy of *Se7en*. "The danger for us," he added, "would have been to get a director who focused on all the prurient details . . . if anything, [Fincher's] got that part out of his system." This is an apt point: while *Zodiac* contains its share of gory moments, the film's aesthetic approach is completely different from *Se7en*,

4.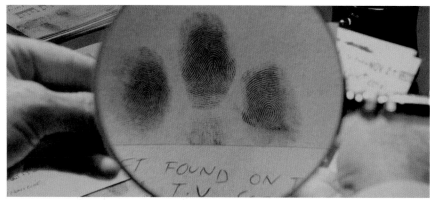

5.

6.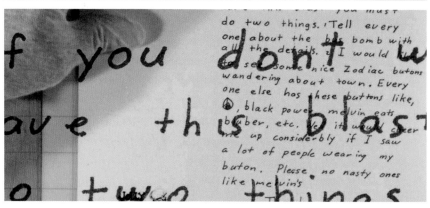

7.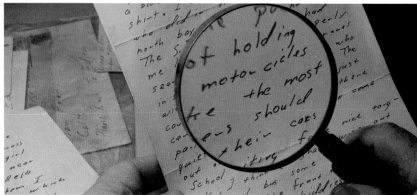

4-7. *Zodiac*'s multiple close-ups of written and photographic evidence are a key component of a forensic aesthetic that measures both investigation and identity in increments; here the spiral of a fingerprint, the imperfections in an old photograph, or eccentricities of penmanship offer potential conduits to criminal psychology.

eschewing neo-Baudelaireian flair in favor of a drab monochrome realism. If *Se7en* was a *wunderkammer*, *Zodiac* is, as Lee suggests, a filing cabinet: where *Se7en*'s signature (though fully subliminal) image is of a severed head in a box, *Zodiac*'s conceptual emblem is bloodless—a simple piece of paper to herald an epistolary epic. At the end of the opening credits, cinematographer Harris Savides plunks his camera in a mail cart carrying the first coded missive from the Zodiac across the newsroom of *The San Francisco Chronicle* and to its unsuspecting editors, an audacious parody of a point-of-view shot that briefly anthropomorphizes a piece of correspondence, imbuing it with perspective and also a wicked sense of purpose. As if to underline the shot's importance, Fincher uses it as the background for his own directorial credit.

The envelope's arrival at *The Chronicle* is a marvelously lo-fi visual effect suggesting the conflation of messenger and message; it indicates that the Zodiac is a shape-shifter, as much an ephemeral, disembodied phenomenon as an actual flesh-and-blood suspect, and all the more threatening for it. The irony that Fincher's film pinpoints is that as much as the Zodiac aspired to mythic resonance, it was in fact the inability of various institutions, including the media and the police, to properly cooperate and definitively identify the man behind the envelope which allowed that same malevolently free-floating persona to take hold of the wider imagination.

Through this lens, *Zodiac* could be described as a meta-horror movie, exploiting a series of terrifyingly verifiable events to access a set of vaguer, more existential anxieties. "I am interested in the hair standing up on the back of your neck," Fincher told Graysmith in 2005. "I'm interested in the things that can't be articulated." In other words: nothing is scarier than an Unanswered Question. *Se7en* is a movie about a serial killer with an idea, one validated if not vindicated by the grisly aestheticism of Fincher's filmmaking. *Zodiac*, though, has been engineered as a movie about the *idea* of serial killers, or an illustration of something even more abstract: the serial killer as idea, transferred from a single, anguished consciousness into the ether. The film is as cognizant of the public fascination with charismatic murderers as *Se7en*, but somewhere during the ensuing decade between his breakthrough and his masterpiece, Fincher's artistic mission shifted, away from perpetuating lurid intrigue to exhuming and examining it.

The primal scene is also a crime scene: *Zodiac*'s prologue, which reconstructs the Zodiac's first recorded attack in Vallejo, offers breathtaking evidence of both Fincher's sociological aims and his multi-levelled directorial technique. *Zodiac* was not only the filmmaker's first work based on a true story, but also his first period piece and his first time shooting fully digitally, a format open to all manner of after-the-fact manipulation. These three threads—history, veracity, and technology—are simultaneously set against each other and intertwined in an Ives-like pattern from the film's first shot.

Or rather, from before it: *Zodiac* opens with the old Paramount Pictures logo, treated digitally to give the impression of ancient 35 mm stock. Certainly, plenty of twenty-first-century movies have employed similar tricks to pay homage to different eras of filmmaking (exactly one month after *Zodiac*'s premiere, Quentin Tarantino and Robert Rodriguez unleashed the strenuously retrograde exploitation-cinema salute *Grindhouse* [2007]), but *Zodiac* offers more reward through its fetishistic play with formats. Throughout the film, Harris Savides faithfully replicates the sterile, desaturated palette of mid-70s movies; a specific point of reference would seem to be Gordon Willis's dark-hued cinematography for Alan J. Pakula's *All the President's Men* (1976).

This textural mimicry has an intriguing, medium-specific subtext—using the state-of-the-art, hi-def Viper Filmstream camera to reproduce the grain of celluloid—and even more evocative surface aims. *Zodiac*'s surface jaundice places its action squarely in the historical, cinematic, and semiotic past. The dateline of "July 4, 1969" locates us in real time as well as a more figurative space: America at the The End of the 1960s, after the escalation of the Vietnam War; the assassinations of progressive figureheads Martin Luther King Jr., Malcolm X, and Robert Kennedy; the politicized chaos of the 1968 Democratic National Convention, Kent State and Altamont; and, most pertinently of all, the visceral horror of the Manson killings. *Zodiac*'s stunning aerial view of Independence Day fireworks in mid-explosion scans on contact as a violent paroxysm of patriotism, and it's into this highly symbolic context—the dissolution of a Utopian dream and the bad vibes of the decade to come—that *Zodiac* projects itself.

"Based on true events," reads another title card, promising verisimilitude while evincing a cinephilic gambit, nodding to the way that vintage grindhouse films

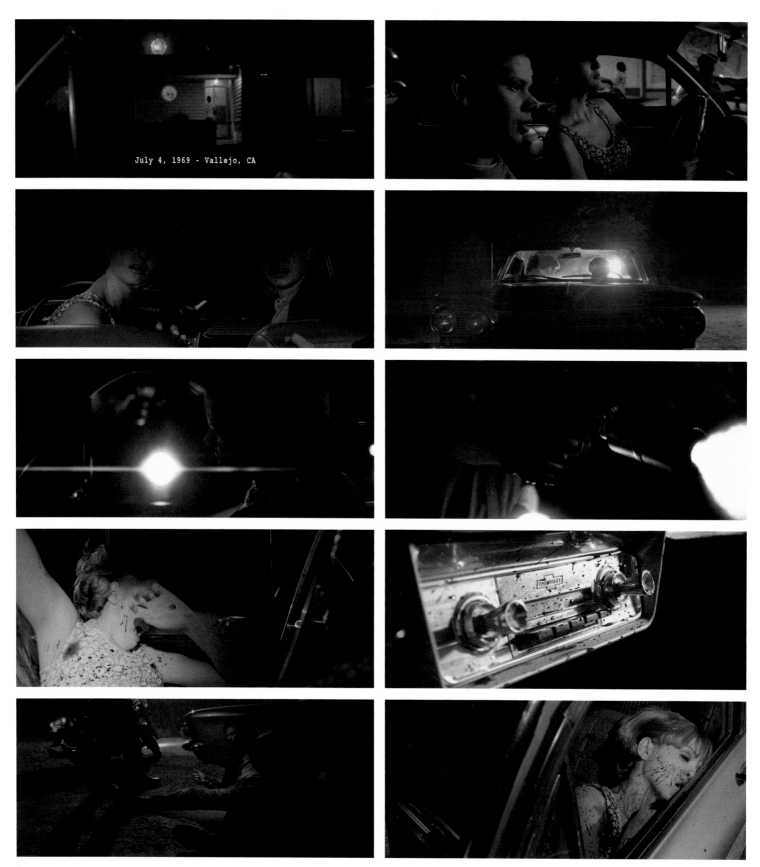

July 4, 1969 - Vallejo, CA

8.

9.

8. The opening sequence of *Zodiac* compresses cultural, filmic and psychic history into a montage that filters the peace-and-love messages of Donovan's "Hurdy Gurdy Man" through the Zapruder-inspired bullet ballet of *Bonnie and Clyde*; the pop of bullets mingles with Fourth of July fireworks as something new slouches towards San Francisco to be born after the summer of love.

9. Brian Cox's attorney Melvin Belli is part of *Zodiac*'s complex pop-cultural weave, recognized by a cop for his guest slot on *Star Trek*.

often advertised themselves as being ripped from the headlines. (The modern progenitor of this strategy was *Psycho*, which begat similar tactics in the promotion of *Last House on the Left* and *The Texas Chainsaw Massacre*.) Fincher demonstrates a real savvy about the visual language and moralistic meanings of early-70s horror films; steeped in the link between sex and death and often set in the world of teenagers, their stories channelled larger cultural anxieties. The boy and girl driving off together into the dark for an Independence Day date in *Zodiac*'s prologue look as wholesome as a Norman Rockwell painting. But there's no true innocence here: she's a married woman and he's a nervous wreck, even more so as he comes to suspect they're being followed by an unknown party en route to a lover's lane.

#

As the Zodiac's first recorded victims, Darlene Ferrin (Ciara Hughes) and Michael Mageau (Lee Norris), the latter of whom survived his wounds, are fated to be footnotes to history. As Fincher films their trials, they're enlarged into allegorical figures—not tragic outlaws like *Bonnie and Clyde*, whose bullet-ridden demise in Arthur Penn's 1967 masterpiece is unmistakably evoked in the ensuing slow-motion carnage—but collateral damage as something new and terrible emerges in the wake of the Summer of Love.

Fincher's use of Donovan's peace-and-love anthem "Hurdy Gurdy Man" underneath the strobing, percussively edited images of the assault is an ingenious contrapuntal music cue. In D. A. Pennebaker's 1967 Bob Dylan profile *Don't Look Back* Donovan had been included as a sort of foil, framed as an inauthentic pretender to Dylan's folk-rock throne. But "Hurdy Gurdy Man" isn't a knock-off novelty: beneath its buoyant melody and lyrics about the singer's visionary encounter with a musician singing "songs of love" lurks a voracious darkness, represented by creeping reverb and a ghostly echo effect. "[The song] may have been inspired by the Maharishi," writes Kevin Courrier in his Beatles study *Artificial Paradise*, "but the abiding spirit on the record could just as easily be [Charles] Manson. . . . Donovan composed a song that was less a celebration of spiritual renewal than a harbinger of bad tidings."

Manson's helter-skelter perversion of the peace-and-love ethos is one inescapable reference point for Donovan's Svengali fable. Another is Jim Jones, the charismatic cultist whose People's Temple was headquartered in San Francisco during the early 1970s—at the height of the Zodiac's predations—before its fatal relocation to Guyana. It's hard to say whether San Francisco's status as the most paranoid location in American cinema is a case of filmmakers harnessing something in the Santa Ana winds or if the city and its population subconsciously

10. The wildly dislocating
    sight of the black-
    clad Zodiac lurking
    around the shores
    of Lake Berryessa
    in broad-daylight
    provides Fincher's
    film with its single
    most nightmarish image:
    an appointment with
    Death reconstructed
    out of the stranger-
    than-fiction details
    provided by one of
    the victims after
    the fact.

started taking behavioural cues from Alfred Hitchcock's *Vertigo* (1958). Either way, the Bay Area has starred in a disproportionate number of classic thrillers, from *Experiment in Terror* (1962) to *The Conversation* (1974) to *Basic Instinct* (1992) to Fincher's own *The Game*, films whose twisty trajectories feel contoured to San Francisco's topsy-turvy topography. (This phenomenon is explored in Guy Maddin's sublime 2017 essay film *The Green Fog*, which intersperses clips from dozens of movies shot in the city.)

"Here is the last stop for those who drifted away from the cold and the past and the old ways," wrote Joan Didion in *Slouching Towards Bethlehem*, describing the lure of California at the end of the 1960s. "They're trying to find a new lifestyle in the only places they know how to look: the movies and newspapers." Didion's essayistic appraisal of So. Cal aspirations could double as a precis of *Zodiac*'s imaginative universe— "movies and newspapers," indeed—but Fincher's own experience of that coastal atmosphere was less literary or rarified. In interviews, the director explained that the proximity of the Zodiac murders to his childhood home in Marin County gave him a personal stake in the story—much more so than in *Se7en*. "If you grew up in the Bay Area, you had this childhood fear that you sort of insinuated yourself into it," he recalled one interviewer. "What if the killer showed up in our neighborhood?"

Fincher's coming-of-age memories are subjective; the civic reference points in *Zodiac* are effective because of how they excavate the audience's collective filmgoing experience. A digitally assisted time-lapse shot of the Transamerica Pyramid being constructed doesn't just mark the passing of time during a flashforward; it calls back to the building's fog-shrouded cameos in Philip Kaufman's 1978 remake of *Invasion of the Body Snatchers*. A predatory overhead view of traffic winding through the streets evokes the voyeurism of *Vertigo*. And the presence of Toschi near the center of the story directly places the film in conversation with local productions *Bullitt* (1968) and *Dirty Harry* (1971)—both of which based their eponymous, loose-cannon cops on the media-sensation detective.

Bullitt was made before Toschi was assigned to the Zodiac case, and its title character is a compelling mix of sullen professionalism and late-60s sensitivity; white-knuckle car chases aside, the drama emanates from how Frank Bullit (Steve McQueen, who studied Toschi's wardrobe and mannerisms before shooting) fears becoming dehumanized by the violence of

11.

12.

13.

11-13. Numerous grim patterns proliferate throughout *Zodiac*, including a recurring motif of victims shown in their cars; a cab driver in Presidio Heights; a weekender at Berryessa lake, and a young mother who hitches a ride on the highway with a deceptively helpful stranger and luckily lives to tell the tale.

14. A special screening of *Dirty Harry* for the SFPD cinches the link between Detective Toschi and his onscreen alter ego, who has no trouble getting his man.

his job. By the time of *Dirty Harry*, however, Clint Eastwood's Toschi *manqué* Harry Callahan has grown comfortably numb, locating moral force in his Zen-like lack of concern. In a gesture of grindhouse solidarity, *Dirty Harry* borrowed much of its plot, as well its setting and the astrological moniker of its villain—a wild-eyed sniper calling himself Scorpio—from coverage of the Zodiac crimes. The film even includes a scene where Scorpio sends a letter to a local newspaper outlining his plans for a killing spree.

Fincher engineers a wonderful hall-of-mirrors trick in *Zodiac* when he shows Toschi at a special SFPD screening of *Dirty Harry*, storming out abruptly, frustrated at seeing his daily grind sensationalized onscreen. (We're watching an actor in a movie playing a real person who's angry at having his life being turned into a movie.) A picture is worth a thousand words: when Toschi leaves the theater, he pauses on the steps and is framed beneath a lobby poster that makes it looks like

14.

Callahan's signature Magnum is pointed right at his head, a psychic sight gag encapsulating the impossibility of living up to one's own exalted fictional representation, as well as the general pressure of being the public face of an investigation firing blanks.

Life doesn't just imitate art in *Zodiac*. It's invaded by it, body-snatcher-style. Toschi isn't the only character with an onscreen doppelganger: the first break in the case comes when Graysmith, played by Jake Gyllenhaal with an air of furtive inquisitiveness, connects a stray line in one of the killer's letters about "hunting the most dangerous animal" to the sociopathic sharpshooter of *The Most Dangerous Game*; *Chronicle* crime reporter Paul Avery (Robert Downey Jr.), is baffled (and bemused) by the younger man's encyclopedic movie-nerd recall, but can't deny the relevance of the "Zaroff-with-a-Z" alphabetical allusion, or the philosophical synchronicity between the fictional killer and the real one. Later, when publicity-hungry attorney Melvin Belli (Brian Cox) agrees to appear on live television to field a phone call from the Zodiac as part of the SFPD's attempt to draw the murderer out for a public meeting, the news anchor recognizes the lawyer less for his career as a lawyer than a campy prime-time cameo on a network space opera: "I loved your *Star Trek*."

That Cox is playing an actor who transitioned into a vain, supercilious celebrity litigator is part of *Zodiac*'s stranger-than-fiction historical record; that Cox's first notable film role came in *Manhunter* completes a subtextual thread binding *The Most Dangerous Game* to *Dirty Harry* to Hannibal Lecter. This is Fincher's postmodern side at its most playful and trenchant, not a Tarantino-style wallow in homage but a thoughtful appraisal of the slippage between popular culture and reality at the edges of the Zodiac case. It's also arguably at the center of the perpetrator's psychology: the Zodiac's aspirations to infamy are apparent in his coded letters, whose confessional depravity indicates a desire to seem larger-than-life. But his messages are also essentially incoherent. Where a fictional creation like John Doe can be granted lucidity by a screenwriter, the Zodiac is bound by the docudrama format to speak in his own words, and in truth, he doesn't say much. What emerges from between the lines of all his baroque coding is the voice of the man-in-the-crowd-as crank (or in the parlance of social networks, a troll) albeit one who has successfully actualized his fantasies.

"This is the Zodiac speaking," croaks the caller after he gets through to Belli. The voice is intimidating, but less interesting in and of itself than the ways in which it manifests throughout the film in different mediums. Not just notes and letters, but on audio tape; the call-in sequence is precisely edited to showcase the bulky reel-to-reel equipment filling up the studio control room. (Later, we'll see the inspiration for the Zodiac's symbol inscribed in the frames of a celluloid print of *The Most Dangerous Game*, as if his very identity had been forged in some photochemical realm.) The analogue technology keeps piling up: as Cox's Belli preeningly plays psychoanalyst for the cameras, we see Avery and Graysmith watching the broadcast from their office and living room, respectively. The police sting is now a media circus. The possibility that the caller is a faker—or maybe a mentally ill man adopting the moniker of the Zodiac as a ploy for attention—only strengthens the scene's implications. "It's very real," cracks another cop, cutting straight to *Zodiac*'s tricky dialectic between fact and fabrication. "I saw it on television".

15.

Fincher gestures again in this direction during a mid-film montage showing notebook doodles and typewritten letters superimposed over various San Francisco locations, imagery that draws on *Se7en*'s opening credit scene, as well as the celebrated sequence in *Fight Club* where Edward Norton's apartment is transformed into a three-dimensional IKEA catalogue. It's also aligned with the visual language and paranoid ethos of *M*, another film where anonymous communiqué, newspaper headlines, and handwriting samples serve as recurring visual motifs. Like Lang with his pioneering use of onscreen text, Fincher literalizes the concept of the public sphere being rewritten in an antagonist's image— a populace under psychic attack. The stylization here has a Godardian sparseness, with onscreen space suddenly invaded and defaced by scribbles and symbols. Fincher's physical graffiti does more than condense and reinforce information already imparted by the narrative: it reorients the story's sense of threat away from the crimes and towards some sort of semiotic vanishing

point. Cryptographic text clusters and metastasizes; the Zodiac has gone viral.

During this sequence, Fincher has each of his lead actors read one of the Zodiac's letters out loud, calling attention to the film's tripartite narrative structure and carefully diffused strategies of identification. *Zodiac* is a rarity for a mainstream American movie in that it has three protagonists, each of whom addresses the same problem from a slightly different angle. The film begins as a newspaper drama, a study of how the media was drawn into covering and escalating the Zodiac case. This section is dominated by Downey's Avery, whose enervating egotism bounces energetically off the *All The President's Men*-style aesthetic. Downey is brilliant here: *Zodiac* captures a generationally talented performer at the moment before his charm and spontaneity were fully commodified and neutered by the Marvel Cinematic Universe. Wielding a charisma derived equally from Robert Redford's pretty-boy Bob Woodward and Dustin Hoffman's earthly cynical Carl Bernstein, the actor

complicates Pakula's noble fetishism of investigative journalism, filling out Avery's ambition and commitment with eccentric flourish while also showing how easily the on-the-job cocktail of arrogance, stress, and deadlines curdles into something toxic. Avery's vainglorious desire to become part of the story—to self-servingly conflate the role of muckraking reporter with death-defying detective—backfires and turns him into a potential target.

The arrival into the story of Toschi, a lumpy, principled striver right in Ruffalo's own hangdog wheelhouse, inaugurates a long middle section styled as a procedural, encompassing the detective's loving, bickering relationship with his partner Bill Anderson (Anthony Edwards); his gruelling pursuit of different leads in different jurisdictions; and his wary dislike of Avery, which is rooted in mutual professional competitiveness. Their impasse fits into the film's overall pattern of one-upmanship, with both men unthinkingly taking behavioural cues from the Zodiac's own egocentric rhetoric. ("Hey Bullitt, it's been a year, you gonna catch this guy or

not?") Meanwhile, in the background of the action, we see the gradual transference of Graysmith's friendship and support away from Avery, who treats the cartoonist like a factotum, and towards Toschi, who comes to recognize a kindred spirit, eventually handing off the baton to watch from the sidelines.

It's this third leg of *Zodiac*'s marathon relay race that fascinates Fincher the most. Where Avery is drawn to the Zodiac case by the promise of glory and Toschi is bound by duty, Graysmith the amateur puzzle aficionado is most naturally attuned to his quarry's obfuscating wavelength. Gyllenhaal took issue with Fincher's "Pavlovian" tactics, sardonically likening the director to a painter and explaining with faux diplomacy that, from his point of view, "it's hard to be a color"; his performance, while less flashy than Downey's or as carefully studied as Ruffalo's, is still remarkable. Even if Graysmith doesn't betray the same outwards signs of psychological ruin as Avery, who spends the last third of the movie sequestered on a houseboat playing

Pong (the video-game equivalent of battering one's head against the wall), or recede into slumped self-doubt like Toschi, he nevertheless undergoes a palpable transformation, peering out from his files at the world through wide, red-rimmed eyes, as if afraid to blink and miss something—anything.

The most perfunctory thing about *Zodiac* is the way that Graysmith's fixation alienates his blind-date-turned-second wife-Melanie. An overqualified Chloë Sevigny escapes the fatal fate of Gwyneth Paltrow in *Se7en* but can only do so much with a disposable role. ("Promise you won't tell Mom about our special project," Graysmith pleads with his school-age kids after enlisting their help as research assistants.) What's harrowing in the character's narrative isn't the question of what he stands to lose by chasing leads but rather what he might find if he keeps at it. The film makes a point of showing that while the Zodiac's victims were chosen primarily at random or out of convenience, Graysmith willingly puts himself in the crosshairs of the killer's

15-17. "This is the Zodiac speaking"; to underline the film's commentary on media, Fincher foregrounds broadcast technology during a live call-in segment; meanwhile, we see the film's other characters—Graysmith and Avery—watching rapt as a story they're already involved in takes a dramatic turn on live TV.

sniper-scope symbol. He's playing the Most Dangerous Game by his own choice.

#

There is a fourth major screen presence in *Zodiac*: the title character, who is played by a number of different actors in various guises before disappearing as a physical presence around the midpoint of the movie, last seen and heard threatening a female hitchhiker who survives her encounter. This set-piece, based on the recollections of one Kathleen Johns (Ione Skye) pays off the ruthlessness of what has come before even as it emphasizes Fincher's restraint. Because we've seen in bloody detail what the Zodiac is capable of in the prologue and the borderline-unwatchable lakeside filleting of a couple in Berryessa, his warning to Kathleen that "before I kill you, I'm going to throw your baby out the window" is hideously credible. But, amazingly, the historical record intervenes as a *deus ex machina*; Kathleen's unlikely escape and road-side salvation constitute this pressurized movie's only moment of true relief.

Zodiac's multiple-casting trick is there to account for the possibility—floated in Graysmith's book, as well as several other studies—of multiple killers, either working in tandem or in a copycat scenario. Broadly speaking, the film follows Graysmith's hypothesis that the most plausible suspect was one Arthur Leigh Allen (referred to in *Zodiac* the book pseudonymously as "Bob Starr"), a disgraced elementary school teacher with a history of animal abuse and pedophilia who died in 1992 surrounded by a veritable mountain of persuasive circumstantial evidence, including a series of supposedly self-incriminating comments to friends and relatives. Allen was ultimately exculpated by DNA testing and inconclusive fingerprint matches, events which *Zodiac* presents without trying to either reinforce or rebut them. "I don't want this [movie] to be about convicting Arthur Leigh Allen," Fincher said in 2005. "Certainly [Graysmith] came to his conclusion and it was good enough for him . . . When [Allen] died, he felt like it was put away. That's not what we want to represent."

Allen is played in *Zodiac* by John Carroll Lynch, best known as Frances McDormand's doting homebody husband in Joel and Ethan Coen's *Fargo* (1996). The sweet teddy-bear quality he essayed for the Coens is replaced by a wicked, low-key flamboyance: the performative streak of a man who likes to play with people. Visited at his factory job by Toschi and Armstrong and Vallejo PD Sergeant Jack Mulanax (Elias Koteas), Allen starts off cooperatively before adopting an oddly patronizing tone; as the interview goes on, he starts displaying taunting body language, flaunting potentially incriminating accessories like a pair of heavy duty boots and a Zodiac-brand wristwatch, which peek mischievously through his work coveralls. The scene is constructed by Fincher and editor Angus Wall as a series of rapt, over-the-shoulder shots, cut in sync with the investigators' skeptical sideways glances at once another.

"With these near-identical, shared looks, the three finally seem to see perceptually, intellectually, the stranger before them," wrote Manohla Dargis in the *New York Times*. "In this moment, sight becomes knowledge however tenuously grasped." As the shots grow tighter and the cutting rhythm accelerates, the impression is of a battle of wills—one that Allen somehow manages to win despite being outnumbered. "I'm not the Zodiac," he says, looming massively in the center of the frame, shot head-on for the first time, his eyes no longer darting but dead and black in their sockets. "And if I was, I certainly wouldn't tell you."

As a confrontation with evil, *Zodiac*'s interrogation scene is tantalizing but maddeningly inconclusive—certainly in comparison to *Se7en*, whose antagonist willingly turns himself in in exchange for an opportunity to use the back of a police cruiser as a bully pulpit. Everything about Lynch's acting allows for the possibility that Allen is lying, but that's not enough: what destroys the film's version of Toschi, who ends up demoted after accusations of forging a Zodiac letter to buttress his investigation, is that he can't translate his intuition into a material case. His seething, impotent certainty energizes Graysmith to pursue a particularly promising lead about Allen's proximity to Darlene Ferrin in Vallejo (he finds that they lived and worked across the street from one another in the summer of 1969). After bringing his findings to Toschi and getting his blessing—a scene soundtracked by the trumpet figure from "The Unanswered Question"—he goes to see Allen for himself.

In Graysmith's book, the author describes repeated visits to observe Allen in Vallejo in 1983, several years after his initial interrogation. Fincher wisely condenses these passages into a single sequence that serves, perversely and ingeniously, as *Zodiac*'s (anti-)climax. Arriving at a nondescript hardware store, Graysmith glimpses his man standing in one of the aisles.

18-20. Fincher likes to shape his procedurals around duos and *Zodiac* features a series of shifting allegiances, with Graysmith gradually moving away from Avery and towards Toschi after the latter is abandoned by his own partner, Bill Anderson.

"I need to stand there, I need to look him in the eye, and I need to know that it's him," Graysmith had told his wife when asked about the ultimate upshot of his quest. Face-to-face with the man who might be the Zodiac, Graysmith freezes; his sudden exit is at least as enigmatic as Allen's face. It's likely that Graysmith is frightened, but Fincher intuitively leaves it open as to why. The opaqueness of Lynch's expression, somewhere between irritation and recognition, becomes a *tabula rasa* on to which Graysmith projects every bit of horrifying knowledge he has about the Zodiac. Because we know what he knows, we're duly obliged to decide if the balding, heavyset cipher in his sights lives up to our to movie-addled expectations: a demonic Hurdy Gurdy Man; a West Coast Hannibal Lecter; a John Doe-style mastermind.

"If we catch John Doe and he turns out to be the devil, I mean if he's Satan himself, that might live up to our expectations," Detective Somerset tells his partner in *Se7en*. "But he's not the devil. He's just a man." There is, perhaps, a subtler form of horror in reading Graysmith's encounter as the desultory confirmation of this rationalist prophecy: a reminder that no matter how large the Zodiac loomed at the time, in the end he was nothing more than a damaged, antisocial, everyday American operating under cover of night—and all the scarier for that. But if Arthur Leigh Allen wasn't the Zodiac, then the possibility of an even stranger human specimen eluding detection—waiting somewhere out there in all that dark, in the enveloping negative space mapped *Zodiac*'s nighttime prologue and Toschi's arrival in the Presidio— remains in play. Would Robert Graysmith recognize that man? Would David Toschi? Would we?

There's an equally devastating ambivalence in *Zodiac*'s coda, which takes place in 1991 in an Ontario, California, airport, where Mike Mageau, the teenage survivor from the first scene, is shown a photo of Arthur Leigh Allen. "The last time I saw this face was July 4, 1969," he says gravely. "I am very sure that that's the man who shot me." The credibility of this statement is compromised by the fact that Mageau still only rates his "very sure" belief at an "8 out of 10," a claim shadowed by doubt, a fraction with a nagging remainder. It's also worth noting that Mageau is literally not the same person that he was in the film's first sequence: actor Lee Norris has been replaced by Jimmi Simpson, whose haggard, haunted expression makes him a mirror of Avery, Toschi and especially Graysmith.

21. As Arthur Leigh Allen, John Carroll Lynch is a dead-eyed enigma whose nonchalance becomes increasingly performative as the questioning progresses.

22. Arthur's Zodiac timepiece is deeply incriminating, but it also develops the movie's theme of time slipping away.

23-24. Tracking Allen to a hardware store years after the fact, Graysmith gets a good hard look at the man who he believes to be the Zodiac; staring into an abyss, neither he nor we know what to think as it stares back.

On one level, the recasting makes practical sense. The scene takes place twenty-two years after Mageau's first appearance, and most actors couldn't convincingly play that age range, with or without makeup. But in a movie where every other character is played by a single actor as they get older, Simpson's presence is a jarring switch, what *Fight Club*'s Tyler Durden would call a "change over." This is especially true in light of Fincher's statements about being hesitant to fully convict Arthur Leigh Allen. How do we watch a scene built around a character's appraisal of a face in a long-ago photograph (and which uses John Carroll Lynch's image to represent Allen) and not clock Mageau's own altered identity? This specific directorial choice deepens the same hairline fractures the film's diegesis opened up by casting multiple actors as the Zodiac (Lynch is not among them). Mageau's comments ostensibly close the case—even Fincher's filmmaking leaves the proverbial filing cabinet open a crack, punctuating *Zodiac*'s epic cosmic drama with a question mark—one awaiting an answer that may never come.

23.

24.

After directing the Panic Room, Fincher began work on an adaptation of author James Ellroy's true crime novel *The Black Dahlia*.

Ives may have been quoting the line "Thou art the unanswered question" from Emerson's 1847 poem "The Sphinx."

Fig C. *In Cold Blood*, Truman Capote, 1966 [Novel]

Truman Capote's true-crime novel served to both popularize and elevated the genre, combining journalism with character study and broader cultural analysis.

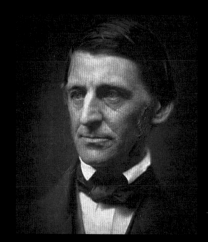

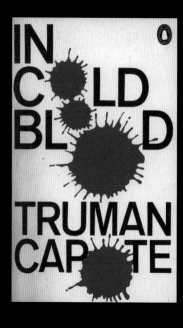

Fig F. *The Texas Chain Saw Massacre*, Tobe Hooper, 1974

It was common practice for exploitation movies to advertise themselves (however loosely) as being based on "true events," a tactic evoked in *Zodiac*'s opening title card.

Fig G. *On Top of the World*, Norman Rockwell, 1928

The wholesome imagery of painter Norman Rockwell is evoked and destroyed during *Zodiac*'s opening murder scene.

Fig H. *Invasion of the Body Snatchers*, Philip Kaufman, 1978 [Still from a movie]

One of several San Francisco classics alluded to in *Zodiac*, notably in the recurring shots of the Trans-America Pyramid.

Fig D. *The Most Dangerous Game*, **1932**

Zodiac's crimes were inspired by "The Most Dangerous Game," a 1924 Richard Connell short story that was made into a movie in 1932.

Fig E. *All the President's Men*, **Alan J. Pakula, 1976**

A key American film of the 1970s, Alan Pakula's fact-based thriller about the *Washington Post*'s investigation of Watergate is used as a visual and rhythmic reference throughout *Zodiac*.

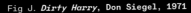

Fig I. *Bullitt*, **Peter Yates, 1968**

Steve McQueen modelled his performance as Frank Bullitt on David Toschi, right down to the way he holstered his gun.

Fig J. *Dirty Harry*, **Don Siegel, 1971**

The sniper pursued by Clint Eastwood in this box-office smash is named Scorpio—a nod to the Zodiac alongside Harry Callahan's Bullitt-like resemblance to David Toschi.

WRITER James Vanderbilt
CINEMATOGRAPHER Harris Savides
EDITOR Angus Wall

BUDGET $65 million
BOX OFFICE $84.8 million

LENGTH 157 min

The eerie superimpositions
of corpses over images
of surveillance and
recording equipment
distills the eerie subtext
of a series where murder
is transformed into
a field of study; the
fleeting, near-subliminal
glimpses of womens'
bodies suggest both the
cold, depersonalizing
perspectives of their
killers and the stakes
that the FBI profilers
are playing for as they
seek ways to better
identify and understand
potential suspects.

1.3
MINDHUNTER

Arriving at an emotionally charged hostage scene in Braddock, Pennsylvania in 1977, FBI Special Agent Holden Ford attempts to negotiate with a paranoid gunman holed up in the back of a warehouse; his soft-spoken entreaties are swallowed up by the chasmic concrete expanse of the parking lot. Three years later, Agent Ford, now officially "expert" in matters of criminal psychology, is summoned to the hospital bed of incarcerated serial murderer Ed Kemper, who rises to enfold him in a suffocating bearhug. What was once a matter of detached professionalism has advanced—or collapsed—into a form of familiarity; for all the time and space traversed in the first season of *Mindhunter*, its thematic arc can be mapped through the steadily narrowing gap between a standoff and an embrace.

These scenes are from the first and tenth episodes of *Mindhunter*, each of which was directed by David Fincher, who also helmed two additional episodes in Season One and three more in Season Two. That makes a total of seven out of nineteen overall—a significant percentage still doesn't square with any kind of totalizing auteurist mythology. To categorize *Mindhunter* as a purely auteur work is to discount its multiple sources of authorship; in the streaming arena, as with "prestige television," the question of creative vision usually resides

1.

2.

3.

1-4.   More than *Se7en* or
       Zodiac, *Mindhunter*
       examines group
       dynamics in
       investigation, with
       Agents Ford, Tench
       and Dr. Carr working
       in sync to establish
       protocols for the
       FBI's fledgling
       behavioral science
       unit. Their most
       compelling interview
       subject is the hulking
       serial murderer Ed
       Kemper, who offers
       himself as an open
       book for study.

with the creator or showrunner. Obvious contemporary examples include David Chase with *The Sopranos*; David Lynch and Mark Frost with *Twin Peaks*; David Simon with *The Wire*; and so on. *Mindhunter*'s officially credited creator and main writer is the British playwright Joe Penhall, a former beat reporter with a stated interest in criminal psychology. But the project did not originate with him. Penhall was recruited to work on the show in 2015, six years after Charlize Theron originally presented Fincher with a copy of retired FBI agent John E. Douglas's 1995 memoir (cowritten by Mark Olshaker), which she'd optioned for miniseries treatment.

Originally slated for production at HBO, *Mindhunter* migrated to Netflix thanks to Fincher's connections following the success of *House of Cards*. "David and I were both fascinated with psychopathy and narcissism and personality disorders because I think we felt, somewhere on the grapevine, there were other people out there who weren't serial killers who were high-ranking politicians," Penhall told journalist Joe Bucher in 2015, nodding perhaps to the cartoonishly Machiavellian characters on *House of Cards*. "I think we were on a mission with *Mindhunter* to show that these people were actually ordinary people, sad to say."

#

Mindhunter's subject matter was sympatico with Netflix's burgeoning investment in true-crime documentaries. In 2015, the streaming giant unveiled one of its most significant conversation pieces in the ten-part miniseries *Making a Murderer*, about a Wisconsin man whose wrongful conviction of attempted murder contributed to his actually becoming a killer. Whether one saw Netflix's braintrust riding a millennial resurgence of serial killer fascination or trying to create one—while simultaneously shoring up an original and cost-effective content library—was a matter of perspective. In the years since *Zodiac*, Fincher had seemingly made efforts to not repeat himself, with only *The Girl with the Dragon Tattoo* qualifying as "genre" cinema in the mold of *Se7en* or *The Game*. "I took on this project in spite of [that notion]," Fincher told *Time* in 2016, responding to a query about *Mindhunter*'s familiar subject matter. "This show is about FBI agents, and how they were able, through the application of empathy, to understand those people who were so difficult to understand," he added. "That's what was intriguing to me. I don't need another serial killer title on my résumé . . . this was not about that."

Mindhunter's overall focus on procedure and investigation marks it a distinctly Fincherian project, with the director serving as considerably more than a hired gun. By the second season, it was widely understood that in addition to serving as *Mindhunter*'s executive producer, Fincher had taken on the mantle of show-runner, overseeing production on location in Pittsburgh and working closely with the other directors and in the editing room. "Even when [David] wasn't directing an episode, he was overseeing it," producer Peter Mavromates told *Variety* in 2020. "It was exhausting."

Fincher's obsessive commitment to *Mindhunter* came with an element of behind-the-scenes drama. While Penhall had been involved in the show's development at HBO, the move to Netflix saw Fincher taking control of the writers' room and decamping to Pittsburgh with the production. Penhall stayed in London, having already written seven of the first ten episodes. He contracted several of his own writers, including Carly Weay, Jennifer Haley, and Erin Levy, whom he referred to as "very classy . . . they'd written *Mad Men*, had Emmy awards . . . They couldn't really be part of a writers' room and be bossed around and paid a pittance and made to rewrite these 25 times"; the various parties communicated by telephone and online while shooting and editing Season One. It was a diplomatic but unsustainable arrangement. By the beginning of Season Two, it became apparent that Penhall had been pushed out, with Fincher's assistant director Courtenay Miles promoted to showrunner. In an interview with *Entertainment Weekly*, actor Holt McCallany referred pointedly to "Joe's departure," citing it as the point at which "[Fincher] sort of really began to rework the scripts and the [show] bible and everything changed a lot."

Mindhunter's compromises with the process and logistics of longform storytelling are real and yet feel subsumed both by the overall quality of the production and a deep sense of connectivity with Fincher's oeuvre. Its impetus is not repetition but refinement, continuing and expanding the dialogue started in *Se7en* and answered in *Zodiac*. Those were, respectively, a movie about a serial killer and a movie about the idea of serial killing; *Mindhunter* is, more than anything else, a parable about the paradoxical nature of expertise, of knowledge as its own vanishing point. Where *Se7en* exhumed *Psycho* and *Zodiac*'s location evoked *Vertigo*, *Mindhunter* could just as easily be titled *The Man Who Knew Too Much*. The show's timeline picks up

4.

almost exactly where *Zodiac* left off in the late 1970s, in a moment when well-publicized figures like the Zodiac—as well as his fellow West Coast boogeyman Charles Manson—captured the public imagination in ways that led to a complex and complementary uptick in media coverage, pop-cultural depiction, and institutional engagement with serial murder, along with the steady proliferation of the thing itself.

These intersecting vertices of practice, perception, and protective measures are made visible in *Mindhunter*'s opening sequence by the geometric clarity of Fincher's direction, which not only emphasizes the space separating Ford (Jonathan Groff) from the gunman by keeping the latter at an indistinct distance from the camera, but also clusters a group of journalists at the far edge of the fray. Swarming together behind Ford as the young negotiator takes over the scene, they're surrogates for the same voyeuristic prurience exploited by the media-savvy antagonists of *Se7en* and *Zodiac* (and foregrounded by Lang in *M*)—the middlemen between criminals and their audience.

Desperate, disheveled Cody Miller (David H. Holmes) is not a John Doe-style mastermind holding court; he's a mentally ill man who's gone off his medication, and his suicide speaks not to a grand design but a lack of control on all sides. The precise configuration of the various parties involved—the cops; the gunman; the FBI interloper; the reporters—is conducive to a sensationalism that heightens the scene's tone while functioning simultaneously as its subject. As in *Zodiac*'s prologue, Fincher arranges genre conventions into a densely self-reflexive pattern before exploding them, here in the form of a startling, borderline-Cronenbergian money shot as Miller turns the shotgun on himself.

"Where do we go when motive becomes elusive?" asks a professor in a criminal psychology class at the FBI Headquarters in Quantico. Out in the audience sits Ford, who's been sent there to train at the behest of his supervisors. It's in this heady, pedagogical milieu that the young agent finds his calling as a man of ideas rather than action. "I'd rather use firearms" snarks a fellow recruit unconvinced by the prospect of a talking cure; later, Fincher shows Ford wincing as he passes a firing range en route to the classroom, an echo of Mark Zuckerburg's head-down, beta-male stroll back to his dorm at the outset of *The Social Network*. (Of all of Fincher's protagonists, it is Zuckerberg whom Ford most resembles: both are mainly interested in systems to the extent that they can

hack them and take a certain satisfaction in being the smartest person in the room; they also both treat their girlfriends pretty badly.) If Ford's motives for getting involved in behavioral science are elusive to himself, *Mindhunter* clearly diagrams how he's part of a larger shift in psychological theory and practice, a move away from assertions of "unknowability" towards a codified, categorical, and clinical method of understanding.

\#

Fincher's previous investigators were cops whose forays into psychology were a means to an end and nothing more: recall Detective Mills's boredom about profiling John Doe versus his desire to catch him. Ford and his new Behavioral Science Unit colleagues are cultivating a different skill set, subject to departmental skepticism. The placement of their office in the basement at Quantico shows where they rank on the organizational totem pole; it's also a funny riff on the idea that serial killers are themselves basement-dwellers, an idea satirized by Graysmith's subterranean encounter in *Zodiac*. By the 1990s, the kind of criminal profiling being pioneered in *Mindhunter* had become standard procedure for law enforcement and duly popularized—and glamorized—through movies and television, protocol effectively distilled into accessible prime-time formula. (The most successful example was CBS's glib and grotesque *CSI: Crime Scene Investigation*, whose formula proved conducive to regionalized spin-offs.) While exercising its fair share of artistic license—and adopting the same tenets of "prestige TV" displayed by *House of Cards* in a move to distance it from its network brethren—*Mindhunter* strives to illuminate the challenges of the described in Douglas's book, and to give a group of trailblazers their due.

The character of Holden Ford is loosely modelled on Douglas; his Christian name, though points unsubtly to the hero of J. D. Salinger's novel *The Catcher in the Rye*, placing *Mindhunter*'s protagonist in a tradition of eager, self-possessed young men seeking intellectual and emotional initiation. Groff, an appealing actor specializing in musical-comedy exuberance (he won a Tony Award for playing King George III in *Hamilton*) plays Ford smartly as a straight arrow who gets bent out of shape, a crooked progression recalling Special Agent Dale Cooper's slide to the dark side in *Twin Peaks*. *Mindhunter*'s fully realist and meticulously Fincherian universe requires a different sort of representation, however. Ford's

5.   Holden's initiation into psychological profiling is juxtaposed against his developing—and increasingly troubled—romantic relationship with grad student Debbie, which suffers as a result of his immersion in his work.

6-8. Traversing the country on an ad hoc lecture circuit, Ford and Tench experience the physical and psychological dislocation of constant, rootless movement; a montage in episode two set to Steve Miller's "Fly Like an Eagle" visualizes the circular, recursive monotony of their routine, moving dazedly from motel to motel.

6.

7.

8.

unsettling transformation over the course of *Mindhunter*'s first season is not as a matter of being invaded by an external force *à la* Coop, but a symptom of internal change. He's not possessed but obsessed, a condition that syncs him with Jake Gyllenhaal's Robert Graysmith, whose wide-eyed Eagle Scout act similarly masked a compulsive intelligence.

Ford's boss Special Agent Bill Tench (McCallany) is closer to *Se7en*'s Detective Somerset: a laconic veteran clinging to principle amidst the careerist jostling of the bureaucrats around and above him. He's also a family man with a wife and adopted son, a vulnerabilizing status that comes more into the foreground in Season Two. The character is based on the FBI agent Roger Ressler, who coined the English-language term "serial killer," and he's acted by McCallany with a watchful authority that genuinely seems to emanate from another era—and not necessarily the one where *Mindhunter* takes place. With his squared-off haircut and slightly sloping ex-collegiate jock's bulk, Tench could be an avatar of the Eisenhower '50s, and there's an old-guard aspect to his behavior. This stolid appearance belies a progressive ethos, however. Tench is sympathetic to his new charge's radical approach, but he's better than Ford at measuring his rhetoric in the company of peers and superiors, and also at identifying and mingling with the hard-drinking, long-suffering, stress-fractured beat cop he resembles at a glance.

Mindhunter is a show about transitions and adaptability—of orthodoxies and institutions in a state of flux. The idea that interviewing already incarcerated killers could generate positive, preventative consequences—and with it, good publicity—is central to the FBI subsidizing Ford and Tench's work; the question of scholarly merit comes second. One key endorsement comes from Cambridge psychology professor Dr. Wendy Carr (Anna Torv) an Ivy League superstar recruited to give Tench's unit some academic ballast. From a more functional perspective, the character is there to open up *Mindhunter*'s macho milieu to a set of distaff dramatic possibilities: Dr. Carr is Fincher's first-ever female investigator, presaging Lisbeth Salander in *The Girl with the Dragon Tattoo* and Detective Rhonda Boney in *Gone Girl*. It's telling that despite Torv's dryly seriocomic performance style—a persona perfectly pitched to Fincher's sensibility—Dr. Carr remains the most remote of the show's central trio. This is not solely a matter of the character's recessive temperament. Carr is a featured protagonist but only in a glancing way, defined mainly by what she withholds

9.

10.

11.

12.

13.

14.

15.

16.

(her closeted sexual orientation) and more often than not serving as a sounding board for Ford and Tench's crises. Her gender is emphasized largely in counterpoint to what feels like an endless litany of unavenged female victims, whether eviscerated on the spot or dissected after the fact. *Mindhunter*'s credit sequence underlines this pervasive, fetishistic misogyny through fleeting, near-subliminal inserts of female cadavers overlaid with images of recording equipment, an unsettling conceptual palimpsest superimposing the technological aspect of behavioural science against the flesh-and-blood reality of serial murder. The imagery also suggests the mechanical, depersonalized nature of the crimes themselves.

The core irony of *Mindhunter*, which works both on the show's terms and in the larger context of Fincher's body of work, lies in how the monomaniacal focus exerted by its main characters on cataloguing the private lives of others becomes its own unusual form of fulfillment at the expense of "conventional" domesticity. It's less that Ford, Tench, and Carr form a de facto "family unit" as that they complement one another's respective solitudes; in the basement, loneliness becomes a shared condition. The show is as attuned to the procedural grind and its discontents as *Se7en* and *Zodiac* and exploits the longform format to put across the impression of characters caught in the gears. During postproduction on Season One, Fincher was concerned that episode two was lacking in pavement-pounding drag, and conceived a stand-alone sequence to convey the mix of fatigue and determination described in Douglas's book. Editor Kirk Baxter compiled a highlight reel of scenes from earlier Fincher movies (mainly *Fight Club*) cut to the Steve Miller Band's 1976 hit "Fly Like an Eagle." "This was to give David an idea of pace and how many shots he wanted," Baxter told *IndieWire*. "Once we had that together, I came back and cut it in isolation."

Like the all-CGI time-lapse sequence which depicts the construction of the Transamerica Pyramid in *Zodiac*, *Mindhunter*'s standout montage compresses and poeticizes the passing of time. In two minutes, it narrates Ford and Tench's quotidian road-warrior exploits as a linear mosaic made up of blink-quick close-ups, two-shots and inserts, sutured together in a steady, driving rhythm by a set of witty graphic matches. We see Ford and Tench flying, driving, eating, drinking, flossing, sleeping, staring and brooding, jet-lagged evangelists on behalf of their fledgling initiative; meanwhile, on the soundtrack, Miller serenely describes the hypnotized vibe of "slipping, slipping, slipping into the future." While serving in one sense as storytelling shorthand—and to show off the breadth of *Mindhunter*'s periodized world-building, from vintage airport lounges to motels to diners—the sequence also stands as an expression of self-contained aestheticism—of style for its own playful, invigorating sake. "Where it really dances," Baxter added, "is when you get repetition of action: four or five plates going down in a row or walking into four or five motel rooms, that musical rhythm of how many am I gonna use? To get the point across with three and then punctuate it with a plop of sugar going into the coffee cup."

Fincher's control of tone in *Mindhunter*'s second episode manifests as a balancing act between the kinetic exhilaration of the travel montage and the more static, head-to-head style utilized in subsequent, re-creations of Ford and Tench's Brief Interviews With Hideous Men. Because *Mindhunter* is a true-crime series, it gets a certain amount of mileage (and caters to a certain viewership) though its expertly cast cameos by household-name serial killers, a murderer's row of American Psychos including David Berkowitz, Richard Speck, and Charles Manson. The towering, heavyset, bespectacled Kemper, played in a tour-de-force performance by Cameron Britton, is the show's most explicitly Fincherian creation: a chatty, self-annotating sociopath along the lines of John Doe enfolded into the forbidding physique of John Carroll Lynch's Arthur Leigh Allen.

"It's my day off," says Tench by way of declining Ford's invitation to join him in deposing Kemper—a highly unofficial visit that, once discovered by their superior Robert Shepard (Cotter Smith), lands both of them in significant trouble. Kemper was a diagnosed paranoid schizophrenic who murdered his grandparents as a teen before being institutionalized and released for model behavior, after which he abducted, tortured and killed a number of young female hitchhikers as well as his own mother—crimes he eagerly confessed to after turning himself into the authorities. "I started feeling the folly of the whole damn thing," Kemper was quoted as saying years later. "I just said to hell with it and called it all off." After being found sane and guilty by a jury and receiving seven consecutive life sentences in lieu of the death penalty (his infamous request for "death by torture" at his trial having been denied) Kemper became a willing interview subject for Douglas as well as number of other journalists and documentary filmmakers. The contrast between the unfathomable savagery of his crimes and the odd sagacity of his conversation (plus his almost comic-book-sized physical dimensions of 6'9" and 300 pounds) marked Kemper as a taboo sort of cult hero, name-checked in the lyrics of underground rock bands and studied by authors like Bret Easton Ellis and Thomas Harris, the latter of whom adapted aspects of his case and persona into *The Silence of the Lambs* via the character of Buffalo Bill.

9-16. Drawing from John Douglas's book about his experiences at the FBI, *Mindhunter* presents a roll call of American psychos including Dennis Radner, Richard Speck, William Pierce, David Berkowitz and Charles Manson, whose various tense interrogations form the series' dramatic spine.

17. Ford and Tench experience their share of pushback during lecturesfrom local police departments whose officers could care less about "why" suspects commit crimes; the gap between theory and practice—between studying killers and stopping them—figures deeply into *Mindhunter*'s thematic matrix.

17.

18. Tench and Ford embark
on their new project
with differing degrees
of resignation and
satisfaction. The
parallel between their
below-ground level
digs and the cliché
of serial killers as
basement-dwellers is a
joke played throughout
the series.

18.   19.

What makes Kemper a locus of fascination for Ford is the way he presents himself as an open book to be studied—an auteur offering behind-the-scenes commentaries on his works. Britton's performance is wonderfully solicitous: even while constrained by leg irons, Kemper seems to be holding court. "Cops like me, because they can talk to me, more than their own wives," he tells Ford brightly, simultaneously laying the groundwork for what he perceives as a friendship and hinting at the deep reservoir of misogyny underlying his crimes. (It also calls back to Debbie's joke to Ford during their first date: "You don't like people disagreeing with you . . . that's very unusual for a guy in law enforcement.") Memorably dubbed the "Co-Ed Killer," Kemper acknowledged the matricidal urges that drove him to use female strangers as surrogates for his true target (a case of real life imitating *Psycho*) and that killing and associated extracurricular activities served as a spur and substitute for sexual gratification.

#

Of all the real-life killers included in *Mindhunter*, Kemper is the one who appears closest to self-actualization. In *Zodiac*, Arthur Leigh Allen made a glib spectacle of his own denial; Kemper hones his own transparency to a fine, sharp point, piercing Ford's authority and reducing him to a sort of student, one who internalizes his lessons all too well. Later in the season, interviewing the Chicagoan mass murderer Richard Speck—a less articulate subject than Kemper with a similarly vicious streak of woman hate—Ford asks him what made him want to "take eight ripe cunts out of this world," a gross deviation from protocol meant to establish the "common ground" theorized

in Quantico's classroom. The audio recording of the interview will, in time, imperil Ford and Tench's project on grounds of inappropriate verbiage (a major plot point as Season One winds to a close.) What it really points to, however, is the extent to which Ford has internalized the pervasive misogyny that has become his area of expertise.

The weakest aspect of *Zodiac*—the dissolution of Graysmith's marriage—is reprised in *Mindhunter*'s first season through the increasingly contentious relationship between Ford and his girlfriend Debbie (Hannah Gross), a sociology major who stoically suffers her lover's workaholic tendencies. (Gross's quick-witted deadpan delivery in the pilot has a hint of Rooney Mara in *The Social Network* and points to a screwball potential that goes largely untapped.) In *Zodiac*, Graysmith's inability to put his family first felt perfunctory, but *Mindhunter* excavates distressing subtext from Ford's struggles on this front. Critic Scott Tobias describes this later iteration of Ford as "a lone wolf, hewing closer to the misogyny and 'organized killer' methodology of his serial-killer subjects than the collaborative effort of his peers," a status at once put across and complicated by Groff's interestingly guileless performance style, which codes the character as a sort of "virgin"—an innocent in thrall to the very different kinds of "experience" represented by Debbie and Kemper.

In the standout ninth episode, which opens with the Speck interview, Fincher cinches the link between Ford's commitment to his craft and the demagnetization of his moral compass. He expresses concern to Debbie about her possible infidelity, mirroring the possessive sexual paranoia modelled by Kemper and other interview subjects; he also carelessly oversteps his bounds with an off-the-clock interview of an

18-19. Following a terrifyingly intimate encounter with Kemper, Ford suffers a nervous breakdown; the final images of season one and the opening moments of season two show a character whose loss of control—and emerging identity crisis—will have to be addressed upon his return to work.

20-21. This sequence of the masked BTK Killer at work emphasizes the series' baroque horror elements that hark back to the likes of *Se7en*, but also an abiding interest in the visual motif of the dark mystery behind the closed door.

elementary school principal, Roger Wade (Mark Kudisch), suspected of pedophilia. As a result of this intervention—but in the absence of anything like proof—the principal is fired and his furious, scandalized wife confronts Ford for effectively destroying their lives.

The staging of this conversation, with Ford standing outside his door and Mrs. Wade (Enid Graham) hanging back at the other end of the hallway, deliberately recalls the standoff in Pennsylvania, with Ford now occupying the screen position of the late Cody Miller. (A great touch: Mrs. Wade is framed by a set of elevator doors that keep straining to close automatically behind her.) The question of whether Mr. Wade is actually guilty is never resolved, but implications of the blocking are disturbing nonetheless. Our hero has achieved the closeness and insight he desired in the pilot, but at the cost of the empathy he's meant to be developing; whatever progress he's made is bumping up against a point of no return.

Crucially, Debbie plays mute witness to this encounter. In the tenth episode, she works up the nerve to confront Ford over their crumbling relationship, at which point he coldly and preemptively psychoanalyzes her motivations using language and techniques derived from his vocation. It's a reversal of her presumptuously sizing him up on their first date, but in this case, turnabout is less fair play than revenge. Their breakup frees him to revisit his true romance with Kemper, who has read a newspaper story in which the agent is quoted as saying that they're "friends."

When Ford enters Kemper's hospital room, Fincher cuts to the latter's point of view, a perspectival switch emphasized by the gesture of the killer putting on his glasses: it is from Kemper's perspective that Ford comes into focus. They talk about whether or not Ford considers Kemper a friend: "in the context of our work together . . . sure." Kemper's eyes light up at Ford's use of the word *together*, with its little shiver of complicity, the same teasing solidarity alluded to by John Doe with his double-edged plea and invitation to "HELP ME," or burlesqued by Arthur Leigh Allen sending Detective Toschi a letter years after his interrogation reading "Dear David, if I can ever be of any help to you, just let me know—I'm sorry I wasn't your man."

Whether Kemper is merely taunting Ford or genuinely seeking a connection, the suggestion that they're on the same wavelength is devastating.

And then comes the hug, with its implied physical threat (he waits until the orderly has departed) and menacing sense of communion with somebody—and something—that even the most curious among us would probably prefer to remain unknown. Ford has become an expert, and it has broken him. His subsequent panic attack, scored to Led Zeppelin's psychedelic pathfinder hymn "In the Light," concludes *Mindhunter*'s first season on an unusually bleak note; the final scene, which shows the as-yet-unnamed BTK killer Dennis Rader (Sonny Valicenti) ominously burning a set of pictures in his backyard doubles down on the ominousness.

The steady weaving of BTK into *Mindhunter*'s first season through a series of cryptic vignettes (we mostly see him at work as an ADT service technician) continues in the first three Fincher-directed hours of Season Two, including a horrifying, Roxy Music-scored cold open in the first episode where Radner's wife discovers him practicing autoerotic asphyxiation in their bathroom, clad in a garish clown mask—a revelation occasioned by an unlocked bathroom door. "In every dream home, a heartache," croons Bryan Ferry, a phrase that Fincher mines for its disconcertingly wide-scale sociological implications while using it to narrow in on his heroes' corrupted domestic lives. Later on in the same episode, Tench notices his own bome's back door ajar, an indication that somebody's been sneaking off in the night: the culprit turns out to be his adopted, pre-pubescent son Brian (Zachary

20.

21.

22-23. Throughout *Mindhunter*, the role of media in driving public interest in the phenomenon of serial murder— and its complicating effect on matters of investigation—is manifested through images of the characters watching coverage of their work.

24. As the work/life scales are tipped towards the former, Tench finds himself alone and abandoned by his troubled family, a dismal cliffhanger that accrues poignancy in the light of the series' cancellation.

Scott Ross), who may be harbouring morbid fantasies of his own.

Fincher does some memorable directorial work in Season Two, like an interview between Tench and one of BTK's surviving victims, who is described as being badly disfigured but whose face is never shown; instead, the camera stays mostly on McCallany's face as he listens, frustrating one set of potentially prurient expectations while engaging our mind's-eye in reconstructing the ordeal. (It's a sophisticated example of telling-*as*-showing.) There's also a sly bit of self-citation in a short sequence showing Radner working in a public library whose glowing desk lamps recall Somerset's nighttime reading session in *Se7en*.

#

Where Fincher's contribution is felt most strongly in Season Two is in the deepening motif of serial-killer-as-celebrity-figure. The character of Ted Gunn (Michael Cerevis), who takes over the Behavioral Science unit from the departing Shepard, exemplifies institutional opportunism, offering Tench, Ford, and Carr increased resources in an attempt to secure media renown, while the casting of Cerevis nods—however obliquely— to the actor's memorable performance as

John Wilkes Booth in the original company of Stephen Sondheim's *Assassins*, a pitch black musical revue set in a purgatorial shooting gallery featuring cameos by would-be Presidential killers. *Mindhunter* mimics Sondheim's conceit in season two by including David Berkowitz (Oliver Cooper) and Charles Manson (Damon Herriman, who also played Manson in Quentin Tarantino's *Once Upon a Time in . . . Hollywood* [2019]), whose infamy rubs off on their interlocutors. Formerly departmental heretics, Ford and Tench are received by their peers as heroes, pressed to share war stories.

The season's final four episodes, all directed by Carl Franklin, are devoted to the media circus around the Atlanta Child Murders of 1979 to 1981, and how it complicated and compromised on-the-ground efforts to locate a killer suspected of having more than two dozen underage victims. Franklin, whose résumé includes the superb 1992 neo-noir *One False Move*, ably navigates the material's racial and sociological undertones, framing Ford's investment in the case as an attempt at personal redemption ringed with guilt over being humiliated and outed in a fashion by Kemper; a scene showing Groff's pale, lanky FBI man carrying a cross through Atlanta as part of a surveillance operation draws a satirical bead on the character's white man's burden.

Franklin's directorial vision is his own, and it coalesces nicely with the show's larger Fincherian project, which, as in *Zodiac*, pivots on irresolution. Ford and Tench's profiling leads the police to a likely suspect in the form of the furtively self-contradicting Wayne Williams (Christopher Livingston), an African American whose racial identity confounds the team's agreed model of a white male assailant. After the arrest however, there is only enough evidence to charge Williams with the murders of two adults, and none of the children. The season ends with Ford helplessly watching a press conference in which Atlanta's political leadership claims its partial victory while conceding a larger defeat. "As of 2019, none of the remaining 27 cases have been prosecuted" reads a title card as the episode—and the season—draws to a frustrating, unsatisfying close.

It's an ending as open as *Zodiac*'s, and it will remain so for the foreseeable future. The plan had been to continue the show's narrative into the 1990s, eventually depicting the identification and capture of Radner as BTK, but in 2019, Groff, McCallany and Torv were released from their contracts and *Mindhunter* was placed on "indefinite hold"—a purgatorial euphemism for cancellation. In October of 2020, Fincher confirmed that the show's second season would be its last for the foreseeable future, citing a combination of high costs and creative fatigue as factors. "It's a 90-hour workweek, [and] it absorbs everything in your life," Fincher told *Vulture*'s Mark Harris. "For the viewership it had, it was a very expensive show, [and] one some level, you have to be realistic—dollars have to equal eyeballs." By cutting loose of *Mindhunter*, Fincher was able to develop and produce *Mank* as part of his deal with Netflix, privileging a more explicitly personal and self-contained project over a series defined by creative and medium-specific compromises and yet strengthened, however inadvertently, by an imposed lack of closure. The image of Ford staring helplessly at the television in an Atlanta hotel room is answered in the final moments by a glimpse of Radner in his own motel in Kansas City, donning a mask, surrounded by news clippings of his exploits and trophies from his victims, tightening a noose around his own neck in implied ecstacy—and in the absence of any authorities closing in. He's still out there, unknowable and undiscovered. Nothing is over; nothing is contained; time keeps on slipping into the future.

24.

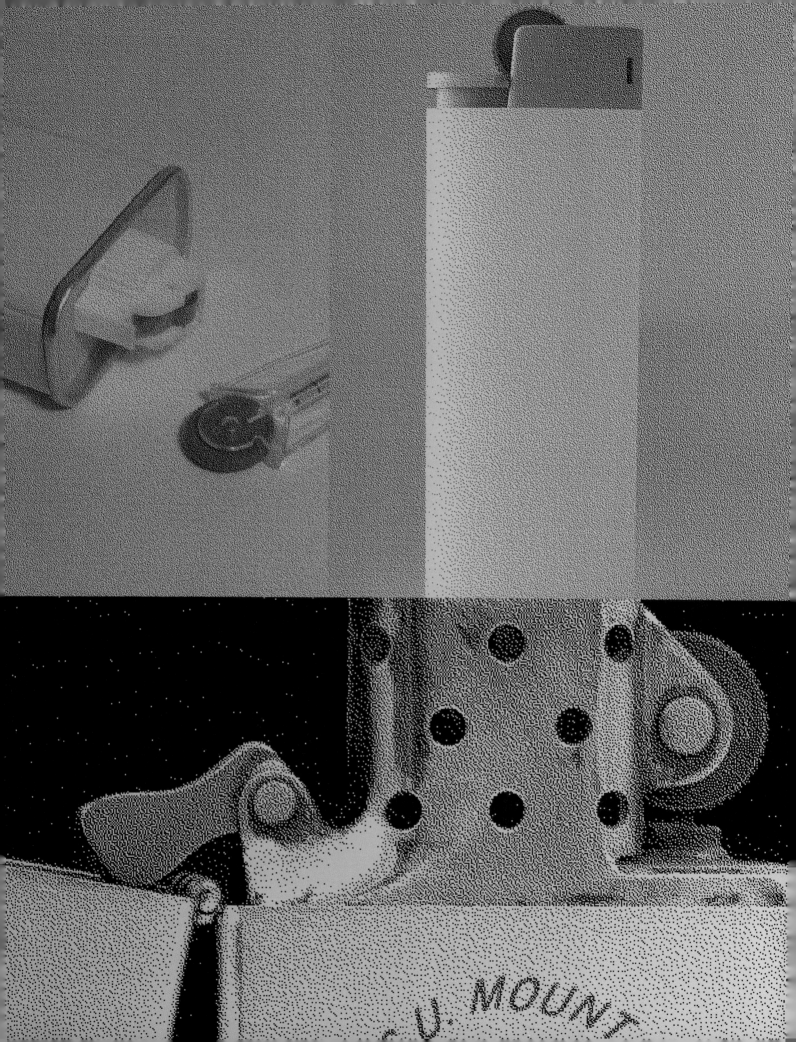

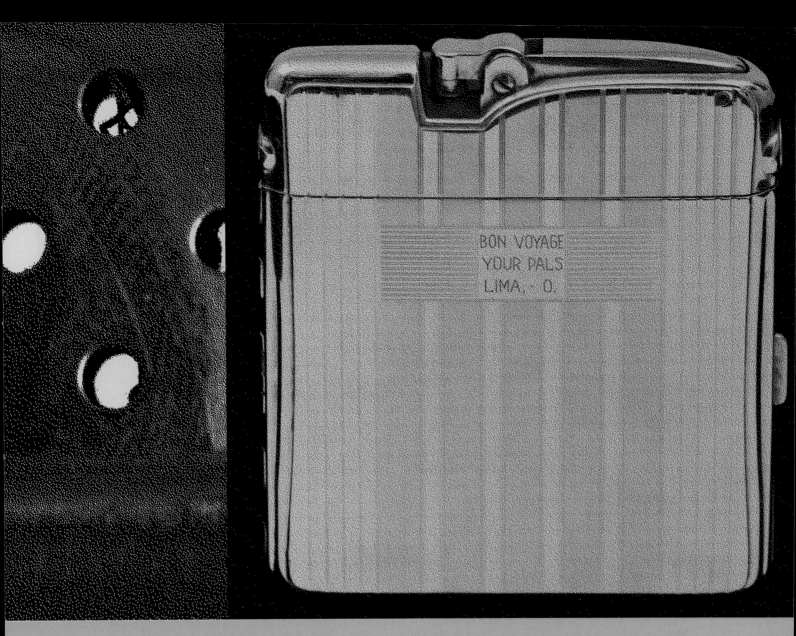

MAXIMUM
SECURITY

< Images of descent, intrusion and troubled slumber start *Alien 3* on a nightmarish note; after the unequivocally happy ending of *Aliens*, Fincher sets about penetrating the audience's sense of security via fleeting glimpses of the Alien stowing away on Ripley's ship.

2.1
ALIEN 3

2007

In his 2017 book *Prison Movies: Cinema Behind Bars*, Kevin Kehrwald analyzes the genre in terms of identification and ideology; he argues that in a true prison film, whether tied to a Depression-era cycle entwined with gangster pictures or set in the present tense, the audience is oriented with an individual or group of inmates against an institutional power structure. As for the prison space, it should be treated simultaneously as "the principal subject of investigation and the

dominant agent of oppression," not simply a setting, but a locus of meaning and morality in and of itself.

Alien 3 unfolds wholly within the cavernous confines of a maximum-security correctional facility on the windswept world of Fiorina 161, colloquially known as "Fury." This nickname could just as easily be applied to the hothouse atmosphere of its lone, man-made landmark, inside whose walls a small group of prisoners and administrators

are perched on different rungs of a panoptic power structure weighted against long-serving and new initiates alike. "We ain't got no entertainment center," observes one hardened lifer, by way of inventory, or a lack thereof. "No climate control, no surveillance, no freezers, no fucking ice cream, no rubbers, no women, no guns . . . all we got here is shit."

The filmmaking resources required to furnish a convincing vision of carceral desperation are considerable: *Alien 3*'s squalid

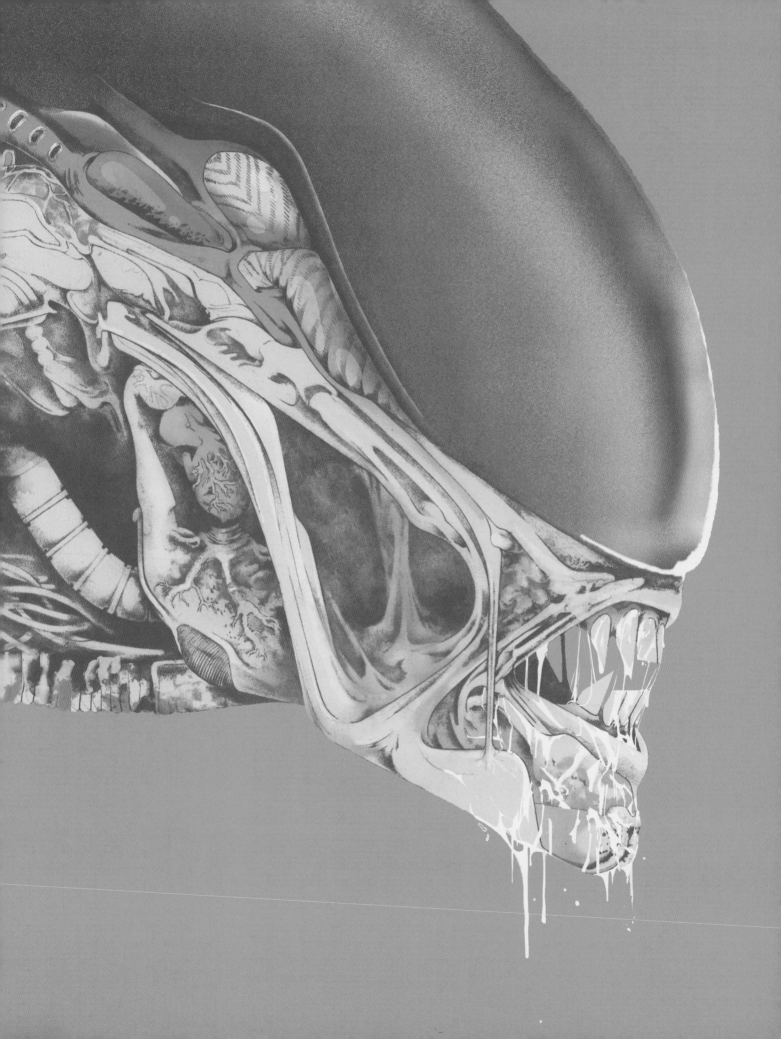

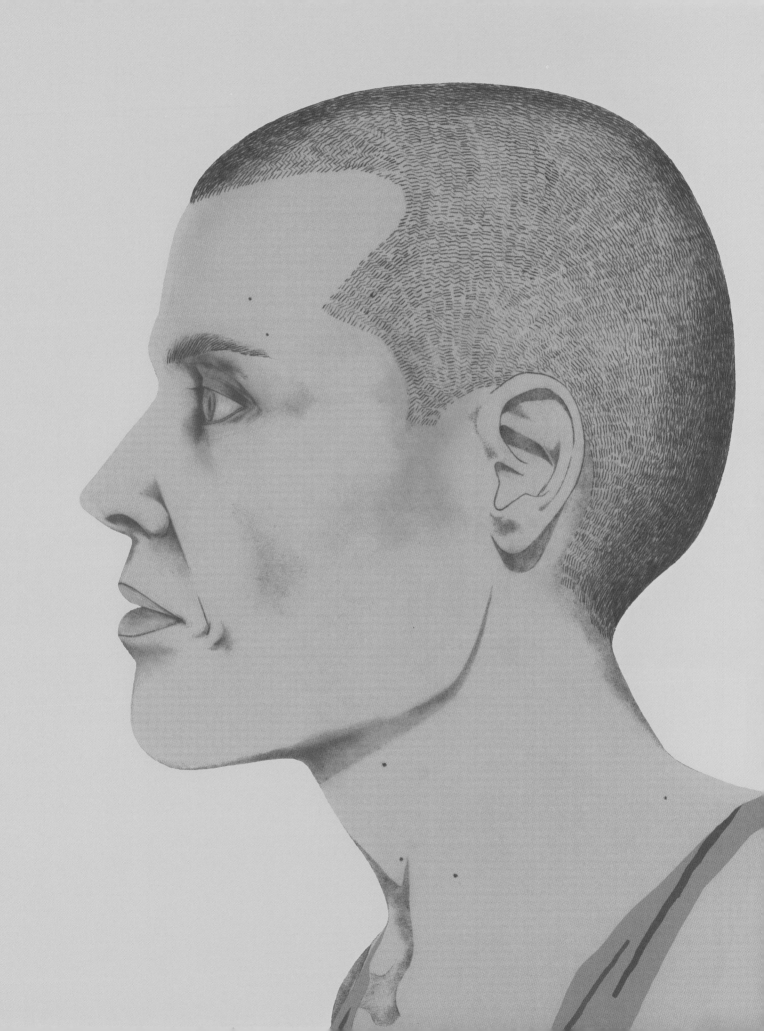

austerity was realized on a $60 million budget from 20th Century Fox, the largest for any film in its franchise to date. But while the film represented a considerable investment for its parent studio, the spare-no-expense mandate didn't necessarily liberate its director. Tasked at the age twenty-seven—and at the apex of his music-video career—with following up two well-loved and phenomenally profitable modern sci-fi classics, David Fincher found himself free, yet everywhere in chains.

"What we have here is failure to communicate," drawls the warden in Stuart Rosenberg's *Cool Hand Luke* (1967), a major entry in *Prison Movies: Life Behind Bars*, not least of all because of the punitive implications of that famous catchphrase. On the eve of shooting his feature debut—and already long-since subject to top-down admonishment by *Alien 3*'s producers—Fincher had dinner with screenwriter Rex Pickett, who'd been hired to finesse one last draft before the cameras rolled. After filling Pickett in on months of creative struggles, the director asked if his side of the story sounded "totally insane" to a third party. "[Pickett] said, 'no, [it] makes sense,'" Fincher told *Premiere* in 1992. "[He said] 'maybe you're just not communicating it well.'"

#

Alien 3 begins with a distress call and a wide-angle shot of an escape pod detaching from the cargo ship Sulaco and plummeting through Fury's atmosphere and into the water. It's an overture announcing a downer, and initial reactions to *Alien 3* characterized the film as too grim for its own good. "Gloomy and inert" was the verdict of the *Boston Globe*'s Jay Carr, while in the

1.

Chicago Sun-Times, Roger Ebert offered a supremely backhanded compliment, calling it, "one of the best-looking bad movies I've ever seen." The negative reviews were compounded by commercial underperformance: while technically *Alien 3* outgrossed its antecedents (without taking inflation into account), it quickly dropped off the box office charts, landing as just

the twenty-eighth-highest grossing film of its year. The film's dismal fate was widely chalked up to the same law of diminishing returns afflicting Hollywood in a period of widespread sequelization: 1992's top earners included *Home Alone 2: Lost in New York*, *Lethal Weapon 3*, and *Batman Returns*. The story seemed a generational cautionary tale about the consequences of MTV colonizing Hollywood, with Fincher the music-video-whiz kid transformed ignominiously into a poster boy for reach exceeding grasp.

"I had to work on [*Alien 3*] for two years, got fired off it three times, and I had to fight for every single thing," Fincher told the *Guardian* in 2009. "No one hated it more than me; to this day, no one hates it more than me." The director's assessment doesn't mince words, but in other precincts, *Alien 3* has been reappraised as everything from slightly underrated to a misunderstood masterpiece. In 2013, critic Scout Tafoya chose it for the first instalment of a video essay series at the website *RogerEbert.com* called "The Unloved"—a title pointing towards a prevalent tendency in millennial criticism to "reclaim" widely disparaged movies with the benefit of hindsight. "Everything that Fincher is known for originates here," Tafoya narrates over a set of clips suggestively interspersed with canvases by Hieronymus Bosch. "The dank interiors, the sense of dread dripping from every vent and furrowed brow . . . the film may be riddled with imperfections, but it transcends them. If Ridley Scott's *Alien* is science-fiction turned into art, *Alien 3* is art maimed until it resembles science-fiction."

Tafoya's enthusiasm locates the major point of interest in Fincher's debut, which is as an auteurist artifact. What doesn't work in *Alien 3*—its slow, punishing pacing; its unindividuated characters; its churlish avoidance of crowd-pleasing moments—cannot in good conscience be recouped as strengths, but nor should its flaws, whether circumstantial or faults of execution, obscure its hard-edged virtues. Chief among these is an orneriness that, in a more successfully realized movie like *Se7en*, registers as evidence of genuine control and directorial temperament. *Alien 3* is a dour, heavy-spirited slog, but it is hardly impersonal. Beneath its tarnished surfaces, it's been engineered by Fincher as a drama of principled resistance and ethical martyrdom in the face of stifling, profitous corporate oversight—a harsh, insinuating fable of its own making.

It is also, in setting and subtext, a prison movie, one powered by a sense of injustice

1. The spacecraft Sulaco is a carry-over from *Aliens*, and Fincher's eagerness to trash the vessel—along with all but one of its human inhabitants—right off the top of *Alien 3* signals the movie's revisionist ruthlessness.

2-9. The production design for *Alien 3* is cold and spartan, with the prison shot variably at low angles like a cathedral and mapped multi-directionally as a labyrinth; after the glistening, militaristic textures of *Aliens*, Fincher's squalid *mise-en-scène* serves a story haunted by suicidal desperation and presages the sense of omnipresent decay from *Se7en*.

that's at once pettily personalized and more subversively aimed at the machinery driving its own production. "I think it's fair to say that our smoothly running facility has suddenly developed a few problems," notes Superintendent Andrews (Brian Glover), placing the blame for Fury's recent slew of fatalities on Ripley, whose knowledge in matters pertaining to the Alien is seen through his megalomaniacal lens as a liability. In *Alien 3*'s pseudo-Foucaultian setup, the prison's ruling class are pseuds who don't know what they're doing, while Ripley's expertise is ignored. Moments after this desperate attempt to consolidate his authority, Andrews is pulled up and into an air vent by the very predator whose existence he refuses to acknowledge. In a film of stark, Wagnerian solemnity, the slapstick nature of the staging registers as a sight gag executed with evident, vengeful satisfaction (all that's missing is a reaction shot of Sigourney Weaver smiling).

Ceilings are a recurring image in *Alien 3*, a film shot mostly at low and often Wellesian angles; the plafonds are lit and framed by Fincher and cinematographer Alex Thomson to emphasize the towering dimensions of the sets. Thomson was not the director's first choice as DP: production began with the venerable Jordan Cronenweth behind the camera, maintaining continuity not only with Fincher's music videos (Cronenweth having shot the 1989 Madonna promo "Oh Father") but also Ridley Scott's *Blade Runner* (1982), a film as deeply seeded in contemporary genre-cinema DNA as *Alien* (1979). In contrast to the largely lateral staging of *Alien*, *Blade Runner* is a surpassingly vertical movie, and in *Alien 3*, Fincher synthesizes both approaches to create a uniquely spacious sense of containment and claustrophobia. The compositions have an uncanny centrifugal force; the spiritual weight of incarceration doesn't so much bear down on the characters as it hovers above them ("everyone prostrate before an absent God" in Tafoya's poetic phrase). *Alien 3*'s cathedral-like spaces are connected by a warren of winding corridors extending in all directions, giving Fury the architectural configuration of a labyrinth, a configuration that also resonates thematically in the film's most powerfully realized moment, which maps an exit strategy for an existentially entrapped protagonist.

Circa 1991, David Fincher was fending off suggestions that he was himself the monster in *Alien 3*'s maze. A set-visit feature by Gareth Pearce from the Fall 1992 issue of *Empire* exposes the bundle of raw nerves that had converged on

2.

3.

4.

5.

6.

7.

8.

9.

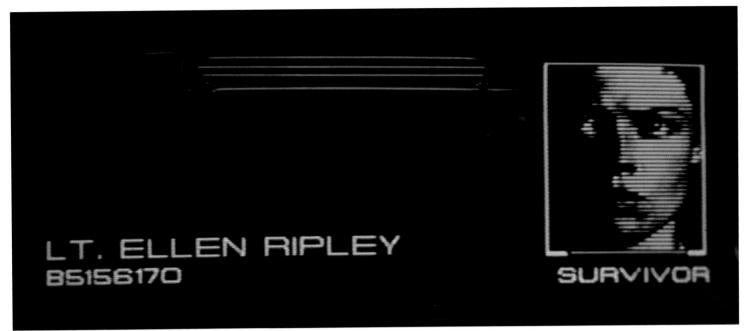

LT. ELLEN RIPLEY
85156170   SURVIVOR

10.

10. "Survivor"; the
official, designation
for Ellen Ripley
in the wake of her
ship's crash on
Fury underlines the
resourcefulness
that makes her a
throughline for
the franchise.

11. *Alien 3* presents
Ripley as a battered,
bruised survivor,
stripped-down and
emotionally drained
from her previous
series incarnations.

12. In the original
treatment for *Alien 3*,
the male characters
were monks; the close-
cropped, prison-issue
haircuts serve a
similar function in
de-individuating the
inmates, sometimes to
the point of confusion.

a London soundstage, describing a movie that seems at every turn to be resisting its own production. "I've been through a tunnel of blood on this one," gripes Weaver, as if channelling Ripley's flinty irritability. "This film has been a nightmare," admits a flustered unit publicist. In Pearce's account, even the studio's spin doctors seem stricken; in the absence of any real advocacy for *Alien 3* one instead hears the sound of gears grinding, as a massive, rusted hunk of intellectual property gets dragged out of storage.

In 1986, James Cameron aced his sequelizing assignment on *Aliens*, updating Scott's shivery interstellar *Gothic* for a higher-octane blockbuster marketplace. Where *Alien* had moved with the methodical creep of a horror movie, *Aliens* was an all-out action extravaganza: the winking pluralization of its title was a promise fulfilled and then some. If Cameron's movie nevertheless felt of a piece with its predecessor, it was largely thanks to the presence and performance of its lead: *Aliens* earned Weaver an Oscar nomination for Best Actress and a secure place in the one-liner Hall of Fame for hissing "get away from her, you *bitch*," while staring down her towering, hyperbolically fertile rival—acid against acid, maternal instinct turned molten. A third *Alien* movie, it was understood, would have to feature Weaver: the rest would be negotiable.

And so it was: Pearce's article alludes to *Alien 3*'s harrowing backstory of conceptual

and developmental strife, a shaggy-dog narrative outlined more fully in Charles de Lauzirka's three-hour documentary *Wreckage and Rage: Making Alien 3* (2003). Essentially an epic-length making-of featurette commissioned for the *Alien Quadrilogy* DVD set, *Wreckage* cycles through the various iterations of *Alien 3*'s screenplay, including a few early drafts written without Ripley in the case that Weaver wouldn't agree to participate. Where the transition in series stewardship from Scott to Cameron followed a certain tech-noir logic (and hewed close to the high end of Hollywood) the carousel of talents attached to *Alien 3*, including directors Renny Harlin, Vincent Ward, David Twohy, and novelist William Gibson, was motlier and suggestive of some larger indecision, of the difference between finding somebody with a story to tell and of finding somebody to tell a story.

Wreckage and Rage is more of a horror movie than *Alien 3*; its structuring absence is David Fincher, who declined to be interviewed, having gone on the record elsewhere about his myriad frustrations. These complaints were anything but mollified by the so-called "Assembly Cut" of *Alien 3* included in the Quadrilogy box-set, which reinstated some thirty minutes of dropped footage but without the filmmaker's input or supervision, a gesture akin to poking somebody in the eye with an olive branch. In his *Empire* feature, Pearce positioned Fincher as at once overmatched and overweening, juxtaposing ostensibly supportive characterizations from cast members ("he's a nice bloke doing his best") with whispers that the director's exacting, repetitive style was dragging an already troubled production even further behind schedule, as well alienating key personnel. "When I ask if [Weaver] can remember the last time [Fincher] made her laugh," writes Pearce, "[she] purses her lips and doesn't reply."

Wreckage and Rage is tinged by a similar ambivalence, albeit more contextualized by Fincher's burgeoning auteur status at the time of its making; the commercial success of *Se7en* and notoriety of *Fight Club* had gone a long way towards rehabilitating his reputation with critics and financiers alike. Adopting the tone of an impartial chronicler, De Lauzirika includes multiple anecdotes describing outright studio meddling while playing up an ugly fracas between Fincher and screenwriter-producer David Giler, who ended up walking off the set. Giler also referred to Fincher during a heated conference call as a "shoe salesman," glibly boomeranging the director's commercial background (and its implied lack of artistic conviction) against him.

It could be argued that Fincher's gift for the hard sell was what made him a viable candidate to manage what was an essentially mercenary enterprise—that and the fact that, as a relative newcomer, he wasn't in a position to push back against the franchise's brain trust. If there is a common denominator amongst the most famous troubled Hollywood productions, it is an obstinate auteur whose track record proves conducive to the issuing of on-set ultimatums: think *Heaven's Gate* (1980), which saw one of the oldest Hollywood studios held hostage and ultimately bankrupted when Michael Cimino leveraged his Oscar statuette against final cut, or *Titanic* (1997), where James Cameron justified every lavish, fanatical act of below-the-line excess on the basis of his past hits, *Aliens* included.

While less of a historical ordeal than *Heaven's Gate* or *Titanic*, *Alien 3*'s shoot dragged on longer than expected, lasting ninety-three days, at which point the studio pulled the plug. The story that got reported was that Fox executive vice president Jon Landau took it upon himself to call Fincher's bluff (a few years later, the producer would be pushed even further beyond his limits by Cameron on *Titanic*). "The lesson to be learned is that you really can't take on an enterprise of this size and scope if you don't really have a movie like *The Terminator* or *Jaws* (1975) behind you," Fincher said in a candid interview with Mark Burman for the BBC in 1993. "When everybody's wringing their handkerchiefs and sweating and puking blood because of the money that's being spent and you're going, 'Trust me, this is what I really believe in,' they turn around and say, 'Well, who the fuck are you? Who cares what you believe in?'"

#

There is ample, ambient evidence of *Alien 3* as a movie directed with a persecution complex, with Fincher balancing his belief in his own methodology against a desultory awareness of hired-gun status. This odd mix of obstinate confidence and reluctance informs the film's treatment of Ripley as an unwilling, disengaged participant in her own heroic narrative. Where Fincher's crusading male heroes imperil themselves via their all-consuming obsessions, the female protagonists of *Alien 3* and *Panic Room* are more aptly described as put-upon, cornered by external forces and forced, backs against the wall, to stand their ground.

Alien 3 takes off from the idea of Ripley as a resourceful survivor—a post-adolescent iteration of the "Final Girl" archetype theorized by slasher-movie scholars like Carol Clover—while also nudging her towards a tragic and stirring act of self-actualization. The character's refusals in *Alien* and *Aliens* to accept her own corporately mandated expendability, as dictated by the tyrannically expedient Weyland-Yutani conglomerate, have left her empowered but also embittered; the sudden, pointless deaths of her would-be surrogate family members Newt and Hicks, combined with the discovery that she's harboring an Alien in her womb, represent a vanishing point in which suffering supplants succor once and for all. *Alien 3* dramatizes the process by which Ripley grows alienated from her own survival instinct.

"I thought, what are the Yuppies coming to grips with?" Fincher explained. "We've come full circle and realized that selflessness is as important as selfishness in order to survive. So I thought that's the obvious place to go with this character because we're not really going to have too much more to do with her." In his adamance that *Alien 3* should wrap up Ripley's narrative once and for all, Fincher rebuked Giler's characterization of him as an "adman," because at its core, the film is about somebody who is no longer willing to buy in. If Fincher's debut is selling anything at all, it's philosophical ambivalence.

The punkish, anti-establishment thrust of *Alien 3* is concisely aestheticized by Ripley's extreme minimalist makeover, which plots the character along a larger pop-cultural continuum of defiant female baldness. In the late 1980s, the Irish rock star Sinead O'Connor shed her hair as a rebuke to record executives lobbying for a more conventionally flirtatious image; the MTV award-winning video for 1990's "Nothing Compares 2U" features the close-cropped singer in an intimate, confrontational close-up. A few years later, Demi Moore would adopt a similar look in *G.I. Jane* (1997), a basic-training drama that used its star's bullet-headed look to jab at patriarchy ("suck my dick," Moore sneers at her sexist

11.

12.

13.

13. The revelation that Ripley is harbouring an Alien Queen culminates the series' nightmarish subtexts of maternity and bodily violation; for the first time, the enemy is within, and the inescapability of that arrangement shifts the movie's tone towards an unsentimental fatalism.

14. The stubborn superintendent Andrews becomes *Alien 3*'s avatar of fallible male authority.

15. The Alien emerges from a stray dog, testifying to its adaptability and setting up its more agile design.

C.O., paraphrasing comedienne Roseanne Barr) while connecting, via the directorial presence of Ridley Scott, to the complex gender politics of *Alien*. Originally scripted as a male character, Ripley's sex was changed to a female just prior to production, a switch that permitted Scott to play some clever games at the film's climax, literally stripping Weaver down and using her statuesque near-nakedness to signify fleshy, permeable femininity versus the nightmarishly phallic solidity of the movie's star monster. In *Aliens*, Cameron reversed Scott's visual language by having the character don chunky, cumbersome body armor for the final showdown, a move synced to his own fetishistic love of military hardware.

If Ripley's haircut in *Alien 3* is a fashion statement, it's not one that she's making on her own behalf. Awakening in Fury's infirmary, she's informed that her coif is a standard-issue prevention measure

14.

against head lice, as well as an initiation rite into a monkishly male milieu. Fincher works Weaver's androgyny for all it's worth, pranklishly scribbling cinephilic references in the margins of his film's prison-movie blueprint. *Alien 3* mimics the focused, religious-iconic close-ups of Renée Jeanne Falconetti as the title character in Carl Dreyer's *The Passion of Joan of Arc* (1928) and the bullet-headed satire of Stanley Kubrick's *Full Metal Jacket* (1987)—also a reference point for *G.I. Jane*—whose wannabe Marines are shown in the prologue being shorn like sheep (or lambs to the slaughter). Furthermore, Fincher is riffing on his own 1989 music video for Madonna's "Express Yourself," which outfitted the singer in masculine drag *à la* Marlene Dietrich and set her to infiltrating and seducing a group of well-muscled, faceless workmen against a menacingly overscaled steel-and-glass backdrop.

The metropolis of "Express Yourself" is knowingly styled on Fritz Lang's *Metropolis* (1927); both the video and its inspiration guide Fincher's expressionist approach in *Alien 3*, which, crucially (and, understandably), lacks the Madonna clip's sense of glamour and humor. While Ripley is a less explicitly sexual (or sexualized)

presence than either *Metropolis*'s sinister gynoid Maria or "Vogue"-era Madonna (or, for that matter, Marlene Dietrich) the disruption she causes within a cloistered, forcibly celibate order—a "Double Y Chromsome Correctional Facility" in the film's doublespeak designation—is comparably seismic. In Vincent Ward's original script treatment, the setting was not a prison but a floating, wooden monastery, whose peaceably Luddite, earnestly God-fearing residents debated whether Ripley was a savior or an avatar of Edenic temptation. Within this quasi-religious framework, the Alien would emerge as a devil in their midst.

Without fully committing to Ward's spiritual vision, Fincher integrates certain of his ideas: the character of Golic (Paul McGann), who goes mad after watching the "Dragon" slay several of his fellow inmates, has the fervor of a true believer. Ripley's haircut pairs her on one level with Joan of Arc, and on another with the smooth aerodynamic physicality of the Alien itself. In the film's signature image, she and the Xenomorph come face-to-face in a tight, probing two-shot, twinning a primal terror of the Other with a repulsion borne of recognition and even intimacy—less a sneak attack than a reunion. "Don't be afraid, I'm part of the family, " Ripley will tell the creature later on, at once Saint Joan (and also maybe Saint Margaret of Antioch, the patron saint of expectant mothers, swallowed by Satan in the form of a Dragon, who carved her way out of the belly of the beast with an irradiated cross) and the Virgin Mary.

The seed of this doubling was planted at the end of *Aliens*, during Ripley's dramatically stirring and gender-coded confrontation with the Queen Alien—a standoff marked by James Cameron's characteristically full-metal feminism. (See also *Terminator 2* [1991], where Linda Hamilton's Sarah Connor is radicalized by her foreknowledge of apocalypse into a pitiless, crackshot human version of a "Terminator".) It's telling that Cameron hated *Alien 3* primarily because of how ruthlessly Fincher killed off Hicks and Newt, calling the decision "a huge slap in the face to fans," because, for all his future-shock virtuosity and love of heavy artillery, he's a fundamentally sentimental storyteller. (See: *T2*'s Spielbergian emotionalism, with its unmistakable trace elements of *E.T.* [1982].) Fincher eschews such putative humanism; if there's any Spielberg in *Alien 3*, it's the Spielberg of *Jaws* (1975), who killed off a bevy of archetypal innocents in the first reel—a

hippie chick, a sweet pre-teen boy, a dog—to show that he wasn't messing around.

Tyro though he was, Spielberg didn't have the stomach to show a Great White munching on a canine; in *Jaws*, the death of the Black Lab Pippit is signified by a shot of a stick floating forlornly in the surf. Fincher enthusiastically shows the prison colony's mascot Spike being torn apart in gruesome detail while giving "birth" to the progeny of the Face Hugger who'd stowed away in the escape pod (an unfortunately predictable plot point after similar developments in the first two movies). The dog's death is one of several legitimate shocks to the system early in *Alien 3*, a litany including not only Hicks and Newt's mutual elimination, but the latter's horrific, rib-cracking autopsy (a harbinger of *Se7en*) and the mutilated, animatronic visage of Lance Henriksen's sympathetic "Synthetic" Bishop [Lance Henriksen], another *Aliens* castaway

15.

who gives Ripley the bad news that her nemesis has tagged along for the ride and expresses his preference to "be nothing" before being switched off. The blunt-force morbidity of these scenes is laced with stabs at transcendence; the cross-cutting between the dog's bloody death throes and Newt and Hicks's funeral rites permits Fincher a bit of stylistic flexing: it's a warm up for the visceral-liturgical dichotomy of *Se7en*, with the eulogy by Charles S. Dutton's stoic, *de facto* prison chaplin Dillon ("within each death, no matter how small, there is always a new life") simultaneously sanctifying and satirizing the film's themes of decay and regeneration.

Looking to significantly reimagine the series' namesake as a hedge against audience expectations, *Alien 3*'s FX team collaborated with the monster's original designer, H. R. Geiger, to brain-storm a quadripedal creature and used mostly analogue techniques to realize it on-screen. To the extent that Fincher can be described as a "special effects director," *Alien 3*'s integration of miniature and full-scale puppets as well as traditional "man-in-suit" work (courtesy of Stan Winston protege Ron Woodruff Jr.) is marvellously achieved—especially because so many of the innovations are keyed to speed.

16. A typically shallow-
focus composition from
Alien 3 distances and
differentiates Ellen
Ripley from the all-
male prison population
of Fiorina 161.

In *Alien*, Ridley Scott displayed his creature judiciously, using the same less-is-more philosophy that Spielberg pioneered on *Jaws*; in *Aliens*, Cameron showed more of his monsters but still treated them as mostly static, slow-moving presences. "Stasis interrupted" reads a computer screen early in *Alien 3*, pointing towards a more mobile threat: *Alien 3*'s Dragon is disconcertingly nimble and quick, and also more mammalian (Fincher suggested putting a Whippet in a costume for certain shots).

#

In a film marked by its stately pacing, the Alien's unexpected powers of acceleration constitute a skittering, staccato counter-melody. This sense of momentum is best expressed in a series of point-of-view shots during a late chase sequence, with Fincher adopting the Alien's perspective in a way that neither Scott nor Cameron ever attempted (and is, again, more sympatico with Spielberg's underwater photography in *Jaws*). Of course the swift, roaming camera movements recall Kubrick, including the prowls through the barracks in *Full Metal Jacket* (1987) and tricycle-rides of *The Shining* (1980); both movies inform *Alien 3*'s omnipresent labyrinth imagery (Kubrick's production company was called Minotaur). The harsh, declamatory acting style of ex-wrestler Glover as Superintendent Andrews is another Kubrickian motif, evoking the

stylized theatricality of *A Clockwork Orange* (1971)—itself a prison movie examining state-sanctioned dehumanization and pent-up male aggression.

The fear of violation, so deeply embedded in the Alien franchise and its invasive, body-hopping monster, are literalized in the attempted gang rape of Ripley ordered by a sadistic inmate (Holt McCallany), an excessively nasty scene which connects to the film's desire to push the blockbuster envelope while also sounding a loud, unpersuasive note of political correctness. Ripley is saved from the attack by Dutton's Dillon, the first

17. "The Dragon": in order to service *Alien 3*'s chase-movie climax, the monster is sleeker, smaller and more mobile than its series predecessors.

18. The POV shots hurtling through Fury's labyrinthine corridors align us uncomfortably with the Alien and call back to the tracking camera movements of Stanley Kubrick—particularly the chase through the hedge maze at the end of *The Shining*.

19. Ripley's rejection of Weiland-Yutani's offer is framed as an act of liberation—suicide as an act of containment against the alien threat.

of several stoic, suspiciously sage African American characters in Fincher's cinema (e.g. Morgan Freeman's Detective Somerset in *Se7en* and Forest Whitaker's similarly conceived ex-con Burnham in *Panic Room*) and an emblem of *Alien 3*'s programmatic dramaturgy. Where in *Alien* and *Aliens* the ensembles were cast and acted with care, Fincher either permits his male actors to overdo it (like Glover and Dutton) or else renders them interchangeable and boringly expendable. The one endearing exception, Dance's charming prison physician Clemons, is rewarded for his warmth by being unceremoniously offed at an unexpected moment—a Kubrickian twist of the knife *à la* Scatman Crothers in *The Shining*.

Clemons's splattery death, skull splintered in a near-subliminal Francis-Bacon-ish insert, immediately precedes one of *Alien 3*'s two great scenes: the aforementioned face-off between the Dragon and Ripley, a meeting that radiates its own revolting mix of fear and desire, the Alien's dripping double-jaws pressed up to Weaver's cheek before their owner pulls away and scurries back up into the ventilation system. It's a bizarre retreat that points to the script's best-prepared and executed twist. Unknowingly impregnated with an Alien Queen—and thus entrusted with the propagation of the species—Ripley has been granted immunity by her tormentor until she's ready for her virgin birth. Here, Fincher changes the

17.

rules of the game, recasting a character consistently defined by being overmatched into an unwilling ally while also giving her a new tactical advantage: no longer required to run and hide, she's able to take the fight to her adversary.

The extended set-piece featuring the "alien-vision" tracking shots unfolds as a chess match of sorts, with Ripley and the inmates trying to herd the Dragon through Fury's corridors and trap it in the fortuitously attached iron works where they can scald it to death: The Minotaur as a casualty of the labyrinth. The lack of differentiation between the film's male characters is exacerbated by the hyperactive swiftness of the camera movement and the cutting, but it's still conceptually satisfying to see a company of prisoners embrace their new roles as jailers, while Ripley's untouchability syncs with Fincher's desire to prod franchise-film conventions. The appeal of widely sequelized action heroes like John Rambo or *Die Hard*'s John McClane is that we know on an extra-textual level that they're death-proof no matter what the onscreen circumstances: If there is one truism at the movies, it's that

18.

"James Bond will return" (and all that that implies). Ripley's "invincibility" in *Alien 3* is of course provisional (she can still come to harm by other means), but it's also genuinely disarming, since it neutralizes the series' traditional source of threat and transforms an ostensible horror movie into a morality tale whose heroine can only triumph by turning her violence inward.

That decision is rendered in *Alien 3*'s other great scene, which also happens to be one of its most contentious. The film's producers were concerned that the fiery foundry backdrop was too similar to the location used at the end of *Terminator 2*, while Ripley's exit was almost identical to Arnold Schwarzenegger lowering himself into a vat of molten metal while offering a thumbs up. Their collective suggestion was to inject a show-stopping moment after Ripley rejects the duplicitous offer of a Weyland-Yutani bigwig (Henriksen) to extract and destroy the Alien Queen embryo; instead of the small stigmata of

19.

blood on Ripley's chest filmed by Fincher, the Alien would emerge fully, shrieking and clawing as Weaver wrestled with it all the way into the flames.

Fincher didn't like the reworked sequence, telling Gregory Moss that he "didn't think it was important to see the monster" and insisting to the producers that "whatever happened, [Ripley] has to be at peace at the end." The reshoots were done under duress, but the scene actually plays beautifully, with the image of Ripley clutching her bastard offspring working both as grandiose, masochistic pulp and as a double-edged tribute to the character—and the audience's—passionately long-standing, love-hate affair with the Alien itself. "You've been in my life so long, I can't remember anything else," Ripley sighs, a distaff Ahab whose hatred has melted into possessive acceptance. While Fincher can't claim credit for the complex semiotics powering the Alien franchise—the metallic sexuality; the unsettling equations between pregnancy and rape; the ominous promise that "in space, nobody can hear you scream"—he distills them into a single image with an alchemist's measured precision while managing his own disappearing act.

"Do you want to go on your feet, or on your fucking knees, begging?" asks Dillon. This is his way of rallying the troops and he effectively becomes a mouthpiece for *Alien 3*'s prison-movie themes: his rhetoric preaches a gospel of literal and spiritual emancipation prefiguring Ripley's uprising of one against Weyland-Yutani, the true, dominant agents of oppression in the Alien universe, seeking to exploit human and Xenomorph alike and forced to watch (via Henriksen's earnestly untrustworthy emissary), as both of their coveted specimens slip from their grasp. No failure to communicate here: Ripley's swan dive offers up a Jesus Christ Pose to rival the symbolic crucifixion at the close of *Cool Hand Luke*. Or, looked at from

another angle, in lieu of the Terminator's sentimental thumbs up, Ripley's silent swan dive registers as a full-body equivalent of an upraised middle finger.

Is the implied "fuck you" perhaps on behalf of her director? Fincher's adamance that his heroine go out "with a sigh, rather than gritted teeth and sweat" ended up being one more battle that he lost, but Weaver's pained, resolute face ends up aligning Ripley with the filmmaker in the decisive moment, as well as for all time: Battered and spent, and stubbornly holding onto a slippery menace in an attempt to keep it from falling into the wrong hands. As the first of Fincher's films to thematize suicide—anticipating not only John Doe's suicide-by-cop in *Se7en*, but the depressive death spirals at either end of *The Game* and the large-caliber-lobotomy of *Fight Club*—*Alien 3* is unmistakably fatalistic stuff, but whatever its flaws, its Pyrrhic victory is earned. Ripley's great escape at the end is a fall toward grace, and she takes the movie with her.

Fig A. *The Big House*, George Hill, 1930 [Still]

George Hill's 1930 drama endures as one of the first prison films, establishing themes and tropes that would carry forward in the genre.

Fig B. *Cool Hand Luke*, Stuart Rosenberg, 1967

Exemplifies the classic prison-movie trope of the angry, violent guard and the inmate with which they fail to communicate.

Fig C. *The Long Tomorrow*, Dan O'Bannon, Jean "Mobius" Giraud, 1975

This comic was important in cyberpunk history because it would go on to be an inspiration for William Gibson's (who also wrote a script for *Alien 3* that was rejected) conception of the Sprawl.

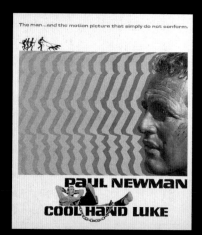

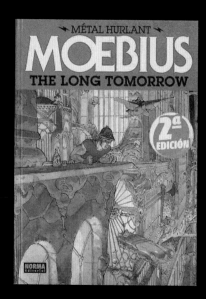

Fig F. "Express Yourself," Madonna, 1989

Alien 3's loaded gender dynamics derive from Fincher's video for Madonna's 1989 hit "Express Yourself," which also isolated its female star in a world of muscled, threatening men.

Fig G. *The Book of Margery Kempe*, 1440

A Medieval text by a fifteenth-century Christian mystic driven by themes of spiritual torment and images of crucifixion.

Fig H. Gothic cathedrals

The high ceilings of *Alien 3*'s location allow for multiple reverent, low-angle perspectives imparting both a sense of town-down authoritarianism and modest awe.

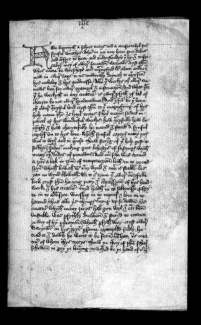

Fig D. *La Passion de Jeanne d'Arc*,
Carl Theodor Dreyer, 1928

Ripley's shaved head and fixation on
martyrdom place her in a lineage with
Renee Falconetti's Joan of Arc in Carl
Dreyer's silent masterpiece.

Fig E. **"Mandinka," Sinead O'Connor, 1987**
[7-inch Record Cover]

In 1990, Sinead O'Connor's video for
"Nothing Compares 2 U" beat out three
clips directed by Fincher; Ripley's
haircut could also be taken as a wry
homage to the victor.

Fig I. *The Minotaur's labyrinth*,
Athanasius Kircher, 1679 [Engraving]

Alien 3 riffs on the myth of the Minotaur,
a monster trapped at the center of a
winding, unnavigable concrete maze.

Fig J. *Terminator 2: Judgment Day*,
James Cameron, 1991 [Still]

During filming, there were worries that
Alien 3's foundry-set climax was too
close to the ending of James Cameron's
box-office smash.

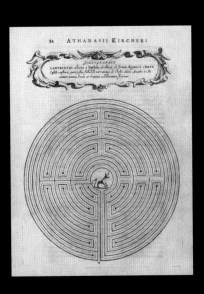

WRITERS David Giler, Walter Hill, Larry Ferguson
CINEMATOGRAPHER Alex Thomson
EDITOR Terry Rawlings

BUDGET $50-60 million
BOX OFFICE $159.8-175 million

LENGTH 114 min

2.2

TITLE SEQUENCE
KEVIN TOD HAUG

< The giant, hovering titles
at the beginning of *Panic
Room* were the result of a
discussion between Fincher
and editor Angus Wall about
the "ontological nature"
of movie credits; here,
they have a heavy, three-
dimensional solidity that
invades the movie's world.

2.2
PANIC ROOM

2002

If *Alien 3* is the David Fincher film least regarded by its creator, *Panic Room* runs a close second. Promoting his fifth feature in 2002, the director made a game of sounding squeezed, subjecting journalists to a litany of complaints delivered with a grin. "Whatever directionour very enjoyable conversation takes," wrote Ryan Gibney in the *Independent.* "[Fincher] always manages to steer it around to one subject: 'The Pitiful and Miserable Experience of the Modern Filmmaker.'"

Two years removed from the tumultuous experience of *Fight Club*, *Panic Room* represented the director's attempt to simplify and downsize his process, the same impulse that had led him towards *Se7en* after squirming free of *Alien 3*. "It's a popcorn movie," the director told *Rolling Stone*, a designation separating him from the insurgent "rebels on the backlot" being hyped at the time for bending the industry to their whims. The subversive, terrorist-

themed action of *Fight Club* had positioned Fincher at the vanguard of a millennial cohort resurrecting the spirit of the '70s; a thriller signed by the writer of *Jurassic Park* (1993)—the keynote popcorn movie of the '90s—looked in comparison like a mercenary move, the difference between pushing the envelope and cashing the cheque within.

Compared to *Jurassic Park*, David Koepp's script for *Panic Room* is pretty vicious stuff, reimagining the earlier film's hide-

seek, stainless-steel-kitchen-set-piece as a full-length feature and substituting murderous burglars for velociraptors and a mother and daughter for their preteen quarry. A high-concept specialist, Koepp had been inspired by a magazine article about a spate of rich families contracting custom-made, impenetrable "safe rooms" in their houses, a phenomenon suggesting that class-based resentment was alive and thriving at a moment of perceived American economic prosperity, and which also abutted closely on the paranoid vantage points in *The Game* and *Fight Club*.

Where those high-concept psycho dramas were predicated on big twists, *Panic Room* is resolutely linear, offering little in

1.

the way of down time and zero character development except via physical action (and arguably a Sid Vicious T-shirt). Reviewing the film for the *Chicago Sun Times*, Roger Ebert likened it to "a chess game...the board and all of the pieces are in full view, both sides know the rules, and the winner will simply be the better strategist." This description accurately captures the terse, adversarial ethos of a thriller where each close-quarters skirmish is pressurized by the slow tick and breathless surge of real time, progressing steadily towards checkmate.

Where *Alien 3* bore visible scars of its creative clashes, *Panic Room* is filmmaking-as-salvage job, as sterile and unblemished as a meticulously tidied-up crime scene. Originally, the film was packaged around Nicole Kidman, who withdrew two weeks into shooting after aggravating a knee injury first suffered on the set of *Moulin Rouge* (2001); there was buzz that Fincher would have preferred to shut down production but Columbia's executives forced his hand. In need of a bankable star, the director sought out Jodie Foster, who'd previously been considered for Sean Penn's role in *The Game*. In a controversial move, the actress stepped down from heading the 2001 Cannes Film Festival Jury only to discover, a little over a month after committing, that she was pregnant. From an *Entertainment Weekly* feature coyly titled "Cause For Alarm": "Fincher's reaction [to the news] was a blood-drained face of shell-shocked disbelief, which the director replicates almost a year later in a hotel suite in Beverly Hills on a January morning." The cast shuffling also extended to the role of Foster's onscreen daughter, with

Fincher's initial choice, Hayden Panetierre, giving way to Kristen Stewart around the same time that Kidman left the production. "When we hired [Kristen] we didn't think she looked like Nicole, but like Jodie Foster, actually," said Fincher in 2002, conceding to at least one stroke of good luck.

Below the line, a considerably more fraught subplot was developing involving the director and his cinematographer, Darius Khondji. In the made-for-DVD documentary *Shooting Panic Room*, the pair can be seen amiably chatting while scouting locations. Less than two months later, Khondji was fired and replaced by his own camera assistant, Conrad W. Hall Jr. "It was hard for me," offers Hall tentatively in the featurette. "You don't really like to replace anybody." There has been speculation that the conflict stemmed from the director's insistence on mapping out *Panic Room*'s shots in advance; the euphemistic explanation was that the two couldn't agree on "aspects of production," hinted at in the anti-analog, digital drift of Fincher's filmmaking. As on *Fight Club*, Fincher solicited input from the Los Angeles-based previsualization company Pixel Liberation Front, whose team used a multistep process called photogrammetry—still images grafted over computer-generated models—to craft a kind of full-scale, interactive 3D storyboard, a virtual space inside which Fincher and Hall could choreograph a series of spectacular camera movements.

Hall shot *Panic Room* on 35 mm film with a handsomely desaturated palette, but the radical digital augmentation of the cinematography couldn't be ignored. In *Fight Club*, Fincher had prankishly kidded pious photochemical purism, using a motif of "change-overs"—the visible blips in the corner of the frame whenever a new filmstrip gets threaded through a projector—as the set-up for a subliminal dick joke. In *Fight Club*, celluloid fetishism is masturbatory; if the floating, disembodied aesthetic of *Panic Room* could be summed up in a catchphrase, it might be, "Look ma, no hands!"

Panic Room's gravity-defying mandate begins during the opening credits, which take the form of elongated, three-dimensional white titles overlaid on the Manhattan skyline—an array reminiscent of Saul Bass's credit sequence in Alfred Hitchcock's *North By Northwest* (1959). In a 2012 interview with the Canadian website *Art of the Title*, Fincher explained that the idea originated from a debate with editor Angus Wall about the ontological nature of movie credits: "[Is it] supposed to be a projection over the scene, or is it supposed to be there?" Viewed through this lens, all of those names levitating in midair could be taken as a winking acknowledgment of *Panic Room*'s artificiality, a subtle bit of rapping against the fourth wall juxtaposing the identities of the film's architects with the monumental, concrete reality of New York City itself—or else ratifying a sense of corporatized empire. A fleeting, thematically appropriate sight gag nestled in amidst the steel-and-glass facades: an electronic billboard flashing the slogan "face your fears."

As *Art of the Title*'s Lola Landekic observes, *Panic Room*'s overture tributes *West Side Story* (1961), moving from the Battery to Central Park in a series of bird's eye views—the same high-angled vantage later exploited to predatory effect in *Zodiac*. *Panic Room* is not a city film in the same manner as *Zodiac*, which recreates its vintage San Francisco down to the millimeter, or even *Se7en*, with its nameless yet indelibly rotten, alternate-universe Big Apple. Instead, the film draws on our collective knowledge of New York as an epicenter of east-coast aspirationalism, dizzying class stratification and materially decadent divorce settlements. In a way, the bustle and flow of the naked city constitutes the *Panic Room*'s structuring absence; the extratextual knowledge that the four-story brownstone that serves as its sole location was constructed fully on a soundstage in Los Angeles clouds the movie's New York state of mind.

Fincher's made-to-order town house testifies to a desire for supreme oversight, perhaps in opposition to the shoot's chaotic personnel issues. In *Shooting Panic Room*, production designer Arthur Max likens his handiwork to a giant, interlocking jigsaw puzzle, an analogy which aligns with Fincher's game-playing side. In fabricating his location rather than grappling with extant architecture and commissioning three versions of the panic room itself— each designed to accommodate different set-ups and angles—the filmmaker was determined to leave nothing to chance, even *Panic Room*'s theme could be described as the limits—or illusion—of control.

#

"I wrote it all down: 4,200 square feet, four floors, perfect; courtyard in back, south-facing garden. Perfect." *Panic Room*'s opening lines are spoken by real-estate agent Lydia Lynch (Ann Magnusson) as she leads Meg Altman (Foster) and her eleven-year-old daughter Sarah (Stewart) around the edges of Central Park on a house-hunting expedition. The image of three women striding purposefully through the frame cutely rebukes the alpha-machismo of *Fight Club*; even if the contrast isn't intentional, there's a very different energy at work than in Fincher's preceding wallow in masculine pathology (set largely in a dilapidated dwelling that becomes a kind of boys' club tree house by the end). By centering Foster's Meg, a recent divorcée leveraging her independence from her wealthy, philandering husband Stephen (Patrick Bachau), *Panic Room* opens up a potentially feminist point of view, albeit one that mostly confers agency by masculinizing a female protagonist—the same tactic as in *Alien 3*, with its seething, no-fucks-left-to-give incarnation of Ellen Ripley.

For *Panic Room*'s home-invasion narrative to work effectively, Meg must adopt the mantle of action hero without being portrayed from the outset as a Ripley-like warrior. While the character's wealth works against the idea of her as an Everywoman— and the film is nothing if not aware of the Altmans' monied pedigree, exploiting it as a source of suspense and *schadenfreude*— Meg's status as a normal person caught up in extraordinary circumstances is central to the story's Hitchcockian conception. "I sold the studio on this by telling them it was a cross between *Straw Dogs* (1971) and *Rear Window* (1954)," said Fincher to writer Robert Epstein in 2002.

The mention of Sam Peckinpah's notorious rape-revenge drama is apt in terms of *Panic Room*'s basic plotline and scarifying bursts of gory violence, although the gender dynamics (and politics) are pointedly inverted. In *Straw Dogs*, Dustin Hoffman's meek writer becomes a lethal man of action after his home is broken into and his wife is sexually assaulted; the film was of a piece with early '70s vigilante-revenge narratives while raising the bar for the triumphal, borderline-pornographic aestheticization of violence ("a fascist work of art," in Pauline Kael's assessment). *Panic Room* undeniably nods to *Straw Dogs* but without Peckinpah's gauntlet-dropping bravado. The conceit of a mother and daughter repelling incompetent male interlopers is ostensibly progessive without ever causing true transgression. Where *Rear Window* enters the equation is on the level of style—in the witty, assured voyeurism of Fincher's technique, and its balance (in the director's words) of "subjectivity and omniscience." Throughout *Panic Room*, the audience is sympathetically aligned with

1. Meg's arrival in the brownstone is tinged not with promise but suspense; the location seems to reflect (and mock) what she imagines as the encroaching emptiness of her new post-divorce prospects.

2-5. The floating, computer-assisted camerawork in *Panic Room* allows for fluid, intimate and at times impossible perspectives on the Altmans' surroundings; in interviews, Fincher said he wanted to create a sense of unencumbered, voyeuristic movement to offset the entrapment of the characters in their high-end living space.

2.

3.

4.

5.

Meg even as the placement and, especially, the movement of the camera complicates the relationship, at once diagramming and exacerbating her sense of entrapment.

"It's got everything you told me you wanted and more," Lydia boasts to Meg, the latter framed with her back to the foreground against a set of stairs leading to the second floor—a composition connoting imminent upward mobility. It's not that Meg can't afford the move so much as she's also buying into a contradictory and compromised version of freedom, a tenuous tenancy subsidized in absentia by her ex. "You could have two families in here if you want," says Lydia, obliviously referencing Stephen's apparently solid new relationship. The brownstone's expanse becomes overwhelming and even alienating—an extension, perhaps, of its prospective owner's psychic state. In *Rosemary's Baby* (1968), a cozy New York apartment concealed an ancient, supernatural evil; here, the cavernous emptiness of the premises is its own sort of haunting, no Satanists required.

Foster may not have been the first choice for the lead in *Panic Room* but there's still something inevitable about her casting as a character determined to maintain her composure in a crisis. As a former child star embroiled in a series of media scandals—first during the reception to her role as a preteen prostitute in Martin Scorsese's *Taxi Driver* (1976) and then again in 1981 after her stalker, John Hinckley Jr., rationalized his attempted assassination of President Ronald Reagan as a Travis Bickle-style courtship ritual—Foster's reticence in the public eye seemed like a useful coping mechanism. Whatever emotions the actress sought to expose were saved for her on-screen alter egos. In *The Accused* (1988), Foster played a rape survivor who refuses to simplify her victimization narrative; in *The Silence of the Lambs*, her ambitious FBI trainee holds her own against sociopaths and bureaucrats while trying to live up to the example of her late lawman father.

What *Panic Room* adds to the Foster formula is the protective impetus of motherhood. *Alien 3* perverted this archetype through Ripley's involuntary pregnancy and desperate, murderous embrace of her unwanted progeny—pro-life and pro-choice ideology wrapped up in a single, pulpy *pietà*. *Panic Room*, meanwhile, plays maternal devotion straight-up, syncing Meg's surprising strength and resourcefulness in the midst of a home invasion to her concern for her daughter. Fincher pits Foster's vibrating concern against Stewart's credible preadolescent petulance. Having survived the teen idolatry of the *Twilight* franchise to become a beguiling dramatic actress, Stewart's career path now resembles Foster's in retrospect, and the two match up perfectly in terms of appearance and behaviour: their mutual dependence is ringed with a terse, almost vaudevillian sarcasm. "It's disgusting how much I love you," Meg sighs while trying to appease Sarah after a fracas involving her father's new supermodel girlfriend; "tell me about it" is the downcast, deadpan reply. (Another funny bit of generational impasse, this one wordless: Meg fills her own glass to the brim with red wine and then pointedly tops up Sarah's Coke.)

Sarah's in-between status means that she's still recognizably Meg's responsibility when all hell breaks loose. Koepp goes even further in establishing Sarah's vulnerability by making her a diabetic: her dependence on insulin in case of a seizure is one of several ominous bits of foreshadowing dropped during *Panic Room*'s prologue. The Kubrickian allusions of *Alien 3* return via Sarah's sulky trundle through the brownstone's hallways on her scooter, which humorously updates Danny Lloyd's trike rides down the funkily carpeted corridors of The Overlook Hotel in *The Shining*. In both films, guided tours serve a cartographical function for the characters as well as the audience, introducing and highlighting specific spaces, objects that will figure in the ensuing carnage. In *Panic Room*, these include a slow-moving, old-fashioned elevator; a complicated alarm system that has yet to be initialized; and the eponymous secret compartment, located behind a mirror in the master bedroom and revealed

6.

by Lydia's colleague Evan (Ian Buchanan) with a magician's flourish. "A safe room," he intones dramatically. "A castle keep in medieval times . . . they're quite in vogue now in high-end construction."

The Arthurian allusion is amusing thanks in large part to Buchanan's practiced hauteur, which flatters Meg as a member of the contemporary aristocracy. "High-end" is the operative phrase here, and Evan's insistence that the panic room's necessity exceeds its novelty (or its extravagance) gives *Panic Room* its initial terse stirrings of subtext. Meg's unease has more to do with the fear of being trapped inside than keeping anything out, but she's clearly susceptible to the anxieties of ownership, and the conditioning by which haves fear have-nots. "Panic is part of American political discourse," wrote Jonathan Sterne and Zack Furness in the online journal *Bad Subjects* in 2003, extrapolating individual pathology into group dynamics and arguing that the common denominator between America's two major political parties during the run up to the Iraq War—the period of *Panic Room*'s production and release—was fear-mongering. "Both sides think that they can best persuade us by scaring us."

Panic Room is meant to be a scary movie, a horror-thriller in the vein not only of Hitchcock and Kubrick, but also heart-in-throat entertainments like Terence Young's *Wait Until Dark* (1967), from which it borrows the gimmick of a home containing a secret fortune. But its subject is also fear itself—specifically, the terror of incursion into the domestic sphere, which popped up in the same year in M. Night Shyamalan's alien-invasion saga *Signs* (2002), which also includes a passage where a sick child requires a life-saving dose of medication. In *The Selling of 9/11*, Bianca Nielsen links Fincher's film and the combination of appeal and anxiety that its namesake manifests for Meg—whose wariness seemingly has more to the thought of getting accidentally trapped inside than keeping anything out—to anguished, contemporaneous fantasies about a compromised national security. While acknowledging that *Panic Room* was entirely written and filmed before the events of September 11, 2001, Nielsen nevertheless perceives an ambivalent anti-consumerist allegory aimed against an American culture of fear. "While the marketing tactics used to promote *Panic Room* (particularly the film's trailers and taglines) capitalized on the economic, social, and political climate post-9/11," she writes, "its content reflects the director's interest in the role violence and terror play in social institutions . . . given the film's setting in New York, these anxieties add a further dimension to the film's post-9/11 relevance."

Nielsen's essay is persuasive in identifying *Panic Room* as a loaded if ideologically incoherent text. While the

6.   Neither Jodie Foster nor Kristen Stewart were Fincher's first choice; both replaced actresses who dropped out after the beginning of production, but they match up physically and temperamentally as mother and daughter.

7-8.   The brownstone's elevator is used in *Panic Room* to signify division and shifting power dynamics between the two factions.

9-11. The behavioral and ethical gradations between *Panic Room*'s three bad guys—the stoic Burnham; the greedy Junior; the sociopathic Raoul (Dwight Yoakam)—subdivide the movie's drama to encompass the possibility of honour among thieves.

script undeniably critiques Lydia and Evan for trying to tempt Meg with the idea of her own private fortress—and to an extent Meg for reluctantly buying into their hard sell—the appearance of the film's villains a few scenes later retrospectively justifies their fear-mongering rhetoric. Similarly,

12.

a key late scene where Meg strategically rejects the help of the NYPD gives way to a conventional, conservative ending where the cops arrive on time to save the day. For his part, Fincher, who'd talked about his explicit attempts at subversion in *Fight Club*, and would have had nothing to lose characterizing its follow-up in similar terms, chose to discuss *Panic Room* strictly in terms of multiplex politics. He characterized the film as an "alternative" based on its intensity rather than its ideology; "there are so many movies out there that tell the audience 'we don't want to make you uncomfortable 'cause this is your Friday night.'"

The punky impudence of Fincher's comments notwithstanding, it's possible to reconcile the two different kinds of discomfort being described by the academic and the auteur. Nielsen's assessment of *Panic Room* as a movie prodding the packaging of safety-as-commodity doesn't contradict Fincher's visceral desire to unsettle his viewers, any more than the film's technocratic patina erases its skepticism about our collective subordination to mechanized systems and processes. "At one point in the film, we travel from keyhole to kitchen countertop, passing seamlessly through the curved handle of a coffee pot," wrote Anthony Lane with a mix of admiration and skepticism in the *New Yorker*. "Is this just showing off, or is *Panic Room* taking a second to remind us where the water boils and where the knives are kept?"

Lane is of course answering his own not-so-rhetorical question. Fincher's long takes are undoubtedly an example of directorial flexing—part of a long line of long takes dating back to the Hitchcock of *Rope* (1948) and Orson Welles's *Touch of Evil* (1958)—but their spatial gamesmanship is also in the service of the story. *Panic Room*'s serene velocity facilitates an end-run around one traditional marker of "realism"—the

practical necessity in most movies of physically embodied cinematography—while inscribing and reinforcing the metallic, material solidity of the film's world. The aim here is metaphysical; no less than those hovering opening credits, *Panic Room*'s airborne camerawork serves as a corollary for a higher intelligence, inviting us to share in and thrill to a weightless point-of-view. It's a twist on Hitchcockian complicity as old as the opening crane-shot push-in of *Psycho*, tweaked for an era of televisual real-estate porn; the cinematography lubricates collective fantasies of access alongside nightmares of intrusion. "The camera is completely unencumbered," Fincher noted. "While the people are [encumbered] . . . they can't get through the wall, and then the camera goes right through it. I think there is something about that that tells the audience, 'scream all you want, no one can hear you. You can only watch.'"

"It's too dark," Sarah tells her mother after climbing into bed during their first night in the brownstone, an endearingly childlike observation that could also be an in-joke on *Panic Room*'s planned visual scheme. Originally, Fincher had wanted to shoot multiple sequences in total pitch-black conditions ("you know, eyes floating in the shadows") but relented after unsuccessful camera tests and settled instead for a sculptural, sepulcral lighting scheme that renders the Altmans' new digs as a kind of jaundiced Twilight Zone—a spacious echo chamber illuminated at odd intervals by glaring bare bulbs. A low-angled shot of Meg's hand dangling off of her bed as she falls asleep (before properly arming the security system) is seen through a wine glass, darkly—it could be a still-life. The next cut

then cues a speedy, startling backwards pan away from the bedroom, moving through the slats of the bannister and down two floors to street level, resting on a window just long enough to show the film's three villains arriving. Their lurking presence reconfigures *Panic Room*'s prowling camerawork into a corollary for their nocturnal craft: it's as if Fincher is casing the joint alongside them. From there, the tracking shot gets synced to the intruders' movements and plans, drifting back up to the top floor (and, yes, through the coffee pot) to observe the intruders jiggling locks and scurrying up fire escapes—and also over top of the brownstone's cathedral-like skylight—before one of them dislodges a ceiling panel with a crowbar and gains entry, forcing an edit after two minutes and bringing the film's tone of creeping, incipient dread into the present tense.

#

Plenty has been written in film studies about the Hitchcockian device of the "MacGuffin," a term coined by the English screenwriter Angus MacPhail to describe an object, device, or event that is of great importance to a movie's characters but insignificant or irrelevant in and of itself. The French director and critic Yves Lavandier later finessed the definition to say that the truest example of a MacGuffin is as a "secret that motivates the villains," in which case *Panic Room*'s example is the $3 million in bearer bonds stored under the floor in the brownstone's panic room—a hidden and untraceable windfall left behind by the property's deceased former owner. As MacGuffins go, a cache of money is

12. Through a glass, darkly: Meg's arm dangling limply off her bed plays up her obliviousness and vulnerability in the early stages of the home invasion.

less fanciful or imaginative than a roll of microfilm (as in *North By Northwest*) or a *Maltese Falcon* (1941) but it dovetails nicely with *Panic Room*'s central architectural gimmick: the criminals require access to the one place designed to keep them out. It also connects the film to another, deeper classical theme: the compulsive, obsessive, and finally self-annihilating nature of greed.

In contrast to the fetishistic serial killers of Fincher's procedural trilogy—or the biologically hardwired killing machine of *Alien 3*—*Panic Room*'s antagonists are a motley cross-section of anti-social types. The prime mover in the group is Junior, the grandson of the previous owner, who feels entitled to more than what he's been left in the will; squirrel-eyed and gaunt with his hair pulled tight in cornrows, he's played by Jared Leto as the seedy antithesis of the prime-time heartthrob persona he created on *My So-Called Life*. Junior's twitchy obnoxiousness is deployed in counterpoint to the stoic, thoughtful calm of Forest Whitaker as Burnham, a cash-strapped security company employee with a chip on his shoulder against his bosses and a vast knowledge of alarm systems and other protocols.

13.

Burnham is hesitant to continue when he realizes the house is occupied; Junior's plan had involved breaking into an empty home. He is convinced to follow through by the prospect of being able to provide for his daughter, a sentimental development implying the coexistence of greed and need, certainly beyond that of Leto's covetous black-sheep blueblood, who's after more than he's already entitled to. If Junior's wanksta ensemble identifies him as a posturing wannabe, Burnham's coveralls register as decisively professional-cum-proletarian costume, complete with an identificatory name patch. The third and most jagged edge of the triangle is Raoul (Dwight Yoakam), a psychopathic freelance hitman recruited by Junior as extra muscle who has no compunctions about dishing out violence even if it's not required. In their different ways, Junior and Burnham are both "inside men" whose

participation complicates the paranoia of urban criminality stoked by Lydia's salesmanship. Raoul, meanwhile proves that a generalized panic and paranoia are not unwarranted. In a nicely executed moment, Leto crosses in front of Whitaker to open the door for Yoakam, a pointed bit of staging which shows that Junior has welcomed the devil inside.

There is, perhaps, an implied satirical contrast between Junior's rushed, bungled plan and Fincher's own immaculate blueprinting, which would make Burnham his surrogate—a connection heightened by the visual prominence of the old pro's surname. "This is what I do," Burnham tells Junior. "If some idiot with a sledgehammer could break in, do you really think I'd still have a job?" (The echo of John Doe's sledgehammer allusion in *Se7en* is no less humorous for being incidental.) Because Leto and Yoakam render Junior and Raoul irredeemable in different ways—the loudmouth moron and the tight-lipped assassin, united solely by misanthropic self-interest—it's left to Whitaker to lend the action some emotional ballast, marshalling a great actor's skill in the service of racially coded sentimentality. The use of a Black man as a savior figure in *Alien 3* indicated a political correctness at odds with that film's self-satisfied depravity, and so it goes in *Panic Room*, which establishes Burnham's reluctance to harm Meg and Sarah as evidence of a decency that will also be his downfall—a flaw that doubles as a saving grace. Fincher establishes the character's moral authority by placing him at the forefront of the subtly diagonalized, deep-focus compositions that punctuate the scenes of the men in the basement; more generally, he hierarchizes *Panic Room*'s ethical universe by keeping the criminals on the lower levels and Meg and Sarah safely sequestered above, an upstairs/downstairs alignment that mocks the old saw of putting women "on a pedestal" while also wittily enshrining their elevated economic position. While the men clamber through the bowels of the house, the women cower inside the safe room, beneficiaries but also prisoners of their own state-of-the-art devices.

They're also stand-ins for *Panic Room*'s audience: Fincher's self-reflexive gambit is to consistently show Meg and Sarah watching the intruders via the panic room's closed-circuit security cameras, a gimmick that italicizes the filmmaker's interest in spectatorship as a theater of cruelty. Any comparisons to *Home Alone* (1990) were laughed off during *Panic Room*'s

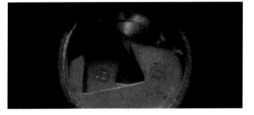

14.

13. The family photos include real ones belonging to Stewart.

14. The claustrophobia of *Panic Room*'s scenario is exemplified via shots framed on either side of the open piping that gives Meg and Sarah their only little window on the world.

15. Stuck in a trap:
     Meg's high-tech
     "castle keep" and
     modern surveillance
     technology do little
     to alleviate her
     terror and frustration,
     only compounding her
     feelings of being
     under siege.

press blitz, but there's a case to be made for the film as a nasty slapstick comedy featuring moments of grotesque turnabout: in addition to being scorched, singed, and otherwise tenderized, the intruders seethe at all times with a comedically profane frustration. Junior's blunt-force stupidity amuses Fincher most, and Leto's acting betrays an awareness that he's as much a crash-test dummy as an actual character, always on the wrong end of Koepp's carefully calibrated, crowd-pleasing set pieces. When Burnham hits upon the idea to smoke the Altmans out using a hose connected to a bottle of propane, the threat of impending suffocation is (literally) exploded by Meg's risky but ingenious response to ignite the gas leak, redirecting the blaze back through the air ducts and towards its source, rendered by Fincher and Hall in hallucinatory hues of neon blue that fill the safe room and then swirl around Junior's body.

Cause and effect, thrust and parry, back-and-forth: *Panic Room* establishes its rhythm and sticks to it, scoring a few visual coups along the way, like the sidelong shot of Junior futilely banging against the locked door of the elevator as Meg and Sarah descend during an early escape attempt, a composition that bifurcates the space of the shaft to create a split screen.

The obstacles that the film keeps throwing up against Meg and Sarah—that slow-moving elevator; the sliced phone lines; the obliviousness of a neighbor to a flashlight-morse-code-distress-signal—all qualify under the film's exacting mandate of physical and psychological plausibility. At times, the inventiveness of the script flags, leading to the feeling that the movie is itself a MacGuffin, its ultimate outcome never really in doubt. The same goes for the series of contrivances that relocate the robbers to the panic room and Meg to the main floor, with Sarah unwillingly but unavoidably left behind as a hostage and to suffer a seizure that requires Burnham—the only one of the criminals with a child of his own—to save her life, the next to last station of the cross in his redemption narrative.

Even amid the grinding of narrative machinery, Fincher delivers a set of extraordinary sequences that sustain the film's narrative tension while accessing the unsettling side of his directorial temperament. The first comes when Raoul executes Junior, the latter having decided—thanks in large part to the third-degree burns marring his face and arm after the backfiring barbecue stunt—that the reward isn't worth the trouble. (Given the supreme annoyance of Leto's performance, Yoakam

could be acting on behalf of the audience, a version of a mercy.) While dragging Junior's body to the backdoor, Raoul encounters Stephen, who'd earlier received a cryptic, half-audible cell phone call from Meg and has ventured out into the night to see what's wrong. Quickly identified as the house's owner, Stephen is subject to a hellacious physical beating that his wife and daughter can only watch helplessly through the panic room's monitors, contradicting Sarah's assumption that her father's new partner wouldn't "let him" come to their rescue if needed and complicating *Panic Room*'s gliding, medium-cool voyeurism with a locked-off, bone-breaking depiction of violence.

The assertion of male dominance through brutality is a theme Fincher explored exhaustively in *Fight Club*, whose amateur pugilists long for identity and control. They eventually redirect their animus away from each other and toward deep-pocket corporate targets, graduating from scattered fistfights to organized terrorism: hence its reception as an instruction manual about punching up. *Panic Room*'s hooligans don't present a comparably unified front—they're greedy rather than idealistic, and have no ideological program to speak of. But the way that Raoul takes his frustrations out on Stephen, reducing him from a potential

16.

17.

16-17. Meg's denial to the police officer serves as one of *Panic Room*'s most provocative moments, inverting the film's tension so that a savior figure becomes a source of threat to her family's safety.

18. Burnham's arrest at the end of the film seems to punish him despite his heroic acts at the climax, and the film leaves his character's fate hanging ambiguously.

patriarchal savior to an enfeebled, hogtied hostage, bristles with some of *Fight Club*'s same allegorical discomfort. It's as if, unable to penetrate the panic room or dislodge or harm its inhabitants, Raoul uses the rich man in the glasses as a punching bag for his grievances.

The implication may be that Raoul's attack is karmic punishment for Stephen's callow abandonment of his family, or else a mockery of *Straw Dogs*; the potency acquired by that film's skinny, bespectacled hero is denied here, with Stephen sidelined upon arrival and failing to hold and aim a long-barrelled gun at the moment of truth. Either way, Stephen's status as one of *Panic Room*'s two designated whipping boys alongside Leto (who also filled that role in *Fight Club*) feels charged with meaning, however inchoate. It permits Fincher a degree of R-rated sadism without resorting to hurt the female characters, whose ordeals, however gruelingly physicalized, stop short of torture; in the film's most excessive image, Stephen's broken collarbone can be seen protruding out from under his expensive trenchcoat.

In another standout sequence, Meg tries to dissuade a police officer (Paul Schulze) from entering the house to investigate a garbled 911 call. As she goes to answer the door, Fincher cuts precisely between multiple levels of the house—Stephen bound and bleeding in the living room; Burnham and Raoul watching on monitors in the panic room; Sarah in their clutches—to set up what must necessarily be a command performance on her part. The entryway creates a cramped, interior frame around Foster, in effect turning her slight, under-shirted frame into a human equivalent of the panic room—the last line of defense against a fatal breach. Back literally to the wall, she fabricates an account of drunk-dialing horniness that rattles the cops just

enough to keep them on the porch and then send them on their way.

The idea of a woman using a sexualized lie to ward off her potential (male) protectors is audacious, put across by Foster's coy mix of defiance and embarrassment—both postures concealing the real sources of threat and tension. But it's the way that Schulze's officer Kenney—filmed by Fincher in a huge, screen-filling close-up—calmly asks Meg to give him a silent signal to indicate if she's secretly in peril ("blinking your eyes a few times, something like that") that touches a nerve. It's a moment that gestures, however indirectly, to the real cycles of domestic abuse and terror that *Panic Room*'s jerry-rigged scenario exploits for escapist terror and suspense; it also outstrips the impact of the actual climax, a desultory throwdown which finds Burnham completing his change of heart and shooting Raoul at the expense of his own clean getaway. When Whitaker wearily puts his hands in the air and the bearer bonds get blown away in the rain, he cuts an existentially crooked figure out of John Huston's *Treasure of the Sierra Madre* (1948) or Kubrick's *The Killing* (1956), both of which end with ill-gotten gains scattered to the wind. A push in on Foster's stricken, blood-stained face underneath Howard Shore's skittering score conveys a measure of psychic damage equivalent to her husband's physical injuries—the shot has a trembling intensity. But the coda is one of the only passages of pure order and contentment in Fincher's entire repertoire, showing mother and daughter together on a bench, bathed in autumnal light as they peruse apartment listings.

In closing, Fincher once again evokes Hitchcock through the use of a so-called "trombone shot," zooming in while tracking backwards to create a paradoxical sense of slippage and equilibrium—a feeling, one

might say, of *Vertigo*, minus that movie's bottomless melancholy and devastation. The actresses remain firmly in focus as the field of view widens, offering up a glorious exterior after two hours of claustrophobia. The impression is one of freedom, not only from the cramped confines of the panic room and of their entire ordeal, but the expectations of "high-end construction." "Do we need all that space?" Meg asks, already knowing the answer.

The finale optimism and openness are a nice touch, but the lack of any return to Burnham—a Black man who has recently saved both women's lives—is a nagging omission: the question of whether the film is making a point about his comparative expendability (and the unseen consequences for his own daughter) or has simply decided in his case that virtue is its own (nonfinancial) reward remains open, giving things at least a scintilla of ambiguity. Typically, Fincher's "happy endings" are highly ironized, either via perversely satisfying, orgasmic images of "completion"—like *Se7en*'s final *petit mort* or the collapsing office towers of *Fight Club*—or else placed in air quotes, as in the unlikely, all-encompassing catharsis served up at the final buzzer in *The Game* or *Gone Girl*'s "happy couple" fade out. *Panic Room* exists in something like its own category, becoming the first Fincher film that doesn't really attempt to leave any residue: its "high-end construction" is also spotless, for better and for worse. In grossing over $200 million worldwide, the film proved that Fincher could pursue his "alternative" vision—and exercise his technological obsessions—while still providing a healthy return on investment (the real happy ending on a job for hire). *Panic Room*'s craftsmanship is undeniable, and yet it's also less a means to an end than an end in and of itself, the suffocating, self-containededly saleable brilliance of a filmmaker thinking inside the box.

Fig A. *North by Northwest*, Alfred Hitchcock, 1967; Opening sequence by Saul Bass

Panic Room's opening titles are styled in tribute to Alfred Hitchcock's cross-country adventure movie.

Fig B. Stanley Hotel, Estes Park, Colorado

A haunted hotel that inspired Stephen King's *The Shining*.

Fig C. *Straw Dogs,* Sam Peckinpah, 1971

Probably the most iconic home-invasion movie ever made, given a gender-specific flip by *Panic Room*'s scenario of a single mother defending her castle keep.

Fig F. Fish in the tank

Fincher wanted to show a burglary sequence from the POV of fish inside a fish bowl looking out and seeing the cats.

Fig G. *Home Alone*, Chris Columbus, 1990 [Still]

Fincher joked during press rounds that *Panic Room* was like a more violent, grown-up version of *Home Alone*.

Fig H. CCTV camera in Lower Manhattan with the Freedom Tower in the background

Post-9/11 fear and paranoia in the US.

Fig D. *Wait Until Dark*, Terence Young, 1967 [Still]

Though *Panic Room* is not technically a remake, it somewhat mirrors the plot and characters of *Wait Until Dark* (1967).

Fig E. *The 39 Steps*, Alfred Hitchcock, 1935

Early example of MacGuffin technique used in *Panic Room*.

Fig I. *Rear Window*, Alfred Hitchcock, 1954

Fincher was inspired by the voyeuristic visual language of Alfred Hitchcock's *tour de force*.

Fig J. *The Treasure of the Sierra Madre*, John Huston, 1948

The bonds scattered to the winds at *Panic Room*'s climax repeat the imagery of John Huston's classic study of greed and hubris.

WRITERS David Koepp
CINEMATOGRAPHER Darius Khondji, Conrad W. Hall
EDITOR James Haygood

BUDGET $48 million
BOX OFFICE $197.1 million
LENGTH 112 min

REALITY BITES

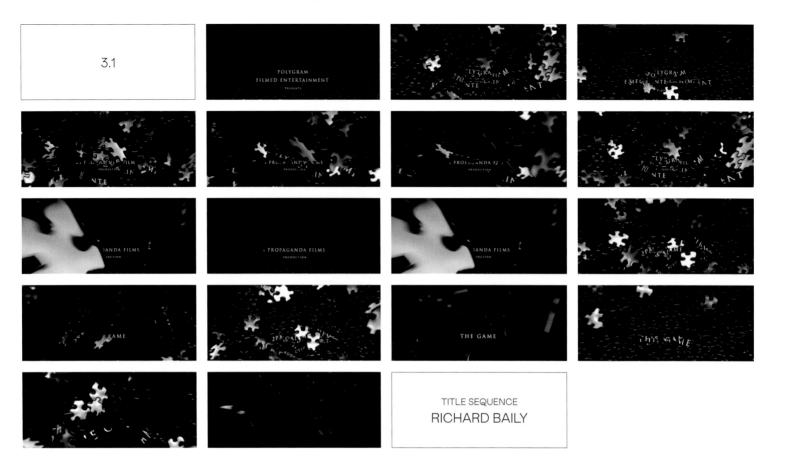

3.1

POLYGRAM
FILMED ENTERTAINMENT
PRESENTS

THE GAME

TITLE SEQUENCE
RICHARD BAILY

< The puzzle motif of
The Game's opening titles
promises a film where
some assembly will be
required; once scattered,
the jigsaw pieces will have
to be recombined by the
film's protagonist
and audience surrogate.

3.1
THE GAME

1997

"Don't call asking what the object of the game is. Figuring that out is the object of the game." So intones CNN talking head Daniel Schorr to Nicholas Van Orton (Michael Douglas), digressing inexplicably in mid-broadcast on behalf of the shady entertainment start-up Consumer Recreation Services (CRS) that has recently taken on the latter as an unwitting—and increasingly unwilling—client. CRS refers to its first-person, live-action role playing set-up as an "experiential book of the month club," but what began for Nicholas as a conventional page-turner transforms during Schorr's address into something more akin to surrealist fiction.

The tactic of using authentic broadcasters to "play themselves" in movies proliferated in the 1990s and remained in sync with a broadening multimedia landscape: in movies like Ivan Reitman's *Dave* (1993) or Rob Reiner's *The American President* (1995), recognizable talking heads became casual guarantors of realism. As an Emmy-winning journalist who was surveilled by Richard Nixon's White House in the early 1970s and placed on the president's infamous "enemies list", Schorr is well-chosen as the implacable face of paranoia in a thriller that draws on that decade's gritty cinematic textures—all muffled Conversations and occluded Parallax Views. But the anxieties that David Fincher's third feature pivots on—or spirals around—are timeless, chief among them the possibility, at once validating and unsettling,

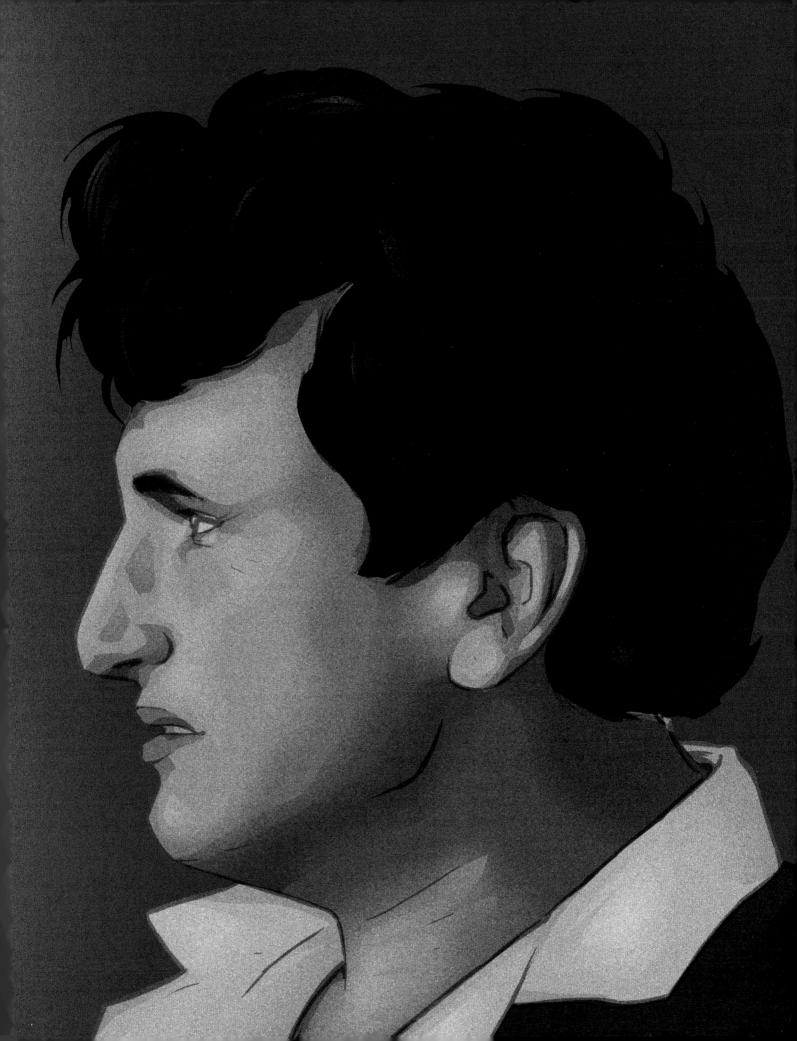

that we are all of us protagonists in some larger, master narrative.

For Nicholas, who is too preoccupied in the moment with wondering why his television has transformed into a two-way communication device, Schorr's warning is just so much ominous, taunting tautology—a scare tactic deployed in the service of a high-tech shake-down. For the viewer, however, the old newscaster's koan-like phrasing provides a hint for the viewer about how to decipher the movie in front of us. Schorr is describing a paradox in which grateful, passive acceptance coexists with the desire for understanding, a warning that's also an invitation. Thus

1.

does the title *The Game* operate on a literal and existential level. To paraphrase the artificially intelligent antagonist of John Badham's *Wargames* (1984)—another fleet Hollywood thriller about a simulation gone awry—for Nicholas, the only losing move is not to play.

Released to mixed reviews and solid box office in the Fall of 1997, *The Game* yoked universal uncertainties to twisty epistemology in a moment of widespread technological transformation. It joined a cycle of high-end genre films, including Kathryn Bigelow's *Strange Days* (1995), David Cronenberg's *eXistenZ* (1999), and the Wachowski siblings' paradigm-shifting action movie *The Matrix* (1999), which sought to examine the collapsing, contingent relationship between embodied and mediated experiences of the world. Where the bulk of these films settle in the sci-fi noir genre and address themes of simulation through digital innovation and biological mutation—the downloadable memories of *Strange Days*; the plug-and-play "body ports" in *eXistenZ*; the immersive virtual reality of *The Matrix*—*The Game* is comparatively bloodless, as well as resolutely analogue in construction and subject matter.

The script by John Brancato and Michael Ferris feints early and often at an uncanny or even science-fictional solution to the question of how and why Nicholas's CRS experience has taken on the contours of a thriller, yet in the end, everything turns out to be explainable in three solid dimensions.

In 1991, Brancato and Ferris sold the original draft for *The Game* to Fincher's Propaganda Films, where it was earmarked for up-and-coming director Jonathan Mostow. By 1993, though, the project had fallen through and was pitched directly to Fincher, who opted to direct *Se7en* instead. That film's success put the director in a position to carefully pick and choose his follow-up, and *The Game* was back on—pending a rewrite. By this time, Brancato and Ferris had been established as hitmakers via their script for *The Net* (1995), about a young woman whose life and identity are hijacked by a cabal of profiteering computer hackers—a near-identical set-up resulting in a decidedly mild crowd-pleaser. Hoping to give the project some of *Se7en*'s edge, Fincher enlisted Andrew Kevin Walker to revise the material, and the biggest switch involved the personality of the story's protagonist, a sympathetic figure in the original draft reworked into a tetchy effigy of karmic retribution. In Walker's updated (and uncredited) incarnation, Nicholas Van Orton is a stingy, master-of-the-universe type, an investment banker born into obscene wealth and determined to increase it. In an interview with the *Washington Times*, Fincher described the character as a "fashionable, good-looking Scrooge"; by invoking *A Christmas Carol*, the director framed his film as a Dickensian tale of redemption, and *The Game* follows that template to the point of sentimental silliness and then—arguably—comes out the other end as a send-up of store-bought self-improvement schemes, or perhaps of

its own existence as a slick, high-concept studio thriller.

Given Walker's participation, *The Game*'s relationship to *Se7en* and its themes of cruelty and control are instructive. Early on in the film, following a lunch date with his semi-estranged, black-sheep brother Conrad (Sean Penn)—during which the latter evangelizes about CRS as a life-changing experience and presents his depressed sibling with an engraved invitation as a birthday present—Nicholas visits the group's offices in midtown San Francisco. There, he submits to a battery of psychological and physical tests ("turn your head and cough, that sort of thing"), including an oddly penetrating pen-and-paper questionnaire and a word association survey structured as a short film sutured together out of glancing, abstract insert shots. The visual reference is to Alan J. Pakula's *The Parallax View* (1973) and its famed subliminal interlude, but the staccato, synaptic editing pattern of CRS's video Rorschach equally recalls *Se7en*'s abstract opening credit sequence, which was also shot by *The Game*'s cinematographer, Harris Savides. A music-video veteran like Fincher, Savides would become one of the go-to cinematographers of the twenty-first century, and if his work on *The Game* is slicker and more classical than the gliding, durational style he developed for Gus Van Sant in *Gerry* (2002) and *Elephant* (2003), it has its own crisp, sculptural beauty, all icy blues and covetous greens, punctuated by spilled-ink nightscapes and gilted around the edges by flashes of platinum, silver and gold, as if marking the boundaries of Nicholas's gilded cage.

Hoping to do some further reconnaissance now that he's agreed to let them run their game ("sign here in blood," jokes genial customer rep Jim Feinghold [James Rebhorn]), Nicholas queries a fellow executive-class player about his own CRS experience. The man responds to the request in a way that a Sunday School stickler like John Doe might appreciate—with a Bible verse. "John, Chapter nine, Verse twenty-five," he tones with a smile that marks him somewhere between a put-on artist and a true believer—the same sweet spot where *The Game* locates its beguiling sense of mystery and cognitive dissonance. "Whereas once I was blind, now I can see," the man adds dramatically, piquing Nicholas's curiosity above his skepticism and recalling the killer's handwritten allusion to exalted, all-seeing vision in *Se7en*: "Long is the way and hard that out of Hell leads up into light."

Vision is a key motif in both *Se7en* and also in *The Game*, which begins with a degraded, home-movie image of the young Nicholas staring directly into the lens of the camera— the start of a scratchy 16 mm montage chronicling a lavish birthday celebration on his family's sprawling suburban estate. (The aesthetic of *The Game*'s opening was shamelessly pilfered for the title sequence of HBO's Emmy-winning series *Succession*, which also focuses on the miseries of the idle rich.) As the prologue ends, Fincher holds pointedly on a close-up of the boy's eyes before match-cutting sharply to Nicholas's aged visage as he splashes water on his face, a bit of staging suggesting a reverie interrupted. If the character of John Doe was truly intended as *Se7en*'s not-so-secret identification point—the all-seeing perfectionist whose plan plays out, however perversely, as a triumph of will over contingency—then Nicholas is his obverse doppelganger, a man who can't see the bigger picture as it takes shape around him, a figure scribbled into somebody else's scrupulous blueprint.

In both appearance and white-collar vocation, Nicholas resembles the lawyer in *Se7en* sacrificed on the altar of "Greed," and while his victimization doesn't prove fatal, it does verge on the proverbial pound of flesh. (Keeping briefly with Shakespeare: the character is like a barren Lear, without even a thankless child to care for him in his dotage.) Nicholas occupies different (if not necessarily elevated) moral ground than John Doe in that any harm he does to others is meted out via the swoops and dips of the stock market but he's imbued with some of the serial killer's harsh, multidirectional contempt for his fellow man. "Notice the way [Nicholas] glares at a bag of Chinese takeout, as if it were a sack of shit," writes *MUBI*'s Greg Cwik, drawing a bead on the privileged misanthropy that tinges Douglas's expertly reptilian performance. "[Nicholas] is a subtly doleful man who uses words carefully, plays racquetball alone, and spends nights watching cable news, a man to whom the capitalist system has given everything except happiness."

Cwik's mention of capitalist corrosion and Nicholas's late-night cable news addiction connects the character, retrospectively and not uncoincidentally, to the scarifying image of Donald Trump in the White House: a snarling, suggestible tycoon taking his cues from a series of television broadcasts. Not that *The Game* makes

Nicholas into a Trumpian blowhard, or even a sociopathic playboy manque like Christian Bale's Patrick Bateman in the movie version of *American Psycho* (2000), a key proto-Trumpian text also embedded in the DNA of *Se7en*. But considering that Douglas's Oscar-winning role as a duplicitous billionaire in *Wall Street* (1987) was based in part on Trump and his nouveau-riche New York ilk, the star's casting as a man whose dolorousness rebukes the mantra that "greed is good" has its own witty inevitability. In the same way that *Alien 3* works simultaneously as a showcase for and an analysis of Sigourney Weaver's screen persona, *The Game* scores many of its effects through the associations

2.

and assumptions prompted by its star and his history of playing front-runners hoisted by their own petards.

Typically, Fincher likes to booby-trap his movies around his characters, who end up wary of making false moves as they maneuver through their respective narrative minefields: think of *Alien 3* and *Panic Room*, with their menacing, maze-like enclosures, or Nick Dunne playing his own version of "the game" in *Gone Girl*, one nursery-rhyme clue at a time. *The Game* sits at the apex of this tendency: while less baroquely violent than *Se7en* and minus the quasi-apocalyptic stakes of *Fight Club*, it's similarly imbued with a sense of lurking, perpetual threat. "Forget political conspiracy, invading aliens or danger from the insect world," wrote Janet Maslin in the *New York Times*, cutting briskly through the film's genre-movie surfaces towards its core of social critique. "*The Game* puts its yuppie potentate through worse terrors, [including] powerlessness, invasion of privacy, temporary poverty and ruining very expensive clothes."

Late in the film, after his assets have been surreptitiously liquidated and he's been exiled to Mexico (where he awakens

1. When Nicholas's television talks to him (in the stentorian tones of CNN anchor Daniel Schorr) it's *The Game*'s first truly surreal moment, marking the character's transition from passive observer to participant.

2. Examining the life-size clown marionette that's been left in his living room, Nicholas realizes he's being watched through the doll's eye; the composition also transforms him into a figure of the fool.

3.

from drug-induced unconsciousness in a mausoleum) the banker undergoes a costume change with a symbolic dimension—a snake forced to shed its skin. In an essay for *The Current*, Gina Telaroli notes that while for the majority of *The Game*, Fincher and wardrobe designer Michael Kaplan style Nicholas as a clotheshorse, his rumpled duds in the Mexico sequence externalize a newfound sense of humiliation: clothes unmake the man. "The dirty white fabric hangs off of him loosely, his hands lost in the arms of the suit and the pants legs gathering at his ankles," writes Telaroli. "He looks small and, in that smallness, there is fear." Telaroli doesn't go so far as to connect Nicholas's appearance to David Byrne's iconic white suit in *Stop Making Sense* (1984) but the "Once in a Lifetime" joke is there for the making; at this moment in the film, Nicholas may well be asking himself "well . . . how did I get here?"

The Game luxuriates in that very precise sense of existential fear: the warm *schadenfreude* of seeing a titan cut down to size. When Conrad refers to his older brother during an argument as a "manipulative fucking control freak," we prick up our ears, not only because the character resembles the remark (manipulation and control being Douglas's actorly specialties) but because it offers a hint as to the shape of his upcoming comeuppance. Turnabout is fair play, and Conrad's not-so-rhetorical inquiry during another loaded exchange—"What do you get for the man who has everything?"—turns out to be a trick question. You don't get him anything: you take something away, and then another thing, and then another,

until he has nothing and remembers what wanting actually feels like. Despite an absence of Chaucer quotes *à la Se7en*, *The Game* is very much a moral tale, elegantly veiled as a nightmare about entering into and being kept in a state of pure, grasping, overmatched helplessness.

"I was always the kind of person who didn't like being victimized by other people's expertise," Fincher told Jenny Cooney for a profile in *Empire* in November of 1997, an admission that partially personalizes *The Game*'s ruthlessness. Drawing in equal measures on his own preference for control and his anxieties about the lack thereof— with the experience of making *Alien 3* as one potential source of inspiration—Fincher engineers Nicholas's reversal of fortune in lucid, excruciating increments. In his video essay "Men on the Chessboard: The Hidden Pleasures of *The Game*," included on Arrow's deluxe Blu-ray release of the film, critic Neil Young zeroes in on the movie punitive aspects, which he boils down in one title-card to "the punishment of luxury," a class-conscious designation that could just as easily apply to the economically-coded skirmishes of *Panic Room*, whose protagonists are also being targeted on the basis of wealth.

Like Telaroli, Young analyzes *The Game* as a study in humiliation, using a chess allusion to identify Nicholas as the story's central, downwardly mobile moving piece—the King Who Would Be a Pawn. The chess metaphor is also derived from the film's most sinisterly funny soundtrack cue, the sudden blaring of Jefferson Airplane's hallucinogenic countercultural

anthem "White Rabbit" over a loudspeaker when Nicholas returns one night to his immaculate mansion to find it ransacked and splattered with black-lit, neon-tinted graffiti mocking and threatening his status as a corporate big shot.

The use of the *Alice in Wonderland*-referencing "White Rabbit" in a movie set in the Airplane's home base of San Francisco is witty on its own terms, and it anticipates Fincher's prickly needle-drop of "Hurdy Gurdy Man" in *Zodiac*, which shares the same Bay Area location. As Young points out, San Francisco's cinematic legacy is one of "surveillance, scams and paranoia . . . a stratified city of wealth and poverty, the two worlds seldom meeting," and through this civically minded lens, *The Game*'s carefully maintained pattern of falling is plausibly a nod to the plunging trajectories of *Vertigo*. Allusions mix with illusions: a shot of Nicholas placing a call from a phone booth is framed deliberately to recall Donald Sutherland's health inspector trying to communicate in secret amidst a clandestine alien takeover in *Invasion of the Body Snatchers*, a film similarly attuned to a paranoid frequency. "I keep seeing these people, all recognizing each other . . . " whispers Brooke Adams to Donald Sutherland. "It's a conspiracy, I know it."

Less abstractly, *The Game*'s location also references the beginning of Douglas's acting career on the 1970s television cop drama *The Streets of San Francisco*, where he played a brash, athletic police detective—a righteous hero not yet hardened into sociopathy like his Bay Area contemporary Harry Callahan (and closer, in shaggy look and spirit, to the soulful tenacity of *Zodiac*'s Dave Toschi). In time, however, Douglas's onscreen persona would come to be coated in a thin layer of sleaze. In the same year that he won the Oscar for Best Actor as Gordon Gekko (he of the cutthroat corporate-raider ethics and alliteratively lizardly name) Douglas carved out an even more iconic status as the put-upon protagonist of *Fatal Attraction* (1987), a family man whose one-night stand with an obsessive, depressive stranger (Glenn Close) threatens his cozy upper-middle class existence.

Douglas's Dan Gallagher is very much being punished in *Fatal Attraction* for the sin of lust (with Close's Alex Forrest nearly as bloodthirsty and calculating as John Doe) but the punishment—stalking, harassment, physical threat, and the abduction of his adorable moppet daughter—is understood to exceed the crime. While *The Game* does conjure up an icily ambiguous blonde in the form of Deborah Kara Unger's shape-shifting CRS-affiliate Christine—an homage not only to Close in *Fatal Attraction* but also Sharon Stone's seductive, yellow-tressed murderess in the San Fran-canonical *Basic Instinct*—Fincher isn't particularly interested in gender dynamics. Christine's unsettling malleability is part of her gig as a CRS operative; both from Nicholas's point of view and that of the movie as a whole (which are basically one and the same), she's a device—less pivotal than Paltrow's sacrificial naif Tracy in *Se7en*, and also less of a performance opportunity. In a movie so fully focused on Douglas and his sour neuroses, the cool, insinuating mystique Unger displayed for David Cronenberg in *Crash* (1996) doesn't get much more than a perfunctory showcase.

A thoroughly conservative movie wedded to the very Yuppie status quo that Fincher's films would go on to prod from a variety of angles (including the direct erotic-thriller parody of *Gone Girl*,

also about a woman who refuses to be ignored), *Fatal Attraction* emasculated its star to prove a point about family values—namely, that they're worth protecting unto the death ("the family that kills together, stays together," in Pauline Kael's deathless formulation). *The Game* is instead concerned with a more professionalized form of predation: namely, the filmmaking process as an exercise in top-down dominance. In a film filled with wonderfully suggestive compositions and expert use of light and shadow, care of Savides, the most striking and ingenious image might be the shot of Nicholas, frustrated with CRS's grueling screening process, standing up and glaring towards the projection booth, light flaring around him as he raises his hand to his eyes.

Backlit in silhouette, Nicholas looks like nothing so much as a deer in the headlights: where once he could see, now he is blind. Besides indicating that the protagonist is having difficulty perceiving what's happening to (and around) him, the shot expressly identifies CRS and its methods as belonging to the world of cinema—an illusionistic enterprise peddling escapism in the form of entrapment (and vice versa). Even as the movie keeps its cards close to its chest for its duration, the shot of the projector, so obviously modelled on the prologue of *Citizen Kane* (1941), is Fincher showing his hand. "This isn't a movie about real life," says the director on *The Game*'s DVD commentary track. "It's a movie about movies."

\#

There have traditionally been two major kinds of "movies-about-movies": films that treat the history or mythology of cinema as their subject—either essayistically, as in Thom Andersen's *Los Angeles Plays Itself* (2003) or Kent Jones's *Hitchcock/Truffaut* (2015) or through self-conscious references

3. Birthdays and aging are central in *The Game*, and Nicholas resents being made the center of attention—an early hint of forces massing in his blindspot.

4-9. Keys, notes, totems and code words; Nicholas's CRS experience transforms the texture of everyday life into the stuff of espionage novels.

4-9.

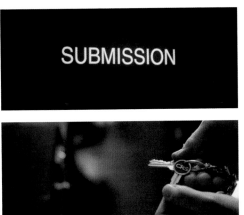

and homages to extant films (c.f. the collected works of postmodernists like Brian De Palma and Quentin Tarantino); and films that document and dramatize the process of moviemaking, like François Truffaut's *Day For Night* (1973) or Stanley Donen and Gene Kelly's *Singin' in the Rain* (1952). These two subcategories are fluid rather than exclusive. For instance, *Singin' in the Rain* uses the conventions of a backstage musical as an armature for a combination history-lesson-satire about the first-half-century of Hollywood; the tale of Gene Kelly's stunt-man-turned-matinee-idol allegorizes popular cinema's shift not only from silence to sound, but also from a preponderance of rough, physicalized slapstick to a technological sophistication negating the need for such death-defying actions.

One of the best running jokes in *Singin' in the Rain* is that Kelly's exuberant Don Lockwood keeps emerging unscathed from what should be fatal situations—an affectionate parody of Buster Keaton's stone-faced derring-do in films like *Our Hospitality* (1923). In 1980's *The Stunt Man*, director

10.

Richard Rush expanded this idea into a more metaphysical dimension through the story of a shell-shocked, fugitive and ex-Vietnam vet (Steve Railsback) who wanders onto a World War I movie set in mid-shoot—another Keaton-esque figure, like the hero of *Sherlock Jr.* (1924) except that instead of stepping through the screen, he stumbles onto the backlot. Later, the film's power-tripping director, Eli Cross (Peter O'Toole) will offer him sanctuary from the cops in exchange for serving as the project's stuntman, blending behind-the-scenes intrigue with pulpy existentialism the semiprofessional daredevil at the beck and call of an obstinate God. *The Game* is probably closer in spirit and philosophy to Rush's underrated curio than any of its carefully annotated San Francisco-set predecessors. Beneath the particular specifics of the plot, what is Nicholas Van Orton but an amateur, crazily committed stunt man? (He even has to pass that physical.)

The telling difference between *The Game* and *The Stunt Man* is that there is no analogue to O'Toole's Eli Cross—no vainglorious authority figure hypothesizing the loss of life and limb as a small price to pay for art. It's an absence that duly strips away any sense of idealism from Fincher's comment that *The Game* is a "movie about movies." If CRS is, as per David Sterritt's Criterion Collection essay, "a fun-house mirror version of the Hollywood film industry," then its output, as represented by the movie that is being staged around Nicholas in real time, is a standard-issue, popcorn thriller of mid-90s vintage. In lieu of an auteur, Fincher envisions an updated version of "the genius of the system," a faceless, technocratic and profit-driven enterprise mobilizing cliches in the service of entertainment.

In a 2014 essay in *Film Comment*, Nick Pinkerton describes *The Game* as Fincher's "most completely realized movie," alluding admiringly to its director's comprehension of "movie logic as opposed to reasonable plausibility." Leaving aside whether or not *The Game* is more "completely realized" than *Se7en*, or *Zodiac*, or *Gone Girl* (which is highly debatable), Pinkerton is apt to invoke "movie logic" as the film's core virtue and interpretive lodestone. To continue with Sterritt's game-as-Hollywood-studio analogy and Pinkerton's mention of "movie logic," CRS's M.O. is to embroil clients in a situation strung together out of generic thriller-isms, beginning with its own self-presentation as a cabal of enigmatic confidence men. From there, all the other elements of the story are recognizable—and, in this self-reflexive context, *permissible*—as tropes, nothing less, nothing more, and nothing new. "[*The Game*] is predictable, yet full of surprises," wrote the *Washington Post*'s Desson Thompson, pinpointing this particular contradiction without even trying to examine it.

"*The Game* is tailored specifically to each participant," notes the ever-smiling Jim Feingold, a line indicating that his associates know Nicholas as well as he knows himself ("you're a left-brained word fetishist") while also signalling Fincher's assessment of his own assignment and also, perhaps his craftsman's bargain in carrying it out. If *The Game* is a "movie about movies," the sorts of movies it's about are focus-grouped, data-mined, market-tested entertainments rather than individualistic or idiosyncratic works of art: it's one thing to insert Nicholas into a revamp of *The Parallax View*, and another to strand him in, say, Michelangelo Antonioni's *The Passenger* (1975). Fincher's

10. The overall ambiguity of *The Game* gets concentrated into the character of Christine, whose level of complicity in what's happening to Nicholas keeps deepening.

11. Nicholas's luxury-class loneliness is a source of humour and pathos throughout *The Game*, marking him (in Fincher's words) as a modern-day Scrooge.

12. San Francisco's twisty topography and breathtaking sightlines are crucial to *The Game*'s atmosphere of paranoia, captured here with unnerving symmetry.

mostly mainstream cinephilia, with its heart squarely in The New Hollywood, determines the precise weave of references knitted into *The Game*'s postmodern texture (no Antonioni here) while his facility with commercial conventions (and the language of commercials) shores up his satirical imperatives. (A brief parody of a soft-sell headache medication commercial, glimpsed on a restaurant television, is a quiet comic highlight.) The indignity of Nicholas's situation is that he's an A-lister (a status reinforced by the casting of Douglas) descending—at first willingly and then unstoppably—into a murky B-movie nightmare.

As with *Alien 3*, *The Game* is filled with images and sensations of descent, beginning with a flashback, visually coded in the same 16 mm style as the prologue, to Nicholas's father standing stock still atop the roof of his mansion before pitching himself silently over the edge—a leap witnessed by his son. The ambivalent emphasis on suicide connecting Fincher's first four movies—not only *Alien 3*, with Ripley's climactic swan dive, but also *Se7en* (John Doe stoically choosing suicide-by-cop) and *Fight Club* (whose narrator "kills" his other self by firing a gun into his own mouth)—is drawn out even further in *The Game*. The elder Van Orton's death serves as the primal scene of Nicholas's loneliness and self-hatred, and generates an extra level of morbid suspense. Not only do we have reason to wonder if the game is going to kill Nicholas, but also if the desperation, paranoia, and shame it elicits will compel him to do it himself.

In between those eerie childhood flashbacks and Nicholas's own climactic leap of faith (following in his father's footsteps from an even higher vantage point) a number of set pieces in *The Game* feature jumps and falls, like a frantic, clambering chase across a fire escape above a Chinese restaurant or a taxi cab splashing off a pier beneath the Golden Gate bridge (staged seemingly as an echo of Douglas's father Kirk plunging into a harbor in *The Fury* [1978]). As a corollary to all this vertiginous imagery, Howard Shore's piano score deploys a circular, vortex-like melody that swirls around the action—the sound of the ground rushing up to meet us, held and distended in hair-raising slow-motion.

#

To return to the idea of "movie logic," there is no way to parse *The Game* without acknowledging the utter preposterousness of its final movements—a wild plunge into implausibility that at once mirrors and inverts the achievement of Walker's script for *Se7en*. No less than *Se7en*, *The Game* is about "the whole complete act": in order for Nicholas to play—and "win"—the game, he not only has to go through the redemption arc crystallized by his adventure south of the border—where, as Telaroli notes, he's forced to confront money (which he suddenly doesn't have) as a finite resource rather than an artificially abundant abstraction—but he must unveil and reckon with the mechanisms of his own torment. The vicarious satisfaction of seeing the prince reduced to pauper reroutes into a more rebellious trajectory; our identification with Nicholas's desire to learn the rules of the game is total. This course correction leads into *The Game*'s most brilliantly absurdist set piece—its pre-climactic money shot and conceptual coup—while also exposing a compromising shallowness at the project's core.

Nicholas's first successful act of retaliation against CRS is to locate and isolate Jim Feingold, while the latter is off the clock; he's tracked down at San Francisco Zoo, where a cageful of prowling, lethal tigers indicate his client's capacity for violent retribution. "Right now, I am extremely dangerous," Nicholas growls, jamming a gun into the actor's stomach and using him—in another straight-out-of-the-movies-development—to gain access to CRS's inner circle, a journey summed up succinctly by a cinematic reference. "I'm

13. The writing's on the
    wall: returning home
    to find his home
    vandalized, Nicholas
    is confronted not only
    with the realization of
    his own vulnerability
    and the violation of
    his personal space but
    also the possibility
    that the things the
    neon graffiti accuses
    him of being—a soft,
    isolated, rich asshole—
    are in fact true.

14.

15.

16.

17.

18.

19.

20.

21.

pulling back the curtain," Nicholas says, coldly from the back seat of Jim's car. "I want to meet the Wizard."

Few American movies have been mined more deeply by critics and practitioners alike than *The Wizard of Oz* (1939), a coming-of-age-fable that is also fundamentally a showbiz metaphor. Dorothy's desire for escape—to go somewhere over the rainbow—is nearly allegorized by her arrival in a full-color fantasia in which every element of her drab Kansas existence gets revised and heightened: in other words, she goes to the movies. In its mix of whimsy and danger, Oz becomes a projection of Dorothy's subconscious desires, just as the trials and terrors of Wonderland manifests as Alice's personalized purgatory. *The Game* stages a hilarious variation on Oz's ending by having Nicholas enter CRS's commissary to see every single one of the film's significant supporting characters gathered together on lunch break. They're even more startled to see him than he is to see them. The key to the scene's audacious affect is the dizzying equilibrium it strikes between the surreal and the banal—a frieze of intricate, unspeakable conspiracy as clock-punching, workaday professionalism. (A year later, Peter Weir would do something similar in *The Truman Show* [1998], a movie not about movies but reality TV, featuring Ed Harris as an update of O'Toole's Stunt Man auteur, manipulating the action from a God's-eye panopticon view in a high-tech command center.)

As Nicholas surveys the room, spotting faces he'd encountered earlier, we're placed in the same position of dazed, slightly hazy recognition. Judy Garland's sleepy protestations as Dorothy awakens back in Kansas and reunites with the local inspirations for The Tin Man, The Cowardly Lion, et. al come to mind: "...And you were there, and *you* . . . and *you* . . . ". *The Game*'s send-up of *The Wizard of Oz* is outrageous and incongruous: Nicholas is not a prepubescent girl, San Francisco is not Kansas, and the wizard is not a magical figure—or even a prevaricating, two-bit showman *à la* Frank Morgan's hucksterish Professor Marvel—but a corporatized collective of charlatans whose interest in the forcible surrender of their middle-aged male Dorothy is merely a matter of money-making.

Is Fincher the wizard behind the curtain? In 2014, the filmmaker told *IndieWire* that he ultimately regretted taking on *The Game* because, in retrospect, he "didn't figure out the third act," a self-deprecating statement that helps to account for how such a carefully thought-out exercise in movie logic still ends up feeling like a cop-out. The moment of truth comes when Nicholas, hopped up on the rage and adrenaline of exposing CRS once and for all, starts brandishing his weapon, at which point Jim, Christine, and the other conspirators begin to protest that things are finally, *actually* out of control—for real, this time. They maintain that even the most convincing moments of Nicholas's humiliation were faked—and totally reversible—but now, armed and dangerous, he's going to genuinely harm somebody. Their terror reaches a crescendo when he fires the gun and, to his horror, hits Conrad, who has arrived on the scene in a tuxedo with a bottle of champagne to toast a successful ruse, as well as his brother's birthday. Devastated at seemingly killing his sibling and tortured by flashes of his father, Nicholas jumps off the roof of the CRS office, only to crash-land, through breakaway glass, in the middle of an elaborate soiree in his honour. Nicholas, it turns out, is the final piece of the puzzle, arriving at high velocity and right on schedule, swallowed up on impact by a giant landing pad marked with an insignia. X marks the spot.

Everything leading up to and after Nicholas's jump is accounted for in *The Game*'s narrative and thematic calculus, and the neatness of all the doubled events and ideas—the visual contrast between the stripped-down commissary and the gussied up banquet hall; the juxtaposition of a suicide dive with a spiritual rebirth; the son following his father's fatal path but surviving

to tell the tale—has a surgical precision that almost obviates the ridiculousness of the proceedings. Almost. The sheepishness with which Conrad, splattered with squibs, presents Nicholas with a T-shirt reading "I was drugged and left for dead in Mexico and all I got was this stupid T-shirt" serves as smug or sheepish acknowledgement of the material's shallowness, the semiotic equivalent of a get-out-of-jail free card.

While legible as a burlesque of Hollywood's *reductio ad absurdum*—of the pains studio movies take to cushion any potential blow to the audience—*The Game*'s wind-up mostly evinces Fincher's own detachment, copping to his not-quite-wizardry with an apologetic smirk. What's missing in the reading of Nicholas's fall as good-natured, *deus ex machina* satire is the conviction visible at the end of a comparatively less accomplished—or "completely realized"—film like *Alien 3*. Ripley isn't manipulated into suicide but chooses it consciously, not out of exhaustion or self-pity or a path of least resistance but as an active, adamant fuck-you to a system that would otherwise exploit her (and the creature inside of her) in perpetuity. There is no true "fuck you" in *The Game*, only a "thank you," proffered humbly from a wealthy man to his peers—lots of them, in fact, as Nicholas brushes himself off and steps into his role as the man of the hour, a grateful Scrooge regaling anecdotes of his own humbling.

Typically, Fincher's provocations at least feel extreme enough to justify their own existence, but in lamenting his own inability

14-21. The screening process at CRS is staged to recall the intake procedure of the Parallax Corporation in Alan J. Pakula's *The Parallax View*, but *The Game* emphasizes Nicholas's impatience and irritation more than his confusion or curiosity; he is less a truth seeker than a man attempting to repress self-knowledge.

22. Blinded by the Light. Staring into the projector at CRS, Nicholas is unable to get a glimpse of his tormentors; the image also associates *The Game*'s faceless, villains with ideas about filmmaking and filmgoing.

22.

to "solve" *The Game*'s third act, the director gestures towards the flaws in the material and maybe also the limiting rigidness of his own sensibility. When a director like David Lynch pastiches *The Wizard of Oz* in *Wild at Heart* (1990) or *Mulholland Drive* (2001)—variations close enough at times to be remakes—he's able to access the story's mythic potency because his style is unbound by rationality or realism, the two qualities at the heart of Fincher's output and worldview. Temperamentally unsuited to embrace or indulge fantasy, he seeks instead to expose or deconstruct it. *The Game*'s acuity as a study of artifice warping perception is offset by its cynical insistence that artifice is all there is. In making a movie about the allure and power of supremely accomplished phoniness, Fincher succumbs to it, stringing his glittering web of allusions around a steadily increasing avoidance of anything like "the real." A generous reading might be that *The Game* negotiates a shift from one narcissistic, unsustainable fantasy to another to psychologize the insularity and fear of America's ruling class; a more skeptical viewer might see Fincher's cinematic hall of mirrors as a structure reflecting little beyond its own intertextual cleverness.

The Game's coda also contains its best punchline: riding high on his public redemption and flush with the spirit of forgiveness (as well with all the cash returned to his accounts) Nicholas agrees to split the—unseen and implied astronomical—bill for his CRS experience with Conrad. This moment is very funny, both as written and played by Douglas (whose glance down at the ledger registers as a silent, full-body wince) and also in light of Fincher's stated "movie about movies" theme. Nicholas's magnanimous gesture terminates his servitude as an actor-cum-stunt man and recasts him as a mix of a paying customer (offering compensation for "recreation services" rendered) and an after-the-fact executive producer/financier. With a single stroke of his pen, he expensively subsidizes his own escapism and suffering: the possibility that Fincher would have liked to sadistically torture studio moneymen after *Alien 3* with some funny games is very much in the mix.

Funny stuff for sure, but funny is as far as it goes, which is to say, not far enough. As befits a movie with a transactional view of human relations, *The Game* scrupulously accounts for its protagonist's paying of dues, in painful self-actualization as well as cold hard cash. But the feeling we're left with after all that expertly jerry-rigged

suspension of disbelief—and all those steep, bruising falls—is that, in the grand scheme of things, Nicholas is just being dinged. He's figured out the object of the game, which was never more than his own justified humbling. The impetus for further change seems weak at best and, certainly, beyond the purview of what Fincher chooses to show.

As a redux of *The Wizard of Oz*, *The Game* substitutes a return to luxury for Dorothy's double-edged, lumpenprole acceptance that "there's no place like home" (even when home is a dust-bowl hovel in the middle of the Great Depression). As a "movie about movies," *The Game* implies that a truly effective, transformative film—one that invites us to imagine ourselves living inside of it, subject to its exhilarations and terrors—can prompt genuine reflection and even personal improvement. This is, to say the least, a suspiciously affirmative and prepackaged sentiment—a rare example of Fincher actually trying to sell something. Even if the finale's vision of "emotional growth" is meant sardonically, with the big reveal unfolding as a fantastical parody of an intervention—or maybe, to extend the film metaphor, a wrap party, with cast and crew all accounted for and enjoying the open bar—the subversion is muted. *The Game* backs off from the genuine fatalism of *Alien 3* and *Se7en*, where "the whole complete act" for Ellen Ripley and John Doe alike requires genuine sacrifice and even self-destruction—the necessity of working without a net. For all its skillful blurring of the line between fantasy and reality (and between life and cinema) *The Game* insists that there is a line and stays on the safe side of it. Like *Panic Room*, it's a film in which inherited prosperity is problematized and even challenged (in the film and in the filmmaking) only to be reinscribed on behalf of a sympathetic protagonist. Besides recalling Detective Mills's sarcastic (and ultimately short-sighted) accusation to John Doe in *Se7en* that the latter's worldview is no deeper than "a fucking T-shirt, at best," Nicholas's ostentatiously cheap memento of his own trials completes *The Game*'s clothes-make-the-man motif on a note of disposable consumerism that's knowing without being particularly profound, a tacky emblem of a movie engineered by a wizard who dares to pull back the curtain and reveal nothing much at all.

23-26. Believing that he's fatally wounded Conrad, Nicholas goes to take the same fatal leap that claimed his father; at this point, it seems the rules of the game have been accidentally violated beyond repair.

27. X marks the spot: Nicholas's leap of faith has a safe landing, the final bit of stage-management in an expensively subsidized humbling carried out with the precision of a Hollywood production.

28. The T-shirt offered to Nicholas by his brother doubles as a punchline on the artificially engineered nature of the movie as a whole.

29. Nicholas's emotional reunion with Conrad after the big reveal justifies the latter's choice to provoke and torture his brother into self-improvement.

27.

28.

29.

Fig A. *The Stunt Man*, Richard Rush, 1980 [Still]

The hero of this underrated 1980 drama is a stunt man who comes to suspect his director is actually trying to kill him, examining the same themes of control and vulnerability in *The Game*'s filmmaking allegory.

Fig B. *The Parallax View*, Alan J. Pakula, 1974

Alan J. Pakula's thriller about a journalist investigating a mysterious corporation inspired the look and feel of Nicholas' interview with CRS.

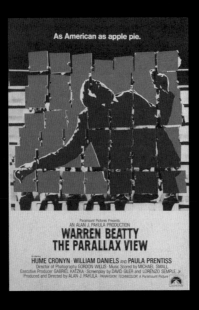

Fig C. *It's a Wonderful Life*, Frank Capra, 1946 [Still]

An angel is sent from Heaven to help a desperately frustrated businessman by showing him what life would have been like if he had never existed.

Fig F. *Mission: Impossible* [TV Series]

Fincher alluded to the 1960s spy show as a reference point for *The Game*'s secret-agent-story tone.

Fig G. *The Streets of San Francisco* [TV series]

Michael Douglas became a star on this location-shot 1970s network cop series.

Fig H. *Basic Instinct*, Paul Verhoeven, 1992 [Still]

The Game plays with the cold, recessive screen persona Michael Douglas developed in thrillers like *Basic Instinct*, with which it also shares a San Francisco backdrop.

Fig D. Jefferson Airplane

The peace-and-love rockers get *The Game*'s funniest music cue, with "White Rabbit" blaring to indicate that Nicholas (and the audience) have gone through the looking glass.

Fig E. *The Wizard of Oz*, Victor Fleming, 1939

Nicholas references Victor Fleming's family classic when he demands to "meet the Wizard" while plotting revenge against CRS.

Fig I. *Bring Me the Head of Alfredo Garcia*, Sam Peckinpah, 1974 [Still]

The white suit Van Orton wears in Mexico was inspired by the one worn by Warren Oates in Sam Peckinpah's squalid quest movie.

Fig J. *A Clockwork Orange*, Stanley Kubrick, 1972

The mental conditioning of the Ludovico Technique sequence is evoked during Nicholas's CRS visit.

WRITER Michael Ferris, John Brancato
CINEMATOGRAPHER Harris Savides
EDITOR James Haygood

BUDGET $48 million
BOX OFFICE $109.4 million

LENGTH 129 min

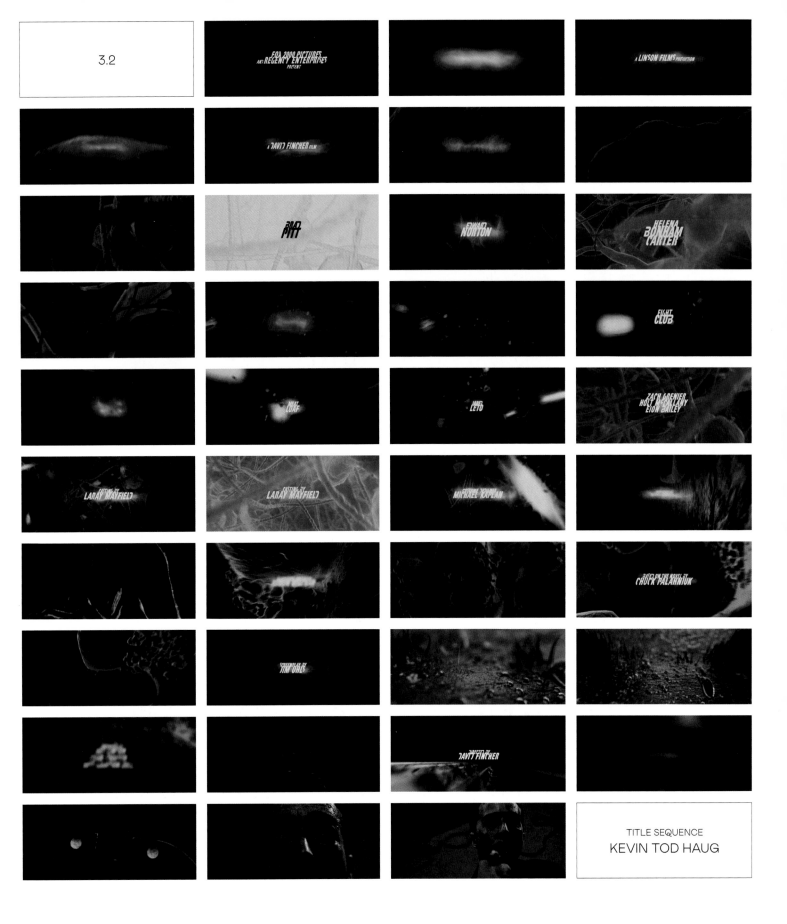

TITLE SEQUENCE
KEVIN TOD HAUG

3.2
FIGHT CLUB

Fight Club begins by mapping a state of mind, its credits displayed over a digitally composed tracking shot emanating in "the fear center of the human brain" and receding at breakneck speed through an inner landscape and out into the real world. It also starts where *The Game* ends, with a gun-toting man ascending an empty office building, racing against time, demanding an audience with the Wizard. There are two significant differences, however. The first is that our protagonist—a nameless, twenty-nine-year-old insurance adjuster played by Edward Norton and heretofore referred to as Jack after his own habit of third-person identification—is easily disarmed and quickly finds himself staring down the barrel of his own weapon. The first thing we see following the title sequence is a rack focus to Norton's wide, staring eyes peeking out above the chamber of the pistol crammed between his teeth. The shot quotes Detective Mills's gun-to-his head encounter with John Doe at the midpoint of *Se7en*; that Brad Pitt is now the one with his finger on the trigger deepens this act of sly self-citation—one of many in movie that also features a theater marquee advertising the actor's earlier flop *Seven Years in Tibet* (1995) in the background.

What looks like an impending murder is in fact a potential suicide; the proverbial man behind the curtain is also a man who isn't there. Pitt's freelance hellraiser Tyler Durden is not so much the Wizard of Oz as the Wizard of Id, a figment of Jack's imagination.

In a movie whose most quotable lines wryly anthropomorphize unconscious biological processes—"I am Jack's raging bile duct," "I am Jack's smirking revenge," etc.—Tyler is Jack's psychic alibi. He enacts his host's anti-establishment urges with the kind of physical and intellectual agility associated with dreams—or maybe with moviegoing.

Tyler's anarchist collective "Project Mayhem" employs a close-cropped contingent of loyally indoctrinated followers called Space Monkeys—a nod to the winged simians commanded by the Wicked Witch of the West in The Wizard of Oz—while the operation's M.O. of elaborate pranks in public spaces recalls CRS's methodology if not philosophy. It's not a coincidence that one of Tyler's side hustles is as a projectionist, surreptitiously splicing pornographic frames into family matinees. Scissors in hand, he proselytizes about the "theatre of mass destruction," another detail-oriented pseudo auteur taking his place in David Fincher's films alongside John Doe, the Zodiac Killer and Amazing Amy.

"It's called a 'change-over,' explains Jack. He's referring to an optical illusion alternatively referred to as "cigarette burns"—barely perceptible blips in the corner of the frame marking the point where one strip of celluloid gives way to another. The projection-booth imagery calls back to The Game's screening room interlude, but it's also a wickedly funny conceptual homonym, threading the needle between Tyler's twin initiatives of "reel change" and "real change." Pitt's chain smoking domestic terrorist in Fight Club is something like a human cigarette burn: an elusive presence shooting the gaps of a fabricated reality.

Like The Game, Fight Club is a movie about paranoia, boomeranging its predecessor's set-up back around by having Jack exposed as the mastermind of his own torment—a puppet-master jerking viciously and helplessly at his own strings. Empowerment or victimization? Passivity or free will? Contradiction is the name of the game here, with the "first rule of Fight Club—don't talk about Fight Club" reinforced by the second (next verse, same as the first). Fincher's film reflects its essentially dialectical themes through the prism of identity crisis, with the big twist doubling as an uppercut of a punchline: the narcissistic fallacy inside every pasty, alienated white-collar labourer bemoaning a consumerist carousel of pointless purchases and "single-serving friends" lurks a chiselled, two-fisted, righteously sloganeering Che Guevara manqué, yearning to break free from it all.

Tyler is not just an apex physical specimen, but a louche truth teller in the radical mode of Lenny Bruce or Abbie Hoffman, hijacking and repurposing the pithy efficiency of late-twentieth-century advertising rhetoric as he proseltyizes about the pleasures of opting out rather than buying in. "You are not your job," he barks during one of the many crypto-motivational monologues that serve as anti-sales-pitches. "You're not how much money you have in the bank; you are not the car you drive; you're not the contents of your wallet; you're not your fucking khakis." Tyler's relentlessly negatory rhetoric extends to his own identity, or, more correctly, his lack thereof—a distinction that provides Fight Club with its second, submerged, and more observant satirical thesis. Tyler boastfully claims to be everything Jack is not—"I look like you want to look, I fuck like you want to fuck," etc.—but his master plan to bring the ivory towers of global finance tumbling down through a series of controlled demolitions in major cities is finally made in the same image of franchised, faceless syndication that serves as its obverse ideological prompt. "Project Mayhem" is a code name and also an imperative, but its third meaning—with an emphasis on "projection"—marks it as something as ephemeral as a shadow, not so much an alternative as a phantom doppelganger.

Duplicates, dupes, and knock-offs abound in Fight Club; an early shot of office Xeroxers buzzing away nods to the philosopher Walter Benjamin and his forward-thinking 1935 thesis about "art in the age of mechanical reproduction." There is no aura here: "a copy, of a copy, of a copy," drones Norton in lobotomized, undergraduate monotone. In the same percussively edited, world building overture sequence, a wittily tilted shot of Jack's garbage can filled to the brim with branded detritus evokes first a rotating space station (complete with extra-terrestrial sound effects) and then the swirling, coffee cup cosmology of Jean-Luc Godard in Two or Three Things I Know About Her (1967)—another movie conflating movie stardom with radicalism that demolishes the fourth wall in between mantra-like reiterations of its own rules.

The caffeinated metaphor is strengthened through Norton's invocation of "Planet Starbucks," a decidedly nineties reference that's no less apt or all-powerful now (and what was Nathan Fielder's much-lauded "Dumb Starbucks" venture, in which the comedian created a pop-up-shop parody of the coffee giant utilizing their

FIGHT CLUB

4.

5.

logos and color scheme, but a more benign strain of the Adbusters-ish hjinks advocated by Project Mayhem?). Later on, while trying to describe the psychological hold that his imaginary friend has over everybody in his orbit—including, of course, himself—Jack settles on a bit of sardonic, symmetry, dubbing him "Planet Tyler."

The doubling is deliberate. In *Fight Club*, the line between soulless conglomeration and dogmatic non-conformity is as thin and permeable as the tissue subdividing cerebral membranes (or the particle board of an IKEA shelving unit). And there's the rub. Tyler may be a know-it-all, but his frame of reference can never genuinely supersede Jack's state of mind. That's why *Fight Club*'s opening, action-movie cliffhanger is such a niftily counterintuitive overture, jacking in to the same turbocharged, reversible polarities that always define Fincher's power dynamics. All is not as it seems. As with John Doe on his knees in a field beneath those high-tension towers, the man on the other end of the gun has the upper hand.

#

Fight Club was adapted by screenwriter Jim Uhls from Chuck Palahniuk's cult 1996 novel of the same name, which traced its gestation to a Portland-based author's workshop specializing in "dangerous writing." The enclave's transgressive, minimalist mandate would be allegorized in *Fight Club*'s eponymous bare-knuckle boxing group, whose members become the acolytes of Tyler Durden Project Mayhem, in effect going from pummelling one another to "punching up" against the forces of late capitalism. In his foreword to a 2004 reprint of the novel, Palahniuk reflects on the book's themes of catharsis and self pity and ties them to a literary moment "[full of] novels that presented a social model for women to be

together." He cites bestsellers like Amy Tan's *The Joy Luck Club* and Whitney Otto's *How to Make an American Quilt* and notes the lack of corresponding masculinist examples; with the calculated humility of a writer who no longer worries about his advance, he proposes that his breakthrough novel's popularity was a simple matter of supply and demand.

The question of whether *Fight Club*, in either literary or cinematic form, fills that void, deepens it, or disappears down it—or if, like Tyler Durden, such a void ever really existed in the first place—was open at the time and remains so. Twenty-five years after its publication, *Fight Club* looks like a signal work anticipating, dramatizing, and perhaps exemplifying a condition recently identified as "toxic masculinity," loosely defined by *New York Times* essayist Maya Salam as "a series of cultural lessons . . . linked to aggression and violence." In his 2019 *New Yorker* essay, "The Men Who Still Love *Fight Club*," Peter C. Baker traced the impact of the novel on various factions and communities treating it not as a cautionary tale but a style guide, including weekend-warrior boxers, hipster pickup artists and reactionary men's rights' advocates claiming victimhood in the face of shifting gender norms and politics.

In the summer of 2019, the blogosphere was inundated with essays and thinkpieces examining what the *Globe and Mail*'s Barry Hertz evocatively called *Fight Club*'s "lingering cultural bruise." "[The film] popularized a version of toxic machismo that has been co-opted by online trolls and the alt-right," opined *Esquire*'s Matt Miller by way of calling *Fight Club* "a bunch of stylized bullshit"; in a *Guardian* thinkpiece, Scott Tobias celebrated the movie's "prescience and power," characterizing it as a "crystal ball that was mistaken for a cultural crisis." The irony is that the long view on *Fight Club* doesn't clarify its quality any more than the instant reactions of critics like Roger

Ebert, whose use of the f-word—that'd be "fascist"—in his horrified *Chicago Reader* pan was a rare case of a mainstream tastemaker propagating moral panic over a multiplex release.

In light of such extreme reactions, Palahniuk's citation of a more obviously canonical novel on his own work is worth unpacking. In the same introduction where he juxtaposes *Fight Club* with *The Joy Luck Club*, he characterizes his book as "apostolic" fiction in the vein of F. Scott Fitzgerald's 1925 classic *The Great Gatsby*, which he describes as "a surviving apostle tells the story of his hero . . . and one man, the hero, is shot to death."

It was Fitzgerald who famously said that "the test of a first-rate intelligence is the ability to hold two opposed ideas in mind at the same time and still retain the ability to function." It is as an illustration of this dictum—of its nobility and also its hubris—that Palahniuk's book and Fincher's movie earn their talking-point status. Not only is *Fight Club* a deeply dialectical novel, but it burlesques the very idea of dialectics by splitting its protagonist—and his first-rate intelligence—into characters who, while superficially defined by their opposing ideas, are one and the same. The spanner in the works is really just a cog in the machine; the dialectic folds in on itself like an ouroboros.

"I read the book and thought: 'How do you make a movie out of this?'" Fincher told *Film Comment*'s Gavin Smith in the fall of 1999, echoing the tagline of Stanley Kubrick's 1962 film adaptation of Vladimir Nabokov's controversial novel *Lolita* ("How did they ever make a movie of *Lolita*?") In both cases, the challenge of translating an epically complex, first-person narrative annotated by asides, digressions, and deconstructions of contemporary popular culture—and even of the act of writing itself—was compounded by the problem of content. Fincher's plan had been to purchase the rights himself, but he was scooped by the very studio whose bosses tormented him on *Alien 3*. "Every time I hear the name 'Fox' it just makes me shrivel," Fincher told Amy Taubin. "But I felt that this was something I had to follow through with, so I met with Laura Ziskin, head of Fox 2000 [the studio's prestige-oriented production shingle]. I said . . . the real act of sedition is not to do the $3 million dollar version, it's to do the big version. And they were like, 'prove it.'"

The greenlight for *Fight Club* was flashed by senior Fox executive Bill Mechanic, who'd underwritten risky ventures like *The Thin*

4-5. Jack's desire to fight back against avatars of authority begins with his boss, but he directs his violence inward; instead of beating the guy up, he takes his bristling anger out on himself and earns a healthy severance package.

6. Jack's insomniac trance is also a parody of the thousand-yard stare of the constant viewer; shots like this one emphasize his blank, mindless passivity (and set up his blackouts as Tyler later on in the film).

7. Jeff Cronenweth's toplit frames give the members of the fight club hollow, sunken eyes, depersonalizing their faces and suggesting an absence of inspiration or hope.

6.

7.

8.

Red Line (1998) and *Bulworth* (1998) and was motivated mostly by the presence of Brad Pitt, whose casting sealed the deal in the same way that Tom Cruise's participation allowed Paul Thomas Anderson to make *Magnolia* (1999). The relationship between Fincher and Anderson's films, with their movie star patrons mutually cast as self-help gurus, helps to place *Fight Club*'s extremity and unlikely studio subsidization in a paradigm-shifting moment for American movies. The film's successful packaging as a $60 million studio production represented a wild confluence of artistic conviction and executive susceptibility akin to Nicholas Van Orton ponying up for his own (metaphorical) funeral at the end of *The Game*.

In opening up Palahniuk's novel, Uhls introduced the idea that Project Mayhem's ultimate goal would be the destruction of credit card companies; once Pitt and Norton were on board, Fincher and Andrew Kevin Walker solicited their input in group brainstorming sessions intended to further crystallize and refine the material's cynicism. "They'd hang at Pitt's house or at an office across from Hollywood's famed Grauman's Chinese Theatre, where they'd drink Mountain Dew, play Nerf basketball, and talk for hours, riffing on the film's numerous bull's-eyes: masculinity, consumerism, their aggravating elders," writes Brian Raftery in his book *Best. Movie.*

Year. Ever., recounting a male bonding ritual of the sort that *Fight Club* would go on to skewer.

Raftery quotes Fincher as literally presenting Fox with an ultimatum at the end of the pre-production process: "You've got seventy-two hours to tell us if you're interested." Further examples of the director's hubris can be found in James Mottram's 2006 book *The Sundance Kids: How the Mavericks Took Back Hollywood*, which describes *Fight Club*'s flowering under the nose of conservative media tycoon Rupert Murdoch as being "as miraculous as the Virgin Birth . . . [*Fight Club* was] distributed by a company owned by the arch-exponent of the very capitalist system the protagonists of the film seek to dismantle, which was also the organization that Fincher clashed with during the making of *Alien 3*." Both authors allude humorously to the "legendary" first screening of Fincher's final cut for Fox's governing braintrust, during which, according to producer Art Linson, the executives were "flopping around like acid-crazed carp wondering how such a thing could even have happened."

Linson's anecdote evokes fish (call them studio barracudas) that have been shot in a barrel, and *Fight Club* is a movie that deploys heavy artillery to hit a series of static, generationally regenerating targets. During the movie's promotional

9.

10.

rollout, Fincher repeatedly mentioned Mike Nichols's 1967, early New Hollywood rallying point *The Graduate* as an inspiration for his own movie's mockery of materialism (which would make the Dust Brothers *Fight Club*'s version of Simon and Garfunkel). The guy who corners Dustin Hoffman's promising collegian Benjamin Braddock beside the swimming pool and whispers "plastics" in his ear is describing his own ersatz humanity. For Fincher, *Fight Club*'s protagonist was an inverted Ben Braddock, "a guy," as the director described him, "who does not have a world of possibilities in front of him." In *The Graduate*, the lure was upward mobility, but financially speaking, Jack already has it made—"plastics" is not a promise but a mortgage-paying reality. His problem is loneliness: an automaton longing to commune with other members of the assembly line.

Fight Club was shot by Jeff Cronenweth, whose use of a bland, desaturated palette in the scenes prior to Tyler's arrival establishes a definitively depressive visual environment. Cutting from Norton's sicky fluorescent office space to his carefully curated designer apartment, the lighting scheme remains identical, proposing the ostensibly optimal condition of "work-life balance" as a form of purgatory—a condition diagnosed in the same year in Mike Judge's *Office Space* (1999), another

comedy about a drone opting out of the hive. The perspectival gamesmanship of Palahniuk's plot gives Cronenweth and his director the chance to play with different levels of realism, including a spectacular feat of virtual mise-en-scène in which Jack's condo is transformed into a three-dimensional IKEA catalogue layout in accordance with his over-the-phone impulse buys.

The effect was achieved with a motion-control camera that created the artificial impression of a seamless pan across an increasingly re-dressed set, calling back to archaic models of cinematic illusionism while anticipating the CGI tracking shots of *Panic Room*. The superimposed product descriptions and price tags play like dry runs for the later film's tactile title sequence, as well as the sinister scribblings in *Zodiac*'s margins. The IKEA sequence feeds Fincher's carnivorous desire to bite the hand that had fed him—or, perhaps, to maul the kind of product-minded producers who had once referred to him as a "shoe salesman." It's telling that after extended passages of scene-setting depicting Jack's cubically compartmentalized life—and his emotionally compartmentalized patronage of various disease and addiction support groups as a salve for his spiritual aridity— *Fight Club*'s plot is catalyzed when that catalogue-perfect condo gets blown up,

8. In the first section of the film, Jack's life is depicted as a cycle of recursive, regurgitative consumerism; shopping on the toilet; standing mesmerized by a rotating baggage carousel; getting bombarded by designer brand names and meaningless slogans—the conditions that lead him to generate Tyler into being.

9. When Marla replaces the penguin as Jack's "power animal" it's a sign that she's successfully colonized his consciousness; she exists as a source of inspiration, strength and frustration.

10. The squalor of the house on paper street repudiates the sterile, anodyne environment of Jack's condo, mirroring his increasingly battered body and suggesting an interior, psychic space thrown into disrepair; a clogged toilet bowl mirrors the wastebasket at Jack's office earlier in the film.

11. The search for human
     connection—and the
     complex psychology
     of homosocial bonding—
     directs Jack into the
     maternal embrace of
     the massive, emasculated
     Robert Paulson;
     a strategically
     placed American flag
     points to some larger
     cultural condition
     of male loneliness.

12.

13.

Zabriskie Point (1970) style. Its destruction forces Jack into cohabitation with Tyler in a dilapidated house on the edge of an unnamed city, "alone for a half mile in every direction."

For the first thirty minutes before Tyler's official entry into the story—not counting the opening flash-forward or the subliminal insert shots that place him flickeringly in Jack's field of view (and our own)—*Fight Club* is carried by Norton's cast-iron deadpan and wearily complicitous voice-over. This authority over sound and image is ambivalent, however; while every aspect of the film's framing, editing and blocking is keyed to Jack's perspective, Norton's performance and sloping, servile, weak-chinned physique connote powerlessness. Gathered into the embrace of the massive, medically gelded testicular-cancer survivor Robert Paulson (Meat Loaf), who's become a confidant (and who will later re-emerge as a martyr to Project Mayhem's cause), he's a shrivelled, helpless figure, his infantilization made total by a shot of him clinging to Robert's massive, pendulous "bitch tits," with their grim intimations of a perverse maternity.

"Men is what we are," chant the members of the testicular-cancer support group, a futile affirmation framed smirkingly against an American flag whose presence mocks their protests of potency. No less than *Alien 3*, *Fight Club* draws on the monastic satire of *Full Metal Jacket*, with its militaristic mantras and hive-like clusters of undifferentiated maleness; it is one of the film's wittier touches that the support group, the *Fight Club*, and Project Mayhem are all depicted as treehouse societies with their own cliques, orthodoxies and initiation rights. (A 2019 *Harper's* expose by Barrett Swanson about an Ohio-based mens' retreat called Everyman reads like a combination parody-homage to *Fight Club*, with the narrator describing "countless unsought hugs" as well as an NDA that seems—unintentionally and hilariously—to follow the film's lips-sealed mantra.)

The aptness of casting an alpha-male rock star like Meat Loaf as an avatar of emasculation is undeniable, and Robert is one of the movie's most indelible creations, a gargantuan, emotionally insatiable golem who exists in a space between empathy and contempt, and as such is a byproduct of the material's neo-picaresque sensibility. And yet *Fight Club*'s philosophical-materialist preoccupations are as invisible from its jabbing, adolescent misanthropy as Planet Tyler is from Planet Starbucks, but to quote *The Simpsons*—specifically the season seven episode "Summer of 4'2," where Lisa infiltrates a group of cool kids—the whole thing smacks of effort, man. In *Alien 3* and *The Game*, Fincher cloaked his anti-establishment attitudes in the vestments of genre, but *Fight Club* is so explicit about its provocations that they graduate from subtext to subject, with mixed if vivid results.

You can feel Fincher straining to cause offense in the support-group sequences, which fail to match the standard of morbid brevity set in "Fetus," with its doomed, in-utero chain smoker. When the skeletal, skull-capped chemotherapy patient Chloe (Rachel Singer) complains to her peers about wanting to get laid before she dies, it's meant as a humanist rebuke to sanitizing platitudes, but Jack's comment that she "[looks] like Meryl Streep's skeleton would look if you made it smile and walk around a party being extra nice to everybody," marks him as the scene's true truth-teller. It's a harbinger of the deceptively self-reflexive misogyny that the film dredges up out of Palahniuk's novel—not so much the flip side of his masculine satire as collateral damage. In his later films, Fincher would address complaints about his work's gender politics by foregrounding brilliant, complex, resourceful female leads, but in 1999, *Fight Club* looked from a certain angle like the early and ugly culmination of tendencies displayed in *Se7en* and *The Game*, with their literally and/or figuratively disposable blondes. (*Alien 3*'s verson of Ripley as an angry, androgynous martyr had gravitas, but was primarily the byproduct of creative inheritance.)

Fight Club's Marla Singer is, in her way, a striking and memorable character. "This is cancer, right?" she asks mid-drag at one of Jack's cancer-survivor group meetings, pale and fetchingly dishevelled behind sunglasses at night. The screwball velocity of Helena Bonham Carter's performance not only obliterated the actress's reputation as a Merchant Ivory "corset queen," but established Marla as a Goth prototype for a millennial movie archetype: the so-called "Manic Pixie Dream Girl," those free-spirited females who, as Nathan Rabin put it, "teach broodingly soulful young men to embrace life and its infinite mysteries and adventures."

12. "A copy, of a copy, of a copy"; Jack's exhaustion with a regimented, photocopied world becomes ironic in the context of Tyler's meticulous terror campaign, which opposes conformity while modelling it on and demanding it in his followers.

13. Project Mayhem gives Jack and Tyler a (necessarily) shared sense of purpose, and results in a more organized living space—albeit one that still reflects a marginal, DIY aesthetic.

14. Tyler's flamboyant ensembles resemble the grunge-glam-chic of early '90s rock stars like Nirvana's Kurt Cobain.

14.

Marla isn't so much free-spirited as depressive, and her stated curriculum is slightly different than the affirmative mandate outlined by Rabin (sample observation: "the condom is the glass slipper of our generation"). Her Manic Pixie status derives mostly from her being a device, one that Fincher and *Fight Club* deploy with a chill, mechanistic precision on the level of plot and theme. In terms of the film's story, Marla is there first to frustrate Jack by horning in on his empathy-tourism racket, activating his guilt over faking pain in the company of true sufferers, and then to serve as a wedge between him and Tyler by becoming not-so-clandestine fuck-buddies with the latter. Of course, because Tyler doesn't exist, what this means is that Marla has been sleeping with Jack, recasting his possessive jealousy as a symptom of schizophrenia and undermining her blithe, give-no-fucks persona with real confusion over her lover's behavioural inconsistency. ("You're Doctor Jekyll and Mr. Jackass," she fumes in the middle of a late-film blowout.)

Within *Fight Club*'s representational matrix, Marla exists as another double for Jack—a behavioral twin with the same self-pitying tendencies—as well as an incursion of atypical but unmistakable femininity into *Fight Club*'s homosocial (and intermittently homoerotic) universe. Like Ripley in *Alien 3*, she's a self-possessed Wendy descending into a nest of Lost Boys; when Jack grabs her in a tight embrace during a group hug session, she's a mother-whore figure even more ambiguous than Robert Paulson. She's also a get-out-of-jail-free card for the gratuitous sexism and "locker room talk" in which *Fight Club*'s male creative braintrust engages under the superficial aegis of critique. "I haven't been fucked like that since grade school!" she exclaims after one athletic sexual session with Tyler, testifying to his (and of course Pitt's) potency while oh-so-naughtily invoking pedophilia: the lack of a laugh track can't disguise the pandering, sitcom-of-the-damned sense of humor.

This tactic of ascribing Marla a set of voracious appetites and vulnerabilizing neuroses in order to score comic points off of them is consistent and exhausting. The "grade school" one-liner is a replacement for Palahniuk's original dialogue, which had Marla telling Tyler "I want to have your abortion"; when Ziskind blanched at its inclusion, Fincher insisted that whatever he offered as a replacement be included no questions asked. As *Looper*'s Sezin Koehler reports in her Collider article "The Untold Truth of *Fight Club*," "when [Ziskind] heard the replacement line . . . she visibly cringed and begged [Fincher] to return to the original script." Autonomy becomes indistinguishable from vindictiveness: "I am David Fincher's Smirking Revenge."

Bonham-Carter's acting in *Fight Club* is above reproach—fearless, inventive, and very much on the same wavelength as her co-stars. It doesn't prevent Marla from seeming like a ventriloquist's dummy (or maybe a Corpse Bride). If, as Paulie Doyle argued in *Vice*, *Fight Club* has "been embraced by the loose collection of radical online male communities (known as the 'manosphere') as a kind of gospel text," it's surely not incidental that its lone female character is styled as an atrocity-exhibitionist, with the added indignity of being reduced in the final act to a quasi-damsel in distress, the unconvincing impetus for Jack to try to intervene against Tyler's demolition initiative, lest the woman he loves accidentally get injured in the chaos.

The logistical vertices of *Fight Club*'s central love triangle are tricky, but they're also Gatsby-ish, with Marla drawn towards Tyler for his mystery and charisma. It's a Svengali-ish dynamic that she shares with Jack even as he resents its implication (i.e. that Tyler has both of them under his spell). Pitt's extraordinary performance testifies both to his gifts and the fetishistic attention of Fincher's direction. A few years removed from being crowned *People*'s "sexiest man alive," the actor is *Fight Club*'s true erotic object: where at first Jack is distracted and unsettled by Marla and her femme fatale act, his Meet Cute with Tyler at 30,000 feet—in his mind as a seat mate during one of his red-

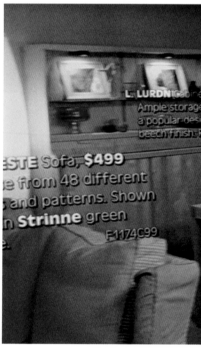

15-22. Life imitates advertising as Jack's condo gets transformed into a three-dimensional IKEA catalogue, a devastatingly funny optical effect that kids Fincher's own background in high-end commercial work.

eye flight—reroutes his fascination-slash-fixation in the other man's direction. From there on, we see the character exclusively through awed and desirous eyes.

Every aspect of *Fight Club*'s mise-en-scène is torqued to celebrate Pitt's sleek, prime-cut body and fashionably tacky wardrobe—an offhandedly trashy elegance that doesn't so much challenge or contradict Hollywood leading-man conventions as reimagine them in Gen-X terms. Tyler's surname evokes Kurt Cobain, and his array of garish-but-glam outfits and goofy accessories (especially his outsized sunglasses) resemble the Nirvana frontman's gleefully sullen anti-celebrity posturing. The character's burnt red leather jacket, meanwhile, nods to the sartorial legacy of another premature youth-culture casualty: James Dean in *Rebel Without a Cause* (1956), who was paid similar tribute in The Replacements' 1989 single "I'll Be You," (a pretty good alternate title for *Fight Club*) through a character referred to as a "rebel without a clue." Paul Westerberg's lyrics jokingly collapsed the distance between idealism and anomie in a way that anticipated Cobain's own lyrical gamesmanship two years later in "Smells Like Teen Spirit," which couched grunge's social insurrection as a kind of anti-intellectual virus: "I feel stupid and contagious."

Westerberg and Cobain were both college radio staples because of how they inhabited and ridiculed rock-star conduct. There are lipstick traces of both singers in *Fight Club*: Westerberg's deathless refrain from "Bastards of Young"—"we are the sons of no one"—is reprised in Pitt's rabble-rousing monologue to his followers about the frustration they feel as "the middle children of history," while Marla functions nicely in image and temperament as a Courtney Love stand-in. A number of gnomic Nirvana lyrics could serve as epigraphs: "I'm so happy, 'cause today I found my friends, they're in my head"; "Just because you're paranoid don't mean they're not after you." As for, "I feel stupid and contagious," it sums up the unquestioning, dead-eyed devotion felt by all of the film's characters for Tyler Durden. What unites Jack and Marla with Robert Paulson or Holt McCallany's hollow-eyed Project Mayhem lieutenant "The Mechanic" is a deeply suggestive headspace that Fincher attempts, in genuinely if agonistically Fitzgeraldian fashion, to construct as an arena for adulation and deconstruction. *Fight Club* allows Tyler's fascist rhetoric to speak for itself through Pitt's offhandedly commanding cadence, and trusts—or burdens—its audience with parsing its content.

#

"My verdict on *Fight Club* is already in," wrote British critic Alexander Walker in the *Evening Standard* after the movie's premiere at the Venice Film Festival. "It's not simply about young guys beating the hell out of each other with bare fists in secret Fight Clubs . . . it uncritically enshrines principles that once underpinned the politics of fascism . . . it promotes pain and suffering as the virtues of the strongest [and] tramples every democratic decency underfoot." Walker's report is at least as hyperbolic as the movie it means to decry, and it gets at a tendency in criticism to draw a one-to-one ratio between a movie's contents and its intentions—a blinkered perspective when it comes to satire.

At the same time, it points to the hazards of Fincher's decision—whether brilliant, miscalculated, or a bit of both—to use his adman's brio in a film that pivots on a series of recruiting pitches. The horrified, judgmental gaze of an Eisenhower-era fable like Elia Kazan's *A Face in the Crowd* (1957),

with its folksy populist demagogue selling snake oil to a nation of innocents, would be too clear-cut for the irony-poisoned nineties. So like Kubrick in *A Clockwork Orange*, Fincher stacks the deck in terms of identification and complicity, binding us to Jack and Tyler through an aggressively subjective storytelling style and presenting the surrounding society as a corporatized hellscape whose easily offended denizens are little more than Margaret Dumonts awaiting their Marxian comeuppance: Karl or Groucho, whichever you prefer.

For the literal-minded critic, *Fight Club*'s appetite to have its cake and eat it—

23.

to present an attractive avatar of revolution and cheer his pissing in the collective punchbowl—amounts to irresponsible hypocrisy. Juvenalia has its uses, however, and it's worth contrasting Fincher's tactical strikes with the timid Boomer maneuvers of another "Best. Movie. Year. Ever." release, *American Beauty* (1999). This is the one about the suburban Dad who opts out of the rat race to relive his wasteoid youth only to wuss out at deflowering a teenage queen and being punished for his decency by assassination at the hands of a repressed, queer, Nazi-memorabilia-collecting closet case. In short, *American Beauty* more than increases the case for *Fight Club*'s necessity. When the Jack concludes a fabricated freak-out in front of his boss with the *sotto voce* aside, "I'd like to thank the Academy," the joke is basically: "I am *Fight Club*'s complete lack of Oscar prospects."

The mantle of anti-prestige prankster suits Fincher, who stages his grotesque pieces with aplomb. In an early entrepreneurial venture, Tyler and Jack pilfer a liposuction clinic, effectively literalizing the self-reliant motto of "living off the fat of the land"; their plan to, "[sell] rich ladies their fat asses back to them" is a pound-of-flesh proposition worthy of John Doe. Bonding

over beers at a shithole diner, the pair make small talk about John Wayne Bobbitt—the tabloid patron saint of emasculation and a significant nineties pseudo-celebrity—and fantasize about beating up William Shatner and Gandhi. The latter is Tyler's pick for a historical sparring partner, and he pays the master of passive non-resistance a tribute when he allows himself to be brutalized to the point of semi-consciousness by a gangster in exchange for keeping the Fight Club's headquarters running after hours—a Christ-like pathos play that grants moral authority by having him beaten him to a pulp.

Such scenes of bone-crunching violence ground *Fight Club*'s headier moments in physical reality, staging an intervention of sorts (call it Project Mayhem) against the anodyne CG spectacle of the late nineties while pledging fidelity to the viscerally embodied phenomenology of picaresque fiction and scarred, ecstatic histories (cinematic and otherwise) of male sadomasochism. A key line, rasped by Jack after demolishing Jared Leto's blonde, symbolically monikered Angel Face, a potential competitor for Tyler's affections, and beneath that a possible object for his alter ego's sublimated desire: "I wanted to destroy something beautiful."

The beauty of destruction is *Fight Club*'s endpoint, and in the same way that the *Fight Club* itself anticipated the bare-knuckled, barefoot quasi-eroticism of modern MMA events—no shirts, no shoes, no mercy—the finale, in which the towers of global commerce topple to the strains of the Pixies sublime 1988 single "Where is My Mind?" plays in retrospect as a shivery, uncanny depiction of 9/11—a surreal special-effects vision that in 1999 jacked into Y2K anxieties of a collapsing planet and would receive a real-world corollary two years later. The shot of Jack and Marla quietly watching the cataclysm from their elevated perch completes the film's Kubrickian cornucopia through its reference to the end of *Dr Strangelove: Or How I Learned to Stop Worrying and Love the Bomb* (1964), which used the World War II era torch-song "We'll Meet Again" in expertly contrapuntal counterpoint to footage of a mushroom cloud. Here, the lovers gaze out at the end of the world as they know it beneath Frank Black's serene description of salvation as disequilibrium: "With your feet in the air and your head on the ground."

"Where is My Mind" also completes *Fight Club*'s major conceptual joke, encoded all the way back in the prologue's not-quite-hostage situation. Realizing that Tyler can't

actually hold him at gunpoint because Tyler doesn't exist, Jack calls his imaginary friend's bluff and, just as he'd physically acted on his Tyler side's synaptic commands in the past—from beating himself up in parking lots and offices to his rough sex with Marla to the masterminding of Project Mayhem—he fires the pistol into his own mouth. Insofar as Tyler is a rock star figure, the title of David Bowie's 1972 single "Rock 'n' Roll Suicide," comes to mind, except that that Ziggy Stardust-era anthem was about a performer languishing past his prime; Jack's conviction in extinguishing his shadow self at the peak of his powers and the pinnacle of his influence is closer to Kurt Cobain's self-annihilating exit strategy.

In their 2003 rock opera *American Idiot*, Green Day riffed on this internalized deus ex machina by having the story's nameless protagonist execute his own revolutionary alter ago as a metaphor for his own disillusionment: "In the State of Mind/it's my own private suicide." *American Idiot* was a record written largely under the influence of the Replacements and Nirvana—and also the Pixies, whose quiet-loud sonic dynamics informed Billie Joe Armstrong's song structures at every turn. It's also a kind of full-dress salute to *Fight Club*, right down to the Gatsbyian love triangle between its nameless narrator, his imaginary friend "St. Jimmy," and the pretty young punk ("Whatsername") who infiltrates an anarchist collective and inflames both of their passions.

As former So. Cal malefactors who became million-sellers on the strength of sneering hook craft, Green Day were easily criticized by haters and disenchanted fans for "selling out," a crime compounded by their durability as a stadium-rock act—a fate worse than death as far as punk cred goes. *American Idiot*'s eventual home on Broadway as a jukebox musical completed the arc; its success as a high-end stage entertainment rendered its deeply felt millennial salvo against the contagious stupidity (and politicized immortality) of the second Bush administration as, if not hypocritical then at least questionable. Armstrong's inspiration to unsettle "a nation controlled by the media" yielded a perpetually profitable piece of intellectual property written in the spirit of the Who's 1973 masterpiece *Quadrophenia*—which also split its protagonist into multiple personalities—but ultimately closer to its Gen-X predecessor *Rent*, a musical exalting off-the-grid living featuring survivor-group interludes and focusing on a heroic experimental filmmaker figure warning us with Durden-esque dudgeon, "In America, at the end of the millennium, you're what you own."

The cultural selling points of *American Idiot* and *Rent* were their unambiguous progressivism—the audience-flattering tactics of musicals tunefully preaching to the liberal choir. Both shows testify to Richard Dyer's claim that musicals present what utopia would feel like rather than how it would be organized, while *Fight Club*—which is not strictly speaking a musical but fully energized by alt-rock and punk energy and aesthetics, and which concludes by hailing the "all-singing, all-dancing crap of the world"—thematizes the organization of dystopia, and fuses flattery and abjection in a way that makes it considerably harder to peg. The stupid human tricks performed by Project Mayhem at Tyler's behest—inventoried through a series of newspaper headlines describing "befouled" public fountains, feces catapults, and shaved monkeys—are at once more benign examples of John Doe's public-facing messaging in *Se7en* and sniggery synechdoches of *Fight Club*'s real-world existence, right down to its corporate sponsorship. Fincher cinches the link between himself and his antiheroes once and for all by splicing a shot of male genitalia in the film's final frames.

Fight Club's subliminal money shot is legible as an X-rated selfie—a portrait of the artist as a pervert (or maybe, circa 1999, a very clever dick). But it's the scene where Jack watches in horror and ecstasy from the passenger seat of a speeding car while Tyler—sitting in the very metaphorical position of the driver's seat—tauntingly lets go of the steering wheel that sums up Fincher's stake in the material as well as his flawed but undeniable accomplishment. Here is the auteur as crash-test-dummy, hurtling himself, his movie, and his audience at and through an obstacle course of industrial pitfalls and onscreens taboos, battered and bruised but never bored.

Such gestures may or may not be examples of a functionally first-rate filmmaking intelligence, and it's tempting in the final analysis to cite one of *Fight Club*'s most quotable moments—that'd be Tyler's sarcastic, not-so-rhetorical query to Jack about, "How's that working out for you, being clever?"—and redirect it back at this very clever movie, a hollow-tipped projectile exploding its Mountain Dew-fueled smugness from the inside out. Tempting, but not necessarily fair, since criticizing *Fight Club* for failing to resolve its myriad contradictions is at least as empty as celebrating its incoherence. As a rock star even more iconic than Kurt Cobain or Frank Black (or Live's Ed Kowalcyzk, whose cameo as a waiter is the jewel in Fincher's collection of glittering I-Love-the-Nineties trinkets) once opined, "It's a fine line between stupid and clever," and *Fight Club* is a high-wire act along the same taut tightrope where *The Game*'s poor-little-rich-man allegory lost its footing. Whatever its flaws, a failure of nerve is not among them.

24.

23. The giant smiley-face singed into the side of an office building is an emoji before the word was coined, and another nod to Nirvana; the newspaper clippings chronicling the Space Monkeys' campaign recall the tabloid headlines marking John Doe's progress throughout *Se7en*.

24. Brave new world: with Tyler exorcised, Jack ends up standing beside Marla, observing his own handiwork as the symbols of global finance crumble before them in an eerie visual prophecy of 9/11.

Fig A. *The Secret Life of Walter Mitty*, **Norman Z. McLeod, 1947**

One of Fischer's favourite films. Flight to fantasy, dream sequence.

Fig B. *Subliminal seduction*, **Wilson Bryan Key [Book]**

A keynote text about the psychology of advertising, and a primer for *Fight Club*'s numerous subliminal, single-frame images.

Fig C. *The Graduate*, **Mike Nichols, 1970**

"It's the story of youthful dislocation and of the feeling of entering the adult world and feeling out of sync with the value system that you're expected to engage in," he says, "and trying to figure out the answer to the question of how to be happy."

Fig F. André Breton

André Breton wrote in his manifesto, that the purest surrealist act would be to go on the street and just shoot around you. Surrealism in the form that Breton and the early avant-garde people intended was a revolutionary movement.

Fig G. *Two or Three Things I Know About Her*, **Jean-Luc Godard, 1967 [Still]**

The famous image of the universe as a swirl in a cup of coffee resurfaces in *Fight Club*'s mock-celestial vision of a discarded Starbucks cup.

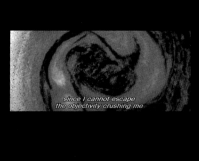

Fig H. "Where Is My Mind?", Pixies, 1988

The euphoric qualities of this anthemic alt rock banger add extra tonal layers to *Fight Club*'s apocalyptic climax.

rsons, Ingmar Bergman, 1966 [Still]
Ingmar Bergman's enduring study of
two characters dissolving into a single
shared consciousness.

Fig E. *Beyond The Valley of The Dolls*,
Russ Meyer, 1970 [Still]
Both films Beyond the Valley of the
Dolls and Fight Club start with a gun
in a person's mouth.

*The meeting of Diogenes of Sinope and
Alexander the Great*, **Mark Quirin after
Peter Paul Rubens 1784 [Engraving]**
Diogenes is a Greek philosopher who
did not want to live by societal norms.
Diogenes lived in a barrel, Tyler lives
in an abandoned house.

Fig J. *The Joy Luck Club*, Amy Tan, 1989
Chuck Palanhiuk contrasted *Fight Club*
with other '90s novels about female
community and comradeship, including
Amy Tan's best-seller.

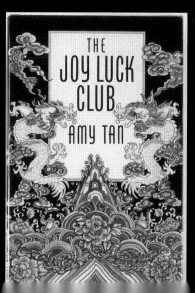

WRITER Chuck Palanhiuk (novel), Jim Uhls (screenplay)
CINEMATOGRAPHER Jeffrey Scott Cronenweth
EDITOR James Haygood

BUDGET $63 million
BOX OFFICE $101.2 million

LENGTH 139 min

UNCANNY VALLEYS

4.1

TITLE SEQUENCE
JAMES J. ATKINSON

< Unveiling his new creation—a massive clock that rotates backwards—Monsieur Gateaux appears to the public as a mad scientist. But it's truer to say that he's a man out of time. The clock becomes a symbol not only of Fincher's desire to craft a throwback melodrama out of Fitzgerald's story but also his protagonist's inverted relationship to life's progress.

4.1
THE CURIOUS CASE OF BENJAMIN BUTTON

"So we beat on, boats against the current, borne back ceaselessly into the past." These are the most famous words that F. Scott Fitzgerald ever wrote; they come at the end of his novel *The Great Gatsby*, sounding a note of mournful acceptance about the exhausting, paradoxical nature of human struggle—the realization that no matter how far any of us get, the ultimate destination is the same unknowable oblivion from which we emerge at birth. It's the perfect epigraph for a fable of innocence overtaken by experience. The novel's narrator, Nick Carraway, is a young man, but as he tenderly eulogizes a friend cut down before his time, he's seeing the world through the eyes of an old soul.

The Great Gatsby was published in 1925 as America rounded the quarter-turn of a promising but unfathomable new century powered by new technologies but stratified along the same divisions of economics and class; the book surveyed the landscape from an elevated vantage. Three years earlier, in 1922, Fitzgerald had released an anthology of short stories called *Tales of the Jazz Age*, a title suggesting the sort of broad yet specific social portraiture that he would narrow to a fine, emerald point in his opus. Mixing genres and styles including tall-tale fantasy, *Tales From the Jazz Age*'s eleven vignettes describe a fledgling country's head-on collision with modernity; the most nakedly allegorical of these is "The Curious Case of Benjamin Button," whose protagonist is borne back ceaselessly—and surreally—into the past by

1. The sophisticated CGI effects used to graft Brad Pitt's facial features onto a series of younger actors are blended into the story's drama. In the midst of his most technologically challenging movie to date, Fincher rarely calls attention to the omnipresent digital trickery, instead focusing on Benjamin's arc from innocence into experience—including a dawning, tender awareness of his own difference.

2-7. "The child is the father of man"; now in his eighties, Benjamin resembles a toddler, and does not recognize his aged caregiver Daisy as his former lover. Of all the images in *The Curious Case of Benjamin Button*, this one distils the aching melancholy of its ideas about the fragile dialectic between birth and death.

forces mysterious to all, including the author himself. "I shall tell you what occurred," writes Fitzgerald in the introduction, "and let you judge for yourself."

Fitzgerald was allegedly inspired to write "The Curious Case of Benjamin Button" in response to Mark Twain's observation that, "The best part of life comes at the beginning, and the worst part at the end." There are traces of Twain's blithe fabulism throughout Fitzgerald's story, which, like several other entries in *Tales of the Jazz Age*, is enchanted around the edges. Benjamin begins life with the body and consciousness of a cantankerous seventy-year old man ("we will call you Methuselah," cracks his father) and ages in reverse in an inexorable march towards infancy, replicating Twain's tragicomic epigram. The progression is absurd, but the light-spirited tone of most of the episode in "The Curious Case of Benjamin Button" can't dispel its melancholy. While its hero is surely a curious case, the tender—and devastating—punchline of Fitzgerald's story is that experiencing life's joys and disappointments out of order does little to mitigate their effects. As Benjamin beats on against the current, he's increasingly tantalized by the promise of youth without youth—of rough waters giving way to smooth sailing. But the far shore is not a safe haven so much as a vanishing point; the story ends with an arrival that is also a disappearance. "Then it was all dark, and [Benjamin's] white crib and the dim faces that moved above him, and the warm sweet aroma of the milk, faded out altogether from his mind."

Fincher's film version of *The Curious Case of Benjamin Button* departs so consistently and significantly from Fitzgerald's text that it doesn't feel like a true adaptation. In this telling, Benjamin is born in New Orleans in 1918 rather than Baltimore in 1860; instead of being

instantly imbued with adult-like thought and speech, he undergoes a linear process of physical and cognitive development, learning to walk on spindly legs and speak through withered lips. Fitzgerald's Benjamin grows up at home, bickering with his siblings and his parents; here, his mother dies in childbirth and his father, a wealthy industrialist, guiltily leaves him on the doorstep at a senior citizens' home. He's taken in by a kindly nurse who raises him as her own son. Benjamin becomes a seaman; he travels the world, takes lovers, and sees combat, all while corresponding with his childhood sweetheart Daisy. The two care deeply for each other but it's many years before they're able to "meet in the middle." They conceive a child and raise her together before Benjamin—as if inheriting the anxieties and absenteeism of his own father—initiates a heartbreaking but necessary separation and flees.

This pattern of painful abandonment and tragic, heartfelt romance is a far cry from Fitzgerald, whose Benjamin becomes gradually disenchanted with his nagging wife and abandons her to star for Harvard's football team. The question of whether Fincher's movie serves as an intuitive, expansive extrapolation on Fitzgerald's themes of loss and mortality or is simply lugubrious in its own register is worth asking, but in the same way that Benjamin and Daisy experience pure, unrestrained joy in the short period where their ages, appearances and appetites are aligned, the moments where *The Curious Case of Benjamin Button* and its inspiration overlap are exhilarating.

To begin at the end—and why not in this case?—there is a shot two hours and thirty-six minutes into the film's running time that crystallizes its metaphysical dimensions. Some eight decades into his life and now as short and smooth-faced as a toddler—with a rapidly narrowing attention span and vocabulary to match—Benjamin is

2.

3.

4.

shown on a stroll with his wizened current caregiver. Walking aimlessly in the manner of a distracted toddler, he stops suddenly and begs his guardian for a kiss, which he receives gratefully before running along. Benjamin, whose memories have faded, is oblivious to the realities of his condition. The woman with him, whose memories have stubbornly remained, is not. The aching potency of the moment derives from this irreconcilable difference.

Fincher shoots the pair from behind at the respectful remove of a medium shot, framed between two tree trunks at screen left and the outer façade of

1.

a manicured hedge maze on the right. It's a composition that a preparation-intensive filmmaker has acknowledged as a sort of happy accident. "We just wanted to see [the woman] sort of tugging this child along as he's forgetting how to walk," Fincher says on the film's special-edition DVD commentary. "They kind of edged over to the edge of the frame and disappeared behind the tree, and right at this moment, the boy tugged at her hand and she bent down to find out what it is that he wants ... He puckers up his lips and gives her this kiss. I'm watching on monitor and I'm going 'oh my God, that's amazing . . . I mean, I wish it was a little more center frame, but it's amazing.'"

This revelation of spontaneity helps to account for why a shot that lasts no more than five seconds remains so imprinted on the mind's eye. Fincher and his

editors Angus Wall and Kirk Baxter grant Benjamin and Daisy's exchange its own hushed, contemplative autonomy; placed in the midst of a montage otherwise cut to the rhythm of a voice-over narration, it's permitted to speak for itself. On one level, the impact of the moment derives from its arrival towards the end of an epic-length dramatic narrative, relying on our gradually accrued knowledge about the identities of—and impossibly complex relationship between—two characters approaching the finish lines of their lives in very different guises. Benjamin's companion is actually Daisy (Cate Blanchett), to whose doorstep he has been returned by providence years after departing—a lover and soulmate transformed into a foundling.

These interpersonal vertices are dauntingly tangled and yet there is also something about the exchange between Benjamin and Daisy that touches the universal, and maybe even the sublime: a mythic distillation of childhood's state of perpetual hope and need; a deceptively plangent tableaux of parental protectiveness and care; a wry archetype of infantilized masculinity. That this single, stolen image can register as devastatingly beautiful in context while also somehow generating a context of its own speaks to Fincher's sophistication as an image-maker, which reaches an emotive peak in his sixth feature even as he's obliged—or forced—to subordinate his instincts as an ironist by Eric Roth's deeply earnest screenplay, in effect, to meet his own movie in the middle.

#

A $175 million co-production between Universal and Paramount, Fincher's follow-up to *Zodiac* edged the director definitively into awards-season territory after a run of genre pieces. The surest sign that *The Curious Case of Benjamin Button* belonged in

a different category was its Christmas Day 2008 release date, as Paramount wagered a blockbuster-sized budget against the box-office record of Brad Pitt and likelihood of a deluxe, golden-hued period piece securing the kind of steady, word-of-mouth attendance earned by positive reviews and Academy Award nominations.

The latter variable fell into place spectacularly, with *The Curious Case of Benjamin* scoring a record-tying thirteen Oscar nods, including Fincher's first for Best Director. *Button* ended up winning three Oscars, for art direction, makeup, and special effects, the latter prize being richly deserved. In addition to creating a number of partially and fully digitised environments that recreate a number of different and disparate moments and locations—New Orleans in the 1920s; Murmansk in the 1940s; New York City in the 1950s—the team at the effects house Digital Domain also used 3-D modelling software to graft Pitt's face onto a series of actors playing Benjamin at either end of his life. More than 150 artists collaborated on a process whereby the star's facial movements were scanned, recreated and synced with his line readings before the "talking heads" were integrated into live-action sequences.

These prizes shored up *Button*'s reputation as a bravura technical achievement, and yet much of the film's reception was centered on its atypical nature, and on the oddness—and perhaps even the objectionability—of a filmmaker previously aligned with the dark and obsessive angling for inclusion with the for-your-consideration crowd. "Two hours and fifty five minutes is a long time to sustain a mood of puckish whimsy," wrote Dana Stevens in *Slate*, adding that, "Fincher's magic can't transform him from [a] coldly dispassionate misanthropist into a sentimental humanist." *Reverse Shot*'s Elbert Ventura concluded a balanced, ambivalent assessment by

5.

6.

7.

calling the director's motives into question: "[Fincher] has created something I didn't think he was capable of . . . prestige kitsch."

It's hard to say which part of Ventura's phrase is more damning: that a formerly adversarial tyro like Fincher was chasing prestige (recall Edward Norton sarcastically thanking the Academy in *Fight Club*), or that, in the process, he ended up producing something even remotely akin to kitsch. More than any of its director's films before or since, *The Curious Case of Benjamin Button* begs the question of why Fincher made it, which was actually less a matter of circumstance than perseverance. In the early nineties, producers Kathleen Kennedy and Frank Marshall tried to get

8.

Steven Spielberg to make the film starring Tom Cruise; when he passed, the project was brought to Fincher, who also opted out. By 2000, the plan was to hire Spike Jonze, and Robin Swicord's screenplay was reworked by Roth, then riding the high of his 1995 Academy Award for *Forrest Gump*.

"[Roth] departed substantially from the book," Robert Zemeckis said in 1994. "The book was cynical and colder than the movie. In the movie, [Forrest] is a completely decent character, always true to his word. He has no agenda and no opinion about anything except Jenny, his mother and God." The director's assessment of his own movie's protagonist is correct, and the case against *Forrest Gump* has to do with its all-consuming gooeyness. Like Fitzgerald, *Forrest Gump*'s author, Winston Groom, was writing in a wry, seriocomic idiom, imagining a stoic, well-muscled simpleton whose mythic physical strength gets channelled, Hercules-style, through a series of heroic feats. Groom's Forrest is a profane, hard-living womanizer who ends up working as a professional wrestler; in Roth's version, the character is a figure of sweet-tempered obeisance driven by pure love for a damaged woman,

and whose passivity, forged primarily out of deference to his no-nonsense mama, is ventured as a state of grace. Shamelessly directed by Zemeckis in unmistakably Spielbergian style, not only does it sanitize the book, but wields Hanks's decency as a bludgeon against cynics, naysayers and subtley itself.

That a hipster like Jonze would blanch at the potential *Gump*-ification of Fitzgerald's story makes sense; when he left the project, Fincher was once again approached, and, emboldened by his experimentation with CGI techniques on *Fight Club* and *Panic Room*, decided to take it on. By all accounts, the filmmaker was gripped by Roth's restructuring of the story into a series of epistolary flashbacks—diary entries written by Benjamin and shared by Daisy on her deathbed with her adult daughter Caroline (Julia Ormond) as a way of unveiling her parentage (shades of *The Bridges of Madison County* [1995], *Titanic* [1997] or even *The Notebook* [2004]). Fincher, who lost his father Jack in 2003 to cancer, connected instantly to the script's depiction of bedside grief and endurance. "You want it to be over as quickly as possible," the director reflects in David Prior's making-of documentary *The Curious Birth of Benjamin Button*, comparing the hospital scenes in the film to his own experiences of watching his father die. "And you don't want it to be over." In the *New York Times*, Fincher additionally told Dave Kehr that it was the morbidity of Roth's script that convinced him to sign on. "When I read the Robin Swicord draft, I thought, this is a love story," he said. "But when I read the Eric Roth draft, I thought, this is a love story, but it's really about death, about the total frailty of humanity."

Viewed this way, *The Curious Case of Benjamin Button* lines up better with Fincher's inventory of death-tinged thrillers,

except that instead of externalizing the threat, mortality here operates from the inside out, with an inevitability that gives the film its own version of a procedural rhythm. The serial killer here is time itself. Notwithstanding the ensuing creative, financial and environmental complications that extended the development process for another five years after Fincher secured the participation of Brad Pitt—with the biggest delays caused by Hurricane Katrina—the filmmaker's realization that his most expensive and elaborate production to date was to be cinematic equivalent of a funeral procession carried through to the finished product.

Ever-supportive of Fincher's work, Amy Taubin nonetheless dropped the gauntlet in a *Film Comment* interview in 2009 when she told the director that she flat-out "loathed" *Forrest Gump*. "What's strange," Taubin added, "is that the two films pose very different worldviews and yet share so many tropes and devices." On the second count, Taubin is absolutely correct: a side-by-side comparison of Roth's two screenplays would reveal at least a half-dozen conceits, characterizations or aphorisms reworked or repurposed from one to the other. As with *Forrest Gump*, *The Curious Case of Benjamin Button* is narrated in laconic, ingratiating voice-over by its title character, whose observations double as offhand pronouncements on the ways of the world around him; "I was born under unusual circumstances," drawls Pitt on the soundtrack by way of introduction. Once again, the narrator's interests are directed mainly towards his (adoptive) mother and his best girl. Like Forrest, Benjamin grows up in a boarding house surrounded by older folk; the ersatz gentility of *Gump*'s Alabama plantation is swapped out and heightened for the cacophony of a senior citizens' home presided over by Queenie (Taraji P. Henson) a childless Black woman who dispenses earthy wisdom like Forrest's beloved Mama.

The race of Benjamin's benefactor changed when the production was moved to Louisiana to take advantage of the state's ample tax breaks; the location also inspired Roth to frame Daisy's deathbed conversation with her adult daughter Caroline against the landfall of Hurricane Katrina, which hit while the film was in pre-production. These elements of history and representation were relatively unprecedented for Fincher, previously a cartographer of stylized, self-contained film worlds. In *The Curious Case of Benjamin Button*, Fincher is telling a comparatively unrealistic story but with one eye always on historical fidelity, and on a considerably larger and more varied

9.

10.

11.

12.

13.

8. The Great War haunts *The Curious Case of Benjamin Button*; here, soldiers are shown advancing on the battlefield in reverse motion, an old-fashioned effect touchingly conjuring life out of death.

9-16. Benjamin's voice-over calls attention to the distinguishing characteristics—and differences—embodied by each of the key figures in his life; late in the film, Fincher edits his observations into a montage that allows each of these characters a final bow.

14.

15.

16.

THE CURIOUS CASE OF BENJAMIN BUTTON

17.

scale than his other decades-spanning opus, *Zodiac*. Both of these films approach the problem of the period piece as a fetishized exercise in nostalgia by thematizing pastness itself; they're constructed as epics of slippage, replete with sensations of things—people, events, evidence, opportunities—receding in the rearview. The common denominator between the true-crime thriller and the Fitzgeraldian picaresque is an incrementalist view of the world that maps progress on both a social and an individual level, with visible changes inscribed in the arenas of fashion, architecture, culture and technology, as well as on the body itself.

Benjamin's own private transformation is yoked to the counterclockwise revolutions of the massive timepiece crafted in the film's prologue by a French watchmaker, M. Gateaux, (Elias Koteas), who is mourning the loss of his son in World War I and hoping that his strategically defective invention might somehow bring the boy back to life. This parable is Roth's most intricate literary conceit, alluding to Fitzgerald's theme of time, while permitting Fincher to meditate on the relationship between technology and temporality. "Few movies in the history of cinema have more fully exemplified [Jean] Cocteau's maxim about the medium itself embodying death at work," wrote Kent Jones in *Cinema Scope* in 2009. His juxtaposition of "Fincher's digitally mediated-end-of-year-entertainment"—a designation alluding to its "prestige" status—alongside an invocation of the French poet and Surrealist filmmaker Jean Cocteau optimistically recodes an

ostensible sell-out gesture as something stealthily avant garde. For Jones, Fincher's methodology throughout *The Curious Case of Benjamin Button* is "not to efface time but to illuminate it."

These seemingly competing imperatives of erasure and showmanship are collapsed in the prologue's most striking passage, which uses a fluid reverse tracking shot to visualize M. Gateaux's daydream of downed infantrymen rising out of the trenches and away from the fray—his late son among them. Thus manipulated, a conventional image of combat signifies in a different direction; what we see resembles a retreat, not from an enemy army but from death itself. The set piece plays as either an inadvertent or deeply ingenious homage to the revivified soldiers at the end of Abel Gance's pacifist epic *J'Accuse* (1919). "A military charge running in reverse and seeing these people fly back together again?" Fincher told Taubin in *Film Comment*. "It's the cheapest trick in cinema . . . it's so simple and yet it's a bold idea. And it's played as such a quixotic moment. It has so much pathos."

As played by Elias Koteas behind heavy black goggles, M. Gateaux is a classic mad scientist figure—a mournfully moralistic craftsman who stands in, however incongruously, for Fincher himself. In *Fight Club*, Tyler Durden's "reel changes" manifested as a vendetta against an imagined middlebrow spectator (or maybe a censor board); M. Gateaux's intervention signifies as more benign. (That Daisy refers to as "Mr. Cake" in her voice-over highlights *Button*'s comparatively saccharine disposition.) As

ever, Fincher delights in coded images of the cinematic apparatus: a shot of the clock's gears being locked into position resembles nothing so much as the loading of a reel-to-reel projector, while its unveiling to a crowd at New Orleans's train station—with Teddy Roosevelt in attendance, another correspondence with *Forrest Gump* and its parade of commander-in-chief cameos—is staged at once like a vintage movie premiere and an archival find in and of itself, with pops and scratches littering the digital frame.

It's easy to read into the crowd's bewilderment at a renowned artisan's presentation of his counterintuitive masterwork and see Fincher himself leveraging his personal investment in *The Curious Case of Benjamin Button* against his audiences' expectations and receiving blank stares. Aesthetically speaking, M. Gateaux's vaguely steam-punk creation is a throwback, a gesture against fashion, progress and modernity itself. Its refusal of progress can be understood as noble and futile. Whether we're meant to believe that its manufacture contributes in some cause-and-effect way to Benjamin's birth or else exists in free-standing, symbolic counterpoint to his experiences, the clock serves multiple purposes as a metaphorical mechanism—including the revelation that its replacement with a digital model in 2003 signals the end of Benjamin's life.

#

The subtle, almost buried equation of digitality with obsolescence is a suggestive postulation in a film whose main character is a partially digital creation. This idea is worth pursuing in depth later on, especially when so many of the film's other elements invite a less sympathetic analysis. Of all the unconvincing things about *The Curious Case of Benjamin Button*, the script's consistently blinkered use of African American characters as helper-slash-saviours rings the falsest, pandering to and flattering an audience conditioned to experiencing universal narratives through the purview of white protagonists. This is not necessarily unusual for Fincher, who grants Dillon in *Alien 3* and Burnham in *Panic Room*—both hardened African American criminals in need of redemption—access to small patches of moral high ground in exchange for acts of sacrifice. Even as Detective Somerset serves as the nominal hero and guiding intelligence of *Se7en*, his worn-out sagacity comes perilously close to a corny, racialized trope.

In *Button*, the New Orleans setting opens up plausible space in the narrative for Black characters, but the writing consistently falls short. Exhibit A: Rampai Mohadi's itinerant African pygmy Ngunda, who arrives at the nursing home during Benjamin's formative years and duly dispenses gentle wisdom about the plight of outsiders in society ("plenty of time you'll be alone"), as well as arranging for his pal's sexual initiation at a local brothel. Ngunda is a jerry-rigged figure, recalling Spielberg's dire "Kick the Can" segment from 1983's *Twilight Zone: The Movie*, with its de-aged (white) senior citizens transformed by Scatman Crothers's homespun interloper into grateful Peter Pans. It's equally difficult to accept Henson's stalwart, emphatic, and endlessly empathetic Queenie as anything other than a sneakily idealized, accidentally retrograde creation: *Film Freak Central*'s Walter Chaw went so far as to term Henson's Oscar-nominated performance as "minstrely", while in the

18.

New York Press, Armond White uncharitably chalked up the film's stabs at solidarity to its star: "Because Pitt does consider himself a socially responsive film actor," he wrote, "he's packed *Benjamin Button* with semi-

19.

20.

topical references to Hurricane Katrina . . . [the film's] superstitious but solicitous blacks don't waken Benjamin's awareness of Jim Crow. Rather, they're inconsequential-corny remnants of old Hollywood stereotypes."

As is so often the case with White, his totalizing criticism of Fincher is spiced with some pungent, unpalatable truths. The equation of "difference" between Benjamin—a white man whose condition has still left him with the blonde, beatific countenance of Brad Pitt—with his surrogate African American family is a tenuous equation that mostly serves to flatter the protagonist—to conveniently place him on a continuum of experience that the movie never really investigates. In light of New Orleans's unofficial designation as America's "city of the dead"—owing to the Antebellum-era outbreak of "yellow fever" that shaped a topography dotted with cemeteries, crypts and mausoleums—the Katrina sequences can't help but feel powerful; more broadly, they bookend a neutral, detached overview of twentieth-century history with a poignant image of Bush-era collapse. Poignant, but not politicized: in response to the charge of exploiting tragedy, Fincher said on his DVD commentary that Katrina's appearance in the film was, "not intended to be an inordinately important beat." This claim scans as disingenuous at best considering its catastrophic significance to the city's African American population—and the impact it had on the national perceptions of systemic inequality. Here, the gathering

17. Benjamin and Daisy's desire for a stable family life slips away in accordance with Benjamin's condition; he abandons his child in the same manner as his own father.

18. The oceanic drift of *The Curious Case of Benjamin Button* is strengthened by extended episodes of Benjamin at sea, where he's a figure of freedom, service and drift.

19. Brad Pitt's matinee-idol looks are played with in different ways, including a brief passage that fashions him in the style of a '50s heartthrob à la James Dean.

20. The revelation that M. Gateaux's analog clock has been replaced with adigital one underlines themes of technological transition.

21

A kiss before dying.
Benjamin's late-life
regression into a
toddler—cared for by
Daisy, who he does not
remember as his lover—
provides the film
with a poetic sense of
pathos and symmetry,
calling attention to
the conjoined states of
fragility and dependence
at either end of the
human experience.

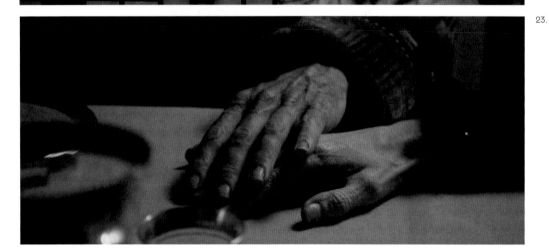

storm's primary targets are a pair of white women, Daisy and Caroline, whose indifference isn't so much satirized as indulged while the filmmakers keep the chaos safely offscreen.

Other aspects of the film feel like capitulations seemingly for the sake of prestige. A sequence placing Benjamin's tugboat in the Pacific Theater circa 1941 as it's strafed by a German U-Boat forms an internal rhyme with the World War I scene, except that here, the bullets fly towards the characters instead of away. It also occasions some risible symbolism in the form of a CGI hummingbird that flies up to greet Benjamin on the sunny morning after a battle of which he is the only survivor. The bird represents the going-to-spirit of the rough-and-tumble tugboat captain Mike (Jared Harris) who had once explained that its vibrating wings could take it backwards (like Benjamin) and, studied closely, traced a figure eight into infinity; it's also as much a cousin to *Forrest Gump*'s signature swirling feather as Mike is to the irascible Lieutenant Dan (Gary Sinise). (In *Fight Club*, Fincher uses Jack's "power animal" to mock the anthropomorphization of complicated feelings.) *Button*'s hummingbird is a symbol of uplift deployed at first without a hint of irony and then brought back for a return engagement in the final passages, flying past Daisy's hospital window. It's a blink-or-miss-it moment, as if Fincher were reluctant to display his film's cloying metaphors with the same pride as his luxurious production design and glamorous movie stars.

To return to Pitt's uniquely augmented performance, it's fascinating to see the ways in which the actor and his director seize on the slight unreality of Benjamin's appearance and use it to key the film's uncanny tone. The technical daring of *The Curious Case of Benjamin Button* is twofold: the film lavishes untold resources on the creation of special effects whose success is largely a matter of being "invisible" and then lets us scrutinize Pitt's famous face to see if it feels "real." It does, and it doesn't. There is a way in which Pitt never quite seems authentic because of his preternatural physical beauty, a desirability exploited in his early roles in *Thelma and Louise* (1991), *Interview With the Vampire* (1994), and *Meet Joe Black* (1999); his otherworldly presence and stillness are just right for a character preoccupied with keeping up appearances and practiced at putting others at ease. Part of the pleasure of the film is waiting for the "real" Brad Pitt to show up while enjoying the speculative spectacle of his older self. In his twenties, Benjamin looks sixty; his affair with a

diplomat's wife (Tilda Swinton) at a hotel in Murmansk in the late 1930s unfolds from his end as romantic initiation even as he looks older than his middle-aged partner, with dishwool grey hair and a lean, sloping physique. Swinton's performance is only a bit more than an extended cameo, but the actress creates a fully realized character as Elizabeth Abbott, a lonely woman whose understanding that Benjamin is not quite normal goes unstated but is signalled by her quiet, smiling bafflement at her lover's transparency—a perfectly calibrated response for the wife of a fusty white-collar spy.

25.

J. M. Tyree describes *The Curious Case of Benjamin Button* as "a string of melancholy vignettes, many of which are as much about mood as they are about plot." The stasis of the hotel scenes in the Murmansk sequence is deepened by Fincher and cinematographer Claudio Miranda's exquisite use of long takes and deep-focus compositions to transform each space—a deserted lobby; a cramped kitchenette—into a locus of contemplation, for characters lost in thought as well as an audience grateful to momentarily slow time's passage and immerse in something like an everlasting moment.

Stylistically, this approach is a way to illustrate that for all the sincerity of Benjamin's attraction to Elizabeth (and vice versa) the pair are both just marking time: she for the duration of her husband's assignment; he until he is able—and willing—to return to Daisy. "It was nice to have met you," reads the note that Elizabeth leaves Benjamin after her abrupt departure, a missive whose simplicity bespeaks not curtness but an acceptance of transience. Rather than being heartbroken, Benjamin takes Elizabeth's message as a spur to focus on the one person he can't imagine ever having to say goodbye to.

"Romance isn't the first thing that the name David Fincher brings to mind," writes Manuela Lazic, once again calling attention to its unusual fit within the director's oeuvre. Fincher's early films are littered with broken, ambiguous or explicitly transactional relationships, with the possible exception of *Fight Club*—with its carefully doubled arc

22-24. In Murmansk, Benjamin forms a bond with a diplomat's wife over their mutual loneliness—a May-to-December romance tweaked by his much older physical appearance. In these scenes, time seems to stand still for two characters at different points in their lives but similarly charged by alienation and attraction.

25. "I want to remember us this way"; finally meeting in the middle, Benjamin and Daisy are moved to contemplate their reflections before time starts to draw them apart once more.

26.

of attraction and obsession turning Tyler into an obscure object of desire—none of his earlier movies really attempt to convey desire or infatuation (or sexuality, at least not directly and certainly without conventional sensuality). And yet, on the other end of *The Curious Case of Benjamin Button*, these sensations begin taking pride of place in Fincher's work. While hardly conventionally romantic, *The Social Network* plays out as a spurned, youthful suitor's grand gesture to reconnect with his ex-girlfriend; *The Girl with the Dragon Tattoo* and *Gone Girl* both pivot on issues of intimacy and compatibility and feature explicit sex sequences as well. In this sense, *The Curious Case of Benjamin Button* is as much a bridging work as *Zodiac*, continuing the earlier film's attempts at historical authenticity while blending in a newfound, steadfastly old-fashioned emotionalism that unlocks something in Fincher's temperament.

The decision to dub Benjamin's beloved Daisy in homage to *Gatsby*'s heroine Daisy Buchanan dates back to Swicord's first script draft, and Blanchett imbues her performance with whispers of her literary namesake. Her Daisy is playful, impulsive, and, as she ages out of childhood, increasingly conscious of her own beauty and sophistication. This narcissism sparks and then torpedoes her attempted seduction of Benjamin when he returns to New Orleans in 1945; a dinner date constructed out of rapid, dizzying dissolves suggests that Daisy's pace is too much for her old friend. Her hurtling verbiage bespeaks the impetuousness of a twentyish striver ("I'm old enough," she purrs by way of a come on) as well as the belief—entirely justified in her case—that her whole life still lies ahead of her. Benjamin, who has been raised to think that his time may be short, takes a warier position.

The interlude where Daisy mounts an outdoor gazebo and performs a private dance for her old friend—while quoting D. H. Lawrence—brings out Fincher's painterly side in a way that stops the movie in its tracks; everything in the moonlight-blue mise-en-scène is frozen around Blanchett's long-legged contortions. As Kent Jones writes, Daisy is "exposing the divide between her own youthfully liquid grace and Benjamin's relative physical frailty"; by offering herself up so readily, she underlines—at least for the moment—her own painful unattainability. Like everything else of importance in *The Curious Case of Benjamin Button*, Benjamin's gentlemanly reticence in the face of temptation is tied to his conception of time, and what feels at first like a missed opportunity (with Daisy left miffed and humiliated) is revealed over the course of the movie as a necessary exercise of restraint, an investment in the pair's future happiness. In *The Great Gatsby*, the eponymous playboy is obsessed with the green light at the end of Daisy Buchanan's dock, an electric lamp that beckons him towards the one he loves like a moth to a flame. Gatsby, the proverbial man who has everything, desires Daisy precisely because, as a married woman, she is off the market and out of reach; the presence of the green light at the other end of the bay shimmers as a perpetual signifier of his want. Nick's closing thoughts envision the "fresh green breast" of the Gold Coast shore, a symbol of American landfall and heritage but also endless, idealistic grasping (and the relationship between the two). When Daisy dances for Benjamin, the main source of illumination is a streetlamp whose beam outlines her with a halo and burns through her red dress; Fincher's composition makes her into a beacon, and Benjamin finds himself drawn to that light for all his life. First in childhood; then as a suitor and a husband; and then again in his second childhood, when he clings to Daisy as a surrogate mother. The film's Daisy is surely a Fitzgeraldian figure, but she is not, in the end, truly unattainable; her

arc is one of changeability, from her decision to compromise her dreams as a dancer after a violent car accident (a karmic punishment for youthful arrogance?) to her acceptance of her aging body and her devotion to Benjamin, whose wants and needs fluctuate in their own maddening, blameless pattern, in and out of sync with her ability to fulfill them.

"I want to remember us as we are just now," Benjamin tells Daisy at one moment during the highpoint of their relationship—a years-long idyll culminating in the birth of Caroline and lasting right up until his decision to leave. These passages fulfill the audience's desire to see the film's glamorous leads finally unencumbered by make-up or special effects: a sight worth waiting for, touched by the knowledge of its own transience. "[Benjamin and Daisy] want to fix this image where time and space have reconciled," writes Lazic, "[but] each new moment soon belongs to the past. Each second that passes brings them further apart from each other." Benjamin and Daisy's salad days in their own private bungalow is depicted as a dreamy fugue of sensual intimacy ("we lived on that mattress") that also cleverly illustrates how, as a person's personal horizons narrow towards the insular perspectives of monogamy and domesticity, in the outside world, history continues apace. The use of the Beatles' hedonistic "Twist and Shout" to punctuate the pair's giddy bedroom choreography is a Gumpian gambit, alluding to a changing pop culture landscape. While the pair sail in the Florida keys, we see a NASA Mercury rocket being launched into the sky above their boat, a symbol of a one-way future.

In *Forrest Gump*, such cultural markers are not only lingered upon, but integrated into Forrest's story; for all his mama's-boy passivity, the idiot-savant ends up shaping the century around him, ending in a Reagan eighties tailored hideously to the hero's "stupid is as stupid does" worldview. (The upshot of *Forrest Gump* is to placate a

Boomer-era audience by reducing history to a highlight-reel-slash-playlist that occludes anything literally or figuratively outside the Top 40; the CGI feather that features in the opening and closing scenes is an answer that's blowin' in the wind.) Benjamin, though, keeps to himself and Fincher's film accommodates this solipsism. In lieu of critiquing or condemning this solipsism it implies that bearing witness to history is as much a part of the human condition as the urge to make it. The second compulsion is still noble, though, and manifests not only in M. Gateaux's clock but Elizabeth's quest, initially thwarted and then achieved in old age, to swim solo across the English Channel. Like so many other narratively significant events in the film, her endeavor takes place in the background, glimpsed on a television set as a news story. (Unfortunately, Fincher can't resist the temptation to show Benjamin smiling beatifically in response.)

Elizabeth's swim evokes Fitzgerald and *Gatsby*'s closing lines: older, wiser, and resolute she reaches the far shore on her own terms. As Daisy ages and tries to rehabilitate her damaged leg, we see her swimming laps in a local swimming pool, pushing through the pain as her body slowly betrays her once again. *The Curious Case of Benjamin Button* is filled with images of water, beginning with the rain beating against Daisy's hospital window and ending with Katrina's arrival. These are all signifers of the great, unstaunchable flow that Fincher's film takes as its subject, and which washes away everything in its spaciously realized onscreen world—including possibly its flaws. A last-second montage presents the film's major characters in a processional sequence, one after the other, head-on to camera; it's as if they're taking their bows as Benjamin sententiously sings their praises in voice-over. This really is prestige kitsch, but the final shot of M. Gateaux's clock, standing disused and abandoned in a basement in New Orleans as the flood waters trickle into frame, is something else all together, equally out of character for Fincher and nevertheless surpassingly beautiful, allowing the film—and with it, the viewer—to be borne upon and then succumb to a swelling current of cleansing and oceanic emotion.

27.

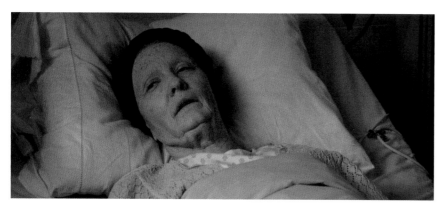

28.

Fig A. Mark Twain (1835-1910)

The Curious Case of Benjamin Button began its life as a short story written by F. Scott Fitzgerald, who, in turn, drew his own inspiration from a quote by Mark Twain: "Life would be infinitely happier if we could only be born at the age of 80 and gradually approach 18."

Fig B. James Dean (1931-1955)

When Benjamin reaches "middle age" in the 1950s, he models himself after James Dean, who tragically died before his time in 1956.

Fig C. *The Great Gatsby*, Francis Scott Key Fitzgerald, 1925 [Novel]

Blanchett's character, Daisy, is called Hildegarde Moncrief in the story. The name change is probably a nod to Fitzgerald and his novel *The Great Gatsby*, which features Daisy as the lead female character.

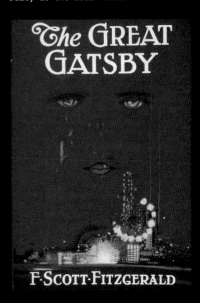

Fig F. *The Kid*, Charles Chaplin, 1921 [Still]

A personal tale of fathers and sons. Within this story, the male characters—the relationships between fathers and sons—a massive underlying thread. Father figures: Tizzy, Captain Mike, Thomas Button.

Fig G. *Essai sur les donnees immediates de la conscience (Time and Free Will)*, Henri Bergson, 1989 [Essay]

A theory of time and consciousness posited by Henri Bergson. He became aware that the moment one attempted to measure a moment, it would be gone: one measures an immobile, complete line, whereas time is mobile and incomplete.

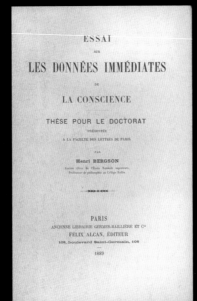

Fig H. *Forrest Gump*, Robert Zemeckis, 1994

Eric Roth's script for *The Curious Case of Benjamin Button* echoes the style and pace of his Oscar-winning work for *Forrest Gump*.

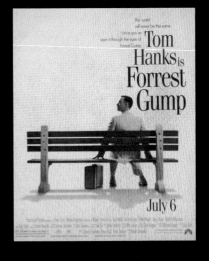

Fig E. *J'Accuse*, Abel Gance, 1919

The soldiers "rising" from the dead
during the backwards-combat scene
manifest as a tribute to the finale
of Abel Gance's silent anti-war epic,
in which the war dead return to life.

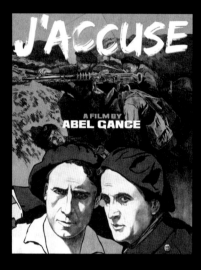

Fig J. *2001: A Space Odyssey*, Stanley Kubrick,
1968

The final images of Benjamin as a baby
recall the Starchild at the end of
Stanley Kubrick's sci-fi epic.

WRITER Eric Roth
CINEMATOGRAPHER Claudio Miranda
EDITORS Kirk Baxter, Angus Wall

BUDGET $167 million
BOX OFFICE $335.8 million

LENGTH 166min

TITLE SEQUENCE
STEVEN DO

< The speedy banter
  between Erica and Mark
  gets contrasted smartly
  with the latter's slow,
  leisurely saunter home
  from The Thirsty Scholar:
  Mark's body is slower than
  his brain, though he picks
  up the pace again once he's
  in front of a keyboard.

4.2

THE SOCIAL NETWORK

2010

"I'm 6'5", 220 [pounds], and there's two of me," says Tyler Winklevoss, taking inventory of his own impressive physicality, as well as the way it's doubled in the presence of his twin brother Cameron. Viewed side-by-side, the siblings—both prospective Olympic rowers and self-proclaimed "Harvard gentlemen" whose obvious victory in the genetic lottery has come supplemented by generational wealth—manifest a surreally symmetrical vision of apex if outdated masculinity. Their slightly bland, anodyne handsomeness embodies a hateful, impressive perfection; they glide through life with the same steady thrum as a racing shell being piloted across placid Cambridge waters. The brothers tower above their fellow underclassmen, including combative computer science student Mark Zuckerberg, whose meeker, lanky build, disheveled dress, and hunched comportment in their presence enacts a deceptive parody of beta-male deference.

The plot of David Fincher's ninth feature *The Social Network* is catalyzed by the high-stakes legal conflict between the hulking trust-fund kids and the slender striver in their midst. The Winkelvosses claim that after contracting Mark to work on a Cambridge-based dating website called "Harvard Connection" he ghosted them and, acting both clandestinely and in bad faith, parlayed their idea into his own billion-dollar social media start-up. "If you guys had invented Facebook, you'd have invented Facebook," Mark sneers at his accusers during a deposition, a taunting

bit of tautology that barely veils his own self-satisfaction at its accuracy. Mark may deny hijacking anybody's intellectual property, but he's pleased to upend his rivals' preternatural sense of entitlement, their deep-seated and newly precarious belief that their heavyweight fraternal tag-team was meant to go undefeated.

The litigious narrative of *The Social Network* is derived from Ben Mezrich's 2009 book *The Accidental Billionaires*, a bestseller chronicling Zuckerberg's rivalry with the Winklevosses as well as a contemporaneous skirmish with his former classmate and Facebook cofounder Eduardo Saverin. A well-mannered rich kid with family connections that ran at least as deep as the Winkelvosses—but minus their sense of imperious conquest—Saverin provided technical support and seed money for "thefacebook.com" which smartly democratized user access and interaction beyond Harvard Connection's blueblooded purview. After relocating their operation to Silicon Valley and taking on a number of other key investors—including Napster creator Sean Parker and subsequent Trump backer Peter Thiel—the partners had a falling out. Through company channels, Saverin found that his ownership stake had been reduced and that he'd been removed from Facebook's masthead (apparently at Parker's urging). Subpoenas ensued—from the Winklevosses as well—with both lawsuits playing out in the public eye owing to Facebook's sudden ubiquity and Zuckerberg's emerging celebrity. By the mid-2000s, the former teenage software prodigy was being hailed as the emperor of the Extremely Online generation, an heir to his fellow Harvard dropout-turned-tech-titan Bill Gates and Reed dropout Steve Jobs, a no-frills Buddha in an ascetic turtleneck.

Subtitled *A Tale of Sex, Money, Genius, and Betrayal*, Mezrich's book mixes petty gossip with Wall Street intrigue, unfolding as a techy picaresque about two ingenious initiates propelling themselves upward through an insular Ivy League hierarchy. (Its drive recalls the author's prior nonfiction hit *Bringing Down the House*, about smart college kids striking rich in Las Vegas, itself adapted into the film *21* [2008].) The story was not only timely, but prescient, a Gen-Y(2K) creation myth describing a society's migration online: let a thousand—or five hundred million—wallflowers bloom. The bulk of the book's information came from Mezrich's conversations with Saverin, who's consequently rendered more sympathetically than his peers, but its star attraction lies elsewhere; in addition

to tallying up Zuckerberg's innovations, *The Accidental Billionaires* conducts a skeptical referendum on a man who went to the trouble of printing business cards reading "I'm CEO, Bitch." (Patrick Bateman could never.)

The Social Network is rigorously structured and bookended by sequences taking up the question of whether the accidental billionaire at its center is an "asshole," an assessment proffered in both the first scene and the last by female characters. Their gender is hardly incidental in a movie whose not-so-hidden gist has less to do with the engineering of social media pathways than a different kind of complex algorithm: the male ego. "*The Social Network* is a cerebral *Fight Club*," wrote Amy Taubin in *Artforum*, and that film's pent-up masculine and millennial anxieties get remapped in Fincher's spiritual sequel along a parallel parabola of ostracization and inclusion. As imagined by Aaron Sorkin in his faithfully non-fiction-ish screenplay and superlatively acted by Jesse Eisenberg, the film's Mark Zuckerberg emerges as an introverted Tyler Durden, recruiting disciples at a distance by offering his fellow outcasts a virtual arena for their grievances. As in *Fight Club*, such succor is by invitation-and-initiation only: more than anything, Mark yearns to climb into one of the prestigious-treehouse-

regimes dotting Harvard's landscape. The first rule of "Finals Club" is that Mark never stops talking about it.

#

"You don't get to five hundred million friends without making a few enemies," declared the one-sheet poster heralding *The Social Network*'s arrival in the fall of 2010, a phrase proudly announcing the film's intentions as what the critic Kevin Courrier smartly termed a "comedy of malice." Besides being the most quotable script Fincher had worked with since *Fight Club*, Sorkin's adaptation—which would go on to win an Academy Award for Best Original Screenplay—represented the filmmaker's first encounter with a writer boasting a creative voice at least as strong as his own. There are a lot of great lines in *The Social Network*, but a portion of the film's satirical eloquence resides (as it does in *Fight Club*) in its director's emphasis on body language, even when the bodies in question exist through cinematic sleight-of hand. What better way to visualize Mark's suspicion about his own (self-)perceived inadequacies as a would-be entrepreneur and also as a man—Harvard, gentle, or otherwise—than natty dual Goliaths who reflect his inferiority complex back at him

in the flawless flesh? And what better way to needle the Nietzschean ideal embodied by Cameron and Tyler (both spelled the normal way), and expose its illusory nature in a movie ruled by realism, than to artificially superimpose the same actor into both roles (an inversion of *Fight Club*'s M.O. of having two actors playing one guy). The performances in *The Social Network* by Armie Hammer are both suavely hilarious, but their effectiveness exists within a digitally assisted framework. Like Benjamin Button, the Winklevi are movie characters born under unusual circumstances.

Such seamlessness is the signature of *The Social Network*, which justly won an Academy Award for editing by Angus Wall and Kirk Baxter—one of three prizes (out of eight nominations) for a movie deliberately positioned by its distributor as an awards season contender. After the "prestige kitsch" of *The Curious Case of Benjamin Button*, Fincher's follow-up seemed like a more intuitive detour into high-end filmmaking, swapping out gilded, end-of-a-century nostalgia for sleek, state-of-the-art melodrama. After a pair of backwards glances, Fincher's third and least distanced period piece—and his second docudrama after *Zodiac*—was understood as a status update. For a computer-literate director driven by fanatical approach to process, the material was a precise fit. "I loved the idea of old-world business ethics put to the test by new-world ability to beta-test and iterate," Fincher said in an interview with *Vulture*'s Mark Harris. "There's this new world where somebody goes: If I've got DSL and enough Red Bull, I can prototype this thing! And then I can get it onto 650 desktops and then eight years later I can get in on 600 million desktops! That is a new paradigm."

The Social Network premiered as the opening night gala at the 2010 New York Festival—the first such selection for one of Fincher's films—and was subsequently promoted as a critics' darling. The mixed reviews that greeted *The Curious Case of Benjamin Button* were supplanted by a series of tastemaking raves; in the opening paragraph of her NYFF report for the *New York Times*, Manohla Dargis characterized the film as "fleet, weirdly funny, exhilarating and alarming." Producing his own competing list of adjectives, Roger Ebert called *The Social Network* "cocksure, impatient, cold, exciting, and instinctively perceptive" and named it the best movie of the year, as did the New York Film Critics Circle, the Toronto Film Critics' Association, and the National Board of Review. The film made

more than one hundred Ten Best lists, by far the most of any commercial release in its year and earned Fincher his second consecutive Best Director nomination at the Oscars (where he lost to Tom Hooper for *The King's Speech* [2010]).

Such universal acclaim was a first for Fincher, whose best-received films (*Se7en, Zodiac*) had still frequently invited dissent or outright dismissal. That this outpouring of respectful consensus (and a healthy worldwide box office of $220 million against a $40 million budget) was directed at a movie stripped of any genre elements suggested that Fincher's reputation was elevated in the bargain; no longer a style-over-substance serial-killer specialist, he had achieved the maturity supposedly sought by serious artists. The most perceptive analysts, however, were the ones who understood that, in auteurist terms, *The Social Network* was more of a mutation than a fruition. The throughline with Fincher's previous movies lay in the use of technology, both as an explicit subject in a movie observing the architecture of the social mediasphere, and as a hybrid divining rod and magic wand in Fincher's aesthetic choices. "Over the past four years, Fincher has gone from an exciting genre filmmaker to the closest thing we have to Otto Preminger," observed Aaron Cutler in

1-2. The conflict between Mark and Eduardo is the dramatic heart of *The Social Network*; the Oscar-winning editing by Kirk Baxter and Angus Wall transforms static deposition-room scenes into pitched battles marked by adversarial body language and rigorous eyeline matches.

3-4. Mark's persecution issues are inflamed by the presence of the Winklevoss twins, who really are ganging up on him; the CGI effects doubling Armie Hammer in the brothers' scenes are like a vision of his beta-male inferiority complex.

Slant, invoking the gifted Viennese émigré who several decades earlier had established himself as Hollywood's pre-eminent adaptor of high-end bestsellers. "[Preminger] made detective stories and legal dramas in which the greatest mysteries were why people behaved as they did rather than who they were, [and] just as Preminger's work gained complexity and reverberation once he began shooting in CinemaScope, Fincher discovered a new way of seeing the world once he switched from film to digital video."

Nick Pinkerton has also pursued the Preminger comparison, using Preminger as a cudgel against Fincher's hard-sell sensibility. "Both filmmakers," he wrote in 2014, "have a nose for material that will get the chattering classes chattering (or, in Fincher's case, the Tweeting classes tweeting)." The topicality of *The Social Network* was a component of its box-office success (over $220 million grossed worldwide), but Cutler's analysis cuts deeper. Even more than in *Zodiac* or *The Curious Case of Benjamin Button* (not exactly a movie for the chattering classes), sensationalism becomes subordinate to storytelling—and the story being told signifies outwards and into the real world. The ostentatiousness of Fincher's early digital experimentations in *Panic Room* and *Fight Club* is either toned down or bracketed off within the film's conceptual design: in every shot and sequence, form follows function. Even the Winklevosses' scenes, which slyly emblematize the director's commitment to digital tinkering, are exercises in virtuoso subtlety, of spectacular craft rendered almost subliminal by design. In *The Curious Case of Benjamin Button*, the audience was invited—and obliged—to scrutinize Brad Pitt's manipulated features at length, an emphasis in keeping with the film's meditative relationship to time and also its requirements as a star vehicle. *The Social Network* features the zeitgeist itself as the main attraction. At one point, the Winklevosses' snide business partner, Divya Narenda (Max Minghella), tells a lawyer that Mark was, "the biggest thing on a campus that included nineteen Nobel Laureates, fifteen Pulitzer Prize winners, two future Olympians, and a movie star." "Who was the movie star?" the lawyer asks. "Doesn't matter," comes the reply.

In lieu of any true marquee names (other than Justin Timberlake as Sean Parker) and thus unburdened by any kind of A-list gravitas, *The Social Network* defines itself through a hurtling forward momentum. The fun of watching Hammer bounce lines back and forth off himself

5-12. Shooting in a tilt-shift format that sharpens and miniaturizes the image, Fincher turns the Henley Royal Regatta into a parody of alpha-male exertion: a faux-Nike commercial that channels and mocks the excitement of the Winklevosses' athletic endeavor (the thrill of victory; the agony of defeat) to the pent-up, repetitive accompaniment of "In the Hall of the Mountain King."

13. A lonely Zuckerberg tramps the Harvard campus byways in the manner of a Pac-Man-like, side-scrolling computer game.

(with expert deadpan support by Minghella) is deepened—and focused, rather than distracted—by our understanding that we're watching a trick. On the page, Sorkin's script draws a bead on the Winklevosses' twitty privilege; onscreen, as rendered by Fincher and his team of collaborators, the brothers are not merely unsympathetic but *uncanny*. It's as if the idea of Ivy League conformity has been distilled into a real-life attack of the clones. The illusion serves, ingeniously, as a suspension system for our disbelief.

Those conjoined sensations of weightlessness and delight—of being caught and held in grateful thrall—is of a piece with the fleetness identified by Dargis and other supporters. Pace is *The Social Network*'s organizing principle and most outstanding feature—a peak in Fincher's later-career project of yoking swiftness to clarity. "It's moving faster than any of us ever imagined," Mark tells Eduardo at one point, referring to Facebook's widespread metastasization while also summing up the movie's need for speed. In the opening sequence, we see Mark on a date at a campus pub called The Thirsty Scholar with his girlfriend, Erica Albright

13.

(Rooney Mara); the brown and amber hues are thoroughly romantic ("golden with barlight and beer" in the words of pub-rock patron saint Craig Finn). Talking with *Time Out*'s David Jenkins in 2011, Fincher said that, "the first scene in a movie should teach you how to watch it," and Mark and Erica's conversation is instructive in this regard. It begins innocuously enough, with a bit of playful trivia—"Did you know that

there are more people with genius-level IQs living in China than there are people living in the United States?"—ramps up through a few flirty false starts (The Thirsty Scholar, indeed) and then plunges roller-coaster-like straight into a vortex of mutual resentment.

The undertow is generated by Mark's need to prove—to his supportive girlfriend, to himself, and perhaps to the unseen, ever-judgemental audience he imagines in his head—that he ranks as an American Brainiac. As in classic screwball comedy, the actors' line readings are so quick as to overlap, but without the madcap harmoniousness aimed for and achieved by a filmmaker like Howard Hawks. *His Girl Friday* (1941)—a movie invoked admiringly in Amy Taubin's review—is about estranged lovers realizing, gloriously, that they're on the same wavelength. *The Social Network*, meanwhile, keeps driving the wedge deeper. "While [Mark and Erica] are speaking face-to-face, they are also foreshadowing a divide between courtesy and clarity that these days is familiar to anyone who spends time online," wrote *The Ringer*'s Katie Baker in 2020. Her observation neatly encapsulates the subtext of a movie in which the perils of face-to-face communication, and the elusive promise of intimacy, are leveraged against a safely disembodied alternative, where body language and tone don't matter and participants can be collapsed into data.

The sequence's headlong velocity invites Erica's bitterly funny observation to her soon-to-be-ex that "dating you is like dating a Stairmaster." Such ruthless dispatch permits the seeding of multiple crucial motifs before *The Social Network* is even five minutes old, the most important of these being the idea of Mark-as-"asshole." As fully inhabited by Eisenberg, who weaponizes the toussled-nebbish tendencies he'd shown in coming-of-age comedies like *The Squid and the Whale* (2005) and *Adventureland* (2009), Mark is an asshole—one who is, as Taubin writes "furiously alive at every moment." In the absence of *Fight Club*'s complicit voice-over—or the endearing, confessional transparency of *Benjamin Button*—we're left to intuit an inner life. Without ever raising his voice or altering his flat affect, Eisenberg inhabits a set of tripwire

14. The Winklevi get humanized during their meeting with Harvard's President Larry Summers, who rejects their naive conception of the school as a meritocracy but also exposes his own blinkered cynicism about the institution.

15. The layout and decor of Facebook's Palo Alto offices are perfectly replicated by *The Social Network*'s production design—brash, abstract artwork that fits its creator's self-image as edgy disruptors.

16-18. Reviews of *The Social Network* criticized Aaron Sorkin's screenplay for a lopsided dramaturgy in which female characters were either minimized, sexualized or otherwise depicted unflatteringly; Erica, Amelia, and Christy are all defined primarily by the male characters they're sleeping with.

14.

15.

epiphanies and defense mechanisms exactly as rapid-fire as the film's editing scheme: no less than *Fight Club*'s credit sequence, with its CGI approximation of the "fear center of the human brain," *The Social Network*'s prologue unfolds as a set of synaptic flashes, this time visualized from the outside-in.

\#

"You've seen guys that row crew, right?" Mark queries Erica not-so rhetorically. "They're bigger than me, they're world-class athletes, and a second ago, you said you liked guys who rowed crew." Besides serving as a sly prophecy of the Winklevi—who, even sight-unseen, occupy a large patch of mental real estate for Mark and the movie at large—the line hints at some irreconcilable crisis about the mind and the body, a Cartesian divide sparking sexual paranoia and a vengeful competitiveness. Mortified by his lack of self-awareness (he tries to de-escalate the situation by chalking this discomfort up to her being "hungry") Erica flees and leaves Mark alone to lurch home in the cold. The hushed, nocturnal beauty of the subsequent credit sequence, shot in graceful, sweeping exterior shots, its wintry nightscapes illuminated by street lamps, provides *The Social Network* with its sole instance of lyricism. It's a gorgeous passage akin to the library idyll in *Se7en*, except that instead of signifying some grateful refuge it expresses solitude—and slowness. Later on, a regatta race will be filmed by Fincher in comically overcranked, sporting-apparel-ad fashion, utilizing stylized tilt-shifted photography (the world seen through a proto-Instagram filter) and scored to the driving, infernal notes of Edvard Grieg's "In the Hall of the Mountain King." But during the mild, descending three-note piano motif of Trent Reznor and Atticus Ross's Oscar-winning score—a melancholically synthetic melody that sounds eerily like software booting up—plays up Mark's laggard passage through the physical world, jogging gingerly through (and out of) lustrous, deep-focus frames that hold their ground irrespective of his presence. The character becomes dwarfed by his surroundings, a mobile figure in a winding, labyrinthine landscape—an analogue Pac-Man.

When Mark gets back to his room at Kirkland House and jumps online, the camera moves closer and the cutting and musical score accelerate to suggest his surging internal tempo. "I'm a little bit intoxicated," he admits in blogging voice-over as he touch-types hateful japes about Erica's family history, personality and

bra size. Mark's facility in the virtual realm is total, a landlocked loser's equivalent of "rowing crew." If his subconscious is telling him anything, it's "Just Do It." Again, form follows function: Reznor and Ross score the flashy montage chronicling Mark's wee-hours engineering of a mean-spirited, hot-or-not-style website—populated by his classmates' yearbook photos and called Facemash, a name right out of *Fight Club* and the Narrator's bludgeoning mandate to "destroy something beautiful"—like an electro-video game fugue. The music bleeds over into interspersed glimpses of elite frat-house bacchanalias, cutaways crammed with smug, model-perfect revellers. Fincher shoots these like a parody of a glossy, circa-*American Pie* (1999) campus comedy—as the projected fantasies of all the dormbound have-nots bonding over their lack of access and acceptance. A telling detail in a blink-or-miss-it montage: a lone, woebegone pothead giggling vindictively beneath a vintage-style boxing poster advertising an all-caps battle of "BOOBS vs. BRAINS."

Inevitably, all of those gorgeous, poreless partiers become hypnotized by the algorithm, crowding around their own laptops to gawk, complicit in a joke originally intended at their expense. Mark's stunt collapses the distance between Harvard's social castes while briefly crashing its online social network. Like Fincher's other disruptors, Mark's innate understanding of medium-as-message makes him a visionary. When Eduardo scrawls out a mathematical equation to help Mark generate the FaceMash code, the text evokes the Zodiac's cryptic chicken-scratches, and recalls how the film bearing his name depicted cryptography—and with it, some wicked, cryptic ideology—infecting everyday reality. In both cases, we might say, the writing is on the wall.

"The ingenuity isn't in the coding," wrote Alison Willmore in *Vulture*, about the sequence in an essay timed to *The Social Network*'s tenth anniversary in 2020. "It's in the social engineering . . . the way [Facesmash] funneled an existing (and in this case, cruel) impulse into an addictive, shareable format." Following a chaotic decade in which Facebook was widely criticized as a hub for data-mining, the wide scale invasion of privacy, and a dangerous, unregulated hyperpartisanship—such addendums felt essential; in *Wired*, Angela Watercutter juxtaposed the film's overwhelmingly popular initial reception against later claims that, in retrospect, its creators weren't nearly critical enough. "Watch *The Social Network* in 2010, and it might feel much darker than anything associated with the company needed to be," she writes. "Watch it today, and it almost seems like the company got off light." Such hindsight recontextualizes aspects of Fincher's film from docudrama to proto-dystopia without compromising its quality; while Facebook's omnipresence means it's no longer "cool"—surpassed in hipness if not users by sleeker, more youth-centered and video-driven apps as well as the scrolling dystopia of Twitter—*The Social Network*'s canonization has not dulled its edge.

In 2010, Zuckerberg was tight-lipped about Fincher's film, shrugging it off in *The New Yorker* as "fiction" and claiming magnanimously to be a fan of Sorkin's television series *The West Wing*. (Around the same time, in *The Hollywood Reporter*, Scott Rudin claimed that he had been officially pressured by Zuckerberg's team to make changes to the final cut.) Four years later, in an interview with the *Guardian*, Zuckerberg was less salutary, declaring that Sorkin had "made a bunch of stuff up." "I think the reality is that writing code and then building a product and building a company is not a glamorous enough thing to make a movie about," he added. "So you can imagine that a lot of this stuff they had to embellish." Considering *The Social Network*'s he-said-he-said structure, Zuckerberg's comments felt less like a repudiation of the film's approach than an extension of it.

Certainly, *The Social Network*'s screenplay is replete with embellishments, starting with all of that staccato, scattershot

19. Like the IKEA catalogue sequence in *Fight Club* or the Zodiac's scribblings, Eduardo's Facemash algorithm is an example of Fincher using written text as a striking graphic element, overlaid on the world of the film in anticipation of Facebook's eventual omnipresence.

dialogue, with its arch, not unpleasing theatricality. Sorkin's reliance on blistering, self-righteous speechifying in nearly all of his scripts is, to use a bit of parlance that the famously Internet-averse writer might hate, a feature that is also a bug. Either way, at this point, it's fully hardwired, and the format Sorkin used in *The Social Network* would be repeated with a few patches in Danny Boyle's inferior *Steve Jobs* (2015). Sorkin's perennial subject is intellectual exceptionalism, and he's preoccupied with the archetype of the politically incorrect truth-teller: think of Jack Nicholson's psychopathic four-star general in *A Few Good Men* (1992) angrily rationalizing murderous military practices, or Alec Baldwin's God-delusional surgeon in *Malice* (1993). Philip Seymour Hoffman's obstreperous CIA fixer in *Charlie Wilson's War* (2009) fits into this category as well. Even when these figures are officially villainous, their powers of articulation—tailor-made for brilliant actors like Nicholson and Hoffman—have a heroic aspect. The crowing, parenthetical, "and I am never ever sick at sea" that's tacked on to the self-aggrandizing rants in *Malice* and *Charlie Wilson's War* is not simply an act of citation (of Gilbert and Sullivan's opera *H.M.S. Pinafore*) but a synecdoche of Sorkin's evident pride in his own grandiloquent consistency.

In comparison to his boldly loquacious men, Sorkin's women tend to be subsidiary or subordinate even when they're brassy, serving as sounding boards for all that bluster (the notable exception being Alison Janney's acerbic West Wing press secretary C. J. Cregg). In this sense, he and Fincher were—at least circa *The Social Network*—considered a match, and the film's lopsided and unflattering gender dynamics were taken to task in various precincts. "How do you do this thing where you manage to get all girls to hate us?" Eduardo whines to Mark at one point.

Besides Mara's humiliated Erica—who largely disappears from the film after the opening scene—the only featured female characters are Eduardo's moody girlfriend Christy (Brenda Song), an apparent gold-digger introduced proferring oral sex in a public restroom, and Amelia Ritter (Dakota Johnson), a Stanford student who concludes her one-night stand with Sean Parker by alerting him to Facebook's popularity with her peers. Johnson is funny and charming in her breakthrough role but she's also a sight gag: we know her alma mater because it's stenciled onto her snug bikini briefs.

Writing in the *Daily Beast*, Rebecca Davis O' Brien did not mince words, characterizing *The Social Network*'s distaff participants as "props . . . buxom extras literally bussed in to fill the roles of doting groupies, vengeful sluts, or dumpy, feminist killjoys . . . foils for the male characters, who in turn are cruel or indifferent to them." *Tech Crunch*'s Sarah Lacy called Sorkin a hypocrite for peddling sexism under the sign of journalistic fidelity: "You're just the messenger, faithfully documenting a world where women routinely take their tops off for men, leave the room when men want to talk about business and a new modern super-nerd hates the women who spurned him." In response Sorkin responded in one of the canonical ways of being Mad Online: by posting through it. "[*The Social Network*] is about a very angry and deeply misogynistic group of people," he said in the comment section of a prominent TV blog, echoing Mark's LiveJournal spiral in the film. "I wish I could go door to door and make this explanation/apology to any woman offended by the things you've pointed out, but obviously that's unrealistic so I thought the least I could do was speak directly to you." (This is the spoken equivalent of Mark throwing two beers to a pal and his girlfriend in an act of solidarity and both cans splattering against the wall.) Sorkin's defensive sarcasm

20.

20. The casting of Justin Timberlake as Napster founder Sean Parker is witty and resonant, and his performance is a marvel of insecurity and needy largesse.

21. Spring break forever: the adolescent hijinks at Facebook's West Coast headquarters underline the immaturity of Mark and especially his compatriots, who treat entrepreneurship as an extension of frosh week.

21.

anticipated his subsequent, semi-infamous encounter in 2012 with the *Globe and Mail*'s Sarah Nicole Prickett, who rattled him during an interview about his HBO series *The Newsroom*. "Listen here, Internet girl," Sorkin snapped at his interlocutor. "It wouldn't kill you to watch a film or pick up a newspaper once in a while." "Then," wrote Prickett, "[he] ambles off, hoping I'll write something nice, as though he has never known how the news works, how many stories can be true."

\#

Like any work of historical fiction, the truth value of *The Social Network* is ultimately secondary to its entertainment value, which is considerable—and which has a lot to do with the dramatic compression of Sorkin's work. The contradiction lies in how much of Fincher's mastery is a matter of meticulously textural verisimilitude, of precisely replicating various places, spaces and early-aughts wardrobe choices until the film becomes a simulacrum. (Zuckerberg admitted that "every single shirt and fleece [in the film] is a shirt or fleece that I own.") The film's surfaces are persuasive, but do they grant some deeper authenticity or insight? This surface-as-depth approach informed *Zodiac*, which adopted the shape of a procedural to get at something about elusivity of true knowledge: working in a genre dedicated to solving mysteries, Fincher left his filing cabinet open a crack. A case can similarly be made that *The Curious Case of Benjamin Button*'s glancing, half-seen evocations of a world that's changing rapidly around its protagonist constitute a commentary on solipsism, with Benjamin resigned despite his remarkableness to his fate as an observer. What links both of these movies is a sense of loneliness—the shared condition of the crusader and the outcast—and what *The Social Network* is trying to convey through its judicious mix of re-creation and embellishment (and realism and theatricality) is the isolating nature of ambition, a truism ironized by the surrounding context of mass-scale interpersonal communication.

Antisocial overachievers are a recurring and resonant archetype in American fiction and cinema; in *Citizen Kane*, Orson Welles created a filmic template for stories about men who gain the whole world at the expense of their soul. Fincher has been quoted as saying *The Social Network* was intended as "The *Citizen Kane* of John Hughes movies," and its final shots of Mark sitting alone in an office, relentlessly refreshing his Facebook page to see if Erica has accepted his friend request, has been widely cited as a nod to *Kane*, implying that Mark's ex is effectively his Rosebud. When the unnamed, friendly law student played by Rashida Jones (an almost parodically Sorkin-esque type) tells him in the film's closing lines, "You're not an asshole, Mark, you're just trying so hard to be," it's as if a kind of sad-sack gallantry is being conferred by a third party. Staring sadly at Erica's profile picture, Mark is less Charles Foster Kane in Xanadu than a new-fangled, un-romantic Jay Gatsby, gazing out at the green light on Daisy Buchanan's dock.

Like *The Great Gatsby*, *The Social Network* is a work of turn-of-the-century satire; like Fitzgerald, it comments on the psychology and mores of its chosen moment by focusing on an emerging, neo-aristocratic American class—what H. L. Mencken characterized in his review of Fitzgerald's literature as "the florid show of modern American life and especially the devil's dance that goes on at the top. . . . The high carnival of those who have too much money to spend and too much time for the spending of it." The Harvard Finals Club parties etched in bump-n-grind montage are as much symbols of decadent excess as Gatsby's Prohibition shindigs; the most carnivalesque character in *The Social Network* is Timberlake's Sean Parker, he of the unforgettably mercenary come-on: "You know what's cooler than a million dollars? A billion dollars." Casting a former boy-band member as the man accused of trying to destroy the economics of the record industry was brilliantly inspired, and Timberlake rises to the occasion, channelling his undeniable charisma into a portrayal of a pariah-turned-seducer. A risk-taker ruled by a set of desperately self-destructive impulses, Sean is a cautionary tale whom Mark sees as a mentor—an aspirational case of arrested development with his own wicked persecution complex. (His Waterloo will be getting caught doing cocaine at a high school house party.)

If *The Social Network* lacks the scope of *Citizen Kane*—or the severe grandeur of Paul Thomas Anderson's Wellesian *There Will Be Blood* (2007), with its epic chronology of rise and ruin—it may be because its characters are comparatively unformed prodigies yet to grow into a true sense of ruefulness or regret. (That Welles could, at twenty-five, believably dramatize the wizened Kane's decline speaks to the singularity of his achievement; it also gives Kane's rise-and-fall narrative the eerie feeling of prophecy.) When Mark wears a

22.

ratty sweatshirt and flip-flops to a hearing in front of Harvard's administrative board, it's less an act of juvenile defiance than a default setting—a shuffle along the path of least resistance that also parodies the nature of an indoor kid who refuses to dress for the weather (hence his desire to go West to Palo Alto, where flip-flops are de rigueur.) When Mark makes a similar scene later with a group of investors (at Sean's urging) it's more like he's forcing the adults to meet him at his level.

The kids aren't alright, but the grown-up world is hardly much better. As much as *The Social Network* constructs the Winklevosses as well-dressed effigies—as straw men in a slow-burning joke about WASPs getting stung—the scene pitting them against Harvard's President Larry Summers (Douglas Urbanski, the former US Treasury Secretary under Bill Clinton) cleverly complicates their roles and our feelings about them. (It also opens up Fincher's film politically.) Clearly irritated at being directly levied in his three-hundred-year-old office, Summers refuses to take his visitors' claims of intellectual theft seriously; he's nonplussed by their account of "Harvard Connection" as well as their literal Harvard connections. The twins' attempts to throw the university's student handbook at its chief administrator, as well

as to use Summers's own freshman address against him—"Letting our imaginations run away with us is exactly what we were told to do," bleats Cameron—activates our *schadenfreude*. It's a hilarious exchange, showing Sorkin at his venomous best: Urbanski's stone-faced composure rebuts the brothers with an arrogance even greater than their own (it also implies that nobody likes a narc in the business world, especially not a Clintonite).

It is our of knowledge of Summers's extracurricular activities, including his role as Obama's chief economic adviser after the 2008 economic crash—where his deficit-hawk policies reduced the size of the administration's recovery-stimulus package—that compromises his claims to expertise, and to authority, moral or otherwise. His seen-it-all attitude disguises a certain blindness. The Winklevosses are hardly visionaries; their intelligence is blinkered by privilege, which is why they only ever thought in terms of "Harvard Connections." Here, though, they are granted a moment of clarity. Read between the one-liners, the sequence evinces Fincher's contempt for anything resembling institutions or establishments, and his rooting interest in their obsolescence; as ever, he's on the side of paradigm shift. "The button on the scene, when Tyler yanks off

the doorknob to the president's office, is a loaded if impotent gesture," writes Brendan Boyle. "The Winklevi have no way in . . . by the time the Winklevi get Mark on the other side of a deposition, the playing field has been leveled, and they're still grasping for the doorknob."

The deposition rooms in *The Social Network* are modest, nondescript spaces far removed from the rich, mahogany interiors of Harvard; their apparent neutrality belies their implicitly adversarial usage. Like the Winklevosses' visit to Larry Summers's office, these on-the-record interludes depict prodigies lobbying for adult intervention. Stylistically, they resemble the interrogations of *Se7en*, *Zodiac* and *Mindhunter*, built around alternating close-ups without being beholden to anything like shot-reverse-shot patterns: the embroidery of point of view is dizzyingly multidirectional.

The sterility of these sequences—their drab, even brightness—contrasts with the burnished cast of the Harvard scenes, so flush with tradition and possibility, their richness heightened in retrospect. The angry splashes of red and green adorning Facebook's Silicon Valley offices through ostentatiously placed abstract canvases—clearly the imports of a high-priced consultant—background Eduardo's climactic burst of rage at being betrayed by Mark; his elegant, black-on-black suit clashes with his soon-to-be-ex-best-friend's North Face jacket and t-shirt, reprising the same gentleman-hipster dichotomy as Mark's battles with Cameron and Tyler. "Sorry my Prada's at the cleaners, along with my hoodie and my fuck-you-flip-flops," he bellows before telling Mark to "lawyer up." It's this line (phenomenally acted by Garfield) that cinches Fincher's fashion conscious, color-coded, and surpassingly cynical take on the coming-of-age fable—more cynical, surely, than *The Curious Case of Benjamin Button*, whose hero gains a measure of wisdom about getting older even if it proves difficult to apply. What we're watching in *The Social Network* is not a progression of innocence (a rare commodity in Fincher's universe) to experience, but instead callowness to consequences in which credit and compensation are inextricably linked as forms of currency. That the financial consequences are comparatively minor for an accidental billionaire doesn't obviate the punitive way that they've been imposed; litigation is the grown-up way of doing business. In the absence of any visible parental figures—except for Mom and Pop Winklevoss, who look like immaculate breeders—the film's youthful ensemble suggests an upscale, young-adult *Peanuts* strip, with Eduardo as Charlie Brown and Mark as Lucy, eternally ready and willing to pull the football away.

Besides allowing the movie to stay somewhat on the record, the quasi-courtroom drama structure leaves room for the viewer to pass the sorts of judgements that Fincher's approach withholds, or else submerges beneath its multiple, interlaced viewpoints (another carry-over from *Citizen Kane*) and stratified layers of monochrome showmanship. "I'm not out to crucify Mark Zuckerberg," Fincher told Mark Harris. "I know what it's like to be twenty-one years old and trying to direct a $60 million movie and sitting in a room full of grown-ups who think you're just so cute, but they're not about to give you control of anything . . . I know the anger that comes when you just want to be allowed to do the things that you know you can do." The reference to *Alien 3* offers further evidence that the dent it left in Fincher's shoulder became a chronic condition—a sign that, in some ways, he will never come of age—but rather than assuming a one-to-one ratio between the director and his antihero, it's more interesting to consider how the film reckons with Mark's motivations and accomplishments. The common denominator between many of Fincher's surrogates is a desire for attention, which leads them to either act out or proselytize, often in public forums and through elaborately designed systems. John Doe's murders, Project Mayhem and M. Gateaux's clock are all in their ways expressive of a nagging dissatisfaction with reality that requires its radical reshaping, whether through pranks, torture-porn or a futile quest to reverse time's flow.

That Mark sees information as power indicates both shrewdness and naiveté; he thinks that if you know somebody is single via their relationship status is "single" they can be had, compatibility and compliance be damned. What finally marks *The Social Network* as a mature work is not its polish or its topicality as a tale of sex, money, genius and betrayal, but the little, shivery sliver of identification described by Fincher, which is not really with Mark's intelligence, ambition or anger, but his insecurity, which gets captured and projected back onto an audience whose members have internalized his resultant innovations as second nature. Even as the ending traps the character in a virtual limbo of his own making, the filmmaking steadfastly refuses distance—or superiority.

The concept of the kind, heart-broken Erica Albright as Mark's own private Rosebud is clever in a writerly sort of way; it also finally sentimentalizes the script's implicit misogyny, transforming Mark into a casualty of his own bad, drunken judgement. But the moment from *Citizen Kane* that comes to mind during *The Social Network*'s closing moments is the tableaux of Welles-as-Kane reflected into infinity as he walks through a hall of mirrors. Without directly quoting the shot, Fincher reverses Welles's idea of an impossibly multifaceted individual—a grandiloquent enigma—into a portrait of helpless, contagious transparency. Mark is not 6'5" and 220 pounds and there's only one of him, and yet he's anything but a singularity: he's a mirror. As the saying goes, he may be the creator of Facebook, but he's also a client, and life under his new paradigm looks an awful lot like what came before. "Let me tell you about the very rich," said F. Scott Fitzgerald, "They are different from you and me." Fincher's movie isn't quite so sure. Like any movie that means to address a specific time and place, *The Social Network* reveals its limits as documentary as well as prophecy. But if any twenty-first century movie contains an image as apt and timeless and prophetic as a lonely boy clicking absent-mindedly into the void for lack of anything else to do—or want, or feel—it hasn't yet been made.

22. Eduardo's betrayal by Mark prompts a moment of beta-male outrage that also plays up the sartorial differences between the two men, with Eduardo's sleek black suit versus Mark's hoodie and "fuck-you flip-flops"

23-24. Clicking into the void: Mark's attempt to add Erica on Facebook is *The Social Network*'s "Rosebud" moment.

23.

24.

Bringing Down the House: **The Inside Story of Six MIT Students Who Took Vegas for Millions**, Ben Mezrich, 2002

Before writing *The Accidental Billionaires*, Ben Mezrich mined a similar real-life story about youthful entrepreneurs bending a complex economic system to their will.

Fig B. *His Girl Friday*, Howard Hawks, 1940

The serene velocity of the dialogue between Mark and Erica in *The Social Network*'s opening was likened by multiple critics to the screwball tradition of Howard Hawks.

Fig C. *Pac-Man* [Video game]

Walking home alone through campus, Mark could be a character from a vintage, side-scrolling video game.

Fig F. **John Hughes**

Fincher joked that his aspiration was to make "The *Citizen Kane* of John Hughes movies."

Fig G. **Propaganda Films**

In 2010, Fincher likened the start-up culture at his old music video and commercial production company to the story shown in *The Social Network*.

Fig H. *Dead Ringers*, David Cronenberg, 1988

David Cronenberg's creepy tale starring Jeremy Irons as identical twin gynecologists set a bar for dual performances.

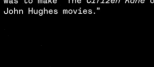

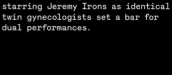

Fig D. *Malice*, Harold Becker, 1993 [Still with Alec Baldwin]

Aaron Sorkin's skill for writing scathing, hyper-articulate monologues (and characters with God complexes) is channelled into *The Social Network*'s script.

Fig E. *Citizen Kane*, Orson Welles, 1941

A clear stylistic and thematic touchstone for *The Social Network*, including the "Rosebud"-style ending.

Fig I. *American Pie*, Paul Weitz, 1999

Underneath its sheen of technological and legal intrigue, *The Social Network* is very much a millennial coming of age comedy.

Fig J. The Harvard Handbook

The Winklevosses' old-fashioned yearning to do things by the book marks them as analog men in a digital world.

INFLUENCES

WRITERS Aaron Sorkin (screenplay), Ben Mezrich (book)
CINEMATOGRAPHER Jeff Cronenweth
EDITORS Kirk Baxter, Angus Wall

BUDGET $40 million
BOX OFFICE $224.9 million
LENGTH 120 min

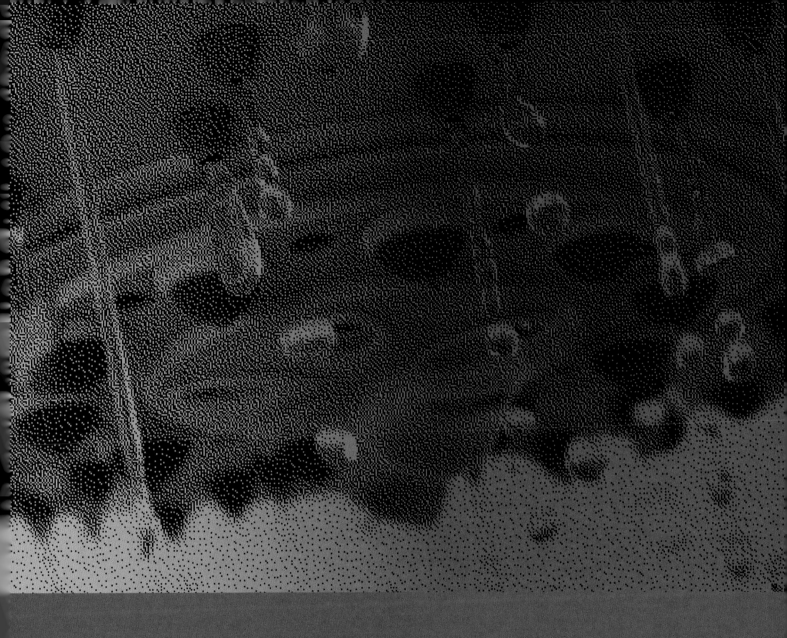

HIS AND HERS

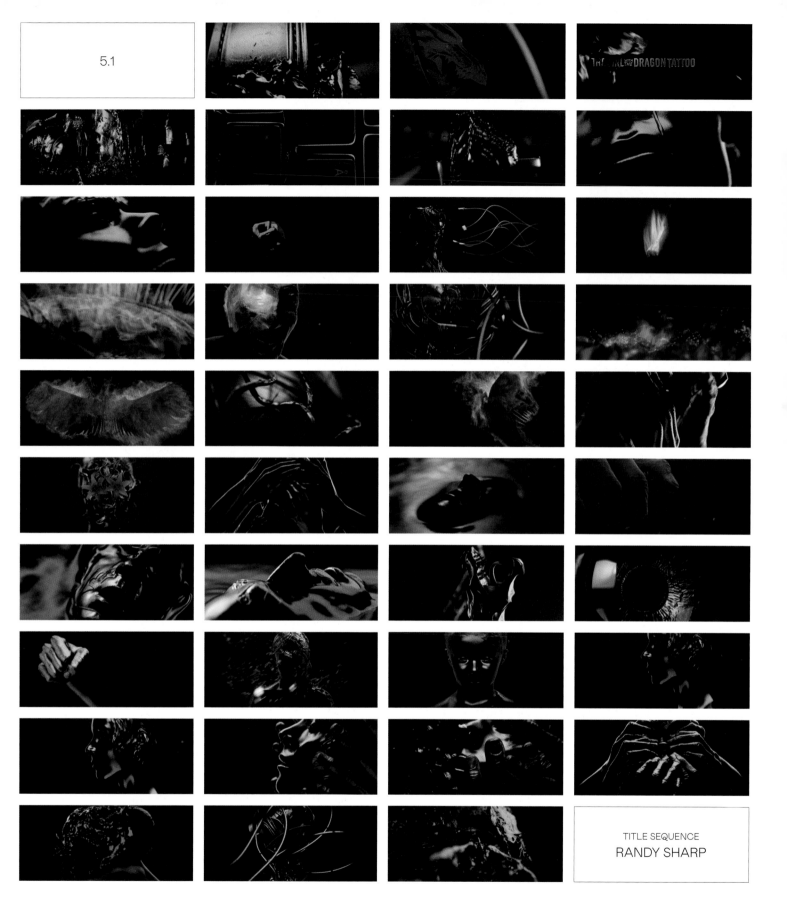

5.1

THE GIRL WITH THE DRAGON TATTOO

TITLE SEQUENCE
RANDY SHARP

< *The Girl with the Dragon Tattoo*'s opening title sequence suggests a pulp-fiction gloss on the James Bond series; here, scenes and characters from several of Stieg Larsson's novels morph and undulate together through an abstract, black-on-black narrative connoting torture, rebirth, and the intersection of the body and technology.

5.1

THE GIRL WITH THE DRAGON TATTOO

2011

There are two significant pop music cues in David Fincher's ninth film, *The Girl with the Dragon Tattoo*, each of which announces his intentions. The first is a cranked-up cover of Led Zeppelin's "Immigrant Song," which blares over the film's opening credit sequence; written in 1970 by Robert Plant as an homage to Norse mythology, its lyrics describe an arrival in a "land of ice and snow," heralding the film's Scandinavian location as surely as Karen O's howling vocals articulate the rage of its heroine. Synced to a set of abstract, black-on-black Rorshach tableaux, "Immigrant Song" surges forth as the eruption of a troubled subconscious. It's also an artistically divergent version of the song, prefiguring the possibilities—and contingencies—of adapting a popular work.

The second is the studio version of Irish singer Enya's 1998 New Age staple "Orinoco Flow," a song whose parenthetical subtitle, "Sail Away," testifies to its meditative drift. The song is the easy listening equivalent of a daydream, but in *The Girl with the Dragon Tattoo*, it's played on a high-end stereo system by a well-heeled psychopath preparing to fillet his guest. If Quentin Tarantino's deployment of the early-70s earworm "Stuck in the Middle With You" to soundtrack an act of torture in *Reservoir Dogs* (1992) was intended in tribute to the Ludovico techniques of *A Clockwork Orange*, Fincher's bit of contrapuntal trickery quotes both movies while tying directly to his own film's theme of evil submerged—however shallowly—beneath bourgeois surfaces.

In between these choice cuts, *The Girl with the Dragon Tattoo* plays its maker's greatest hits. "The film has a pleasingly dialectical place in the Fincher oeuvre," wrote J. Hoberman in *The Village Voice*, observing the film's synthesis of, "the serial-killer procedural *Zodiac* and the computer-nerd biopic *The Social Network*"; he could have also mentioned its array of stage-managed crime scenes (*Se7en*), or that the antisocial hacker at its center cuts an androgynous swath through patriarchal institutions (*Alien 3*), en route to electronically defrauding a misanthropic billionaire (*The Game*). The "Orinoco Flow"-scored climax takes place in a house that resembles nothing so much as a live-in IKEA catalogue (*Fight Club*) with its own fortified secret compartment (*Panic Room*). At its heart, *The Girl with the Dragon Tattoo* is a May-to-December romance that riffs structurally on the *The Curious Case of Benjamin Button*; after keeping his lovers on separate tracks over an hour of screen time, Fincher permits them finally to meet in the middle.

In these ways and more, *The Girl with the Dragon Tattoo* is a super-sized compendium of Fincher-isms—not only plot points and character types but visual strategies, from that stylized sequence to a stridently digitized mise-en-scène which renders bodies, objects and places with pristine pitilessness. Cinematographer Jeff Cronenweth's grimy palette color-codes locations and time frames: the past captured in amber; the present frozen in ice. A gliding point-of-view shot through swirling snowflakes towards a looming ivory tower crystallizes the film's white-on-white aesthetic—keyed to a story probing Sweden's fixation on racial purity—and its thick atmosphere of immanence. As in *The Social Network*, editors Kirk Baxter and Angus Wall (who won a second consecutive Oscar for their work) relentlessly subdivide sequences into interlocking component parts, pressurizing establishing shots and expositional dialogue into a state of perpetual dread. The pulsing, minimalist electronic score by the Reznor/Ross duo is threaded like razorwire through Ren Klyce's buzzy soundscapes, like room tone for an abattoir. In sound, image and attitude—a sullen, implacable virtuosity—*The Girl with the Dragon Tattoo* flaunts its authorship at every turn. The question is whether the final product adds up to more, or less, than the sum of its monogrammed parts.

Such a dispassionate calculus might seem beside the point of the movie's entertainment value and artistic merit

(both of which are debatable), but it befits a thriller mesmerized by its own assembly. The gliding, explicitly Kubrickian tracking shot towards that forbidding country manor emblematizes *The Girl with the Dragon Tattoo*'s unnerving convergence; like *Se7en*, it's a film awash with the tactile sensation of pieces locking into place. "Fincher turns data into drama," writes Ignatiy Visnevetsky, "and then places it into sequential order . . . although [he] has his expressionist bursts,

1.

his current style is mostly forensic, [and it] turns the movie into an investigation of an investigation—a thriller about a thriller."

This assessment might seem a bit tautological, a more pretentious way of saying—with apologies to Muriel Spark—that for a director who often makes one sort of movie, *The Girl with the Dragon Tattoo* is the sort of movie he makes. By this logic, the people who liked those other movies would like this one as well, and yet one constant refrain in the film's mixed critical reception was that its contents were somehow in Fincher's wheelhouse and beneath his abilities. Or did the problem lie somewhere else? In *The L Magazine*, Mark Asch quoted Amy Taubin's observation that "[David] Fincher has never had a screenplay worthy of his talents" before asking, sarcastically: "At what point does that become [his] fault?"

For a skeptic like Asch, Fincher's brand of auteurism had long since detoured from the classical conception of a skilled innovator working inside a top-down hierarchy. By the 2010s, Fincher was in the rare position to pick and choose projects and exercise control over studio capital; his eager and willing selection of a mechanically tacky bestseller could be taken as a lack of case or an abundance of cynicism—or a hint that, for all his self-possession, Fincher was a helpless practitioner-slash-victim of the same pathological recidivism featured in his serial-killer films. "Maybe I am too insulated," Fincher told the *Guardian*'s

1. Beyond being a rumpled, handsome avatar of old-school journalism, Mikael is a passenger, conveyed back and forth from Stockholm to Hedestad by car and train.

2-9. Lisbeth has some of the same sullen defiance as Mark Zuckerberg, and takes a quiet pride in appearing out of place in the sleek, functional spaces favored by her corporate clients; where Mikael is passenger, she pilots her own motorcycle from place to place.

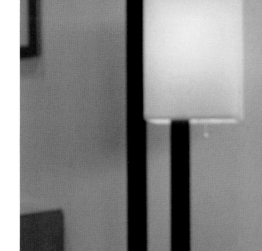

Benjamin Secher. "Or too confident, or simply sociopathic. But I can only do what I think is best."

There is a difference between doing what one thinks is best and doing it as best as one can, and for a number of critics, *The Girl with the Dragon Tattoo* fell into the latter category. "As classy a film as could be made from Stieg Larsson's sordid page-turner, David Fincher's much-anticipated return to serial-killer territory is a fastidiously grim pulp entertainment," wrote Justin Chang in *Variety*; "That Fincher has silk-pursed this swine . . . is no cause for celebration" sneered *Reverse Shot*'s Andrew Tracy. These swipes at the movie's source material were fair enough given that Larsson's book—published in 2005 after its author's unexpected death by heart attack at the age of fifty—was a potboiler passing itself off as progressive social critique.

The Girl with the Dragon Tattoo concerns a crusading, middle-aged journalist who teams up with a punkish computer expert several decades his junior to investigate a decades old cold case on the remote Swedish island of Hedestad. For forty years, businessman Henrik Vanger has agonized over the fate of his beloved grandniece Harriet, who disappeared from the family home one afternoon; every year on her birthday, he receives a gift of pressed flowers in a picture frame from an unknown sender whom he presumes

10.

must be her killer—and suspects to be a member of his own dysfunctional clan. The book's conversation-piece status was less a matter of its laboriously engineered plot than a matter of its posthumous publication and political utility. A prominent left-wing journalist who'd spent decades surveilling far-right groups in Europe via his self-founded magazine *Expo*, Larsson had been celebrated in life as a truth-teller; his death on the eve of his blockbuster transition to fiction was seen in some quarters as the result of a sinister conspiracy like the one in his novel. In his only interview about the book in October of 2004, the author observed that crime stories "are one of the most popular forms of entertainment that exist," adding that he was only writing one because he, "[had] something to say."

"The enlightened socialism and political passion of Stieg Larsson is not possible to fake," wrote a prominent Swedish critic after the publication of *The Girl with the Dragon Tattoo*. There is, nevertheless, something off-puttingly phony about the book's approach, which saleably packages anti-capitalist broadsides with putative feminist empowerment. The latter comes in the slender, spiky form of Lisbeth Salander, the eponymous "girl," of the title, a skilled hacktivist with an eidetic memory described by her creator as a "total outsider . . . with no social competence whatsoever." Larsson claimed that his inspiration for the character was the kid-lit heroine Pippi Longstocking, a rebellious orphan beloved around the word as a distaff Scandinavian Peter Pan: "What," he wondered, "would she look like as an adult?" Larsson's own prose supplies the answer: when Lisbeth makes her first appearance in the novel, she is described as a "pale, androgynous young woman who has hair as short as a fuse, and a pierced nose

and eyebrows"—signifiers of difference that the character wears as a badge of honour.

The same goes for that dragon tattoo, with its twin intimations of rough trade and fairy-tale archetypes; within Larsson's neo-picaresque conception, Lisbeth is knight errant, orphan princess and fire-breathing monster all rolled into one. The character's bristling, nocturnal distance from the world, flouting of sartorial and behavioural norms and capacity for savage violence in self-defense, are revealed as the byproducts of individual and institutional abuse. As the book opens, Lisbeth has been released from a psychiatric clinic, and later suffers brutal sexual assault at the hands of her court-appointed guardian. Her urge for retribution, both for herself and on behalf of victimized women everywhere, leads her to work with Mikael Blomkvist, an old-school muckraker reeling from a legal judgement that may bankrupt his independent magazine. In need of cash—and a respite from the public eye after being shamed in court—he accepts Henrik's offer to investigate Harriet's disappearance under the pretense of writing a Vanger family memoir. His motives are purely mercenary, while Lisbeth's are ideological; he piques her curiosity and secures her loyalty by inviting her to "help [him] catch a killer of women."

Mikael is stoic, nobly rumpled, and deceptively hopeless in a grand tradition of liberal kitsch dating back to Humphrey Bogart's reluctant anti-fascist Rick in *Casablanca* (1943), and a quote by Umberto Eco about Michael Curtiz's classic comes to mind re: Larsson's dramaturgy: "The cliches are having a ball." As a study in romantic authorial self-projection, the character—who is not only an ink-stained wretch but a hangdog Romeo, bedding his married co-editor Erika, a Vanger sibling and the girl with the dragon tattoo herself—is as transparent as cellophane, whereas Lisbeth's seething anger and inscrutability expose Larsson's hackier and more speculative impulses. It's one thing to wonder whatever happened to Pippi Longstocking, and another to rewire her into an atavistic avenging angel. In *The New Yorker*, Nora Ephron kidded Larrson's hard-boiled style, facile pathology and deceptive sexism in a short story slyly titled "The Girl Who Fixed the Umlaut." "Lisbeth Salander was entitled to her bad moods on account of her miserable childhood and her tiny breasts, but it was starting to become confusing just how much irritability could be blamed on your slight figure and an abusive father you had once deliberately set on fire and then years later split open the head of with an axe."

Ephron's joking is meant affectionately, as a gentle chip off a newly minted literary monolith. But it identifies what is so objectionable about *The Girl with the Dragon Tattoo*, which stokes and satisfies blood lust under the aegis of moral superiority. For the book's cabal of serial-murdering Nazi sympathizers and dissembling corporate bogeymen—avatars respectively of Sweden's questionable World War II-era neutrality and its contemporary neoliberal agenda—it's simply not possible for the punishment to exceed the crime, and Lisbeth in particular is granted ethical carte blanche to dispense with them as needed. After five hundred or so pages of stone-faced sadism, Larsson's penny dreadful tendencies blow past the point of self-parody, umlauts and all—which didn't stop him from sketching out an entire repetitive decalogue entitled *Millennium*.

With 40 million copies sold worldwide by 2010—including the sequels written by Larsson and farmed out to his countryman David Lagercrantz—the *Millennium* series was not only hugely profitable but also massively influential, sparking an entire cycle of so-called "Nordic noir" recombining sex, violence and culturally specific social commentary. Of course, Larsson had been less a genuine innovator than a canny synthesizer of popular taste, and it was not a coincidence that producer Scott Rudin purchased the movie rights for the books with Fincher in mind. Given how much *The Girl with the Dragon Tattoo* cribbed from *Se7en*, the filmmaker's participation felt like the closing of a creative feedback loop. Sony contracted Fincher to direct an entire *Millennium* trilogy, handing a potentially lucrative franchise to a filmmaker who'd spent the decades since *Alien 3* railing against the franchise mentality. "It's a totally different thing [than *Alien 3*] because [that] was a cinematic franchise as opposed to a literary franchise," Fincher told *IndieWire*, sounding like a man diplomatically (or perhaps facetiously) splitting hairs. "My job in this was just to try and take a book and put it into cinematic terms."

In this interview and others, Fincher downplayed discussions of Niels Arden Oplev's 2009 Swedish-language version of *The Girl with the Dragon Tattoo*, an international box-office hit that won plaudits for its star Noomi Rapace, who parlayed her performance there and into two sequels—*The Girl Who Played With Fire* and *The Girl Who Kicked the Hornets Nest*, both also released in 2009—into Hollywood stardom. Taken on its own "cinematic terms," Oplev's *Dragon Tattoo* is competent, but then there are no other terms on which to take it. Its faithfulness comes at the expense of achieving any kind of distance—critical or otherwise—from Larsson's text. Like any worthy cover version, Fincher's film, scripted by Steven Zaillian (like Eric Roth, an Oscar-winning hired gun) finds the seams between fidelity and invention.

Without taking its masterful craftsmanship for granted—or completely throwing away Tracy's silk-purse/sow's-ear analogy—the movie's relative superiority to Larsson's book and Oplev's adaptation is less a matter of formalism than a feat of dramatic aptitude, of forging coherence out of contrivance. The metronomic alternation between plotlines makes *The Girl with the Dragon Tattoo* feel like two different movies, but it's more like the film is a double feature superimposed over itself, at once a rote, lurid murder mystery ("Agatha Christie plus anal rape" per Tracy) and a wry, lucid allegory about the confluence of analogue and digital media. It converges as an unrequited love story that etches Fincher's perennial fascination with loneliness. The film's steely exterior belies an ache; what gradually seeps

10.   Martin Vanger, a paragon of svelte Swedish sophistication and lover of Gaelic ethereal pop music, is able to shroud a secretive double life in the shadows of wealth and status.

11-12. The Vanger fortresses straddle architectural eras and represent decades of social dominance—but they also symbolize a shift from classical elegance to cold precision.

THE GIRL WITH THE DRAGON TATTOO

through, like the dark, primordial ooze summoned in the opening by "Immigrant Song," is a sense of melancholy, infusing the alienation of a character who appears either forced or determined to live a solitary existence on her own terms.

#

The casting of Rooney Mara as Lisbeth Salander marks an interesting kinship between *The Girl with the Dragon Tattoo* and *The Social Network*. The original Swedish title of the book, *Män som hatar kvinnor*, translates in English to "Men Who Hate Women," a phrase that could also apply to *The Social Network*, whose writer claimed to be crafting an indictment of misogyny (the same mandate that Larsson carried to and past the point of hyperbole). After two months of auditions, Mara got the part over more bankable actresses like Scarlett Johansson and Natalie Portman; in an interview with *Entertainment Weekly*, she recalled going into a meeting with Fincher "pissed" and "ready to fight" about his drawn-out decision-making process. What Mara brings to *The Girl with the*

Dragon Tattoo is a brazen, brilliantly malleable physicality that's perfect for a character who experiments with her own self-presentation. But she also commands an intertextual aura that illuminates the film's connection to—and rebuttal of—its more prestigious predecessor.

As Erica Albright in *The Social Network*, Mara was not playing a character so much as a structuring absence—the ex-girlfriend who launched a thousand shitposts, reduced (and inflated) to the dimensions of a Facebook profile picture. Lisbeth, though, is the driving force of the movie around her—the catalyst and carrier of its all-consuming linearity. Her agency and mobility are encoded in her jet-black motorcycle, which she pilots through the film as a helmeted, armored presence, a three-dimensional manga illustration. It's satisfying to watch Mara go from a foil for Jesse Eisenberg's pent-up awkwardness to inhabiting a similar character type with even more furiously sublimated intensity, as Lisbeth navigates male dominated social networks. Within the film's economically stratified hierarchy of evil, the nasty venture capitalist Hans-Erik Wennerström,

who operates the corporate windmills that Mikael has been tilting against in a losing battle, occupies the highest level—you can imagine that his business cards read "I'm CEO, Bitch!" in Swedish. In the end, he'll be brought down by Lisbeth's digital skill set and shape-shifting invisibility—an introvert's decisive intervention.

More than any other single element of *The Girl with the Dragon Tattoo*, Mara's acting reconciles Fincher's slick, graphic-novel surfaces with a plausible interiority. "I don't think I've seen an actor do more with deadpan expressions than Mara in this movie," wrote Wesley Morris in the *Boston Globe*. "Her face doesn't move, but whether she's tasing a man or standing in front of a mirror watching a cigarette dangle from her mouth, we respond to her." In line with the reading of *The Girl with the Dragon Tattoo* as a self-reflexive highlight reel, Mara's flinty acting and flat-lined affect evoke Helena Bonham Carter as Marla Singer in *Fight Club* and especially *Alien 3*'s tetchy, short-tempered iteration of Ellen Ripley, adopting the latter's action-hero posture during a climax that plays smartly with star personas. When Lisbeth rescues Daniel Craig's Mikael

13. The limitations of Mikael's journalistic nous come to light in Martin Vanger's basement. He discovers that his target—a "killer of women"—is happy to make an exception.

14. Reversing the classical damsel in distress motif, *Dragon Tattoo* sees Lisbeth enacting the role of cavalry as she single-handedly puts an end to the violence.

from certain death at the hands of Stellan Skarsgaård's Martin Vanger, it's not just a reversal of outmoded damsel-in-distress tropes but a wry deconstruction of Craig's fame—and marquee virility—as the latest incarnation of James Bond.

There is an odd correspondence between Stieg Larsson and Ian Fleming in that neither author lived long enough to see their novels made into films. *The Girl with the Dragon Tattoo* works the 007 connection on a number of fronts, including the opening credits, which pay homage to the Bond series' model of multiplex impressionism— its distinctive audiovisual overtures tailored to each instalment. Because *The Girl with the Dragon Tattoo* was meant to be the first film in a series, the "Immigrant Song" sequence (created by the LA based studio Blur) draws on imagery from the first three *Millennium* novels, compressing exposition and character development into a gooey fugue. Fincher's creative brief to designers Tim Miller and Neil Kellerhouse was abstract: "very adult, super dark, leather, skin, blood, snow, breasts, vaginas, needles, piercings, motorcycles, vengeance"; the final product drenches the director's fetishistic inventory in viscous black fluid, ringed with bursts of burnt-orange fire to signal Lisbeth's phoenix-like rise throughout the story. In an interview with the *Art of the Title*, Fincher praised Miller's process in terms similar to descriptions of his own approach. "He has this incredible eye," said Fincher, "but it's always in service of function—it's got to move the heart, or the mind, or the groin. It's got to engage you on some other part of your being."

It's a fine line between eroticism and disgust—between moving the groin and moving it the wrong way. Fincher's penchant for shriveled-up set pieces sprawls across his filmography, back to the unseen but indelibly suggested death-by-strap-on the "Lust" murder in *Se7en*, and also the Space Monkeys' attempted castration of the narrator in *Fight Club*. When Mikael has his manhood threatened by Martin's Exacto knife, it's a callback to the scene in *Goldfinger* (1964) where Sean Connery is menaced by a strategically placed laser, but also the scourging of nether-regions suffered by Craig in *Casino Royale* (2006) at the hands of Mads Mikkelsen's sadistic Le Chiffre—a moment awash in sinister homoeroticism. More than any Bond since Connery, Craig had been sexualized as 007, starting with the reverse-Ursula Andress allusion in *Casino Royale* of the actor emerging shirtless from the surf. *The Girl with the Dragon Tattoo* pushes the actor in

a different direction, towards a soft-bodied passivity that undermines his license-to-kill heroism and calls attention instead to Lisbeth's tensile strength. In an interview with *GQ*, Craig emphasized that Fincher didn't want him to cut a secret agent figure. "He just used to send me bowls of pasta and bottles of wine," Craig said. "He said you don't look like a journalist, you're moving like an action hero."

Craig can't help but be more dynamic than his Swedish version counterpart Michael Nyqvist, whose Blomkvist is a shuffling non-entity, but he's still emphasized as a figure of middle-aged frailty, reading glasses perpetually dangling from his ear and resting on his clavicle. Where Lisbeth slices through scenes on her motorcycle, Mikael is always being transported or chauffeured, by train or by car. Whenever he arrives, he can't get cell service: Fincher repeats the image of Craig holding his phone aloft as a structuring device. Mikael the print journalist is an analog man, and such visual shorthand works wonders in a movie so packed and weighed down by narrative information. What makes Mikael compelling and attractive—to us, and gradually to Lisbeth as well—is a plodding, dogged determination that's emblematic of old-school sleuthing.

Fincher typically works best inside tightly written scripts, and Zaillian's adaptation is impressively strict about maintaining its his-n-hers structure. The second strand is stronger and more detailed, and Lisbeth's development from a subject of voyeuristic, depersonalizing curiosity—"the girl with the dragon tattoo"—into a locus of identification and subjectivity is considerably more interesting and engaging than the whereabouts of Harriet Vanger. Mara's riveting performance obliges us to see the world through the eyes of a woman who refuses to meet the gaze of others; the first time Lisbeth makes active eye contact it's with Mikael, who arrives at her apartment seventy-five minutes into the movie's running time, a distinctly non-threatening presence as non-plussed by his host's groggy, female one-night stand companion as by her succinctly stenciled t-shirt: "FUCK YOU YOU FUCKING FUCK."

It's a charming-enough introduction, and it sketches out a recognizably Fincherian dialectic *à la* Mills and Somerset in *Se7en* or Tyler and the Narrator in *Fight Club*, or, closer still, Benjamin and Daisy in *The Curious Case of Benjamin Button*: male and female; old and young; idealist and subversive; editor and freelance; analogue and digital. These dichotomies all derive

15. At almost the exact
    mid-point of the film,
    Mikael and Lisbeth's
    paths finally cross as
    he secures her unique
    services. With Lisbeth
    mired in a state of
    perpetual (if ambient)
    anger, Fincher asks us
    to weigh up the levels
    of irony displayed by
    her T-shirt slogan.

from Larsson, whose sense of romance and sops to millennial relevance are as gimmicky as his story's multiple MacGuffins: anonymous letters; amateur numerology; gone girls hiding in plain sight. Fincher, though, is temperamentally inclined towards the technocratic aspects of filmmaking, and clearly identifies with and admires Lisbeth on that plane. He converts data into drama; she uses surveillance to process suspicion and move towards certainty (and like Detective Somerset or Robert Graysmith is totally capable in a library setting). At the beginning of the film, Lisbeth is hired by one of Henrik's subordinates to create a dossier on Mikael, an assignment marking her as the film's true protagonist: for Fincher, knowledge is power, and Lisbeth is a repository of information. Her verdict to her employers is succinct and definitive, and guides our opinion: "he is clean, in my opinion."

Such genuine cleanliness is rare in *The Girl with the Dragon Tattoo*'s antiseptic hellscape, especially on the male side of the ledger. Fincher has never strictly glamorized masculinity (not counting the satirical pin-ups of Brad Pitt in *Fight Club*, which has its cheesecake boy and eats him too), but this film in particular is filled with male grotesques. Not only Skarsgaård's effete, urbane Martin, whose identity as a "killer of women" is identified as part of a familial lineage beginning with his abusive father Gottfried, but also Dutch actor Yorick van Wageningen as Lisbeth's guardian, Nils Bjurman, who leverages his charge's financial need and lack of attachments into extortive sexual servitude. We don't see a lot of Lisbeth's previous trustee, Holger Palmgren (Bengt C. W. Carlsson) before he suffers a debilitating stroke, but the symbolism of a decent man incapacitated and replaced by an opportunist is in keeping with Larsson's misandry. Fincher's use of van Wageningen here is pure, old-school typage: the actor has darting, porcine eyes and a massive, protruding gut, which juts out from his tucked-in waistline and later provides Lisbeth with an ample flesh-and-blood canvas for an act of righteous messaging that also serves as a semiotic punctuation mark, spelling out the movie's agenda in jagged all-caps type.

"I AM A RAPIST PIG" reads the legend soldered into Nils's stomach, scarlet letters carved as a makeshift mark of Cain. In *Se7en*, social critic-slash-body-artist John Doe inscribed his guilty verdicts in viscera, refuting accusations of sadism by deferring to a just cause of "turning each sin against the sinner." "It's more comfortable for you to

label me insane," he says evenly to Detective Mills, a bit of dialogue answered by Lisbeth when she cites her own skewed institutional history back at the man who'd used it to his advantage. "The reports that have followed me around all my life, what do they say, if you had to sum it up?" she asks the prone social worker. "They say I'm insane . . . it's ok, you can nod because it's true. I am insane." On the last line, Fincher cuts to an extreme close-up of Mara's face, eyes ringed black with makeup like a *Blade Runner* Replicant. It's the first such close-up in the film, and it's staged and acted as confrontation—for Lisbeth as well as the audience—with a damaged but lucidly self-justifying pathology. In place of the judgemental detachment of John Doe—or the ecclesiastical savagery of Gottfried and Martin Vanger, who mine the Book of Leviticus for a series of gruesome executions in which the method of death mirrors the sin of which the perpetrator was guilty—Lisbeth embraces and then enacts her own classification as a dangerous woman, internalized shame and rage as self-actualization.

Referring to the "lurid thread of sexual violence" running through *The Girl with the Dragon Tattoo*, A. O. Scott denounced Fincher's "queasy, teasing sensationalism." Such criticisms are on the whole difficult to refute in light of Larsson's prurience and penchant for eye-for-an-eye moral equivalences, which the film cannot help but replicate; once again, the question of taste—more specifically, of Fincher's appetite for a certain kind of chic depravity—comes into play. In *The Atlantic*, Richard Lawson called the filmmaker out for expressing what he terms "a slight flicker of uncertainty" in the scene where Nils ensnares and rapes Lisbeth: "'Should we really be doing this?' the movie almost whispers. And then it goes and does it, rather pointlessly when the film's greater needs are considered."

Lawson criticizes Fincher's direction but he doesn't describe it; those "flickers of uncertainty" wedge a sliver's worth of separation between the book and the film and suggest that the latter's mandate—its organizing principle and "greater need"—may be more multifaceted. The rape scene is punctuated by repeated backward pans away from the apartment and down the hall, twinning the character's entrapment with our own desire to be spared unpleasant details best left behind closed doors. These feelings are thwarted—deliberately and painfully—when the editing plunges us back into the bedroom to see Mara chained, spread-eagled and violated—a victim of prurient

16.

urges shared in some configuration by the character, the filmmaker, and a portion of the audience. The complexity is furthered by our understanding that while Lisbeth is, if not remotely culpable or complicit in what happens to her, her victimhood is twinned with a form of control: she's surreptitiously filming her own assault, collecting the hard evidence that will unambiguously free her from Nils's guardianship as well as ensuring her own spectacular act of retaliation.

An eyeline match between Lisbeth crying, face down on the bed and the lens of the digital lens stowed away in her knapsack—which pushes in where the previous shots panned out—conveys the horror of her humiliation as well as its multiple usages a piece of voyeuristic mise-en-scène. For Lisbeth to achieve real emancipation, she has to bring her camera behind closed doors, and Fincher, whether guided by callous provocation, an attempt at empathy, or sheer commitment to his story's themes of gendered sadism and all-seeing surveillance, takes us with her.

#

The surveillance motif carries and ramps up in the second half of *The Girl with the Dragon Tattoo*. Arriving at Mikael's guest house in Hedestad, the first thing that Lisbeth does is install a series of video cameras around the edge of the property. As critic Niles Schwartz observes, everything in Lisbeth's sphere is similarly mediated: "When [a] friendly adopted cat is found massacred on [Mikael's] doorstep, he is apoplectic and shocked, whereas Lisbeth cooly takes her camera and photographs it." It is Lisbeth's technological facility that allows Mikael to not only digitize but animate a series of old photographs revealing Harriet Vanger's whereabouts and state of mind in the hours before her disappearance; our analog man can hardly run iMovie. Like Fincher's other detectives, Lisbeth's immersion in information—libraries, files, archives—induces a state of exhilaration ("a world of knowledge at your fingertips," in Detective Somerset's words). But Lisbeth's excitement barely punctures the iron veil of neutrality she's woven for herself: her steely

17.

16. The lens peeking out
from Lisbeth's bag
contextualizes
Fincher's decision
to show us her sexual
assault—she knows
it's being recorded
as evidence.

17. Lisbeth's act of
revenge is staged
first as distorted
mirror image of
her own assault and then
a head-on confrontation
in extreme close-up;
she calmly describes
herself as "insane,"
weaponizing the
implications of her
guardian's bogus
psychological profile.

21.

22.

efficiency in physical combat and sexual copulation would be a deadpan sight gag if not for the way that Fincher and Mara use it to signal—and access—the greater need that electrifies *The Girl with the Dragon Tattoo* in its final stretch: not closure or comeuppance, both of which are doled out dutifully in accordance with Larsson's text, but intimacy.

The psychological architecture of Larsson's novel is sturdy in a thick, deterministic way. Lisbeth's traumatic relationship to her monstrously abusive father (revealed more fully in the sequels) gets replayed through the episodes with Nils. Her attraction to the middle-aged Mikael is as much about the yearning for a stable, decent father figure—one more potent than the upstanding but enfeebled Holmer Palmgren—as attraction and sexual compatibility, which is more situational. Because Zaillian's script withholds most of Lisbeth's backstory, the romance between the characters unfolds more organically in the film, or as spontaneously as possible within such an artificially twisty narrative. In the same way that Fincher's inclusion of the rape-revenge subplot exposes (and only arguably interrogates) the exploitation encoded in the novel, his replication of the novel's plotting leads to a dramatic dead end: by the time a monologuing Martin tells the hogtied Mikael "we're not so different, you and I," *The Girl with the Dragon Tattoo* has entered a dead zone of generic cliché. (One redeeming detail: Mikael's fellow Boomer Martin plays "Orinoco Flow" on a tape recorder rather than an iPod.)

What cuts through the gory torpor is the intensity of Lisbeth's protective, proprietary affection for Mikael, which Fincher charts in increments from her first initiation of sex—an almost comically robotic seduction—to the wonderful moment when, gazing together at a laptop on a hotel bed, Mikael places an arm around her and is instructed brusquely "put your hand under my shirt." It is Lisbeth who sets the pace for their relationship, and Fincher locates tenderness in the tension between her hardwired, experience-based need for control and compartmentalization and a growing trust in her lover's decency. (Craig's self-effacement is praiseworthy and he does well to convey Mikael's befuddlement at Lisbeth's devotion; he has the look of a man caught in an ongoing double take.) This humanizing vulnerability cuts another way as well: in one of the film's most striking bits of staging, we see Lisbeth turning away while Harriet Vanger—not dead but hiding away from her psychopathic cousin Martin under an assumed identity for forty years—is reunited by Mikael with Henrik.

"Harriet Fucking Vanger," Lisbeth calls the subject of her investigation, and she isn't joking. In refusing to separate a terrorized innocent from the other members of her appallingly deep-pocketed family, she expresses a generalized contempt for their wealth as well as a tragic, furious jealousy for a woman who's welcomed at the other end of her trauma into a warm, loving, paternal embrace—what Schwartz identifies as the "climactic 'Hollywood Happy Ending' moment of sentimental closure and reunion."

The last act of *The Girl with the Dragon Tattoo* blows right past this Hollywood Happy Ending in pursuit of an ambivalence that puts it on a continuum with Fincher's other work. Lisbeth's first impulse—of righteous, retaliatory contempt for a corrupt Swedish ruling class—finds a cathartic outlet in an elaborate scheme to defraud and ruin Wennerstrom on Mikael's behalf, the last in a series of events in which she either saves or bails out her lover. Here, Fincher reactivates the film's latent James Bond elements to transform Mara into a combination 007/Bond Girl. After securing a phony passport, she dons a platinum wig and designer threads (both subsidized by a loan from Mikael) on an excursion to Zurich to secretly steal and redistribute Wennerstrom's wealth into a series of private accounts.

Lisbeth's high-fashionista incarnation "Irene Nesser" puts Mara on display in a different way than the rest of the movie: the character becomes a satirical obverse of Lisbeth's usual self. If it feels as if we're suddenly watching a different movie, as ever, Fincher takes his stylistic cues from Lisbeth's and her greater needs, which is now to believably inhabit her glow-up. Instead of shrinking from the gaze of others, Lisbeth embraces her conspicuousness, flaunting her new persona for bank security cameras and administrators alike; in one meeting, she makes sure to leave a red smear on a coffee cup. The entire escapade is lipstick traces, the "invisible hand" of the market given a high-end manicure.

Lisbeth's temporary willingness to be seen cues the film's desirous gaze, and Fincher's camera takes her in without leering, remaining objective and observant

18.

19.

20.

23.

24.

25.

of the process and psychology of masquerade. Returning to her hotel room after an appointment, Mara is glimpsed in an in-between-state: wig off, black hair pinned down, body girdled, dragon tattoo peeking out from beneath a padded white bra. She tosses her fancy jacket aside and pulls a black leather vest over her half-naked body before getting down to work, as if slipping back into her old skin. Later, returning to Stockholm by high-speed train, mission accomplished, it's Goodnight, Irene; she lights a cigarette, tosses the wig out the window and waits to exhale. The close-up of her face lasts only a few seconds, but Mara's expression stays in the mind's eye. Is that relief? Fatigue? Satisfaction? A moment of identification with Harriet Fucking Vanger, forced to spend her life under an assumed name? Or is it regret over her own high-rolling, conventionally beautiful alter ego's disposability?

The primacy of clothing in the closing moments of *The Girl with the Dragon Tattoo* offers perhaps the finest example of the film's visual shorthand, compressing a series of complicated emotions about love, ownership, heartbreak and independence into the process and outcome of a single purchase. Lisbeth buys Mikael his own expensive leather coat, as if to bring him closer to her. Arriving at the Millennium offices after hours to deliver the gift, she sees her lover leaving with Erika—a natural blonde. Lisbeth isn't discovering anything new here; Mikael's relationship with Erika—with whom he shares a history, a business, a lifetime of experience—isn't a betrayal so much as the confirmation of his distance from a younger lover, a gap that can't be collapsed by a commodity. Silhouetted in black against a streetlight, Lisbeth tosses the gift in a trash bin, climbs atop her motorcycle and drives off down a cobblestone path and out of one last precise, deep-focus frame, which tracks forward but only so far before losing sight of its

subject. In a movie suffused by sensations of immanence and approach, the final beat captures a lonely departure.

It's an incredibly sharp, abrupt fade-out, and Fincher styled it that way pending two more installments that would inevitably bring Lisbeth and Mikael back together in accordance with Larsson's epic—and epically profitable—vision. In 2012, Sony confirmed that Fincher would direct *The Girl Who Kicked the Hornets' Nest* and *The Girl Who Played with Fire* back-to-back; by 2014, the studio backed off on the plan and opted for a "soft reboot" of the franchise, recasting Mara's role with Claire Foy and treating 2018's *The Girl in the Spider's Web*—adapted from one of David Langercrantz's "official" follow-ups and directed by Fede Alvarez—as a sequel. A case can be made that this was the best possible outcome not only for Fincher, no longer bound to a franchise likely to bring diminishing returns, but for the film, which paradoxically gains a certain standalone integrity for remaining so open-ended.

The third key musical cue in *The Girl with the Dragon Tattoo* is a cover of Bryan Ferry's "Is Your Love Strong Enough?" by the post-industrial supergroup How to Destroy Angels. The song tells a story of love at first sight shadowed by doubt: "I knew at a glance/There'd always be a chance for me/With someone I could live for . . . Am I asking too much?/Is your love strong enough?" (Fincher would later use Roxy Music's "In Every Dream Home, a Heartache" in *Mindhunter*; both singer and filmmaker are arch formalists with one keen eye on the mainstream, easily and enjoyably taken at face value while giving the impression of hidden agendas.)

The strength Ferry refers to is the power of trust, and Lisbeth's willingness to take a leap of faith for and with a man whom she knows to be good—to be "clean, in her opinion"—is the opposite of the suicidal plunges at the end of *Alien 3* and

The Game, or the ecstatic self-destructions of *Se7en* and *Fight Club*. Larsson wrote a cliffhanger; Fincher zeroes in on the idea of isolation as the cost of independence, and extracts pulpy emotion from the cold bones of his material. Lisbeth's binning of the jacket is less a rejection of Mikael than of the notion that that you could (or should) try to remake anybody other than yourself. (Fincher gives us an insert shot of the clothing bag's designer label as it lands in the trash—an indicator, perhaps, of a certain ambivalence about well-stitched silk purses.) Where Mark Zuckerberg keeps refreshing his browser impotently into the void, this not-so-accidental billionaire moves on and through a world of men who hate women, resolute yet changeable, insane yet inured, in no need of rescue or reunion. She isn't asking for anything; her love is strong enough, and so is she.

18-20. Assuming an alternate identity for her final act of revenge: Lisbeth becomes a mirror of the blonde, affluent Harriet Vanger; in her hotel room, Fincher shows her in a state of in-between-ness deconstructing the masquerade.

21-25. Arriving at the *Millennium* offices to surprise Mikael with the gift of a leather jacket, Lisbeth spots him leaving with his lover; stricken at the realization of her own disposability, she throws the present in the garbage and rides off alone.

Fig A. Pippi Longstocking

Stieg Larsson explained that Lisbeth was his vision of the Scandanavian kid-lit heroine as an adult.

Fig B. David Hume (1711-1776)

The Scottish philosopher David Hume also mentioned our tendency to dehumanize enemies in his 1738 *Treatise of Human Nature*.

Fig C. *A Man Without a Country*, **Kurt Vonnegut 2005 [Novel]**

A close shot of a book thrown by Mikael is a swedish translation referring to Mikael's overt opposition to xenophobia.

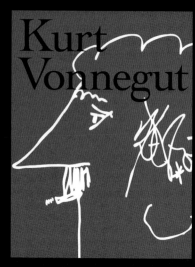

Fig F. *Dress and Identity*, **Kim K. P. Johnson, 1995 [Book]**

A collection of readings discusses the relationship between dress and identity. Selections from many disciplines present a examination of subjects, such as textiles and clothing, anthropology, sociology, social psychology and womens studies.

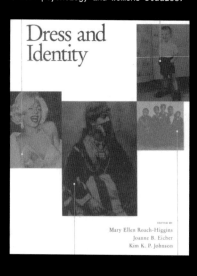

Fig G. *A Clockwork Orange*, **Stanley Kubrick, 1971**

The humorously contrapuntal use of Enya's "Orinoco Flow" recalls Stanley Kubrick's use of "Singin' in the Rain" in *A Clockwork Orange*.

Fig H. *Goldfinger*, **Guy Hamilton, 1964 [Still with Sean Connery]**

Mikael's predicament in Martin Vanger's basement plays on the Bond film tradition of 007 being regularly threatened with castration.

Fig D. *Expo*

Mikael's publication *Millennium* was based on Larsson's magazine dedicated to observing and critiquing the European far-right.

Fig E. *My 60 Memorable Games*, Bobby Fischer, 1969 [Book]

Lisbeth can be seen buying a copy of a book on chess by Bobby Fischer as a gift for her guardian. This is most likely an inside joke, as screenwriter Steven Zaillian also wrote and directed the film *Searching for Bobby Fischer*.

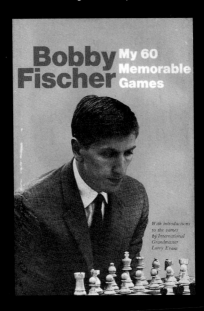

Fig I. *Blow-Up*, Michelangelo Antonioni, 1966 [Still]

Reconstructing photos of a parade as part of their investigation, Mikael and Lisbeth could be in a millennial remake of Michaelangelo Antonioni's Mod landmark.

Fig J. *Blade Runner*, Ridley Scott, 1982

When Lisbeth takes revenge on her court-appointed guardian, she's made up to resemble Daryl Hannah's Replicant Pris.

WRITER Steven Zaillian
CINEMATOGRAPHER Jeff Cronenweth
EDITORS Kirk Baxter, Angus Wall

BUDGET $90 million
BOX OFFICE $232.6 million

LENGTH 158 min

TITLE SEQUENCE
RANDY SHARP

< *Gone Girl*'s credits flash
  by with unexpected speed
  over shots of an empty,
  underpopulated town with
  plenty of places to hide
  (or be lost); an unnerving
  overture for a chronicle
  of a disappearance.

5.2
GONE GIRL

Meet Cute: Asked about herself by a handsome stranger at an upscale New York City house party Amy Elliot proffers three possible backstories: "(A) I'm an award-winning scrimshander; (B) I'm a moderately influential warlord; (C) I write personality quizzes for magazines."

The correct choice is the last one, but only by a matter of degrees; over the course of *Gone Girl*, Amy will display artisanal and combat skills commensurate with her offhandedly phony alter egos. She will also inhabit a variety of physical, behavioral and literary disguises or aliases: Amazing Amy; Diary Amy; Abducted Amy; Cool Girl; America's Sweetheart; "crazy fucking bitch"; suicidal Ophelia; bloody succubus; Virgin Mary. Rosamund Pike's Oscar-nominated performance as a woman compelled and capable of self-renovation propels David Fincher's eleventh feature through the preposterous implausibilities of its plot; Amy's changeability complicates the answer to the deceptively simple query asked at the outset by her suitor: "Who are you?"

What is *Gone Girl*? If *The Girl with the Dragon Tattoo* was a combination cover version-slash-greatest hits album, its follow-up is something headier and less easily pegged: a simulacrum of a skilfully scrimshawed thriller, a multiple-choice test made up entirely of trick questions. Gillian Flynn's 2012 novel emphasizes Amy's riddling nature, and variations on the final-exam format were prevalent in

the book's reception, as critics struggled to parse a book determined to preemptively corner every argument about its contents. In *Vulture*, Amanda Dobbins wondered whether *Gone Girl* was "(A) a gothic portrait of marriage; (B) a confession of a mythically unstable woman; (C) a misandrist revenge fantasy; or (D) a misogynistic summary of all the ways that a woman can falsely accuse a man."

Even more than *The Girl with the Dragon Tattoo*, *Gone Girl* came with talking points attached. A former writer for *Entertainment Weekly* whose first two novels, *Sharp Objects* and *Dark Places*, had featured deeply flawed, self-destructive female protagonists embroiled in Midwestern Gothic plots, Flynn was praised in the *New York Times* for channelling the "discreet malice" of Patricia Highsmith, whose 1954 novel *The Blunderer*, in which a cheating husband fantasizes about murdering his clingy, neurotic wife and ends up being investigated after she winds up dead, offers a possible model for *Gone Girl*'s plot.

A high priestess of pulp, Highsmith's criss-crossing thrillers were couched in cynical class commentary; Flynn's recession-struck urban professionals bristle against their forced relocation to the great state of Missouri, but the novel's hook—taken line and sinker by the commentariat

1.

and fifteen million readers—was barbed with questionable gender politics. In an interview with the *Guardian*, the author responded to accusations that *Gone Girl* and its multiple-choice-test of a heroine were "bad for feminism." "The one thing that really frustrates me," she said, "is this idea that women are innately good, innately nurturing. To me, that puts a very, very small window on what feminism is. For me, it's also the ability to have women who are bad characters . . . there's still a big pushback against the idea that women can be just pragmatically evil."

Pushback—with extreme prejudice—is where *Gone Girl* locates its sense of thrust, and also literary history. Five decades after Betty Friedan's *The Feminine Mystique* pulled back the veil on "a problem that [had] no name"—the stifled frustration

of American women contemplating the sources of their fulfillment, or lack thereof—Amy Dunne's brand of "evil" pragmatism struck a cultural chord. After discovering that her husband Nick has been cheating on her with one of his students, Amy stages a murder scene at their home and disappears; after a period of absence during which she and Nick both go through the wringer, she returns to clear his name and unofficially renew their vows, leveraging her newfound celebrity status as a loveable survivor to keep him from revealing her deception.

Well-bred, preternaturally poised and surpassingly insecure beneath her queen-WASP facade, Amy is a poster girl for the idea of having—and being—it all: victim; manipulator; kept woman; gone girl. Flynn's device of having the character narrate her own treachery directly through a series of journal entries recalls the epistolary style of seminal second-wave feminist texts like Sylvia Plath's *The Bell Jar* and Sue Kaufman's *Diary of a Mad Housewife*, novels that critic Réka Szarvas notes dramatize the same intimate, domestic psychodramas probed in Friedan's non-fiction study—"the 'vicious circle' [of] domestic life."

Viciousness is prevalent and multidirectional in *Gone Girl*, and Fincher's movie—written by Flynn herself—stays faithful to the book's free-floating misanthropy. By doubling down on the attraction to tacky paperbacks that drew him to *The Girl with the Dragon Tattoo*, Fincher was once again open to criticisms of bad taste, but Flynn's book is a wryer and more playful piece of work than Larsson's distended penny-dreadful—and an even better fit for the filmmaker's highly ironized sensibility. Instead of trash gussied up as social commentary, *Gone Girl* is social satire slumming as trash. Fincher's direction—speedy, fluid, and haughtily removed—duly places the action in scare quotes. There is no need for comic relief in *Gone Girl* because it's been fully torqued in the direction of farce. In her *London Review of Books* essay "Laughing at *Gone Girl*," mystery novelist Steph Cha recalls watching the film in a full theater, where "each new twist generated a substantial amount of communal laughter . . . the film sprawled out of darkness into the realm of the absurd." "[*Gone Girl*'s] structure of two halves . . . is perfectly suited to its actual genre," observed the *New Statesman*'s Philippa Snow, "which is arguably not that of the thriller, but of the marriage or re-marriage comedy."

The comedy of remarriage has a simple structure, mapped out by critic Stanley Cavell in his 1981 book *Pursuits of Happiness*,

1. Fincher has downplayed the significance of the Mastermind board game in *Gone Girl*'s opening scene but it nevertheless shades our initial perceptions of Nick (though Amy is the story's true mastermind).

2. The spectre of Amy's kid-lit alter ego hangs over her every move; she resents her parents for fictionalizing (and "improving") her childhood while still straining to live up to that pure, idealized image of "Amazing" Amy.

which takes off from the idea that the screwball farces of the 1930s and '40s were "fairy tales for the Depression"—escapist love affairs pairing glamorous movie stars for an exhausted, appreciative, populist audience. The films analyzed in *Pursuits of Happiness* typically feature a couple that is married and gets divorced either before the beginning of the film or during the film only to remarry at the end, achieving in the process not only "genuine forgiveness" of past slights but what Cavell calls a "reconciliation so profound as to require the metamorphosis of death and revival." In its A-list casting, anxious economic subtext and mock-resurrection imagery, *Gone Girl* fits as snugly into Cavell's scheme as any American studio movie of the twenty-first century; it's a mordant update of a vintage tradition.

Talking to *Film Comment* in 2014, Fincher referred to *Gone Girl* as "high seriousness in little dishes of candy." In what may be the film's funniest sequence, Ben Affleck gets pelted with Gummi Bears. Nick Dunne—Amy's one-time house-party suitor and eventual husband—stands accused in the court of public opinion for murdering and disappearing his wife. His presumed guilt is a matter of circumstantial evidence planted by Amy but also his own lack of media savvy. The ex-big-man-on-campus has stupidly allowed himself to be photographed several times during the search for Amy flashing the dopey, shame-faced grin of a frat boy; in lieu of an alibi, he needs an extreme makeover. "Every time you look smug, or annoyed, or tense," says his attorney Tanner Bolt (Tyler Perry), "I'm gonna hit you with a Gummi Bear." "I didn't kill my wife," Nick insists. His eyes are too wide, his voice too intense. Ping. Try again.

Gone Girl's Gummi Bear interlude functions, (A) as a rib on Affleck's somewhat undeserved reputation as a "bad" actor, as well as his long-standing status as tabloid and social media pariah with a high-profile love life; (B) as an acknowledgment of Fincher's own mythos as a directorial taskmaster; (C) as an encapsulation of the movie's very particular, pressurized tone, which integrates smugness, annoyance and tension on a subatomic level; and (D) as an illustration of the material's endlessly rich theme of authenticity subordinated, filtered and metamorphized by media perception. Nick's dressing room hot seat faces a vanity ringed by halogen lights; the composition obliges us to see two Afflecks acting side-by-side. Popping flashbulbs, jutting microphones, and parked news vans dot the film's mise-en-scène; if *The Girl with*

the Dragon Tattoo romanticized muckraking as a check against corporate power, *Gone Girl* perceives the cable-news landscape as a web strung together from opportunism, abasement, and exploitation, and whose puppet masters suffer no consequences for errors of judgment.

#

Released in October of 2014, *Gone Girl* arrived coated in its own carefully applied tarnish. Decked out with brutal violence (including a throat-slitting by boxcutter) and full-frontal nudity (including two shots of male genitalia), here was an awards-season movie too extreme for awards season, its selection as the Opening Night Gala for the New York Film Festival notwithstanding. Such prestige signifers differentiated *Gone Girl* from *The Girl with the Dragon Tattoo*, which didn't gross enough money to guarantee a sequel but was still successful enough to land Fincher a $60 million budget for a stand-alone, R-rated genre movie with no franchise potential. (The book had originally been optioned as a star vehicle for Reese Witherspoon, who has a producer's credit.)

On *Dragon Tattoo*, Fincher found a way into (if not out of) the material by forging an alignment with an unconventional, incorruptible heroine and riding it through the turns of the plot. *Gone Girl* is similarly set in a world of Men Who Hate Women, but Amy navigates her environment with a demagnetized moral compass, and she's less of an obvious behavioural outlier than Lisbeth Salander. Her looks and heritage are more reminiscent of Harriet Fucking Vanger, herself a gone girl, albeit one whose reasons for fleeing are rendered fully sympathetically. Amy's appeal to Fincher lies primarily in her sense of flourish: the director loves aesthetes, micromanagers and truth-tellers, and he finds some mixture of the three in a character who's as adaptable as Ellen Ripley or Meg Altman with the showmanship of Tyler Durden, the Zodiac or John Doe.

If the ostensible exploitation-flick nadir of *The Girl with the Dragon Tattoo* was Lisbeth videotaping her own sexual assault as a means of entrapping her abuser, *Gone Girl* peaks—or flatlines—when Amy violates herself with a wine bottle and then pantomimes the aftermath of a non-existent rape for a security camera. Her

2.

ersatz abjection is not simply a provocation or a plot point; like so many things in this perspective-obsessed movie, it's about what a particular character is choosing to show, and to whom, and why. "There is a specter haunting *Gone Girl*," wrote Kent Jones in *Film Comment*, who said that that the film had "the feel of science fiction set in an instantly recognizable present," before zeroing in on the ghost in the machine: "Once Amy's disappearance is announced," [the film's] mood grows into something coarser, eerier, and more subtly pervasive . . . [*Gone Girl*] becomes a hyper-acute rendering of a world filled with people forever checking and re-checking their own media-ready self-presentations, acting on their every emotional impulse and mortally afraid of being disliked."

"They love you," Margot reassures her brother, checking her social media feeds after his triumphant interview with Sela Ward's Katie Couric-ish Sharon Schreiber, which bears the fruits of Tanner's Gummi Bear assault. Played humorously by Perry as a thoroughbred clotheshorse with deliberate notes of Christopher Darden and Johnny Cochran—allusions that tease out the plot's deracinated O. J. Simpson trial riff—Tanner is as much a creature of the 24-hour news cycle as the disgraced men he defends in his role as the self-described "Patron Saint of Wife Killers." He's a frequent guest on *Ellen Abbott Live*, a sensationalistic current-affairs talk show whose namesake (Missi Pyle, impersonating Megyn Kelly by way of Nancy Grace) fans the flames of public outrage in whatever direction the wind is blowing. Even further out on the periphery, we get characters determined to actualize Tanner's mandate to "realign public perception"; introduced spilling out of her tank top during a late-night tryst, Nick's underage mistress Andie (Emily Ratajkowski) piously buttons up during a press conference in which she reveals her affair. ("Why is she dressed like a nun?" snarls Amy of a woman she'd referred to as "the girl with the giant, cum-on-me tits.") Standing in between blow-up photos of their missing daughter, Rand and Marybeth Dunne (David Clennon and Lisa Barnes), shamelessly plug a fundraising website that links back to their own series of childrens' books; magnanimity and grief vie with self-promotion in Marybeth's deliberate pronunciation of "www.findamazingamy.com."

"[The book] talked about narcissism in a really interesting way," Fincher told *Time Out* in 2014. "The way we concoct not only an ideal version of ourselves in the hope of seducing a mate, but in hopes of seducing someone who is probably doing the same thing." Describing Flynn's novel as "elaborately marbled"—a diplomatic way of noting its epic length—Fincher praised the writer for her willingness to hone the script's focus and "slaughter her darlings" during an exhaustive back-and-forth streamlining process. An *Entertainment Weekly* story published on the eve of *Girl*'s release hinted at creative tensions regarding the movie's ending, but both Fincher and Flynn—who received sole WGA credit—stressed that they were on the same wavelength throughout. "As someone who covered movies for many years, I know that most of the time it doesn't turn out so well for the original author," Flynn said in an interview with the *Kansas City Star*. "What was different this time around was that I had a great director who really liked the book and didn't want to turn it into something other than what it already was."

Gone Girl preserves Flynn's he-said/she-said structure, which alternates between chapters written by Nick in the present tense—where he insists on his innocence and tries to outpace a police investigation in which he is the only suspect—and ones written by Amy. The two voices are vivid and distinct: Nick is sullen and judgemental—a "righteous ball of hate"—while Amy mitigates cynicism with a precious, preening self-regard. "I am fat with love! Husky with ardor!" she crows in

one of the first journal entries chronicling her relationship with Nick, a love-at-first-sight pairing that, in her telling, descends into paranoia and threats of violence. "This man I love may kill me," she writes in her final missive, after which it's revealed that the diaries—and the vast majority of what they reveal about the Dunnes' marriage—are fabrications. "I'm so much happier now that I'm dead," Amy crows, rejoining the narrative in real time, speaking not from beyond the grave but a campground in the Ozarks where she'd been hiding out under an assumed identity. Amy's frame-up of Nick is supposed to build to a suicidal coup

3. Amy's plan originally involves killing herself, and *Gone Girl*'s lone subjective image illustrates her self-pitying fantasy of a watery grave.

4-9. "And he thought he was the writer:" righteous vengeance and the mind-numbing boredom of a woman who feels ignored at every turn combine in Amy's meticulously forged diary entries, which not only fabricate her relationship with Nick but become a more interesting (and dramatic) substitute for the life she's barely living.

3.

4.

5.

6.

7.

8.

9.

de grâce, but she decides that living well is the best revenge until she's waylaid by a pair of strangers who see through her Southern-fried disguise and snatch her fanny pack of hoarded cash. Presumed dead and facing limited options, the trust-fund striver is suddenly in exile on the wrong side of the tracks, and must find her way back—to life, (economic) liberty and the pursuit of happiness—with Nick, whether he likes it or not.

Flynn's big twist is a nifty bit of engineering, short-circuiting and rerouting our sympathies in a book defined by the self-serving unreliability of two professional scribes. Both Nick and Amy have an elastic relationship to the truth; where they are decidedly unequal is in their ability to draw the cord taut. The same qualities that make Nick a passable, if garden-variety, liar in his personal life—a hangdog cheater harboring seething fantasies about divorce or worse—render him publicly untrustworthy, even when, as in his practiced protestations to Tanner, he's speaking the truth from behind what Amy refers to during their first date as a "very villainous chin." The fabulism practiced in print and in person by his wife is something else, and of an exponentially higher calibre than Nick's sloppy concealment. When Amy journals, she breaks the gendered covenant of "confessional" writing, which assumes that female authors should dutifully perform autobiography; freely mixing truth and lies and adjusting the ratio to suit her purposes, she displays the pervasive, persuasive, detail-oriented dissembling of a natural-born manipulator.

Or a Mastermind. Just after *Gone Girl*'s opening credits, we see Nick trudging through his less-than-picaresque hometown hamlet of North Carthage carrying a battered, telltale board-game box under his arm. Devised in 1970 by an Israeli postmaster and telecommunications expert named Mordecai Meirowitz, Mastermind is a game for two players, designated respectively as the codemaker and the codebreaker; the goal is for the latter to discern and identify the surreptitious patterning of colored pegs on a game board. Given Fincher's fascination with code-making and breaking—from *Se7en* to *The Game* to *Zodiac* to *The Girl with the Dragon Tattoo*—and the extent to which *Gone Girl* is a narrative about pattern recognition, the Mastermind box is as legible a directorial self-reference as Tanner Bolt's Pavlovian gambit. Protesting too much in an interview with *IndieWire*, Fincher claimed that "it was the only [game] we could legally clear . . . red herrings are fun but they are

10.

also irritating and distracting." Indeed they are: When Nick places Mastermind on the shelf at the bar he owns with his twin sister Margo (Carrie Coon), it slots alongside Let's Make a Deal, Emergency, and The Game of Life, three living room favorites that could serve as alternate monikers for the movie we're watching. "There's no significance at all," Fincher added. It's enough to make you reach for the Gummi bears.

#

Gone Girl is a many-splendored thing—fun, irritating, and distracting; tense, smug, and annoying—but above all, it's a movie made by a mastermind of self-awareness, a filmmaker who has always conferred considerable significance on games and game-playing, code-making and code-breaking. Nick relates his marital problems to Margo over The Game of Life and is shown zoning out to a Call of Duty-style Xbox title ("I just felt like shooting a lot of people"). Amy's obsessive ex Desi—Neil Patrick Harris—who comes to her aid after she's been robbed and offers her safe harbor in his fortified, secluded lair in the hopes of rekindling their relationship, rhapsodizes about a potential night of "octopus and Scrabble." Margo's nickname, "Go," refers to an abstract strategy game that turns a grid into contested territory, and Gone Girl's parade of reversals and turn-based approach to storytelling create the impression of a live-action board game,

one whose rules, boundaries, and objectives are inscribed within the mise-en-scène. In The New Yorker, Joshua Rothman wrote that Gone Girl "crosses the thin line that divides genre fiction from postmodern fiction . . . it is decisively unreal, in the manner of Fight Club—a movie in which the actual and the symbolic occupy the same slice of reality."

Rothman's point is apt. More than any of Fincher's films after Fight Club, Gone Girl presents a satirical panorama, calling attention to its own construction and the constructedness of the characters and situations therein. A website glimpsed for perhaps one second in the middle of the quick-cut, five-minute montage that visualizes Amy's vituperative "Cool Girl" rant—a hyper-articulate indictment of pre-programmed, performative femininity positioned by Flynn as the book's rhetorical coup—scribbles semiotic shorthand in the margins of the monologue. It reads, simply, "Lifestyle Robots."

The Lifestyle Robot that Amy orders for Nick to establish his wasteful spending practices as part of the case for the prosecution is an animatronic dog, which becomes his soulless spirit animal as surely as the Dunnes' fickle housecat—shown skulking around the edges of the action—is Amy's. The incriminating items have been stashed in Margot's woodshed, which Fincher transforms into a veritable wunderkammer of branding: there's even a flatscreen television bearing the Sony

logo, a nod to the director's working relationship with the studio-slash-electronics-conglomerate.

Logos pop off the screen in Gone Girl with the same Godardian playfulness as Fight Club's Starbucks-logo-space station or walk-through IKEA catalogue. Rooting around for supplies at Big Lots, Amy buys designer sheets inscribed with "Rampage." The old mystery-movie cliché that nothing is as it seems gets turned on its head: Everything here is exactly as advertised, and maybe even more so. "We have our first clue," says a cop in Nick's kitchen, brandishing an envelope (left, of course, by Amy) reading "Clue #1." "Sometime around the point that the lead detective investigating Amy's disappearance compliments the name of Nick's bar (The Bar) as 'very meta,'" wrote Nick Pinkerton in Bombast in 2014, "I decided I'd had just about enough of exemplification-as-exoneration."

Pinkerton's put-down prods Rothman's observation about Gone Girl's deliberate artificiality, characterizing it as a bug rather than a feature. It's a fair assessment of how Fincher's game-playing side, left unchecked, can manifest its own form of smug, tense, annoyance, but there's a difference between revelling in meta-ness and yoking it to a specific milieu or moment. The "very meta" line—spoken onscreen by Detective Rhonda Boney (Kim Dickens), the film's designated scion of plain-talking honesty and one of Fincher's sharpest sleuths—is modified from

Nick's explanation in the book that "people will think [he's] ironic instead of creatively bankrupt." Put-ons abound at every level of *Gone Girl*'s visual environment, with its sprinkling of punchable hipsters and their paraphernalia (i.e. Margot's "Protect Your Nuts" T-shirt or a hideous tuxedo T-shirt glimpsed during a party scene). In this irony-poisoned universe, where else would aspiring Lifestyle Robots go to drink but a place called The Bar?

The impassive, all-caps signage of Nick's establishment is one of several outstanding bits of production design by Donald Graham Burt, and the location serves as background for the film's emotional pivot point—a flashback to Amy's discovery of Nick's infidelity. This episode is distinguished as an "authentic" flashback, as opposed to the miniature fictions in which Amy "forged the man of her dreams." The snowflakes falling around Nick and Andie as they clinch in the dark outside The Bar rhyme with another one of Amy's "true" memories: A walk with Nick on their first night together past a bakery truck's "sugar storm," which dusts the happy couple and sweetens their first kiss.

The "sugar storm" and the scene at the Bar are shot, edited and scored so similarly that Amy's retelling of the former slips over the latter like a palimpsest: In both memories, Nick uses two fingers to wipe his lover's lips clean, a gesture that sours Amy's sugar-coated recollection. "He did the exact same thing with *her*," Amy tells her campground neighbor Greta (Lola Kirke), genuine sadness cutting through her husky, faux N'awlins accent. Pike's acting in *Gone*

11.

Girl is consistently poker faced (and rarely does anyone call her bluff) but her stricken reaction shot upon seeing Nick and Andie replaying a moment that Amy believed belonged to her alone contextualizes the character's subsequent machinations more powerfully than the scorched-earth, confessional rhetoric of the "Cool Girl" speech. Pike's avid, reddened eyes take *Gone Girl* out of scare quotes; the scene's distanced sightlines and swirling CGI snow recall Lisbeth Salander silently watching Mikael and Erika departing arm-in-arm

from the Millennium office at the end of *The Girl with the Dragon Tattoo*.

Larsson's citation of Pippi Longstocking as the inspiration for Lisbeth is interesting in light of *Gone Girl*'s pairing of Amy with her own fictional kid-lit alter ego "Amazing Amy"—a blonde, prepubescent overachiever created and marketed into a perennially profitable property by child psychologists Rand and Marybeth. (The line-drawn cover art and paraphernalia help further fill out the movie's media landscape; *Gone Girl*'s Blu-ray came with an *Amazing Amy* book.) *Amazing Amy* represents something distinct from Pippi's plucky, principled non-conformity—an aspirational (and all-American) exceptionalism somewhere between Barbie and Beverley Cleary. The idea that Type-A Amy grew up in the shadow of her own unblemished, universally beloved doppelganger explains her frustrated literary ambitions as well her competitive streak. "Your parents literally plagiarized your childhood," Nick says ruefully during the splashy launch party for *Amazing Amy*

12.

and the Big Day, a presumable series capper in which the grown-up protagonist gets married (a development that prompts Nick's own on-the-spot proposal). "No," Amy replies. "They improved on it, and peddled it to the masses," with practiced, sarcastic resignation at being "regular, flawed *real* Amy"—as opposed to "perfect, brilliant, Amazing Amy."

Gone Girl makes it clear that Amy's compulsion to control the narrative of her life—and the lives of those around her—is a byproduct of having her story continually hijacked: by her parents' well-meaning, self-enriching exploitation; by Nick's cheating and taking her for granted; and even by the dubious white knight Desi, who rescues Amy only to passive-aggressively bribe her into sexual servitude. "I'm not going to force myself on you" he says, but Amy—who surely saw this coming—looks more annoyed than afraid. (The casting of Harris as a beta-male with a control fetish is wittily double edged, riffing on his knowingly obnoxious ladies man character on the CBS sitcom *How I Met Your Mother*.)

10. A perfect visual for a sugar-coated romance: Passing by a bakery early on in their courtship, Nick and Amy find themselves unexpectedly dusted. One way to trace *Gone Girl*'s arc is as a journey from sweetness to bitterness, as the "sugar storm" dissipates and fades into memory.

11. "I'm Punch"; discovering his marionette doppelganger in Amy's cache of presents, Nick realizes the depth of her puppet-master manipulation.

12. Lifestyle Robots: The high-end items Amy secretly purchases to implicate Nick in her murder are emblems of *Gone Girl*'s consumerist critique.

13. As Amy hits the road in a car she bought with her own money, the terse, pent-up images of the film's first half give way to an ecstatic tableau of sun-dappled liberation—with just a tiny pinprick of blood to evidence Amy's self-mutilating sacrifice in the name of vengeance and freedom.

14.

The not-so-hidden subtext of the Cool Girl rant, which is ostensibly about the speaker's distance from and contempt for women who willingly turn themselves into fetish objects for presumptuous unappreciative partners, is Amy's shame at her own complicity in the cycle. The way she asserts herself is by disappearing, transforming from an afterthought to a structuring absence; to be "gone" is not to be dead, but emancipated. Amy's flight from New Carthage is heralded by a brief, ecstatic shot of a feather-topped pen—Diary Amy's mightier-than-the-sword weapon of choice—flying out of a car window.

The broad comedy of Amy's stint as the Cheezie-eating, pool-lounging, bottle-brunette Nancy reverses Lisbeth's glamorous blondes-have-more-fun excursion in *The Girl with the Dragon Tattoo*. Ducking out of her bungalow for a smoke after watching Nick skewered by Ellen Abbott, Amy-as-Nancy leaps and kicks up her heels—dancing like nobody's watching. The Post-It notes marking different dates in Amy's calendar with the prompt "Kill Self?" (etched in perfect pink penmanship) point towards the orgiastic, negation-in-completion sought by John Doe and other suicidal Fincher protagonists; combined with the eerie image of the dead Amy "floating down amongst all the other abused, unwanted, inconvenient women"—and Nancy's Southern accent—these evoke the depressive Edna Pontellier in Kate Chopin's *The Awakening*, but Amy makes a different choice. When she removes those morbid Post-Its once and for all, it's weirdly exhilarating, initiating a wild final section of fight and flight scenarios driven by Amy's survival instincts.

Fincher said that he picked Pike to play Amy because while he'd always liked her in movies, he "didn't really know her"—as opposed to Affleck, whose casting as a man sweating in the glare of the media spotlight possesses an even greater metafictional potency than the director's use of Michael Douglas in *The Game* or Brad Pitt in *Fight Club*. Supposedly, Pitt was offered the part first; he's a more versatile actor than Affleck but, in this case, the latter's slightly lachrymose charisma—a clenched agony that makes him uniquely meme-able among male stars of his generation—is perfect. (The much-circulated paparazzi shots of Affleck staring out to sea, his back marked by large scale body art of a phoenix rising from the ashes, made him a Twitter punchline—the Boy with the Dragon Tattoo.) If Pike's performance is a marvel of shape-shifting inventiveness—as if Amy was a liquid metal Lady Terminator—Affleck carves Nick in granite. He's slow-moving, slouchy, and indignant behind that "villainous chin," and when he thoughtlessly poses for a selfie with a well-wisher, it's like somebody's flipped a switch. The grin is put-on, automatic, and doesn't reach his eyes. "I flipped through Google Images and found about fifty shots of Affleck giving that kind of smile in public situations," Fincher told Vanity Fair. "You look at them and know he's trying to make people comfortable in the moment, but by doing that he's making himself vulnerable to people having other perceptions about him."

Supposedly, Affleck objected to two things during the shooting of *Gone Girl*: wearing a New York Yankees cap for a scene where Nick tries to evade recognition at an airport (the lifelong Red Sox fan ultimately agreed to model a Mets hat) and delivering the line, "I'm so sick of being picked apart by women." The actor's reservations may have had to do with his own highly publicized love life; that aside, the dialogue draws a bead on how, even with Amy out of the picture, *Gone Girl* is replete with needy, grabby, and otherwise unflatteringly depicted females: disingenuous media mavens like Elizabeth Abbott and Susan Schreiber; disdainful mothers-in-law; slatternly baby-baking neighbours; unscrupulous groupies slinging "chicken frito pie"; self-deluding Cool Girls; flip-flop wearing grifters.

15.

14. *Gone Girl*'s most deliberately shocking set piece plays out as a hybrid parody of porno and giallo, with a bloody money shot that drenches Amy in Deep Red.

15. Tanner Bolt's taskmaster approach to preparing Nick for his media appearance could be taken as a joke on Fincher's directorial reputation: Multiple takes, over and over, until he gets it right (or else he gets pelted with a Gummi Bear).

When Margo discovers Nick's affair with Andie, she reacts like a jilted lover, and she doesn't seem to have a life outside her brother's embroilment, leaving the siblings open to whispers of "twincest." (The "Protect Your Nuts" T-shirt is like free advice to her twin.) Even Dickens's level-headed Detective Boney views Nick through a half-wary, half-desirous lens. Not since *Basic Instinct* (also about a guy named Nick) has a Hitchcock pastiche thrown up such multi-directionally threatening femininity. Like Paul Verhoeven, whose filmography is crammed with inscrutable, dangerous, rootable women—from Sharon Stone in *Basic Instinct* and Elizabeth Berkeley in *Showgirls* to Isabelle Huppert in *Elle* (2016), another limber exercise in exemplification-as-exoneration—Flynn and Fincher play up their insidious ideology until it flies over the top. Once there, it's rendered that absurd, and cathartically so at that.

That's the idea, anyway. *Gone Girl* the movie doesn't go as hard on Nick as the book, with its dueling, contradictory subjectivities. Because Fincher stays above the fray, he never gets inside the seething rage and inherited woman-hate that informed Flynn's original version of the

16.

character; the script carefully offloads several objectionable zingers to Margo, who deems her sister-in-law a "crazy fucking bitch" and suggests that an appropriate present for her fifth wedding anniversary would be for her brother to "take [his] penis and smack [her] in the face with it . . .' There's some wood for you, bitch!" Affleck is surely credible as an entitled, paranoid lummox and a sexual opportunist (he's very funny when Nick is shushing Andie during a late-night, living-room tryst at Margot's house) but he doesn't convince as a possible wife killer, underselling the threat embedded in Flynn's opening voice-over: "When I think of my wife, I always think of the back of her head. I picture cracking her lovely skull, unspooling her brain, trying to get answers." As Affleck speaks, we get a head-on close-up of Pike, head tossed affectionately or contemptuously over bare shoulders, eyes lowered and opaque.

Gone Girl begins and ends with this same composition, which calls back subliminally to *Se7en*'s blonde-head-in-a-box denouement and the CGI head trip of *Fight Club*, but mostly evokes Stanley Kubrick and his trademark dialectic of fear and desire. The "Kubrick Stare" is usually associated with the director's antisocial men, suturing the audience in a form of vicarious complicity: Think of Malcolm McDowell's sociopathic Alex DeLarge gazing out from his booth at the Korova Milk Bar in *A Clockwork Orange*, or Private Pyle (Vincent D'Onofrio) putting his abusive C.O. in his murderous sights in *Full Metal Jacket*. *Gone Girl*'s emblem is closer to the iconic shot of Kidman's Alice Harford in *Eyes Wide Shut*, grinning at her husband (and us) from behind lowered glasses—a tousled, teasing, barely domesticated Sphinx.

The plot of *Eyes Wide Shut* is catalyzed by Alice unexpectedly recounting her fantasies to Tom Cruise's Bill, keying jealous anxieties that unfold as a phantasmagorical "dream story" set, at least partially, inside his head. *Gone Girl* unspools its characters' brains (Nick's and Amy's both) without sacrificing objectivity: Fincher's style remains realistic while admitting some judicious expressionism. The small-town trappings of New Carthage (its name an allusion to a sacked Roman city) are fully recognizable until they're not. A visit to a deserted shopping complex populated by meth addicts reveals Stygian depths, symbolized by a massive downward escalator. A pullback on a highway-side filling station frames a chasmic expanse prowled by monstrous tanker trucks. The threatening vibe of these spaces is the terror of flyover country as experienced by city mice, and Amy's masquerade as Nancy is laced with a condescension that's called out by Greta after she and her drawling boyfriend Jeff (Boyd Holbrook) shake down the impostor in their white-trash midst. "There's worse people out there than us," Greta shrugs as she departs, a mock apology that boomerangs back on Amy's disingenuous class tourism. Greta's ability to see through Amy's slumming disguise suggests that her eyes are wide open even as she's shown to be as susceptible as anybody else to Amy's form of media brainwashing: "Amen," she hollers after Ellen Abbott reminds the viewers at home following the Nick Dunne saga that Missouri has the death penalty.

Pike's comic high point comes when Amy watches Nick's Sharon Schreiber interview while spooning creme caramel into her mouth, slack-jawed and half-hypnotized as she sees exactly what she wants to see—Nick taking it right on the villainous chin about his failures. "I've taken myself to the woodshed for how I've treated you," he says, looking directly into the lens—now fully playing the same game of Mastermind as his wife and effectively telling her "no harm, no foul." Fincher cross-cuts between Nick and Margot and Desi and Amy watching the show, as if enfolded into the movie's own audience; the crucial multiple-choice question is whether Amy—who no longer wants to kill herself but is also not amenable to living under Desi's well-manicured thumb—is ultimately entranced by the medium, the message, or something else. "This is the greatest joke of all," writes Kiva Reardon. "The chink in this clever woman's armor is love . . . How could it not be? Raised on fairy tale rom-coms, as we are, to hold love and marriage as the be all and end all . . . romantic love shackles women to the narrow part of playing wife . . . [those] who take Amy's return home to Nick as proof of her intellectual deficiency fail to see the bigger picture: Love doesn't make us do crazy things, it's the pressure to find and keep love—and thus happiness, stability, respectability—that does."

Amy's love is strong—strong enough that after performing captivity and abuse for Desi's omnipresent security cameras, she offs her host in a stunningly gory sex-and-violence set piece that brings all of *Gone Girl*'s latent, lurking violence to the surface. The film's inventory of playful props includes a pair of heavy, oaken Punch and Judy dolls gifted to Nick by Amy for their fifth anniversary—"there's some wood for you, bitch"—and besides fitting in with the overall game-playing motif, they suggest a way of watching the movie: As a a full-contact battle between fully poseable archetypes. Amy's transformation mid-coitus into a killer casts her as Punch-as-Judy, a kept woman lashing out at an ineffectual Bluebeard. The scene is scored by Trent Reznor and Atticus Ross like a sine-wave, and edited in pulsating flashes by Kirk Baxter; Jeff Cronenweth splatters the antiseptic bedchamber in the deep-red palette of a *giallo*. Look at all that passion all over the wall, and also those high-thread count sheets (remember that the brand is Rampage). The conflation of Desi's arterial spray with a pornographic money shot, with Amy drenched in blood, is an example of Fincher exercising his bad-boy side; the visual allusion to *Carrie* (1976) and its all-annihilating prom queen namesake keeps things very meta.

From there, *Gone Girl* waves goodbye to traditional realism, with Amy arriving on Nick's doorstep after driving interstate all night in her stained nightgown, stumbling up the driveway and finally swooning into his arms. Even as she feigns unconsciousness, she has the upper hand. As Nick and Amy are joined in front of a throng of reporters, we realize that this is the first time that they're truly occupying the same space, finally liberated from flashbacks and half-truths. A shot from the perspective of the Dunnes' front hallway after they've returned home from the hospital—where Amy's story of being abducted and imprisoned by Desi convinces everyone that it has to—closes the door on their public show but only briefly.

It's in the space between Amy's very public resurrection and the return of prying eyes to her household that *Gone Girl* evokes a pop-Buñuelian stasis; now safely housebound after a month in the public, Nick exists at the mercy of an exterminating angel. After keeping its stars separate for most of its running time, *Gone Girl* makes an eerie game out of their sudden proximity and intimacy, starting with a mock-baptismal that moves from *Carrie* to *Psycho*, reimagining Janet Leigh's slashed Hitchcock blonde as a purified survivor. Amy invites Nick into the shower as she washes the blood right out of her hair, a seduction that's also a way to ensure her loving husband isn't wearing a wire. Later, she'll invite Ellen Abbott over to provide a prime-time update on their reconciliation. The host comes bearing a mechanical cat to pair with Nick's electronic dog, a peace offering to a pair of Lifestyle Robots.

"When one is in love, one always begins by deceiving one's self, and one always ends by deceiving others," writes Oscar Wilde in *The Picture of Dorian Gray*. "That is what the world calls a romance." The patent irony of *Gone Girl*'s conclusion is that after their very public trials the Dunnes are settling back into the same terse, performative groove as before, except with no illusions about each other—those are saved for Amy's adoring public, who learns via the interview with Ellen Aboot that a baby is on the way. This is Amy's final and most insidious trick: Knocking herself up with a fertility clinic sperm sample she claimed she'd destroyed. In doing so, she conjoins revenge with regeneration, an act of immaculate conception reversing *Se7en*'s climactic abortion—final move in what John Doe calls "the whole complete act." At the end of *Zodiac*, Robert Graysmith studies Arthur Leigh Allen's face as if to consider what the man in the hardware store aisle is capable of, and whether it matches up with the killer living in his mind's eye. Nick knows full well what his partner is capable of. Whether this knowledge renders him more or less equipped to deal with the situation is more uncertain. "What have we done to each other," Nick wonders over the closing close-up of Amy. "What will we do?"

What's powerful here is that any couple could pose these same questions to one another and they'd be meaningful without the generic baggage of murder and mystery. As usual, when Fincher is at his best, *Gone Girl* is airtight but also spacious, leaving plenty of room for viewers to project onto its vision of neo-bourgeois domestic bliss as an interpersonal, thermonuclear detente. Looking for a way out of this particular happily-ever-after, Nick reminds his wife that their history together is one of resentment and attempted control. Because *Gone Girl*'s final one-liner doubles as the last word on its Punch and Judy show, it's worth asking if her retort—"that's marriage"—attains the bite-size "high seriousness" alluded to by Fincher. Is it: (A) a glib commentary on monogamy; (B) a commentary on the glibness of characters who've internalized its myths; (C) a very meta critique on how those myths have been encoded into the glib romantic comedies *Gone Girl* burlesques before subjecting them to a shotgun wedding with psychological horror; or (D) a sincere case for loving compromise coming strangely from a filmmaker more typically inclined to leave his protagonists alone, bitterly nursing their untenable principles. In *Pursuits of Happiness*, Stanley Cavell describes the lovers of Howard Hawks's *His Girl Friday* (1940)—which happens to revolve around a falsely accused killer and his own private media circus—as being "just at home with one another, whether or not they can ever live under the same roof." His point is that the characters played by Cary Grant and Rosalind Russell are destined to be together despite their best efforts at pulling apart, and *Gone Girl*'s protagonists are similarly magnetized. Every codemaker needs a code breaker; in this very meta movie, playing house is no different than the real thing. Even after checkmate, the Game of Life goes on.

16. Biding her time while Nick is investigated, Amy revels in no longer having to appear "Amazing"; she dresses down to go shopping and relax by the pool, soon to experience delight after watching an episode of Ellen Abbott that seems to seal her husband's fate as a wife-killer.

17-19. Image is everything, and Amy understands instinctively how to present herself for the camera's eye; a swooning damsel in distress; a poised and perfect housewife; an expectant mother lapping up a nation's empathy and admiration.

17.

18.

19.

Fig A. *The Awakening*, Kate Chopin, 1899 [Novel]

Amy's suicidal ideation links her to the heroine of Kate Chopin's influential novel.

Fig B. *The Blunderer*, Patricia Highsmith, 1954 [Novel]

Gillian Flynn's novels have earned comparisons to Patricia Highsmith, and the plot of *The Blunderer*, about a man accused of killing his wife, hews close to *Gone Girl*'s plot.

Fig C. *Eyes Wide Shut*, Stanley Kubrick, 1999 [Still with Nicole Kidman]

Fincher mentioned Stanley Kubrick's valedictory drama as an inspiration during filming.

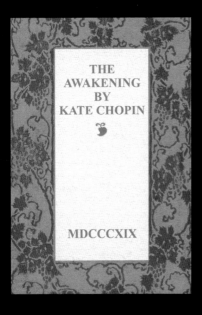

Fig F. **Johnnie Cochran**

As played by Tyler Perry, Tanner Bolt appears as an updated version of O. J. Simpson's savvy lawyer Johnnie Cochrane.

Fig G. **Nancy Grace**

The sensationalistic Court TV host is the model for *Gone Girl*'s Ellen Abbott.

Fig H. *Leave Her to Heaven*, John M. Stahl, 1945 [Film]

John M. Stahl's Technicolor thriller stars Gene Tierney as a as a beautiful sociopath who prefigures Amy Dunne.

Fig D. *Gone with the Wind*, Victor Fleming, 1939 [Still]

Amy swoons into Nick's arms Scarlett O'Hara style after returning to their home.

Fig E. *The Feminine Mystique*, Betty Friedan, 1963 [Book]

The first edition of this book paved the way for the second-wave feminist movement in the USA.

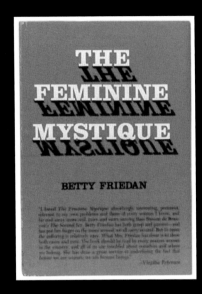

Fig I. **Beverly Cleary**

The books by the best-selling childrens' author serve as a possible template for the look and subject matter of the Amazing Amy series.

Fig J. *Carrie*, Brian De Palma, 1976 [Still with Sissy Spacek]

The image of a woman discovering the extent of her powers who coated in head-to-toe in blood is namechecked in one of *Gone Girl*'s key set pieces.

WRITER Gillian Flynn
CINEMATOGRAPHER Jeff Cronenweth
EDITORS Kirk Baxter, Jeff Cronenweth

BUDGET $61 million
BOX OFFICE $369.3 million

LENGTH 149 min

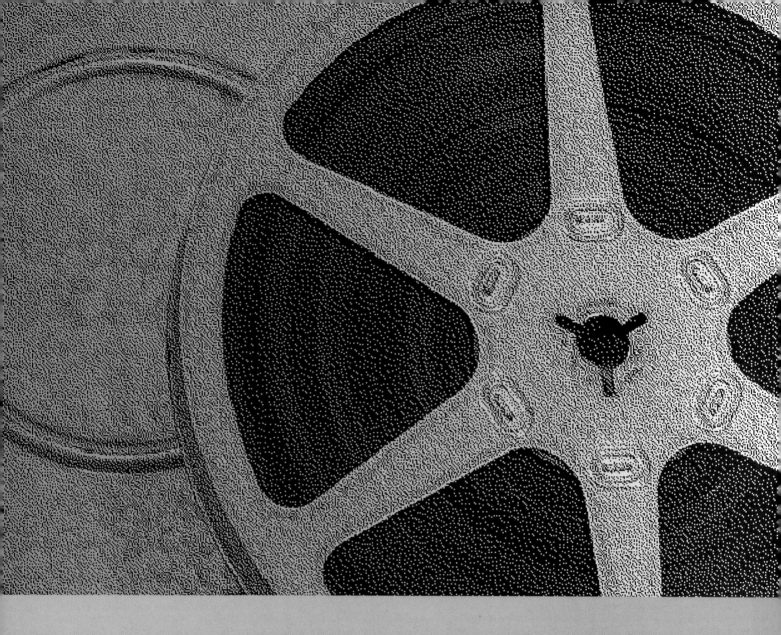

THE MAGIC OF THE MOVIES

< The CGI skies of *Mank*'s
opening titles conjure
clouds on the horizon.
They also locate us safely
outside the studio towers
of Hollywood, framing the
desert town of Victorville
as an isolated backdrop—
the topographical equivalent
of a blank page lodged in
a typewriter.

6.1
MANK

2020

Stop me if you've heard this one before. Dining in MGM's studio commissary with his younger brother Joe (Tom Pelphrey) in 1933, Gary Oldman's Herman Mankiewicz resists an offer to lend his prestige to the newly formed Screen Writers Guild: "As Groucho always said, 'never belong to any club that would have someone like you for a member.'"

In theory, it's apt that the producer of *Duck Soup* (1933) would quote history's most enduring Marxist maxim (non-Karl-division). But Groucho's elegantly self-deprecating statement actually dates to the early 1950s. So unless culture-vulture Mank has also read John Galsworthy's 1906 novel *The Forsyte Saga*, where the turn of phrase originated, his joke doesn't make such sense. Ditto the young screenwriter trying to sell a skeptical David O. Selznick on a "different kind of Paramount Picture," that's, "like *Frankenstein* and *The Wolfman* all rolled into one." The pitch takes place in 1930, a full year before Boris Karloff donned the boots and bolts for James Whale; George Waggner's *The Wolf Man*, meanwhile, was still a decade away.

The question of whether these and other anachronistic gaffes ·truly amount to a hill of beans—an expression we hear in a scene set in 1934, nine years before Rick Blaine bemoaned the problems of three little people in this crazy world—or an invitation to pedants is at the heart of wrangling with a movie that turns viewers into attributionists and sleuths. Either way

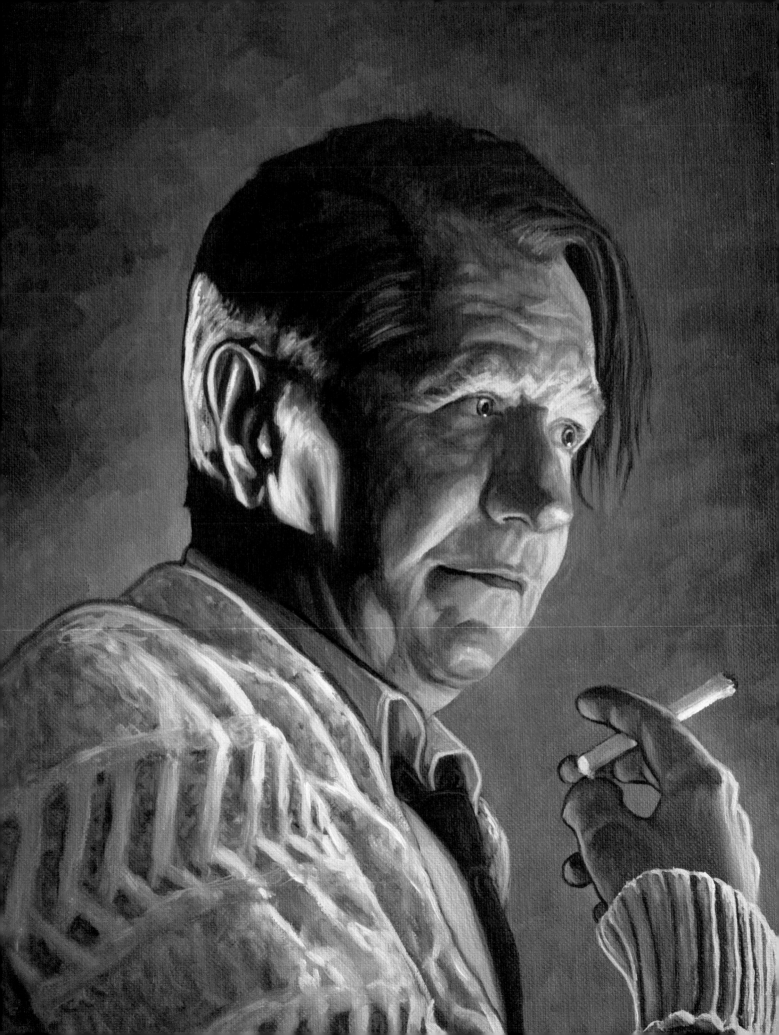

it would seem to be a losing battle on both sides. Are a few botched datelines enough to revoke a movie's artistic license? Probably not. But given that David Fincher's film wears its period references as a suit of armor—or maybe a costume-party ensemble; "come dressed as the sick soul of Old Hollywood"—it's unfortunate that they also double as its weak spots. Joel and Ethan Coen's phantasmagorical *Hail, Caesar!* (2016) deliberately fudges its backlot mythology, yet feels nevertheless like the work of genuine buffs with a stake in the period being depicted. *Mank*'s lapses suggest a Gen X director's lack of care for a bygone era, even as the movie was packaged as his most "personal" work to date.

With *The Girl with the Dragon Tattoo* and *Gone Girl*, Fincher continued his gentrification of genre cinema—an upscale trajectory that could just as easily be seen as him choosing to slum it. The guilty, principled ambivalence of a cynical pro used to going low and striving to aim higher informs *Mank*'s fictionalized biography of Herman Mankiewicz, and makes for a tidy behind-the-scenes narrative as well. Fincher's twelfth feature is a movie that no other contemporary American director (save, perhaps, for the Coens) would have even tried to make, for hire or otherwise; its relatively obscure subject matter and lavish black-and-white presentation testify to auteur *carte blanche*. The mythical art-and-commerce equation of "one for me, and one for them" sketched by Martin Scorsese in the mid-80s not-so-coincidentally tied to the production of a movie called *The Color of Money* (1986)—is usually invoked whenever a name filmmaker embarks on a self-described "passion project." The six-year gap following *Gone Girl*, during which Fincher was linked to a series of highly commercial ventures, including a remake of Hitchcock's *Strangers on a Train* (1951) featuring Ben Affleck, gives *Mank* the ring of a one-for-him proposition. The director brought the project to Netflix as part of an exclusive content deal granting him freedom of choice beyond the purview of brick and mortar studios, and *Mank*'s opening titles cite Orson Welles's RKO pact for *Citizen Kane* as a relevant parallel: "He was given absolute creative autonomy, would suffer no oversight, and could make any movie, about any subject, with any collaborator he wished."

Fincher's selection of a script that had been, in his words, "languishing" for nearly thirty years—and passed on by multiple studios—suggests a movie guided not by market forces but a sense of filial piety: Not one for the proverbial "me" or "them," but a gesture on behalf of a dearly departed third party. The grief of losing a parent suffused *The Curious Case of Benjamin Button*, with its nagging pangs of paternal absence and grim images of terminal illness; *Mank*, which opens with its protagonist in traction, is similarly attuned to frailty and slippage. Herman's sudden immobility following a near-fatal car accident prompts him to reflect on his life and times, catalyzing a memory play with obvious structural echoes of *Citizen Kane*. Except that instead of prismatic glimpses at an enigmatic world-beater, we're positioned at the subject's own termite-like vantage point. The result is something like *Kane* in reverse.

An intricately conceived chamber piece with a bifurcated timeline, *Mank* intersperses sequences of Herman's working internment circa 1940 in Victorville, California (a dry county parched further by his employer's removal of booze from the alcoholic writer's rented bungalow), with flashbacks to his eventful Depression-era MGM residency, churning out fast-talking newspaper comedies, losing bad bets, and keeping company with the moguls and power brokers that he curses under his breath. Besides recalling *Kane*'s experimental narrative architecture, *Mank* has been patterned after the two soberest and most-prestige coated titles in Fincher's filmography: *The Curious Case of Benjamin Button* and *The Social Network*. Like those films, *Mank* was showered in Academy Award nominations, and similarly open to charges of being dangling Oscar bait. "[The film] develops like an award ceremony with only one nominee," wrote *MUBI Notebook*'s Kelley Dong, a nifty bit of critical jiu-jitsu using Fincher's industry heavyweight status to trip him up; besides mocking *Mank*'s sometimes sober sense of self-importance (which mixes uneasily with its raucous comedy), Dong's comment hints at an aging provocateur's not so secret aspirations: To belong to a club that would finally have the guy who made *Fight Club* as a member.

What's really being probed in this pithy put-down—and the bulk of the film's critical reception, positive and negative—is the question of *Mank* as a movie made for posterity. "At 30, [one isn't] as connected to the idea of what one leaves behind as you are when you're close to 60," Fincher told Mark Harris, and the progression from the Juvenalian delinquency of *Fight Club*, to the meditations on impermanence encoded into *Zodiac* and *The Curious Case of Benjamin Button*—as well the measured nostalgia of *The Social Network* and the midlife-crisis subtext offsetting *Gone Girl's* disposability—

1-3.   As played by Gary Oldman—who appears in and dominates nearly every scene—Herman Mankiewicz is a wry, voluble observer of his industry; he serves simultaneously as the film's dramatic center and tour guide through a painstakingly recreated era.

4.   5.

resonate in light of this comment. *Mank* may be a movie that Fincher felt he had to age into—and one he couldn't have made at any other point in his career—but it's another of the director's press-round observations that truly pinpoints its perplexing laxity—its sense of having been made by a perfectionist with his guard down. Asked by Harris whether he and his father had been able to satisfactorily develop the film's script during Jack's lifetime, Fincher's reply was simple: "We never quite cracked it."

As Joseph McBride can attest, *Mank* doesn't quite crack it as a history lesson, or as a fair-minded portrait of Orson Welles—even if the script's initial "anti-auteurist take" was tempered after the fact by Fincher and an uncredited Eric Roth. If it's possible for a movie to be simultaneously too broad and too insular—to alienate a mainstream audience while irritating hard-core cinephiles—*Mank* manages it; at times, it's like watching a game of inside baseball that keeps missing the strike zone. The film's ensemble is at once overcrowded and underdeveloped, stranding Lily Collins in a thankless role as Herman's live-in stenographer Rita Alexander (a mere sounding board for his oratory) and contriving a hyperbolically fusty version of Welles's Mercury Theatre producer John Houseman (too-preciously played by Sam Troughton) to spoon-feed us exposition about the period and its players, as well as the style and themes of the in-process screenplay entitled "American." ("It's Lear ... the dark night of the soul . . . I never thought I could care so much about a sled" . . . it goes on like this.) Kirk Baxter's editing is characteristically supple in juggling the story's multiple time frames and channelling the script's streams of syncopated, Sorkin-esque dialogue, but *Mank* never approaches the hypnotic convergence of *The Social Network* or *Gone Girl*. For every ingeniously engineered sequence—like the briskly Kubrickian tracking-shot constitutional through the MGM backlot with Arliss Howard's arrogant Louis B. Mayer (a self-styled general traversing his own personal paths of glory)—there are passages weighted with stasis, as if the movie itself were in traction. *Mank* idles more than it drives; no other Fincher feature has such an inverse ratio of urgency to inertia.

What's more odd than *Mank*'s dramaturgical flaws is how compromised it feels as a technical accomplishment, not in spite of Fincher's creative freedom but as its byproduct. It's a movie of conspicuous and contradictory aesthetic choices, beginning with its very modern widescreen aspect ratio of 2:21, which instantly rebukes the director's claim that he wanted it to look like "something that was found in Martin Scorsese's basement." (In truth, it looks more like something Marty recorded from TCM on his DVR.) Everything about *Mank*'s aesthetic is recognizably and impressively *achieved*, and yet for all of its meticulous-cum-playful re-creations of vintage filmmaking techniques (rear-projection, day-for-night lighting) and exquisite in-camera artisanry (sets, costumes, and the same kind of invisible, world-building CGI that buttresses all of Fincher's features), *Mank* never truly resembles a movie of the 1930s or '40s. Instead, it plays as a semi-beguiling hybrid, one that views the past through an 8K Monstrochrome sensor, all inky, noirish shadows and soft, pooling backlight. The silvery sheen and digitally augmented depth-of-field wrought by cinematographer Erik Messerschmidt has been overlaid by artificial slivers of decay—faux scratches calling attention mostly to their own phoniness (and authorship). "When *Mank* throws up those changeover marks (i.e., "cigarette burns"), writes Walter Chaw, "it doesn't make the picture seem more period-specific . . . it reminds of Fincher's own *Fight Club* and puts one on guard for subliminal genitalia."

The hairline fractures in *Mank*'s classical simulacrum orient it very much in the present tense, which is also where it happens to be addressed. Of all the critics who took a good crack at the film's array of formal and historical anachronisms, the *New Yorker*'s Richard Brody did the best job of breaking things open (instead of just rapping its maker across the knuckles or patting him on the head). Noting aptly that *Mank* is at its most engaging in its scenes of "high-society machinations"—like the extended, mid-film set-piece at Hearst Castle where a Cheshire-grinning Herman provokes the host and his cronies with provocative talk of Adolf Hitler's rise to power and Upton Sinclair's EPIC (End Poverty in California) initiative—he smartly characterizes it as a "do-over" of *The Social Network*, one that "deals with the political implications that [the director] overlooked in the earlier film." What Brody means is that *The Social Network*'s information-age creation myth was applauded before Facebook's spurious influence could be fully perceived, and the site's emergent status as a hub for disinformation gets recontextualized by *Mank*'s big twist. Shooting his mouth off to his boss Irving Thalberg (Ferdinand Kinglsey), Herman suggests that the "magic of the movies" could easily be used for propagandistic sleight-of-hand ("You can make the world swear Kong is ten stories tall or that Mary Pickford is a virgin"). After securing the tacit approval of Hearst and Mayer—fellow members of a coastal ruling class none too eager to have their taxes raised by a socialist governor—Thalberg commissions a series of ersatz, xenophobic newsreels casting Sinclair as an enemy of the people; the result is a landslide victory for conservative candidate Frank C. Merriam.

To the extent that he has ever been a political filmmaker, Fincher is more apt to deal in anti-establishment attitudes and abstractions than concrete ideology; when he makes period movies, he's more interested in how history is textured—in the exactitude of how things look and sound—than the larger currents churning away underneath. Writing in the *American Prospect*, former Democratic Socialists of America vice-chair Harold Meyerson referred to *Mank*'s inventions as "fake news about fake news," but unlike McBride's complaints about Orson Welles, he meant the characterization as a compliment.

4-5. *Mank* features a number of vintage filmmaking techniques like visible rear projection; it also contains a number of camera set-ups patterned after *Citizen Kane*, like an extreme low angle close-up of a quarter spinning after it hits the floor.

6. As Orson Welles, Tom Burke is glimpsed in swift interstitials drawing on the filmmaker's various flamboyant filmic alter egos: Not only the Shadow and the Stranger, but also Kurtz in his unmade adaptation of Joseph Conrad's *Heart of Darkness*.

6.

Meyerson argues that the film's approach sacrifices accuracy for acuity; that while "there's no record of Mankiewicz inspiring Thalberg, imploring MGM not to distribute the newsreels, or even favoring Sinclair . . . it's only because of these Fincher-created motivations for their protagonist, and the quarter-century delay in finding a studio willing to produce the script, that the issues of socialists breaking out of the third-party ghetto by running as Democrats, and the efficacy of fake news to defeat any liberal candidate, have come to the screen at the very moment when they've never been more timely." In a 2016 *Los Angeles Times* editorial Meyerson had predicted that grassroots Presidential candidate Bernie Sanders would be subject to the "same calumnies as Upton Sinclair"; *Mank*'s inadvertent and despairing election-year allegory must have made him feel like a prophet.

#

If *Mank*'s explicitly political valence is atypical for Fincher, the way its embellishments also narrow the scenario into a revenge story—with Herman sublimating his guilt over his peripheral role in Sinclair's defeat by taking aim at its architects—intersects with the director's perennial interest in the smartest guy in the room: An archetype he imbues with equal measures of superiority and self-loathing. To paraphrase Robert Kolker, Fincher's is a cinema of loneliness, of isolated and sometimes self-deluding truth-tellers trying to find a way to spread the good word: Artfully staged crime scenes; acts of domestic terrorism; letters to the edtor; a hot-or-not website; flowers under glass; a forged diary. Everywhere the director looks, he sees messengers in search of a medium, and *Mank*'s syllabus of Old Hollywood quotables includes the possibly apocryphal jibe by Samuel Goldwyn (alternatively credited to Moss Hart and Humphrey Bogart) that, "If you want to send a message, call Western Union." The line is uttered late in the film by the reptile-eyed Mayer (who buys and sells the idea that screenwriters should keep their ideologies safely submerged), but it's also evoked in an early sight gag of the Paramount studio tower being blocked out by a sudden, screen-filling close-up of a telegram. Below the Western Union logo, it reads: "Charlie—come at once: There are millions to be made and your only competition is idiots—Mank." The recipient is Charles Lederer (Joseph Cross), who buys into the sender's flattery before apprehending the sting in the tail. "I hate to tell you, but anyone

7-8.   The loving, platonic bond between Herman and the actress Marion Davies—the much-younger wife of his patron and rival William Randloph Heart—provides *Mank* with its emotional fulcrum; when Herman accuses his friend of being a "marionnette" for her media baron husband it prefigures the veiled acts of character assassination in his new screenplay.

9.   The 1934 gubernatorial campaign of socialist muckraker Upton Sinclair serves as *Mank*'s key political subplot; the economic and ideological threat posed to Hollywood moguls by Sinclair's End Poverty in California Campaign results in a studio-subsidized smear campaign that tips the election to the right.

7.

8.

who can rub three words together to make a sentence gets one," explains Joe Mankiewicz to the newcomer, revealing that he too had journeyed to Los Angeles after being so hailed. If Herman truly believes that Hollywood is a confederacy of dunces, he's also strangely insistent on initiating his pals into the ranks, or else he's implying unkindly that it's where they (and he) belong.

There are mixed messages, then, and Herman's tendency to say what he thinks rather than think about what he's saying is a hypothetically ennobling trait that Oldman's performance casts daringly as an alienation effect. Critics singled out the sixty-two year actor as a flagrant case of miscasting, but the extra miles that Mankiewicz logged on his odometer through decades of compulsive drinking justify Oldman's sagging, sallow physicality as a man in his forties. Sydney Ladensohn Stern's 2019 book *The Brothers Mankiewicz: Hope, Heartbreak and Hollywood Classics*—a measured and intelligent dual biography of Joe and Herman exponentially less in thrall to the latter's Algonquin-table legend than the 1996 Richard Merryman book from which Fincher's film takes its name—provides evidence of the writer's reflexive, contrarian bellicosity: What Joe once termed (and not admiringly), "binges of perversity and extremism."

In both books it indicates that Mankiewicz was propelled and paralyzed by annoyance about excelling in a low medium that recognized his gifts as a satirist and a satyriasist more than the legitimate theater to which he aspired. ("If I'm ever electrocuted, I'd love to have you sitting on my lap," goes one deathless innuendo in 1930's *Love Among the Millionaires*, another vintage *bon mot* duly repurposed by Fincher Sr.) A transplanted New Yorker who cut his teeth as a critic and reporter in Weimar-era-Berlin, Mankiewicz found himself dashed like Clifford Odets (or Barton Fink) on the rocks of the Pacific. Thus stranded, he proceeded to complain about and condescend to a trade of which he had an innate and uncanny understanding. The picture that emerges is of a self-loathing virtuoso, whose narcissism belies a shame-faced self-effacement; the legend that Mankiewicz offhandedly proposed the switch from black-and-white to color in *The Wizard of Oz* makes him the (uncredited) man behind the curtain for the most innovative special effect in cinema history.

\#

In the '90s, Jack Fincher told his son that he believed *Mank* was about a man "finding his voice"; writing in *Artforum*, Amy Taubin praised Oldman's hoarsely flamboyant performance for "the myriad ways [he] can make a line sound like he's whistling past the graveyard." The actor's braying, mechanical delivery can get wearing, but it captures a script-department lifer's contempt for his own protean gag reflexes, and the contrast between Herman's grandiose Cassandra act and Welles's Promethean ambition—the spent force rekindled by the *wunderkind*— serves as the movie's dialectical spine. *Mank* synthesizes aspects of behind-the-scenes accounts by Pauline Kael and Robert Carringer (as well as plenty of scenes taken from Merryman) to suggest that a movie as dazzling and multifaceted as *Citizen Kane* could only have been engineered via a mix of experience and experimentation. It positions the veteran and the tyro initially as grinning coconspirators. "Ready to hunt the Great White Whale?" Welles asks, alluding to the duo's mutual acquaintance and enemy William Randolph Hearst. "Call me Ahab," responds the older man, drolly.

The line between Hermans Meville and Mankiewicz intersects in several places with Welles's legend; in 1956, he made a ceremonial cameo in John Huston's movie of *Moby Dick*, and both Harry Lime and his descendant Gregory Arkadin could be described as Melvillian confidence-men (as could the forgers of *F for Fake*). *Mank*'s other guiding literary light is Miguel Cervantes, and Herman's harangue during the film's climax as an uninvited dinner guest at San Simeon nods to Welles's own unfinished version of *Don Quixote*. "How about we make our Quixote a newspaperman?" Herman asks his host not-so-rhetorically, proposing a fable about a progressive white knight who ages into a jaundiced yellow journalism. "Who else could make a living tilting at windmills?" With his chiselled, sinister features and hearty growl, Charles Dance makes for a wonderfully solicitous Hearst, hanging on his pet writer's every word not only because

9.

10. In his own surreal riff on Oz, Fincher has a hungover Mank wander from harsh reality to the make-believe—and amusingly de-romanticized—world of Hollywood movies, right in William Randolph Hearst's back yard.

he finds him amusing, but because he knows he can literally afford to ignore him. The Quixote sequence, with its volleying close-up reaction shots, is thick with self-consciously clever touches, like a massive fireplace modelled on the one at Xanadu and Herman's *sotto voce* portmanteau of "marionette," mocking Hearst's young wife Marion Davies's (Amanda Seyfried) thwarted attempt to play Marie Antoinette. (Our hero's truth-teller status is underlined by having him be the only one undisguised at a costume party.) What's being set up via all these thick-fingered metaphors is a view of *Citizen Kane* as an act of metafictional harpooning, and in the spirit of Herman's bilious admission, "The white wine came up with the fish," another line from *Moby Dick* bubbles up: "For hate's sake, I spit my last breath at thee."

Where *Mank* surely shortchanges Welles is in sidelining his anti-fascist activism while celebrating his cowriter's efforts to sponsor Jewish refugees from Europe during World War II. In fact, it wasn't only Hearst who resented *Kane's* anti-authoritarian critique, but also the Federal Bureau of Investigation, which smeared the film as Communist propaganda—an unlikely agenda for a screenwriter who in reality leaned to the right. To Jack Fincher's credit, some of the film's other fabrications are rather witty: A running joke in the '30s set sequences about the chaotic making of *The Wizard of Oz* insightfully frames *Kane* as a kind of conceptual cousin, a cathartic fantasy populated with real-life figures via thinly fictionalized alter egos (". . . and you were there, and you and you . . ."). Here, not only is Hearst the obvious model for the imperious, decaying Kane, but the cowardly, lying Mayer closely resembles Everett Sloane's toadying Bernstein.

While Herman relishes his act of literary vengeance against these men of pernicious influence, he's stricken whenever it's mentioned that the character of Susan Alexander—a status-climbing songbird trapped in Kane's gilded cage—seems like an attack on his pal Marion. Herman and Marion's chummy rapport—a well-documented cornerstone of *Citizen Kane* lore—is at once *Mank's* best-developed and most tellingly compromised dramatic strand, while Seyfried, sly-eyed and savvy while firing off her lines in ratatat Brooklyese, is easily the film's most charming performer. As filmed by Fincher, the actress doesn't resemble Davies so much as Jean Harlow, or Madonna in her own early '90s retro-ingenue phase; she's styled plainly as an object of glamorous, brightly haloed desire. And yet when the long-suffering Sara Mankiewicz (Tuppence Middleton) refers her husband to his own history of "silly Platonic affairs," it dulls any illicit edge, clarifying Herman's chivalry in Marion's presence—beginning with the very funny sight gag of him lighting her cigarette as she pretends to be burned at the stake in a Hearst-financed private screen test at San Simeon—as just so much harmless flirting.

This supposed innocuousness reflects *Mank's* habit of trying to have it both ways with its namesake: A bold Quixote tilting at the windmills of Hollywood and Hearst, but harmlessly avuncular when he dubs the young woman resting on his shoulder during a nighttime jaunt through San Simeon "Dulcinea" (and not out of bounds for dubbing her a puppet of her husband.) "I hope if this [movie] gets made, you'll forgive me," Herman tells Marion after the actress ventures to Victorville; "I hope if it doesn't, you'll forgive me," she answers. It's a lovely, humane, exchange that's also a wholly invented act of absolution, and the last act of *Mank* is informed—and made fascinating—by a sort of processional sentimentality, as Herman's friends and loved ones all try to talk him out of his kamikaze venture before resolving

11. The final act of *Mank* finds Herman's friends and colleagues trying to protect him from his own kamikaze campaign against Hearst; here, a man who tries his best to alienate others is sentimentally shown to be the beneficiary of a loyalty and respect at odds with Hollywood expediency.

12. "How's that?" Accepting his Oscar for *Citizen Kane*, Herman takes potshots at Welles but seems secretly concerned whether or not his put-downs live up to his usual standard, as if seeking approval even in a moment of total validation.

11.

to stand by him. In addition to burying the hatchet with Marion, Herman is embraced and celebrated in turn by Charlie, Joe, Rita, and Sara; as staged by Fincher, these visions of steadfast familial devotion have the feeling of a long goodbye, addressed to a man who identified with Mankiewicz's

12.

raconteurish spirit. Or, to quote Welles on *Kane*'s legendary MacGuffin—the humble sled "Rosebud," supposedly inspired by Mankiewicz's memories of a stolen childhood bicycle—this reading of *Mank* as "Oh Father: Part II" is "rather dollar-book Freud."

Ideally, movies should be watched rather than psychoanalyzed. To borrow a joke from Manohla Dargis about Woody Allen, *Mank* climbs onto the couch and winks of its own volition. In the absence of any official annotations, it's hard to know exactly what was added or subtracted from Jack Fincher's script after the fact, but a phone call between Joe to Herman includes references to the author of *Benjamin Button* ("Last night at a party, F. Scott Fitzgerald referred to you as a ruined man") and a warning—big wink—about "hunting dangerous game." If these are indeed knowingly post-dated citations, are they any more significant than the "Seven Days in Tibet" marquee in *Fight Club* or *Gone Girl*'s Gummi Bears? Or do they suggest, as per McBride's accusations, of projection and "delusional hubris," that Fincher's insecurity in making a movie partially about Orson Welles had motivated him to scribble his own history in the margins.

Mank is at its weakest when directly aping *Kane*, with Exhibit A being a misguided attempt to fill in one of Welles's most eloquent blanks—the unseen image of the girl with the white dress and parasol described in reverie by Bernstein—with Herman's mind's-eye view of Sara smiling beatifically on a ferry. This really is dollar-store Freud, while the

moment where Welles hurls a case of whisky against the wall as he grudgingly concedes to a cowriting credit—only to have Herman integrate the tantrum into the script as a necessary act of "purging violence"—provides ample ammunition for charges of cartoonish opportunism. The scene's attempted grace note, that Welles agrees with Herman's inspiration, quickly places the pair back on the same wavelength; it unconvincingly equalizes *Mank*'s not-so-hidden message about the essentially compartmentalized nature of filmmaking, which has been designed—much like its political allegory—to apply equally to an era of vertically integrated studios and the streaming behemoths—a thesis crystallized around Fincher's own singular, contradictory practice of absolute control and open-minded collaboration.

The film's inventory of repurposed quips concludes on a verbatim note, reproducing the catty, media-proxied back and forth between Welles and Mankiewicz after their Oscar win for Best Original Screenplay in 1942. Holding court in Rio De Janeiro, Welles says, "Tell Mank that he can kiss [his] half" of the statuette; addressing reporters outside his home, Herman says that he is, "Very happy to accept this award in the manner in which the screenplay was written—which is to say, in the absence of Orson Welles." What sticks here isn't the character's snide claim to solo greatness, or the even sarcastic kicker added a few seconds later, suggesting that the shared credit for *Kane* is "the magic of the movies." Rather, it's a short, barely audible two-word sentence in between insults, as Herman leans into the microphone and asks the assembled journalists, "How's that?"

Critic Colin Brinkmann writes that this line, and especially Oldman's halting, small-voiced delivery, "[seem] to embody all the pain and bitterness and cynicism that's holed up in the character"; if *Mank* has a Rosebud, "How's that?" and its fleeting, interlaced sensations of aggrandizement and diminishment—as well as the very Fincherian idea of image maintenance and manipulation performed in the public eye—may be it. In a movie filled with durable one-liners, these two words, and the contradiction they express of a contrarian in search of approval, stand out as something we haven't heard before (and might miss on a first viewing). They also double as a query on behalf of the tender, ambitious and exasperating film they're attached to, which may or may not have been made for posterity and may or may not get there; for now, that outcome may be best left as an unanswered question.

INTERVIEWS

Cutting his teeth as an assistant to his father Jordan Cronenweth on *Blade Runner* and *Stop Making Sense*, cinematographer Jeff Cronenweth has worked predominantly in music videos, his first being alongside David Fincher (George Michael's "Freedom! '90"). Following a brief pause in their collaboration, Fincher later signed him on for *Fight Club*, which became his first major feature project as cinematographer, and the pair worked again over the years on *The Social Network*, *The Girl with the Dragon Tattoo*, and *Gone Girl*.

I want to start with *Alien 3*. You're there, and it's not a credited cinematography job for you. Your dad left the film. He was replaced by Alex Thomson. So, you would have had enough exposure, I guess, to the production from a variety of angles. Could you see that it was a bad fit creatively for Fincher?

Well, here's the thing. Obviously, it's his first picture. It's a big one and there's an enormous amount of pressure there. But it's the third film in that series, right? Each time you do one, there's another group of producers that are attached. I think there were twelve producers attached. David wasn't the first director that they inquired about. There was Renny Harlin and someone else who was considered for it, and then so he came in. Everybody had a say in it. It was being shot in London. At the time, it was almost impossible to work there as a crew member, and it wasn't necessarily the best atmosphere for my dad to work in. Don't get me wrong, I love London. I love shooting there. But at this time, with the unions and the lack of work and it was the only picture going on, really. It was *The Sheltering Sky* and us.

[Chuckles.]

[Vittorio] Storaro was shooting it and [Bernardo] Bertolucci was directing it. It just was very difficult. There was a lot of underlying resentment, I felt. And then for David to be such a young director with such strong opinions to come into that world. And I thought there was a misunderstanding of what he could bring to it and actually how talented he was. He pushed boundaries. He put cameras in positions that people didn't quite understand. "Why are you looking up at all these people?" "Why are you looking up at Sigourney Weaver?" "Why can we hardly see anything in this position?" Because he's building a . . . it's not just the shot, he's building an experience around this monster that you've seen three times now and that still has to be scary. She's come back from somewhere, so we already know the story, so now you have to go deeper. And he was going deeper. He took bold, *bold* steps. I was flabbergasted. The first day of shooting, we have Sigourney, shaved head, naked, bugs crawling on her face. Actually, I think, if I remember correctly, one went in her ear and we had to get a medic to come take the bug out. That's the first shot on the first day of your first feature. Wow. That's uh . . . that's *cajones* right there, man.

So, it was difficult then?

Yes, oh yes. I know that, from our perspective, my dad and I loved David with all of our hearts and saw the talent early on, and so we couldn't have been more invested, but my dad had Parkinson's disease. We were shooting on different stages at Pinewood, and there was the Bond stage, which was like a concrete airplane hangar. It's literally colder in there than it is on the outside because the way that the concrete stores the cold. Parkinson's isn't great in the cold, and the studio didn't really want us there, and when it came down to it, Fincher just said, "Look, this kills me, but it would be better for me to be able to fight one-on-one without them having anything to use against me, and at the moment now, you're the apple that they keep dangling over my head, and I don't want you to go through this," and so we left. In a way, it was a miracle for us. It was painful and we felt for him, and there was so much dissent at that moment.

I think later on it got a little bit better, but it was always a difficult set. It's a difficult subject. It was uncomfortable. It was super cold, everything was wet, monsters, all of that stuff going on. The night that that happened, I called my stepmother and said, "I'm going to call Phil Joanou," who we had done *State of Grace* with and who I had gone to film school with at USC, and who had reached out to us to do *Final Analysis* but we had already signed on to do *Alien 3*. I called him and he's like, "That's the most bizarre thing. I did a screen test today. I left and asked it to be lit a certain way, came back and it was lit completely different, and I said, 'I'm not going to spend the next six months going through this.' I need a new DP." I called that night, we flew back and started *Final Analysis*, and it was in LA, in San Francisco, with my dad's crew, and a much better environment for his illness. So that worked out really well for us, and I remember towards the end of that movie, Fincher came to visit, which was interesting because I don't think Phil and David were ever good friends, and he brought us T-shirts that said "Aliens" on the front and "Fuck it" on the back.

<u>Did it cross your mind at that point that there's a progression for you to shoot a movie like *Fight Club*, or was it more of a spontaneous thing?</u>
No, no. Truth be told, I was learning an enormous amount. I found it extremely easy to understand his aesthetics. They were much in line with mine, and when he gave me an assignment—an insert, a pick-up shot, a scene, a B-, C-, D-camera to go do—it was easy for me to find those, and I think that's what kind of intrigued him. And then I thought I would do films, but they weren't gonna be with him, at least not for a while. As I've said before, when I first met him for *Fight Club*, I thought that was to address second unit in an expanded role, but not to get asked to shoot it.

<u>What was the talking point on a movie like *Fight Club*, visually, for you guys?</u>
Well, understanding what the story is first and understanding what visual language we're going to try to support that story. So, going through references that had the kind of contrast or had the kind of shadow and used colors in a way that we wanted to manipulate them for that movie. We needed to understand who was important and what those characters meant, you know? It was ironic because *Aliens* is a dark movie, *Se7en* is a dark movie, *The Game* is a dark movie at times. Photographically speaking. And so, he said, "This is going to be a *really* dark movie," and I'm like, "Well, what are we gonna do? Just turn the lights off?" So how would this be different? It comes together in the scouts, in the pre-production meetings, in the locations, from looking at sets and wardrobe. You start to see the shape of things and the world that these guys live in, and then you see how it should be lit. And *Fight Club*, it's dark sometimes, and sometimes it's not. The discussion was, "It should feel like you're stoned and you walk into 7/11 at two in the morning," and that's what I want the inside of the store to look like or feel like, because it was about connecting emotionally to what you're seeing and what's happening in the story.

<u>With Fincher, one of the myths around him is that some actors get driven crazy by takes and it's to excess and it's all about showing power. I'm not asking you to defend or criticize him. You're there and I just want to hear about it.</u>
No, I don't look at it that way at all, and I think actors that have done a whole movie with him, the majority would beg to differ. I mean,

certainly, in certain situations, it will be wills. It always is. That's the personalities of leading actors or actresses, and the director, it's that kind of position. They do it all the time, whether it's Fincher or anybody else. But for me, you know, I've learned how he processes things, and it's about dissecting a particular shot or scene, maybe into thirds, and arranging with each of those thirds. But he also has this kind of method in that he doesn't like to necessarily cut and re-set. He likes to get people in a rhythm and break the too-much-thought-processing, get you into things happening organically, and it's not just with the cast. It's with all of us.

Well, it has to be, yeah.

It's with me or my camera operator because usually there's two of us. There's two cameras, traditionally, on most of our films, and so it's us kind of muscle memory-ing, working out the marks with the actors. We all seem to arrive at the same time, and takes one through seven, everyone's tripping over each other or we're just starting to get into the groove. But then he may go onto something where we do four in a row without cutting and that's to get people's energy going. Somebody has something in their head that they want to do, but it feels mechanical, so if you say, "Go back. Start over again. Go back. Start over again," you find this kind of organic thing that comes out that's more from the heart and less from overthinking things. So, those are some of the things that get perceived as being indulgent when, in fact, I think, once you see the performance and once you see the same integrity put into everything, you're good with it. It's rare that I find people that don't appreciate it.

One of my favourite scenes in any Fincher movie is the opening back-and-forth discussion at the beginning of The Social Network between Mark [Jesse Eisenberg] and Erica [Rooney Mara]. The way it's shot, but also the editing too.

It's a combination. It's Aaron Sorkin's writing, but it's the way David understood how to cover it, and it's the actors' performances. Right off the bat that was going to be one of the harder sequences because it necessitated having two cameras opposing each other, which is never a cinematographer's ideal situation because you compromise lighting no matter what. You can't have that overlapping dialogue as quickly as they do it and not have both sides of that because you'll never be able to cut two pieces together, right? So, the coverage started one over the top and one underneath for the master and the tighter two, and then we went this way and this way and this way, and uh . . . I don't know if you can see my fingers, but . . .

No, no, I got it.

And so that was like day one challenge, but I was so happy that he afforded me some leeway that he doesn't normally, and it just worked out so great. And this is a fantastic line of his, so I can repeat it, but the first time we screened it in front of a big audience, he's like, "Watch, watch," and it starts off and you see them and you start to realize you're supposed to look at them, and everybody in the theater kind of leans forward to get a better look. The volume of the background noise is at such a level, you can barely hear what they're saying. He's like, "Once they lean forward, I'm not letting them off the rollercoaster until the end of the movie."

To quote the name of an experimental film by Ernie Gehr, it's "serene velocity" that Fincher's work has. It is speed that is not uncomfortable. It is just not calm, exactly. It's like a silenced pistol. They just go.

They go because there's a lot to look at. The performances are really good, and you lose track of time. Also, this brings me back to something about that scene and about him and about the volume in that: One of the reasons we do so many takes is because it's this notion that once he gets you on that ride he doesn't want to give you an excuse to get off, and that's whether it's obvious or whether it's subconsciously. And by that I mean if there's a soft shot, if there's a camera move that does something, if an actor's timing wrong, if the glass was here and now it's over here. Are those subtle? Yeah, of course. Do they stack up over two-and-a-half hours and 900 shots? If you have one bad shot a day on a 100-day shoot, you have 100 bad shots in your movie.

It doesn't seem like such a big deal at the moment, but when you accumulate, then you've kind of numbed your audience and you've given them opportunities not to be fully engaged, and that goes for every aspect. That goes for performances, too. He's not being a perfectionist for that, he's being a perfectionist to protect the work that we all do collectively.

With *The Girl with the Dragon Tattoo*, am I to understand correctly that you came onto that one late?

That's right. I didn't start the film. David and Ceán, his partner and producer, felt like it was so close to the release of the Swedish version of *Dragon Tattoo* that their intent was to bring as much authenticity as possible. By that I mean immersing in the culture and utilizing a primarily Swedish-based crew. They hired a young Swedish DP who, in his defense, I had reservations how he was going to pull it off with just a few music videos, commercials and small naratives under his belt. It was a big ask to first collaborate with David on a movie that scale. And also, stylistically, they kind of were different in that he didn't come from a formal school of thought, and this kind of goes hand in hand with what we were talking about before—he is more of an organic filmmaker.

If the sun was over here in one shot and the sun was over here in another shot, who cares? It looks great. That's not the way it works in David's world. It's like, everything has to have a plan. Four hours from now, when we're still shooting in this direction, what is your plan? The sun's going to be over here now. What do you do when you come around and cover it? So I was on my way to a commercial at about five in the morning in LA, I'm on the 405 driving down to Manhattan Beach Studios, which is now Marvel, I think, and the phone rings, and I knew the area code for Sweden, and I'm like, "I know what this is. I know what this is." He's like, "Hey. What are you doing?" "Now?" "No, for the next six months." [Laughs.] Oh, God. "Uh, sure, I'll be there Monday." Met them in Switzerland. They were scouting in Switzerland, in Zurich for all the bank scenes and that interaction. I met him there and that was it until August the following year.

The last word I'd use for *Dragon Tattoo* is "ugly," but it's not soft the way that you shoot that movie.

I mean, this was the mandate. The weather is such an integral part of the movie and how cold it is and what they're going through. So you had to make that a character in the movie, and you had to figure out a way that you can convey that. And sure, you can have the wind howling and you can have the actors shivering and you can have frost on the windows, but there had to be something that was coming from the camera, too. And it was color: color of light; color choices on the camera, like what temperature we're shooting things at; time of the day we shot stuff at; atmosphere. All these things help convey that cold.

For me, that's one of the proudest things, like when you watch that movie and people say, "Oh, it looks like it was really cold."

Well, it was. When things are too pretty and you're outside and the snow's there, it's like, "Oh, let's go make snow cones and a snowman." Like, no. You wouldn't be doing that.

With *Gone Girl*, visually, I'm interested in it as a movie that is about reality, because there are subtle differences in the realities of the two narratives. Can you speak on that?

Yeah, because we don't have the advantage of having as much time to tell the story as the book does. We have to create an image where you can kind of instantly start to question the character of this person, of what's real and what's not. It's a weird thing, because she rejects it at the beginning, but then embellishes it and uses it to her advantage when she needs to. His character meanwhile is pretty obvious and it's easy to make him look like an empathetic guy and it's easy to make him look like the bad guy, and it's genius casting for Fincher because Ben's lived through all that. That's his life.

There's a driving montage in the film and, to me, it is a perfect translation, visually, of how Gillian Flynn writes the "Cool Girl" monologue. As a cinematographer, how do you shoot something like that?

For me, it's extremely exciting because it's a lot of . . . you're not matching, in this case, to a sequence. You're matching to time travel. It's time travel. And the purpose of the montage is to show the passage of time and the passage of location. It gives you a unique opportunity to break away from the constraints you would have if you're sitting at a dinner table and had to do twenty shots. Now you can make each of these beautiful as long as they convey the message of time's passage and the point of, like, whether it's the pens being thrown out because each of the diaries had a different color pen, or the kids driving by and mocking her, or somebody else, or any of the things that happen. As long as you feel like you're engaged in that journey, it's super exciting, and it becomes a bit of a burden because there are so many shots. And in the day when you see there's twenty-seven inserts, you're think, "Oh my God. You're never going to use twenty-seven inserts." But that's just human nature fighting back against the time you know it's gonna take to do these things. Once you get them all and you know how it's gonna cut together, it's brilliant to have all that and have those choices.

CASTING DIRECTOR

LARAY MAYFIELD

Casting director Laray Mayfield connected with David Fincher early in her career, but was unable to work for him initially due to her social situation. But a return to Hollywood in the mid-90s saw the pair reconnect, and she has gone on to cast every one of his films (and TV series) from *Fight Club* onwards. Over the years, Mayfield has accrued an almost preternatural feel for Fincher's casting choices, giving top-billing to recent discoveries and helping to launch careers (Rooney Mara in *The Girl with the Dragon Tattoo*) and locating new angles in an old reliables (Ben Affleck in *Gone Girl*).

Your association with Fincher extends beyond your first credit for him, which was *Fight Club* in 1999. Are you able to talk a bit about the early days you spent with Fincher and also the evolution of the David Fincher brand?

Yeah, well, it wasn't with the general public, but it was there when I met him in 1986. We'd both just gotten to LA He was twenty-two, and had a name for himself. He was represented by CAA. He had high-power attorneys. He had worked at ILM. He directed that incredible smoking fetus PSA that received a lot of attention. There definitely was a buzz about him already. Of course, I was oblivious to it because I'd just come to LA from Tennessee and everything was, like, "Wow! It's crazy!" But yeah, Dave was well on his way, even at twenty-two.

And I imagine that's a self-possessed quality that defines someone as a director, right?

Well, I've always said about Dave he is the only person I've ever met that knew at conception what he wanted to do. He had a passion . . . a dream and drive. I think that sets Dave apart because that's just unique in general having that focus so early in his life. The other thing to touch on, which we'll get deeper into that's unique about Dave, it's going to be really hard to talk to anybody that works with Dave just on a business level because we're friends. He is my family.

This runs parallel to some of the mythology around certain directors, and it was true of Kubrick, and for the people who don't like them, they use it to say, as critics, "This work is hermetic. This work is closed off. This work is impersonal," or the industry writing is, "Oh, he does a lot of takes." And yet the loyalty that people have, and the desire to keep wanting to work with filmmakers like this, I think is very indicative of a completely different attitude. It must not be that difficult to work with somebody like that or people wouldn't work with them for thirty years.

Exactly right! Common sense will tell you that. It couldn't be that bad, or none of us would do it. It's interesting, you put it so eloquently when you said there's these myths that people, if you don't like somebody, that's what they use, you know, Dave doesn't give a shit. Neither do the rest of us.

You were David's first assistant in the fifteen-year period before Fight Club. *Which covers a lot of his music video and commercial work, plus* Alien 3.

I met David the first day I was in LA, and within nine months, I was working as his assistant. Within 18 months, I started casting his videos and commercials, and it was a whirlwind. It was like going downhill on ice, because once Propaganda took off, work was coming furiously and it was this great team and great fun. When Dave went to do *Alien 3*, I said, "I can't do that. I can't go to London." I brought my son to LA when he was five, and we had just been in LA two-and-a-half, three years. When I first got to LA, I had no car, I had no place to live. And at this point, I had a little house and had a car, and so that is the point where Dave said, "You're right. That's too much to ask. You should go off and set up your own casting company, and I'm going to be back and we're always going to work together and it has always been that way. He did reach out to me on *The Game* and *Se7en* to see if I would come and work in the casting departments, but I was living in New Mexico with a boyfriend and my son and we had a bunch of horses and a big life going on, and I was like, "No, I don't want to do that right now."

Fight Club *is a pretty auspicious movie to kind of start as a casting director with a feature filmmaker because you're dealing, at that time, with one of the big movie stars of the millennium. How did you secure Brad Pitt for the Tyler Durden role?*

Well, Dave had done *Se7en* with Brad, so I had nothing to do with that, and then we did a casting process for Helena's role. Back then, did we even have cellphones? Maybe we had a cellphone. I don't remember. You know, I can't remember if Helena came and met him—I'm sure she must have. "Helena Bonham Carter" there's nobody else in the world like her, she's brilliantly talented— so unique and powerful, and that's who we need in this role.

Edward Norton, who plays the everyman counterpoint to the rock star guru Pitt, is a movie star in 2000, but not the way Brad Pitt is.

That was a very, very important part of it because *Fight Club* is so deep, it's so psychological, and it really spoke to me because

I was raising a male child on my own, as were a lot of women I knew during that period of time, and I think it's a juxtaposition because he's not real, if you're going to imagine somebody, wouldn't you imagine somebody who is more magnificent than how you present yourself to the world?

I love the idea that inside every corporate drone, Brad Pitt is just waiting to jump out . . .

Exactly.

Looking like he does in that movie, which is as attractive to me as any male actor has ever looked in a film. It's incredible.

Yeah, he's awesome. I only know Brad from when I've worked with him with Dave. Brad is a very nice person.

It's so interesting because you watch movies throughout your life and you're like, "I wonder if I'll ever talk to that filmmaker," but you never think you're going to talk to a casting director. On *Panic Room*, even the first time I saw it when I was like a teenager, I was like, "Boy, Jodie Foster and that little girl match up well."

Yeah. Well, you know, that was a disaster—it started out being Nicole Kidman and Hayden Panettiere. There were a lot of issues and Nicole had to drop out. So, when we started to get it back up and going, I had met Kristen Stewart early in the casting. She had only done a couple of commercials, she was so interesting. Jodie wanted the role very badly. She had wanted to work with Dave for a while. I kept getting phone calls from Jodie's agent, saying, "Hey . . . " (I had done a movie with Jodie, *Altar Boys*, that she produced and she starred in.) "Hey, just can you please tell David Jodie would love to be considered if anything changes," and so it was one of those things that organically fell in to place. Jodie was available, she really wanted the role, she made it known to Dave, and Kristen had done a movie in between that was nice, so it was a no brainer. Jodie, Kristen, perfect. My friend David Hogan is how I got to LA. He was super-close with Harry Dean Stanton and he said that Harry Dean always told him that, "There's never any real mistakes, it all works out how it was meant to be." And in this case, that's exactly what happened. It worked out with the two people who were actually supposed to be in the film.

Did you and Jared Leto have an understanding that he's just going to get the shit beaten out of him every time he works with David Fincher?

[Laughs.] Yeah, he did. We got the shit beat out of him in the audition process, too. [Laughs.] He knew exactly what he was getting himself in for. And he was all for it.

Now, I cannot think of a better cast American movie than *Zodiac*. Can you tell me how you did that?

That was an easy movie to cast and it was a really pleasurable movie to cast. I love that time period. They were all actors that I thought were fabulous. It was a dream job. David's whole thing is always, "Find me the best people. Find me the best actors for the role. Just show me who they are." And authenticity is super-important. If you're doing a movie about real people, there's a reason why you're doing that, and they have a great story, but Dave's whole thing is you feel as if you want to pay homage to the people, and so if you can cast actors that are physically very similar, then that's a plus.

For *Benjamin Button*, was there a casting process for Pitt, or is it just he's attached to the film and then you cast around that?

No. He came on right away. I'm sure he and Dave talked about it for quite some time before. *Benjamin Button* was something we tried to get going for a while. I don't remember exactly the moment that it happened, but Brad was who David wanted, always.

On *Dragon Tattoo*, you're not casting or making a remake of a Swedish film, you're casting an adaptation of the book.

Yeah. Much different. In fact, I have never seen the films.

It might seem like a weird person to ask about for *The Social Network* because it's not a huge part, but I'm interested where Rooney Mara came from for that part.

I've known Rooney and [her sister] Kate for a long time, from when they first started acting in New York. So, I was very familiar with Rooney. But you know, Rooney is like Helena in that way she is unique, so is Kate. Rooney was perfect.

It's a very swift movie. So is the acting style in that. Everybody's really, really accelerated. I wonder how it informed the casting, as the acting style is almost screwball in that movie?

Yeah, we considered this A LOT in casting. He needed actors we were sure could do that, manage the pace, who are immensely articulate—wouldn't stumble over words, could translate the dialogue with soul and emotion like it was normal language. The auditions were fun because they were like sprints, and sometimes we'd even bring Aaron [Sorkin] in and go, "Okay, come on. I'm fast, he's faster." I always thought it was timing, some of that. This scene can only be this long, this scene . . . It was meticulously cast on that level.

And the brilliant stroke of casting Justin Timberlake as the face of Napster.

He was great. I was super-proud of that. I thought it was fun and he was so game for it, and I have never been in a room with an actor in an audition that could do what I saw Justin Timberlake do. His mind is magnificent, we would send him 14, 16 pages, and a day-and-a-half later, he'd show up, off book. Not even off book, he didn't even bring the pages in from the car to the office, and he would run those scenes and David can say, "Okay, alright, let's stop right here. Let's pick this scene up and blah blah." It was pretty phenomenal.

With *Gone Girl*, is Ben Affleck inevitable in that part? Was there a "Eureka!" moment between you and David where you're like, "Well, yeah, of course it's going to be Ben Affleck for this."

Yeah, I mean, I think we started running a list early on, and it was just like that. David was like, "Ben." I really like Ben. David *loved* and enjoyed working with Ben. I only got to know Ben in some of the casting process and read-throughs. He's a very nice guy and he's a very hard worker.

On the one hand, you have Affleck who fits to the contours of that part. With Amy, that poses a really interesting question. Do you cast a big star? Do you cast an unknown? How do you cast that part?

She's super-cool. She's another hard worker, and she wanted that role, and she went to the mat for it. I was very keen on Rosamund [Pike] early on. I put together a list for David and we looked at lots of all different types of actresses, but the feeling that we both had was that this book was so, so popular that it was important for whoever played the role of Amy to hold their own space in that character. But to also allow this audience of readers to project whatever their ideas about Amy were. Because, of course, we all know who Rosamund is, and probably people saw her in the film would go, "Oh, who is it?" But she wasn't that well-known. She is also a classic beauty. She didn't give away any of the darkness. I was excited when we were able to cast her.

ANGUS WALL

A man of many talents, Angus Wall began a long run of Fincher collaborations on the director's second feature, *Se7en*, where he helped design the film's now-iconic title sequence. His first editing gig for Fincher arrived with *Panic Room*, where he worked alongside James Haygood, and that led to a solo editing job on *Zodiac* and then a partnership with Kirk Baxter on *The Curious Case of Benjamin Button*, *The Social Network* and *The Girl with the Dragon Tattoo*—the latter two netting a pair of Academy Awards for Best Editing.

There's this interesting layer of Fincher collaborators that's back before the beginning, and it really seems like a pretty tight consistent group.

I met him when I was twenty-one and he was twenty-five or twenty-six or something. I was working in the video vault at Propaganda, duplicating tapes and making show reels, and he was already the superstar. There are certain people who are just born to do what they do, and he's one of them. He kinda does know everybody's job better than they do . . . I'm sure you've heard that before. But that makes it possible for him to work with people who lack experience but have passion. It serves everyone well because it inspires fierce loyalty that's met with fierce loyalty. So he sticks with those people and vice versa.

When you're talking about your own age being twenty-one at the time, I mean, we're talking about the late '80s/early '90s now, and I'm interested to hear about that period.

That was the golden age of music videos and commercials. David turned everything he made into a story. There's a narrative—even if it's an oblique narrative—in everything he did. There's a beginning, middle, and end. There are characters, plot development, and certainly tone. If you look at his early music videos, you can see him learning. Steve Winwood's "Roll With It" showed his ability to use technology—in that case the snorkel cam—in service of story. In his "Loverboy" video, he learned and mastered, basically devoured, everything Joe Pytka took years to figure out and put it in that one video, which must've rankled Pytka to no end. I mean, that's a terrible way to put it, but that's the truth, that's how talented David is. He just kept learning voraciously with every project.

There's also something like the anti-smoking PSA, which was made by Fincher in his early twenties, and it just does Kubrick, right. He just does the Star Child *in utero*, you know, smoking, and it's one of the greatest sight gags I've ever seen. And you look at that, and you go, "Well, of course the guy was gonna make feature films."

You can see that dark humor in everything, and that was from the start. That's imbued in every layer that goes into his work. David works in a fractal way, both in terms of how he builds a shot or a scene or a film . . . but also in how he works with his team. And by that I mean, he gives you what you need when you need it. If you're editing a film with him and you need an idea about how to approach a scene, he can give you that. Later in the process, if you need feedback about the pronunciation of a certain syllable in a certain line, he can also give you that when it's time. Also, a lot of people find themselves boxed into a certain genre or medium, whether it's commercials or music videos or films. David is equally adept at all of them, and to your point, he can make a single shot, like the anti-smoking PSA, or he can make an ongoing series like *Mindhunter*, and be equally adept. He can keep that quality across the board, which is really rare. You see feature people trying to make forays into commercials or music videos, or vice versa, and they just can't do it.

How does your work as an editor feed into his world?

He's a master of film syntax or syntagma. He knows what the rules are, how to bend them, and he also knows how to break them. There's no end to the amount of coverage you could actually generate in shooting a scene. So you always talk about film as a matter of nouns and verbs and adjectives and adverbs and then compound sentences with different clauses and phrases. It's a language. And you can get to a ballistic pace in language if you have the right building materials in service of the right blueprint. The building materials are what is generated on set, and the blueprint is the script. The editing, then, is the construction of the final product using those materials. It becomes about how transparent an experience watching the film can become. How can you be in the exact right place on the right lens with the precise, most concise action? Essentially, how precise can you be without being reductive? How many thousands of tiny decisions can you get right in order to achieve that state?

When I watch his work, that's what I appreciate. The acute level of detail: The synthesis and the crystallization of thinking and the crystallization of a moment inside very specific performances. The thing about having watched him for more than thirty years is that his continual development—and I say that word with all due respect—is really, really interesting. Because you look at the early stuff, and you talk about, say, "Loverboy". "Loverboy" is a sort of a technical exercise. You can picture David saying I want to learn how to do these things and I'm going to do them better than how I've seen them done before. He accrues all of this technical knowledge, and then ultimately he starts really focusing on performances, which is interesting. On *Zodiac* he seemed to relax about the technical stuff and just focused on performance and story . . . perhaps a more '70s approach to filmmaking.

The opening credits of Se7en, which you worked on, is where I think you have his birth as a feature filmmaker, where he's going to force the audience to adjust to a certain tempo. If there's more of a stylebook for the last thirty years of genre film in America, I can't think of it. So, maybe talking about how that came together and how much you guys knew this was going to set the tone for the movie.
I mean, *Se7en*'s sort of a grudge movie in a weird way. I feel the grudge in that movie. It's low key, but it's there. Really, it's like a grudge that, I think, probably developed on *Alien 3*. But I'm projecting. I mean, what the fuck do I know?

No, I'm with you. I think it's a good read.
I can tell you what it feels like to me. So, um . . . I was a pretty young editor at that point, and he called me up, and he said, "Hey, will you work with this guy Kyle Cooper on the titles for the movie?" and I was like, "Fuck yeah. That sounds great." I worked with Kyle. And Harris Savides who, you know, rest in peace, shot the main title. The footage was beautiful. I worked on it with Kyle, and I remember David saying later, "I knew we were fucked when I walked in and looked at your face before you even played it." The whole sequence just kind of laid there. I knew it too, and David was like, "Hey, maybe try a different tack and cut it up like you're John Doe working on his notebooks." OK? I mean, awesome direction. So, I literally worked on it like that for six weeks. And it was great, and he got this guy called Findlay Bunting, this cameraman . . . don't look that up in rhyming cockney slang. [Laughs.] How anybody can name their kid that . . .

Way ahead of you. Go on.
. . . is beyond me. Findlay in his basement shot 16, I think, of the titles and, played with the gate as he filmed. That's why you get all that great filmic distortion that people have tried to emulate so poorly for so long. Doing that main title was a really eye-opening

experience. We went to the premiere at Mann's Chinese and seeing that play on the big screen like that, I was like, "Holy shit."

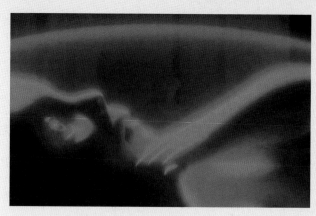

There's no way to do the calculus on this, but you guys also did at least as much for Trent Reznor as he did for *Se7en*. That's a 50/50 to me.
The music is really the foundation of that whole sequence. It's really didactically cut to the track.

Was the credit sequence for *Panic Room* something that came out of a conversation he had with you or was it with Kirk Baxter?
That was before Kirk's time.

So, it was with you then, right? Because it was a conversation he had with an editor.
Maybe. I mean, Jim Haygood and I cut *Panic Room* together. David talked about showcasing New York in the titles because the rest of the film is set in the Brownstone. It was a way to give breadth and expanse and set the stage for the rest of the film.

But also, this wonderful idea that the credits occupy physical space.
David approaches a lot of images in a layered way, and sometimes that's for technical purposes because he needs to do a composite shot and it's literally impossible to get everything in one. There are other times where it's a creative choice, which *Panic Room*'s main title would be. There are other times when it's not completely necessary, but it's convenient in terms of getting each individual layer as perfect as possible, and when you put three different layers of something that is as close to perfect as a production can make it, you get a pretty awesome shot.

One of the things I'm trying to wrestle with in the book is that he's one of the signature special effects filmmakers, it's just in an opposite way than, say, a Cameron or a Spielberg or a Ridley Scott are. Do you think there is any truth to that?
In psychological terms, David lives in the shadows. There's a certain joy to being in the shadows, and the visual effects work is also in the shadows—it's in service of this deep sense of reality, a really peel-your-eyeballs-back sense of reality. It's interesting that somebody who has such a high level of craft and manufactures things, creates things artificially that simulate reality, that, you know, is all in service of actually examining the shadow.

Benjamin Button feels atypical in the way it's edited. Where Fincher's films are known for that strictness, and rigour, this feels like it's cut with a mind on something more laconic and contemplative.
That might be more to do with the story instead of the editing but I think I know what you mean. You think it's going to be a movie about love, but it's a movie about death. You look at *Mank* and clearly there's a very deep relationship with Jack that David had and continues to have. You know, he lost his father just before *Benjamin Button*, and there were critical choices, I think, for him to make in *Benjamin Button*, about whether it was going to be a love story or whether it was really going to be about loss, and the movie ended up being about loss. And I think that the contemplative part of it may come from that. It's not an uplifting movie.

Am I right in thinking that, with *The Girl with the Dragon Tattoo*, every time Daniel Craig's character goes somewhere in that movie there's a shot of him looking for cell phone service?
I don't know.

You don't know. I mean, I love the repetitive, recursive aspect to the way that movie is cut. I love the establishing shots in that movie. Every location he goes to is just described in like two shots. It's so tight.

I'll tell you an interesting story about that. I think we spent a day with Soderbergh. And David and Steven are friends. You couldn't have two more stylistically different directors. Soderbergh is all about, what's the fillet of the scene? Cut all the fat off, trim it to the quick, and give me the fillet. With David, there's always a beginning middle and end to a scene and he's constantly making you work to understand the space. He's giving you just enough so you completely understand it. So we spent the day with Soderbergh, I think he was with us on *Dragon Tattoo*, trying to speed it up and getting rid of some of the sort of ins and outs of each scene, and it kinda broke the movie. It was really interesting. With David, each scene is sort of its own little Swiss watch, and if you take a piece out, it doesn't work anymore. Do you know what I mean? It's really designed to be what it is.

The pace and the sense of place, especially, is just dazzling in that movie.

Yeah. It doesn't have a sense of humor about itself the way that a lot of his other movies do. I personally miss that being-light-on-its-feet aspect that, say, *Zodiac* and *The Social Network* and *Fight Club* have. There's a mind at play in each one of those movies that I don't— I don't necessarily know if you feel that in *Dragon Tattoo*.

I know that those two movies, Social Network and Dragon Tattoo back-to-back, are just a feat of cutting, and, you know, there's Oscars to prove it. It just seems like a Herculean task.

Listen, as an editor he's one of the easiest people to work with. It's not like you're cutting the movie three different times, which you do with certain people. He knows what he wants. He shoots within a five-percent range of performance. There's a very clear goal, and if you can get into that slipstream with him, it's like you're moving at speed towards making that thing. Do you know what I mean? So, it's a little embarrassing to win an award for that because it's not rocket science. You have to trust your bullshit detector and you have to do the job, but it's not like you're inventing something. You have all the pieces there to make something great.

ACTOR

JOHN CARROLL LYNCH

The actor John Carroll Lynch had his breakthrough moment in 1996 when he played the lovably laconic Norm Gunderson (doting husband to Frances McDormand's Marge) in the Coen brothers' *Fargo*. His workrate over the ensuing quarter century has been nothing short of astounding, but it's his pivotal role as suspected serial murderer Arthur Leigh Allen in David Fincher's *Zodiac* that remains one of his defining achievements, proving that it's no small feat for an actor to create a character who is supposed to be a tundra of emotion and readability.

Arthur Leigh Allen, the character you play in Zodiac, only became a public figure posthumously. There's stuff about him that's on the record, but very little about what he was like or what he thought.

Well, the advantage of working with Fincher is the exhaustiveness of the research, particularly on this subject. When I was hired and first met with him, I was brought out to the center of his office where the historian for *Zodiac* laid out the timeline of the people who might or might not have been the Zodiac, and there was the Arthur Leigh Allen timeline, where he was in various locations when the murders took place. He also had a box of transcripts and videotapes for me, digital recordings of him being interrogated, and so I was able to watch actual footage of him in an interrogation room. That was the video that was available, and in terms of his body language and his ability to mimic human behavior, it was very telling. I mean, the degree to which he could transform from a victim to just dropping it was really shocking. It obviously took him years of practice. Then there was the process of working on the material I was given, and working with the actors and also working with David. But I was given books—the two [Robert] Graysmith books—I was given transcripts, I was given a digital tape, so it was quite a bit of research for the character.

It's interesting you talk about mimicking and performance. Right up until you're shot head-on, the interrogation scene is a very angular scene in the way it's constructed and edited. Your acting is also angular. There's so much going on with your arms, your legs, your posture. There's nothing that's straight on about the way Allen is sitting. And yet, I don't read him as uncomfortable; there's like this weird, seething flamboyance to him. He's performing a bit, particularly the uncrossing of the legs, the flashing of the watch.

It's also directing. I mean, these things are all of a piece. There's nothing that happens in a Fincher movie that doesn't happen for a reason. He sent me about that particular task in a particular way. When we did the folding and everything, all of those things were from that videotape, from the way in which he sat in the interrogation room. It was almost serpent-like. He was coiled. The beauty of shooting that scene was we had all the time in the world, so the lighting never had to change. We shot a lot, and it didn't matter where the cameras were sitting. The light was the same for everybody. So, there was no specialty or character lighting being done. Then to sit down with those three other actors, who are spectacularly good at staying present, it allowed for a lot of freedom inside a very constricted pattern of shooting.

There's such an interesting power dynamic to that scene. It should feel like they're ganging up on Allen, but weirdly he seems to gang up on them. It's really something.

Yes, and all for the beauty of, "Does anyone else think this person is a person . . . " That's the funniest line in the movie. In terms of what Allen was like as a person, I know he liked the attention. Whether or not he was actually the Zodiac can still be debated, but his desire to have attention brought to him, for good or for ill, was part of what he was doing, all the way to the end of his life. I think that was an important part of how David wanted the character to be portrayed, and certainly it was part of what I saw in the videotape of him at the interrogation. It was maybe the only time people talked to him.

When you talk about attention, that scene is interesting because, on top of all the foregrounded stuff—"Is Graysmith satisfied? Is Allen guilty? Does he recognize he's being seen?"—given that Allen is factually a pedophile, I read that into his expression at the end, too. Not so much that he's been found out, just the idea of being seen and being suspected. This is someone who probably got a lot of bad looks in the latter part of his life; when he got attention, it was always negative attention, whether he liked it or not.

The movie is a meditation on obsession. Each person is destroyed by the virus of obsession. Each person spreads it to the other. In one way or another, the only person who survives it is Anthony Edwards and that's because he doesn't catch it.

Yeah, he taps out.

Yeah. And he never gets to the point of ingesting a full viral load. Whenever I think about that scene, and whenever I see it, it makes me think, "And the whale looks at Ahab, and Ahab looks at the whale." It's them recognizing, in each other, the hunter and the hunted. It works on the basis of whether or not he is actually the Zodiac, or whether or not he wasn't. David was very wise in the way in which he went about directing me to play the character as an innocent man, and then also to four or five different actors to portray the Zodiac, and to mix in, even in the ADR [Automated Dialogue Replacement] sessions, a variety of voices. The only time you hear my voice, fully and completely my own voice, is in the scenes with Ione Skye in the car, when you don't see the face of the Zodiac at all but he's not wearing a mask.

You know, my dad was an attorney. He was once prosecuting a case in which one of the people was an eyewitness, and he went down to the cafeteria to eat lunch and the person was sitting in the cafeteria. My dad said, "Why is that defendant sitting down here without his lawyer? That's really weird." And when he finished his lunch, he went back upstairs and realized that it wasn't him. Our understanding of what we actually see . . . I recently watched a television show about what we are genetically predisposed to see and understand. It's based on the way in which light hits natural objects, how we perceive light hitting natural objects. So, when you start to create artificial worlds, you can fool the eye very quickly, very easily, because we don't see what we think we're seeing anyway. We're interpreting the world of what we see, and our sense can be fooled pretty easily. When it comes to this movie, it's clear to me that the movie is not about catching the Zodiac. If Fincher wanted to have that movie, he could have that movie. He wanted us to think about what it is to not be certain.

There's also something very contemporary about the Zodiac. It's not like he was sitting around being a prophet. But his time has come, I think, in terms of the society we live in. We're now so interested in these lurid, prurient, coded things.

I can understand why you see it that way. There's another thing, too, which I think leads into that, which is a desire for certainty. Graysmith, as a character in the film, is motivated like an Eagle Scout is motivated because he describes himself as one. He wants to be certain. He wants to have a moral universe in which the bad guy is caught and punished. That's not the moral universe Fincher sees, I don't think, and that's certainly not the moral universe in the script. In our world, the desire for righteousness and certainty, it seems to me, leads to conspiracy theories, because you can't always trust what you're being told. There is no institution that can give you the certainty that used to be presented as 100% fact—that God exists, that you can take the government's word for something, that even the post office is a safe place. Nothing is certain. I think that desire for certainty leads to the mania that the Zodiac exposes in the film. And then from *Fight Club*, that comes back again even bigger role in *Mindhunter*.

In *Se7en*, the serial killer is a pop creation. He's this guru, he has a worldview, there's a coherence. It's very much in line with that post-*The Silence of the Lambs* glamorization of this subject, and when you see the killer in *Se7en*, he's this creepy, heavy-set guy. He's kind of pathetic. The fact that Fincher could make both *Se7en* and *Zodiac*, and have one examine the other, is an amazing thing about him.

I recently watched *The Man Who Shot Liberty Valance*. It had been a long time since I'd seen it, and I was talking to a friend of mine who's brilliant when it comes to this kind of examination and this understanding of film. That movie is like an endtime John Ford movie—he mocks everything that he set up in every other movie he ever made, and he saps romance from it.

Yep. And saps moral authority, too.

Moral authority, absolutely. Everyone is a sham. Everybody agrees to a corrupt version of the past that everybody's living with, and it's a lie. You know, all of David's movies are, to one degree or another ... there's no way of getting out of a Fincher universe.

With the Coen brothers, who you worked with on *Fargo*, the easiest thing to say about them is that they're mean, which says nothing about what their films are. And that scene at the end of *Fargo* ... it's terrifying. "Two more months." Because we see the world that they live in. I've always found that last scene tender and beautiful but frightening as well. I think the Coens manage to have an ambivalence in their movies where they're never just mean, they're mean and they're humane. With Fincher, people are pretty quick to judge him as a nihilist, or to say that his movies are kind of mean, which, to me, doesn't say enough about them.

The thing I appreciated most working with him—and this is true of Joel and Ethan and every person I've ever worked with who's a master—is he drops anything out of the process that he doesn't care about. People can complain about a wide variety of things with Fincher—I know that there's a lot of people who talk about the amount of takes he does, and all the other things—but all of that is part and parcel with what he's actually going after. *Zodiac* reflects back a clarity. Each of his movies, there is a clarity that one could see as unforgiving to humanity, if one wanted to, but you can't not see the humanity of it. With the Coens, the thing that makes *Fargo* so fundamentally different is Fran [McDormand]. She can't be cold. There's not a performance of hers that isn't filled with blood and spit. Margie is the same, and my relationship with her can't be dismissed in a sense of being. . . . It's interesting that you experience fear in that moment. That certainly wasn't how we felt it, or at least I played it, which was all about joy and anticipation. Without that joy and that anticipation, what does Margie's life look like? She sees the world. She's in it. He's not. He's safe.

Well, she has a power in that movie; it starts with that belly, but there's a moral authority she has where the evil men in the film fall at her feet, you know? And when she lectures Peter Stormare at the end, it's like she's practicing for motherhood. He's like a teenager in the backseat. She's like, "Dont'cha know that?" The way the film ends, the joy and anticipation is very real. I think great movies are not the ones whose intentions are unclear, but where the intention and, as you say, the clarity is so clear while still allowing people to take different things away from it. It's about subjectivity. It's a very spacious movie, *Fargo*, even though it's tight as a friggin' drum, as editing and staging goes.

It really is about space, isn't it? It's about open space. It's about cold, white beige. When it comes to Fincher, the thing that's clear, in the brief times I've talked with him and worked with him, is his absolute mastery of every level of filmmaking, and every level of the equation of film. Nothing is left to chance, and that goes from him negotiating with the studio to make the thing, whatever it is he's making, all the way to the time when he's going to make another. It's never one thing. He is present to the creation.

When you talk about that precision and that intention that Fincher has, what does that do for you as an actor?

I'd describe it as a dance floor. There are directors who set a very solid dance floor, and you know that you're in the right place; you are free inside a space that's presently created though it naturally flows in no particular direction. There's not an intention of having to force many moments. You are free. When I've had the good

DAVID FINCHER: MIND GAMES

fortune of directing, I've tried to maintain a sense of freedom for the actor. It's very similar to what free will is, I think, in philosophical terms. One has complete free will and will always end up where one is fated to be. When I'm acting, and I've decided something and it flows, and I realize the camera's already sitting where that decision will be made, that is the mark of somebody who leaves you free to be yourself and knows exactly where you're headed. That's one of the reasons why [casting director] Laray Mayfield is such a great collaborator, because she is exhaustive for David in his desire to find exactly the right person. You know, in the second portion of my career, throwing elbows was an important part of that, and there was a time when people would say, "I don't think we can see him for that because he doesn't have an edge."

ACTOR

HOLT McCALLANY

This New York–born character actor has become something of a totem in the Fincher oeuvre. Two small but crucial supporting roles in *Alien 3* and *Fight Club* gave his career in film a jump start. But McCallany also symbolises Fincher's judiciousness and memory when it comes to selecting collaborators, as he returned nearly two decades later to play the complex role of Detective Bill Tench in *Mindhunter*. At time of writing McCallany was in the middle of shooting Guillermo del Toro's *Nightmare Alley* in Toronto.

Although you're probably most associated with being in *Mindhunter*, you were also in David Fincher's first movie. Are you able to recall your first interaction with him?

Sure. I was a young actor in New York City, and really very much at the beginning of my career. I had had a couple of small parts in films; one scene in a movie with Sean Penn; a horror movie. Really nothing. I was mostly just a stage actor. I was an understudy in the Broadway production of *Biloxi Blues*. I replaced Woody Harrelson when he got *Cheers*. I did a lot of off-Broadway plays. One day, I got a call from a casting director, a gentleman named Billy Hopkins. It was for *Alien 3*, and he called me in, and I got to read for David. You have to understand that, at that time, I wasn't aware of who David was. He was a young guy, approximately my age. It was his first movie. Obviously, it was a big film. It was part of a franchise. He had founded Propaganda, and he was a very successful commercial and music video director, but I didn't know him and I came in and I auditioned and he seemed to like me. Then I got a call and Billy said that he was offering me a part. I was excited. But what happened was, I was living with a girl at that time, and the job was like five months in London. In the original script, the role of Junior, which was my part, it was a very small part. The girl was saying, "You have to go to England for five months and it's only this small part. I don't want you to leave for that long. Why don't you stay with me?" We had an argument about it, and finally, I called Billy and I said, "I guess, you know, I'm not gonna go," and he said, "You know, well, I think that David is going to want to speak to you. He's going to want to call you at home." I said, "Really?" Then David Fincher called me and he said, "Listen, don't worry about the script. I have a lot of ideas for your character, and I'm going to shoot with you a lot." And I said, "Okay, then I'm in. Thank you." I was very young. I had no résumé. Why me? If you look at that film, what you see is all of these very accomplished British actors: Charles Dance; the late Brian Glover; Paul McGann and Ralph Brown, who had done *Withnail and I*, which is a film that I know David really liked. I didn't know why I would merit being invited to come all the way to England and to work with these very accomplished British actors. But I didn't ask questions and I just showed up and I did the film and, you know, true to his word, David put me in a lot of scenes, and the film was a great experience. As you're aware, I'm sure, the studio eventually took the film away from David in the post-production process and recut it.

There are problems with the film, but there's such a visceral clarity to, I guess I would call it, your one, big scene, which is a really unpleasant sequence.
I remember it very clearly, as if it were yesterday.

For a Hollywood film, it's a pretty nasty scene.
Well, here's what I would say to you regarding that. I have a lot of admiration and a lot of gratitude to Sigourney Weaver, and the reason is, she came up to me and she said, "Holt. It's very important to me that this scene feels real. So, I want you to know that whatever you think it is that you would do in this kind of a scene, or that the character would do, I want you to know that that's okay, whatever that may be. If you need to grab me, or slap me, or whatever you think it is, I want this to feel real." And what I really appreciated about that is the fact that it kind of freed me from a lot of the inhibitions that I had felt prior to that because she's the star of the movie, one of the highest paid actors in the world, and I'm like a young actor who's basically on his first big movie. I didn't want to step out of line. But I wanted the scene to be good. I wanted David to be happy, first and foremost, but I also didn't want her to be uncomfortable. The fact that she said that to me, it made me feel like, "Okay, let's go for it. Let's do whatever it is. Let's let those emotions out and let's let that element of violence that needs to be there in that kind of scene." It is the expression of this subtext that exists throughout the whole movie of these guys are on this forgotten planet and they haven't seen a woman in God knows how long and my name is Junior. I'm the youngest guy. I see a woman and I can't control myself. But I'll always be grateful to Sigourney for having that attitude because that conversation she had with me was really helpful to me before we shot that scene.

In addition to being grateful for the opportunity that Fincher gave you, and being aware of the studio's meddling, was Fincher's own frustration palpable while he was directing the film?
I think that it was. David has a certain directing style that's very much his own. All the things you know very well without me saying it. He's very meticulous, very driven to make something as good as it can possibly be. Very, very specific about the notes he will give to the actors and to the crew. He wants to get what he wants to get and he's going to stay there as long as it takes. Let's be honest, he's not very tolerant of mistakes. He doesn't like you to slow him down. He expects a very high standard of excellence from every department, and I think that some of the British crew bristled a little bit at his directing style. I remember Sigourney and Charles Dutton and I threw a wrap party at the Groucho Club for the British artists and for the crew, and David attended, and this was really at the end of the shoot, and I remember saying to David, "Did you have a good experience here, David, in England?" He looked at me, he said, "I'm never coming back here."

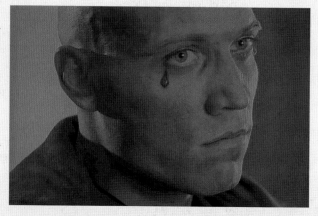

You have a bigger part in _Fight Club_ than you do in _Alien 3_. You have a couple of very memorable scenes. I'm sure millions of people would recognize you and your face from that movie because, you know, it really stands out.
You're absolutely right, and you know, for many, many years after I did _Fight Club_, it was the performance for which I was most frequently recognized by the public, even though it's a small part.

The film is essentially almost like a two-hander with Brad and Edward, a two-hander with a girl, you know what I mean? But you know, me and Jared Leto and Meat Loaf, yeah, we're there, but it's very much a supporting character. And yet, I can't tell you, I can't count how many times I would have people walk up to me and go, "His name is Robert Paulson."

I bet.

"Hey, you're the guy from *Fight Club*!" And you know how I felt about that? I felt deeply gratified, because if I was going to be recognized for anything, let me be recognized for having been a part of such a unique and original and special and memorable film. I can tell you that every actor in Hollywood wanted to be in *Fight Club*. *Se7en* was this remarkable film. I think it's a masterpiece. Also, the script for *Fight Club*, there was certainly nothing else at any of the studios that resembled that. Even when we were shooting, we all had a very clear sense of the fact that we were a part of something special, and I don't think that any of us could have predicted that the film would become what it has become. We were all kind of a little mystified when it launched and there was kind of a lukewarm reception to the film in many quarters. As I've said before in an interview, I remember very well Rosie O'Donnell coming on her show to say, "Whatever you do, don't see Fight Club. It's demented. It's depraved." There are a lot of people who had problems with the movie, but that did not describe those of us who were part of the project. We were really proud to be in that movie.

And then from Fight Club, *you have an even bigger role in* Mindhunter.

He promotes people. Erik Messerschmidt, who was our director of photography on *Mindhunter*, was a gaffer on *Gone Girl*. One of the head writers in season two of *Mindhunter*, a very talented woman named Courtenay Miles, had been our first A.D. in season one. Josh Donen, who was a writer on the show, had been David's agent! He'll give you an opportunity that another director or producer wouldn't if he feels that you can do the job. But then you better deliver. You better do your homework and you better show up and be prepared and be ready for work and be able to sustain your focus and your concentration.

What was your basic preparation for Bill Tench then?

At the risk of sounding slightly pretentious, Orson Welles famously said that in each of us there is a poet and a priest and an assassin and a revolutionary, that you remove the things about yourself that don't correspond to the character that you wish to create. I'm not Bill Tench, but I have certain things in common with him, and it was about identifying those and accessing those. Issues of fatherhood and what that means, and what it means to be a detective in that kind of job. I think these guys really believe that they fulfill a very important role in society, and they're not wrong about that. They feel a certain responsibility. An obligation. John Douglas, who wrote *Mindhunter*, one of the most famous FBI agents probably of all time, had a complete nervous breakdown and was unable to work for a very long period of time. Why is that? It's because they obsess about these cases. They're always thinking about them. They're always trying to walk a mile in the shoes of the killer. So, it's a very dark place to inhabit, because in the back of your mind, you're always kind of thinking about it and processing information and poring over crime scene photos and talking to the families of victims and trying to put together the pieces of the puzzle. So that's part of it: How can I think? How can I change the way that I think about these crimes and about these criminals, and put myself into the mentality of these detectives?

I would answer it in this way: David Fincher is in charge of every aspect of the production, and he oversees the entire thing. Even in an episode that he's not directing, he's still watching those dailies every single night. And if things aren't working, then he's gonna step in. Now, having said that, he is also going to afford his guest directors every courtesy that he would insist on if he were directing. Though, if he's seeing stuff in the dailies that isn't working, you better believe we will be reshooting that. And we are reshooting it because, ultimately, it's his name. Netflix isn't greenlighting the project because Holt McCallany wants to do it, and they're certainly not greenlighting because Joe Penhall wrote something. Joe, coming from a theater background—and I'm just giving you my impression—didn't fully understand that television is a very different animal. Unlike in a play, where the playwright's words are sacrosanct. It ain't gonna work that way in TV. We got into rehearsals and we go through every script line by line, and we talk about every line. "Okay, why am I saying this? Is there another way to say it? Is there a better way to say it? Am I stating something that I've already stated in a previous episode? Is there an element of redundancy? Is there a more direct, more dramatic, more interesting way to express what I'm trying to express?" We have those conversations. This is in the production office sitting around the table. I loved those moments because that's when I have an opportunity, having done my homework, to say, "Would it be possible, do you think, for me to say X instead of Y? Because it just feels to me . . . " and then you better make your case, and you better have thought it through, because you're allowed to ask questions, but they had better be relevant. And Joe, you know, didn't seem to get it! So, we were having one of those rehearsals that I'm describing, and talking about the dialogue, and David was suggesting some modifications, and Joe was bristling.

I don't want to not give Joe any credit because he deserves credit. He wrote an entire season of the show. But when we got under the hood, David made a lot of changes. David put his stamp on it. You can't challenge David on that set. You can present an idea. You can ask questions. You can express a different point of view. But don't for a moment allow yourself to be confused about who's in charge. This is a David Fincher production, and David is going to be the final word on every decision regarding every aspect of the production. Now, I personally think that's a great thing, because who else would you want? You know, part of the reason that most television is so bad is because they produce it by committee, and they've got the studio executives weighing it and then the network executives weighing it, and, you know, to be very candid, and this is probably a controversial opinion to express, but I wonder, in many instances, how solid is the judgement of some of those people is? They're not writers. They're not directors. They're not actors. And yet, they often proclaim themselves to be experts on every aspect of the production. Well, some of them may be! So, what I like about being with David is that if I have an idea of something that I want to do with the character, I have to only convince one guy, David Fincher, and if David signs off on it, that's it and I get to do it.

ERIC MESSERSCHMIDT

Erik Messerschmidt is one of Fincher's more recent recruits, and yet another example of a creative collaborator who was rushed up the pecking order for his ability to execute the director's famously exacting vision. His first job for the director was as a gaffer on *Gone Girl*, and just two years later he was given his first major cinematographer gig on both seasons of *Mindhunter*. He also took on the not inconsiderable task of shooting *Mank* in black-and-white and in a fashion which harked back to Hollywood's classic era, and won an Oscar for his troubles.

You worked with David Fincher for the first time as a gaffer on *Gone Girl*. I'm interested in hearing about that experience, but also the evolution of your professional relationship, which led to the point where you're shooting a feature with him.

I was a young man when I got the job on *Gone Girl*. I had done a few commercials with Jeff Cronenweth but never a film, and Jeff's gaffer was doing *Interstellar*, the Nolan film, so he wasn't available. When you're staffing a movie with David Fincher you want to make sure you get a very particular type of person. You want someone who's thoughtful and intelligent and can speak for themselves and is not intimidated, it's a short list and one I'm thankful Jeff included me on. David has a very particular way of working that is incredibly unique, and you either get it or you don't, and I think those of us that see that and see the value in it and recognize the importance of how he works and can communicate with him with some sort of mutual sensibility fit well in the system.

But I think David's reputation precedes him in a way that's not really accurate. People accuse him of being a taskmaster, or a control freak. He is actually incredibly collaborative and generous and curious about the world; curious about human beings and interested in storytelling. He is one of the most generous people I know.

How did you develop the specific visual perspective of *Mindhunter*?

I think it probably is more in terms of camera direction than lighting, actually, in the case of *Mindhunter*. It's like, let's—and it absolutely came from David, was, "We're going to look over people's shoulders. We're going to look around, we're going to observe the conversation from outside the conversation. Until we allow the audience to be inside it, but we're going to be very particular about when we do that." That, to me, is incredibly interesting, and I had a great time working that out with the directors and figuring out when we were going to do that.

When you say, "looking over the shoulder," it's like it seems the interrogation scene in *Zodiac* is one style book for *Mindhunter*. Not meaning you copy it over and over again, but that's a scene that you feel echoes of in a lot of the set-ups and a lot of the framing and the direction of that show.

I think some of that is just David's cinema vocabulary, to be honest. You know, when I first met with him about the show, I was like, "What is this show?" and he said, "We're gonna shoot two people sitting across a table from each other with a Styrofoam cup in the middle and we're gonna make it fascinating." I was like, "*What*?" And I had done procedural TV in my career. I had done really bad procedural TV. But that was before I read the scripts and before I had seen Cameron Britton play Ed Kemper and before I kind of understood what it was.

What an actor. What an actor that guy is. Wow.

Yeah, he's spectacular. But I think David—and I think you would agree—is a classical filmmaker. I mean, he's classically trained. He responds to classical composition methodology. He's not interested in being different for the sake of being different. I think he's gone through that in his career. If you watch *Panic Room*, he's experimented with things that didn't work and learned from his mistakes, and fallen back to classic film techniques that work for him. They also support the way he wants to tell the story. In terms of cutting sequence and stuff, I think the things that we did in *Mindhunter* absolutely echo some things he learned in *Zodiac*. Although, I think there are moments of playfulness in *Zodiac* that aren't really in *Mindhunter*.

There are color values in this show that are very sort of deliberately chosen, but I'm interested, too, in the contrast between the seasons, because season two strikes me as more exterior. I don't know if you'd agree with that, but there's more exploration of the different cities and spaces.

I think that's absolutely true. I believe that what we call "style" or "aesthetic" or whatever in filmmaking is much more the result of working practice than intent. In the way that you can never predict the way a dish is going to taste when you read the recipe. It's all about the application of technique. So, you know, we filter our technique, we make decisions about what we're going to do, we set our visual rules which we may or may not choose to later break, and then the result is the combination of those—of the application of that technique. So in the case of *Mindhunter*, where, at least in the first season, we're in these very restricted rooms with very formal framing and very minimal camera movement, the show feels restrained and small and contained and containable. And then in the second season, when the script takes us outside, and we're able to see more of the world, the scope of the show expands. That's not really anything other than just the practical realities of those locations, you know. We could now move the camera because the characters are moving through the space and we can follow them through the space. I think the two seasons are very much different shows in that way, you know, but it's because the story is different. The first season is sort of the exposition and the second season is kind of the second act in a way, and unfortunately, we don't have a third act.

Yeah, well, that sucks a lot. Even though he doesn't direct all the episodes, Fincher is understood as the guiding intelligence of this show. Is that the case?

I felt a tremendous responsibility to oversee the stylistic application, at least in terms of camerawork, because episodic TV directors, and obviously not all of the directors we had are sort of journeymen directors, but it's an interesting thing that doesn't really happen in feature film. If a director like Andrew Dominik comes in, and he is ostensibly an auteur, right, and he makes his films very differently from David and he also writes his own films, so for him to step into that situation was a big change. TV directing is a little bit like being a for-hire prose writer. It's like, "Okay, this week you're writing for *The New Yorker* and I need you to write Shouts & Murmurs." Well, if you normally write for *Vanity Fair* and now you're gonna write Shouts & Murmurs, you're gonna read the previous columns and you're going to work in that style, right? You have some editorial staff that helps you through that and I felt a responsibility to do that to some extent, and I definitely applied some pressure to the directors with regard to trying to protect the integrity of the show in totality. Not because I didn't feel as if the directors were going to hold the integrity, but the show is so specific and particular that it was important to kind of stay within the boundary lines of what it was that we had set up. But David was there every day. He was in the blocking rehearsals. He's on the tech scouts. He's on the director scouts. He assisted in the selection of locations. He weighed in on the costume fittings. He is absolutely there.

Would you say he's interested in procedure as a subject?
Yeah, well, that's a really interesting question. I hadn't thought of that. David is not a sentimental filmmaker, you know?

No kidding.
He is not interested in nostalgia as a theme. I think he's interested in nostalgia as a point of reference.

Absolutely. It's a big distinction.
And he's not tongue-in-cheek or exploitative of those sorts of things. Not to be too critical of *Mad Men*, but the kind of "put pomade in their hair and backlight everybody and make them look glossy" is not David's view of the 1950s or the 1960s. I think it's interesting what you say about procedure. I think David is a logical human being. He's interested in rational decision-making and practicality. One of the tenets of the set is if you have an idea—and it went for everybody on the crew—of how to improve the shot, speak up. But only do it if it's something he needs to hear, not if it's something you need to say. Don't make it about you. Make it about the show. So, when you have that kind of environment where it's like, "no, let's work on this together, but it's not about ego at all, and in fact what it is, you have someone who will call it out as ego," which, unfortunately, most of the creative energy in the film business comes from that.

Is there a time where you can definitely remember putting something forward that not just got through but that was, you know, what's the famous Fincher line? "There's two ways to do something and the other way is wrong." Do you have a time where you had the right one?
Well, uh . . . yeah. I mean, there's probably more examples in *Mank* than there are in *Mindhunter*. By the way, when David says that, he's not making the assumption that his way is always right.

I've always liked that line because, as much as it's a kind of brazen, provocative thing, it's essentially how everybody works at the end of the day.
They're difficult things to point out because the alternatives are hard to articulate, but like, you know, *Mindhunter* is essentially told in cuts, and it's told, in many cases, in very complex staging and screen direction issues. Depending on your cinema vocabulary, those scenes can get incredibly complicated very quickly. There is a mathematical way that I started to break these scenes apart in terms of figuring out how to cover them. There comes a time in a lot of these scenes where you have to make screen direction choices. You have to exclude certain shots because of scheduling. They turn into kind of logic puzzles when you shoot scenes with this formal framing and you're dogmatic to screen direction. So, there are, I think, several instances where David and I would not argue but debate which side of the line to shoot a scene from, or how to approach a cutting sequence. Probably the best example is there's a scene in the Montie Rissell episode, which David actually directed as a reshoot. Montie sat down, and in the blocking rehearsal, he faced the window, he didn't face the interviewers, and a lot of the scene is played like this. And I had lit it through these front windows, and David's amazing to work for as a cinematographer because he takes light into consideration. He laid it out and he's like, "This is great, we can shoot it from here and it'll be backlit because you're going to want to light them from the windows and it'll all be edge-lit and that'll be fantastic, right?" and I said, "Yeah, great."

Then it came time to shoot Montie's close-up, and from Holt's point-of-view, he's sort of in profile for part of the scene, and in the blocking rehearsal, I was like, "We should shoot a close-up where he's lit like I am right now," and David was like, "In the front light?" I was like, "No, no, it'll be beautiful, it'll be all pearlescent and he's sort of talking about his father and we'll put this—" and David was like, "I don't know, man. Like, the whole scene is back lit, you've got all this edge shape, and then you want to cut to a close-up of a kid looking in flat front light." I was like, "Yeah, let's do it." It turned out—you know, we put the camera there, and it turned out to be the right decision, and it's not about my authorship or whatever, it's just like, I think it's the process of advocating for certain things and why you want collaborators, you know? And David agreed in the end. He was like, "Yeah, that is really beautiful," and it worked out.

When you're making a black-and-white movie like *Mank*, what are you saying we're not going to do?

Well, at this point, David and I don't pontificate very much about the movie. There isn't a lot of, "Oh, what are we going to do?" There isn't a lot of sitting down in the office and, like, poring over stuff. What I do when I work with him, and what I did on *Mank*, was I read the script, obviously, and I just pulled like two hundred stills. Movie frames, fine art photography, paintings, things like that, and I assembled it into a kind of look book and I just cold emailed it to him, with some contextual notes. Like this for this scene, this for this scene, this for this scene. But merely as a conversation starter, not as a like, "This is what I see." It's like, "This is what I think is interesting about this." What's great about David, and what a lot of directors are not capable of doing, is David's incredibly reflexive with his notes. Like, he doesn't have to consider it very much. He can sort of see. He's like, "Yes, no, I need to see more like this, I think this is interesting, absolutely not, we're not doing this." Like, he's very clear, but it's not because he's not receptive to the ideas, he's just really good at assessing things. I took basically those two hundred stills and whittled them down.

But to answer your question, it wasn't like, "Let's remake *Citizen Kane*." I'd shot some black-and-white commercials and I'd shot some black-and-white music videos and obviously I'd shot black-and-white in film school. Black-and-white for a cinematographer is seductive and almost like a siren. It can lead you down this path, I whispers to you: "No, come this way, hard shadows and Venetian blinds and it'll be great, and people will look at it and be like, 'Oh, he did the . . .'" and I was so worried that I was going to do that and draw attention to the work or make the wrong choice because I was excited about shooting black-and-white. You see it, you know it happens a lot. You know these TV shows do these kind of token black-and-white episodes, like, "Let's do the noir episode!" I was like, I'm terrified of that, because you don't want people to be like, "Oh, it's tongue in cheek," or "He's being coy or cheeky with it," you know?

So, there were definitely early conversations with David and I where we said, "Okay, within the canon of black-and-white photography exists this incredible spectrum of technique and style, from glamor to noir to realism—and we can be reverential to all of those within the context of the scene and the sequence of scenes." And you see it. There are moments in *Mank* where I may have overreached a little. I'm always a little worried about that. Thalberg's office is very classic Hollywood day interior noir kind of look, with these Venetian blinds, patterns on the wall. The movie is stylized but hopefully it doesn't draw so much attention to itself visually that you lose the connection to what's happening on screen.

I can't square this idea that, per many critics of the film, *Mank* is a love letter to the movies. I'm like, have you read a love letter before? This is not a love letter. There's affection, but that's not all there is.

Right. I've lately got a lot of questions where people are like, "Well, why didn't you shoot on film? It's supposed to be a black-and-white movie. Why didn't you shoot on film?" And my answer is always the same. The answer is, "If you want consistent, predictable results, film is the worst medium to shoot on." If you're interested in spontaneity and unpredicted magic and the sort of happy accident, it's a wonderful medium, and I'm not suggesting that one or the other is better, but David is not interested in being surprised. And he's absolutely not interested in being surprised tomorrow about something he spent $200,000 shooting today.

ACKNOWLEDGEMENTS

ILLUSTRATION

This is the author speaking:

They say that good things come in threes. Which doesn't stop me from hoping I'll someday do a fourth book—a fifth? A sixth? With rising coastlines and Donald Trump considering another White House run?—in tandem with Abrams and *Little White Lies*. Or maybe we've run out of worthy auteurs. To the judicious Eric Klopfer, the ever-flexible Clive Wilson, and especially serious mensch David Jenkins—who calmly oversaw the writing, editing and execution of *Mind Games* (and came up with its title) during a period where workspaces were transformed into panic rooms and collaboration was dependent on social networks—I say: thank you and [extreme William Somerset voice] I'll be around.

Mind Games was designed by Fabrizio Festa, Olesia Lipskaia, Hannah Nightingale, Tertia Nash. Their work, I believe, speaks for itself. Thanks also to *Little White Lies* MVP Adam Woodward for the usual behind the scenes help.

Whether it was a fear of being unable to think clearly in the midst of a strange year or the fact that David Fincher is a tough nut to crack, I picked more brains than usual on this one. Respect, gratitude and socially distanced hugs to Steve MacFarlane, Sydney Urbanek, Neil Badahur, Kam Collins, Devika Girish, Haley Mlotek, Lydia Ogwang, Courtney Duckworth, Bart Testa, Danelle Eliav, Felipe Furtado, Elizabeth Nelson (and Mr Style), Darrah Teitel, Blake Howard, Iman Bundu, Mark Peranson, Jesse Hawken, Michael Koresky, and the Wife Guys (Bronwyn, Meg, Mallory, Ben, Tina, and Adara) Special thanks to my *Ringer* editors and fellow Fincher-heads Sean Fennessey and Chris Ryan, who allowed some writing I did for the website a few years back to be repurposed into the *Zodiac* chapter, and also to Jason Gallagher, Andrew Gruttadro, Miles Surrey, and Mose Bergmann.

For anybody thinking of writing a book—of any length, in any style, and on any topic—my good advice would be to seek out people who will actually give you good advice. Sofia Majstorovic, Brendan Boyle, and Madeleine Wall each did their part for this book by way of subtraction, substitution, and sarcasm. The latter in my experience is the truest indicator that somebody cares; by that metric, they care a lot.

Gone Girl evangelist (and senior Wife Guy) Anna Swanson pulled double duty, serving simultaneously as our main researcher and interview liaison; she was instrumental in securing the participation of most of the artists who appear in this book. I'd like to thank Jeff Cronenweth, Arthur Max, John Carroll Lynch, Laray Mayfield, Erik Messerschmidt, Holt McCallany, and Angus Wall for their time and candor. Vikram Murthi, a fine film critic, provided timely, verbatim transcription and helpful thoughts about the interviews and the project as a whole.

I am indebted to Dooho Choi for enlisting Bong Joon-ho to write the concise, beautiful foreword that precedes this book, and to Director Bong for his words and his of course his own cinema, which I would classify (according to his chosen taxonomy) as beautifully curvilinear but still cutting—figure eights traced with razor wire.

I'm grateful, as always, to an inner circle that doubled as a life preserver over the last year: Matt and Suzie; Sandy (Grandma) and Vesa (Papa); Evelyne (Granny) and David (Zayde). And, forever in my heart (and more than ever, my personal space) Tanya, Lea, and Avery. The latter was born under unusual circumstances as *Mind Games* was reaching the finish line, and as of this writing, she is cute as a Button. I only hope that she doesn't grow up too fast.

Se7en/Zodiac	Ana Godis
Alien 3/Panic Room	Margherita Morotti
The Game/Fight Club	Kingsley Nebechi
The Curious Case of Benjamin Button/ The Social Network	Freya Betts
The Girl with the Dragon Tattoo/ Gone Girl	Hsiao-Ron Cheng
Mank	Jaxon Northon

IMAGE CREDITS

Key (tl) top left   (bl) bottom left
     (tm) top middle   (bm) bottom middle
     (tr) top right   (br) bottom right

Every effort has been made to identify copyright holders
and obtain their permission for the use of copyrighted
material. The publisher apologizes for any errors or
omissions and would be grateful if notified of any corrections
that should be incorporated in future reprints or editions
of this book.

INDEX

BIBLIOGRAPHY

Abbott, Megan. "Gillian Flynn Isn't Going to Write the Kind of Women You Want." *Vanity Fair*, June 28, 2018.

Acocella, Joan. "Man of Mystery." *The New Yorker*, January 2, 2011.

Allen, Valerie. "Se7en: Medieval Justice, Modern Justice." *Journal of Popular Culture* 43 (2010): 1150-1172.

Andrew, Geoff. "Fritz Lang's *M*: The Blueprint for the Serial Killer Movie." British Film Institute. Updated April 24, 2019. https://www2.bfi.org.uk/news-opinion/news-bfi/features/fritz-langs-m-blueprint-serial-killer-movie.

Asch, Mark. 2011. "Trash Hit: The Girl with the Dragon Tattoo." *L Magazine*, December 21, 2011.

Bailey, Jason. 2019. "'Mindhunter': What to Know and Read About the Killers in Real Life." *New York Times*, August 19, 2019, Arts.

Baker, Katie. "The Opening Evisceration of Mark Zuckerberg in 'The Social Network.'" The Ringer, September 21, 2020.

Baker, Peter C. "The Men Who Still Love 'Fight Club.'" *The New Yorker*, November 4, 2019.

Barfield, Chrales. "'Alien 3' Effects Person Talks the Time David Fincher Dared the Head of Fox to Fire Him." Playlist, February 26, 2019.

Beaumont-Thomas, Ben. "*Fight Club* Author Chuck Palahniuk on His Book Becoming a Bible for the Incel Movement." *Guardian*, July 20, 2018.

Bereznak, Alyssa. "Ten Years Later, Mark Zuckerberg Is Still Trying to Overcome 'The Social Network.'" The Ringer, September 22, 2020.

Bernstein, Jacob, and Guy Trebay. "George Michael's Freedom Video: An Oral History." *New York Times*, December 30, 2016.

Bishop, Bryan. "Author Chuck Palahniuk Tells Us Why It's Time to Re-Open *Fight Club*." Verge, May 27, 2015.

Bitel, Anton. "Why *The Game* Remains David Fincher's Trickiest Thriller." *Little White Lies*, July 27, 2020.

Blauvelt, Christian, and Christian Blauvelt. "Ben Mankiewicz Shares What Happened After the Events of 'Mank'—and His Role in the Film." IndieWire, December 8, 2020.

Blomqvist, Hakan. "The Man Behind the Dragon Tattoo." *Jacobin*, October 20, 2015.

Boorsma, Megan. "The Whole Truth: The Implications of America's True Crime Obsession." *Elon Law Review* 9, no. 1 (2017): 209–224.

Boyle, Brendan. "Witness for the Prosecution." Stars in My Crown, October 31. 2020. https://brendanowicz.substack.com/p/witness-for-the-prosecution.

"Brutal, Relentless, Disturbing, Brilliant: Chuck Palahniuk's *Fight Club*." Book Marks (Literary Hub), September 22, 2017.

Bucher, John. "Joe Penhall on the Nature of Criminality in MINDHUNTER and THE KING OF THIEVES. LA Screenwriter, January 31, 2019.

Burkeman, Oliver. "Gillian Flynn on Her Bestseller *Gone Girl* and Accusations of Misogyny." *Guardian*, May 1, 2013.

Carter, Jimmy. "Fight Club: Brad Pitt and Edward Norton TALK about Fight Club...an Interview." June 9, 2008. https://www.youtube.com/watch?v=7VaA6_CDRyY.

Cha, Steph. "Laughing at 'Gone Girl.'" *Los Angeles Review of Books*, October 22, 2014.

Chang, Justin. "*The Girl with the Dragon Tattoo*." *Variety*. December 13, 2011.

Chiarella, Tom. "Daniel Craig Is a Movie Star from England. Any Questions?' *Esquire*. August 1, 2011.

Chitwood, Adam. "How Fincher's *Dragon Tattoo* Marked the End of the Big Budget Adult Drama." Collider, November 7, 2018.

Cohen, Anne. "Marion Davies' Scandalously Glamorous Life Deserves Its Own Movie." Refinery29, December 4, 2020.

Collins, K. Austin, and K. Austin Collins. "David Fincher's 'Mank' Brings Old Hollywood Thrills—and Eerie Political Chills." *Rolling Stone*, November 12, 2020.

Cooke, Tim. "Why Zodiac Remains David Fincher's Most Puzzling Masterpiece." *Little White Lies*, February 26, 2017.

Cutler, Aaron. "New York Film Festival 2010: David Fincher's *The Social Network*." Slant magazine, September 27, 2010.

Cwik, Greg. "For the Man Who Has Everything: Close-Up on 'The Game.'" Notebook (MUBI), March 26, 2019.

Dargis, Manohla. "Hunting a Killer as the Age of Aquarius Dies." *New York Times*, March 2, 2007, Movies.

———. "Millions of Friends, but Not Very Popular." *New York Times*, September 23, 2010, Movies.

———. "No Job, No Money and Now, No Wife." *New York Times*, September 25, 2014.

Denby, David. "Influencing People." *The New Yorker*, September 27, 2010.

Desowitz, Bill, and Bill Desowitz. "'Mindhunter': David Fincher and Editor Kirk Baxter's Dance of Death." IndieWire, May 29, 2018.

Dibdin, Emma. "The Five True Crime Stories That Inspired 'Mindhunter' Season Two." *Esquire*, August 15, 2019.

Dobbins, Amanda, Sean Fennessey, and Chris Ryan. "The Everything David Fincher Ranking." The Ringer, September 25, 2020.

Dong, Kelley. "Millions To Be Made: David Fincher's 'Mank.'" Notebook (MUBI), December 14, 2020.

Dowd, A.A. "*Alien3* Is so Much Better than David Fincher and Its Reputation Insists." A.V. Club, May 14, 2018.

Doyle, Paulie. "How 'Fight Club' Became the Ultimate Handbook for Men's Rights Activists." VICE, January 5, 2017.

Ebert, Roger. "Chris Burden: The 'Body Artist.'" RogerEbert.com, April 8, 1975.

———. "Panic Room." RogerEbert.com, March 29, 2002.

———. "Seven." RogerEbert.com, September 22, 1995.

———. "The Curious Case of Benjamin Button." RogerEbert.com, December 23, 2008.

———. "The Girl with the Dragon Tattoo." RogerEbert.com, December 19, 2011.

———. "Zodiac." RogerEbert.com, August 23, 2007.

Edelstein, David. "Movie Review: Fincher's *The Girl With the Dragon Tattoo* Brings the Hate." Vulture, December 19, 2011.

Emile, Evelyn. "Prison Films and the Idea of Two Worlds." *Brooklyn Rail*, June 20, 2019.

Ephron, Nora. "The Girl Who Fixed the Umlaut" *The New Yorker*, June 28, 2010.

Evangelista, Chris. "Watch: David Fincher Directed a Super Bowl Commercial Scored by Atticus Ross." Slashfilm, February 4, 2021.

Every Frame a Painting. *David Fincher - And the Other Way Is Wrong*. October 1, 2014. https://www.youtube.com/watch?v=QPAloq5MCUA.

Fagan, Kevin. "Zodiac Killer Case: DNA May Offer Hope of Solving the Mystery." *San Francisco Chronicle*, May 3, 2018.

Fear, David. "'Fight Club' at 20: The Twisted Joys of David Fincher's Toxic-Masculinity Sucker Punch." *Rolling Stone*, December 16, 2019.

———. "David Fincher: The Rolling Stone Interview." *Rolling Stone*, January 12, 2021.

Fienberg, Daniel. "'Mindhunter' Season 2: TV Review." *Hollywood Reporter*, August 15, 2019.

Fight Club. *Kirkus Reviews*. June 1, 1996.

Freer, Ian. "The Curious Case of Benjamin Button Review." *Empire*, January 1, 2000.

French, Philip. "Film of the Week: Panic Room." *Guardian*, May 5, 2002.

Garber, Megan. "One Way *The Social Network* Got Facebook Right." *The Atlantic*. February 3, 2019.

Goldberg, Matt. "'Alien 3' Revisited: The Films of David Fincher." *Collider*, October 4, 2017.

———. "'Se7en' Revisited: The Films of David Fincher." *Collider*, October 5, 2017.

———. "'The Game' Revisited: The Films of David Fincher." *Collider*, October 6, 2017.

Gregory, Drew. "I Didn't Understand 'Gone Girl' Until I Was a Woman." *Bright Wall/Dark Room*, November 26, 2019.

Groves, Tim. "Murder by Imitation: The Influence of *Se7en*'s Title Sequence." Screening the Past, April 2018.

Gullickson, Brad. "The 'Alien 3' That Could Have Been." Film School Rejects, August 16, 2019.

Halbfinger, David M. "Lights, Bogeyman, Action." *New York Times*, February 18, 2007.

Harris, Aisha. "How Faithful Is David Fincher's *Gone Girl*?." *Slate*, September 30, 2014.

Harris, Mark. "Nerding Out with David Fincher." Vulture, October 23, 2020.

Harris, Paul. "Focus: So Who Was the Zodiac Killer?' *Observer*, April 15, 2007, sec. Film.

Harvilla, Rob. "Decoding David Fincher's Gorgeous, Goofy, and Iconic Music Video Career." The Ringer. September 24, 2020.

Heaney, Katie. "Is True Crime Over?" The Cut, August 19, 2019.

Heffernan, Teresa. "When the Movie Is Better Than the Book: *Fight Club*, Consumption, and Vital Signs." *Framework: The Journal of Cinema and Media* (Detroit, MI) 57, no. 2 (Fall 2016): 91–103.

Hertz, Barry. "The Lingering Cultural Bruise of David Fincher's *Fight Club*, 20 Years Later." *Globe and Mail*, October 13, 2019.

Holmes, Linda. "'The Social Network' Is A Great Movie, But Don't Overload the Allegory." NPR, October 1, 2010.

Honeycutt, Kirk. "'The Curious Case of Benjamin Button': Film Review." *Hollywood Reporter*, November 24, 2008.

Horowitz, Josh. "David Fincher Didn't Want to Make 'Another Serial-Killer Movie' . . . Until 'Zodiac' Came Along." MTV News, January 2, 2008.

Howe, Desson. "'Alien 3.'" *Washington Post*, May 22, 1992.

Hunter, Rob. "37 Things We Learned from David Fincher's 'Gone Girl' Commentary." Film School Rejects, August 5, 2015.

———. "50 Things We Learned from David Fincher's 'Panic Room' Commentary." Film School Rejects, June 30, 2016.

———. "48 Things We Learned from David Fincher's 'Zodiac' Commentary." Film School Rejects, August 25, 2016.

———. "29 Things We Learned from David Fincher's 'The Game' Commentary." Film School Rejects, November 10, 2016.

———. "33 Things We Learned from David Fincher's 'The Girl with the Dragon Tattoo' Commentary." Film School Rejects, November 17, 2018.

Jagernauth, Kevin. "David Fincher Says He Shouldn't Have Directed 'The Game,' Dislikes Superhero Movies & Talks 'Crazy' '20,000 Leagues.'" IndieWire, September 16, 2014.

Jenkins, David. "It's All True: A Conversation with David Fincher." *Little White Lies*, December 2, 2020.

Jensen, Jeff. "Cause for Alarm: Jodie Foster in "Panic Room.'" *Entertainment Weekly*, February 15, 2002.

Jordison, Sam. "First Rule of Fight Club: No One Talks about the Quality of the Writing." *Guardian*, December 20, 2016.

Kashner, Sam. "*Gone Girl*'s Rosamund Pike, Oscar Nominee, Spills on Her Pregnancy, David Fincher, and That Unforgettable *Gone Girl* Scene." *Vanity Fair*, January 20, 2015.

Kehr, Dave. "A Curious Life, From Old Age to Cradle." *New York Times*, October 31, 2008.

Kettler, Sara. "Why the Zodiac Killer Has Never Been Identified." Biography, October 10, 2019. Updated December 17, 2020.

Kilday, Gregg. "The Making of 'The Girl with the Dragon Tattoo.'" *Hollywood Reporter*, January 14, 2012.

King, Angela. "The Prisoner of Gender: Foucault and the Disciplining of the Female Body." *Journal of International Women's Studies* 5, no. 2 (2014): 29–39.

Koehler, Sezin. "The Untold Truth of *Fight Club*." Looper, May 7, 2020.

Lacy, Sarah. "Memo to Aaron Sorkin: You Invented This Angry Nerd Misogyny Too." *TechCrunch*, October 11, 2020.

Lambie, Ryan. "Alien

Landekic, Lola, and Ian Albinson. "*The Girl with the Dragon Tattoo*." Art of the Title, February 21, 2012.

———. "*Panic Room*." Art of the Title, November 29, 2016.

Landekic, Lola. "The Game." Art of the Title, January 11, 2013.

Lane, Anthony. "Home Fries." *The New Yorker*, March 31, 2002.

Lang, Brent. "David Fincher on 'Mindhunter': 'I Don't Know If It Makes Sense to Continue.'" *Variety*, November 18, 2020.

Lawson, Richard. "*Mindhunter* Review: An Appealingly Repulsing Serial Killer Study." *Vanity Fair*, October 17, 2017.

Lazic, Manuela. "Fincher Moments: The Pure, Painstaking Romance in 'The Curious Case of Benjamin Button.'" The Ringer, September 23, 2020.

Lee, Nathan. "To Catch a Predator." *Village Voice*, February 20, 2007.

Lessig, Lawrence. "Sorkin vs. Zuckerberg." *New Republic*, October 1, 2010.

Levy, Emanuel. "Curious Case of Benjamin Button, The: Interview with David Fincher." EmanuelLevy, December 4, 2008.

Lincoln, Kevin. "What David Fincher's Fascination with Serial Killers Says About His Filmmaking." Vulture, November 9, 2017.

Macfarlane, Steve. "Beer Money." Element X Cinema, March 5, 2021.

Marchese, David. "Even Jodie Foster Is Still Trying to Figure Jodie Foster Out." *New York Times* magazine, January 31, 2021.

marty288. "Gone Girl: The Murder of Feminism or Unconventional Female Representation?' Marty28blogs, November 14, 2015.

Maslin, Janet. "FILM REVIEW; A Sickening Catalogue of Sins, Every One of Them Deadly." *New York Times*, September 22, 1995.

———. "FILM REVIEW; Terrifying Tricks That Make a Big Man Little." *New York Times*, September 12, 1997.

———. "FILM REVIEW; Such a Very Long Way from Duvets to Danger." *New York Times*, October 15, 1999.

Mason, Paul. "Systems and Process: The Prison in Cinema." Images, May 1998.

McCarthy, Todd. "The Game." *Variety*, September 5, 1997.

Mccluskey, Megan. "The True Story Behind David Fincher's New Movie *Mank*." *Time*, December 5, 2020.

Miller, Matt. "Have We Finally Grown Out of Thinking *Fight Club* Is a Good Movie?" *Esquire*, October 15, 2019.

Mills, Bart. "In 'Forrest Gump,' Historical Figures Speak for Themselves." *Chicago Tribune*, July 8, 1994.

Morris, Wesley. "The Girl with the Dragon Tattoo." Boston, December 20, 2011.

Morrow, Martin. "Review: The Social Network." CBC, September 30, 2010.

Mukherjee, Stotropama. "Charles Pierre Baudelaire: The Man of the Crowd." Accessed March 15, 2021.

Mulcahey, Matt. "'We Don't Find Shots, We Build Them': DP Erik Messerschmidt on *Mank*, Lens Flare Painting and Native Black and White." *Filmmaker*, December 22, 2020.

Myers, Scott. "Interview: Eric Roth on The Curious Case of Benjamin Button." Go Into The Story, December 27, 2008.

Naughton, John. "An Oral History of 'Fight Club,' 20 Years Since Its Release." *Men's Health*, November 11, 2019.

———. "Daniel Craig: A Very Secret Agent." *British GQ*, March 29, 2012.

Nayman, Adam. "How David Fincher Puts Himself in His Movies." The Ringer, September 23, 2020.

Newell, Chris. "Zodiac (2007): Never Let Ethics Get in the Way of a Good Story." Scriptophobic, May 9, 2019.

Newman, Kim. "Alien 3 Review." *Empire*, January 1, 2000.

Nielsen, Bianca. "Home Invasion and Hollywood Cinema: David Fincher's *Panic Room*." In *The Selling of 9/11: How a National Tragedy Became a Commodity*, edited by Dana Heller, 233–53. New York: Palgrave Macmillan, 2005.

Orr, Christopher. "The Movie Review: 'Zodiac.'" *The Atlantic*, July 30, 2007.

Panther, BL. "David Fincher's Madonna Videos Hone Her Style, but Dull Her Radical Edge." The Spool, December 6, 2020.

Pearce, Garth. "Alien3 – Empire's On Set Interviews With Sigourney Weaver And David Fincher." *Empire*, May 22, 2017.

Perez, Rodrigo. "Interview: David Fincher Talks Violence, Unpleasant Revenge & The Odd, Perverse Relationship That Drew Him To 'The Girl with the Dragon Tattoo.'" IndieWire, December 21, 2011.

Phillips, Brian. "Murder, We Wrote." The Ringer, January 22, 2020.

Phillips, Maya. "'The Social Network' 10 Years Later: A Grim Online Life Foretold." *New York Times*, October 5, 2020.

Phipps, Keith. "*The Social Network*." A.V. Club. September 30, 2010.

Pinkerton, Nick. "Bombast: Gone Finching." *Film Comment*. October 10, 2014.

———. "Fake It After You Make It." Employee Picks, December 31, 2020.

Poniewozik, James. "Review: 'Mindhunter' on Netflix Is More Chatter Than Splatter." *New York Times*, October 12, 2017.

Power, Ed. "Mindhunter, Season 1 Review: So Much More than Your Average Serial Killer Drama." *Telegraph*, October 15, 2017.

Prickett, Sarah Nicole. "How to Get under Aaron Sorkin's Skin (and Also, How to High-Five Properly)." *Globe and Mail*. June 23, 2012.

Radish, Christina. "Rosamund Pike Talks Gone Girl, 'That Scene,' and More at SBIFF." Collider, February 4, 2015.

Raftery, Brian. "The First Rule of Making 'Fight Club': Talk About 'Fight Club.'" The Ringer, March 26, 2019.

Rapold, Nicolas. "Curating Reality: Cinematographer Erik Messerschmidt and 'Mank.'" Notebook (MUBI), December 4, 2020.

Reardon, Kiva. "Patriarchal Parody: The Rom-Com Logic of David Fincher." The Hairpin, June 2, 2016.

Rebello, Stephen. "Playboy Interview: David Fincher." *Playboy*, September 16, 2014.

Reed, Atavia. "The New Face of the Home Invasion Thriller Is Black and Female." A.V. Club, May 31, 2019.

Rehling, Nicola. "Everyman and No Man: White, Heterosexual Masculinity in Contemporary Serial Killer Movies." *Jump Cut*, no. 49, Spring 2007.

Rohrer, Finlo. "Is the Facebook Movie the Truth about Mark Zuckerberg?" BBC News, September 30, 2010.

Romano, Aja. "Horror Movies Reflect Cultural Fears. In 2016, Americans Feared Invasion." Vox, December 21, 2016.

Romano, Evan. "This David Fincher Anheuser-Busch Super Bowl Ad Really Makes You Miss Beers with Friends." *Men's Health*, February 3, 2021.

Romero, Dennis. "After Arrest in Golden State Killer Case, Zodiac Killer Case Could Be Cracked by Decades-Old DNA." NBC News, May 5, 2018.

"Rooney Mara and David Fincher." *Interview*. November 28, 2011.

Rothman, Joshua. "What 'Gone Girl' Is Really About." *The New Yorker*, October 8, 2014.

Russell, Nicholas. "10 Years On: 'The Curious Case of Benjamin Button.'" Medium, December 25, 2018.

Salam, Maya. "What Is Toxic Masculinity?" *New York Times*, January 22, 2019.

Salisbury, Mark. "Seven Review." *Empire*, January 1, 2000.

———. "Transcript of *Guardian* Interview with David Fincher at BFI Southbank." *Guardian*. January 18, 2009.

Schwartz, Niles. "'Fuck You You Fucking Fuck': David Fincher's Cyber Fairy Tale of (Mis)Communication, 'The Girl With the Dragon Tattoo.'" The Niles Files, December 27, 2011.

Schwarzbaum, Lisa. "*Panic Room*: EW Review." *Entertainment Weekly*, March 27, 2002.

Scott, A. O. "FILM REVIEW; Luxury Home, Built-In Trouble." *New York Times*, March 29, 2002.

———. "It's the Age of a Child Who Grows from a Man." *New York Times*, December 24, 2008.

———. 2020. "'Mank' Review: A Rosebud by Any Other Name." *New York Times*, December 3, 2020.

———. "Tattooed Heroine Metes Out Slick, Punitive Violence." *New York Times*, December 19, 2011.

Seale, Jack. "Mindhunter Season Two Review – Still TV's Classiest Guilty Pleasure." *Guardian*, August 16, 2019.

Seitz, Matt Zoller. "Gone Girl." RogerEbert.com, October 2, 2014.

Semigran, Aly. "'The Girl with the Dragon Tattoo': Behind the Scenes of the Opening Credits." *Entertainment Weekly*, February 21, 2012.

Sepinwall, Alan. "'Mindhunter' Season 2: A Killer Instinct Slightly Softened." *Rolling Stone*, August 19, 2019.

Seymour, Tom. "The Real Mindhunters: Why 'Serial Killer Whisperers' Do More Harm than Good." *Guardian*, August 19, 2019.

Shooting "Panic Room.' Directed by David Prior. Culver City, CA: Columbia TriStar Home Entertainment, 2004.

Simpson, Philip L. *Psycho Paths: Tracking the Serial Killer Through Contemporary American Film and Fiction.* Carbondale, IL: SIU Press, 2000.

Sims, David. "'I'm Not Lamenting the Existence of Marvel.'" *The Atlantic*, December 4, 2020.

Smith, Gavin. "Inside Out: David Fincher." *Film Comment*, September–October 1999.

Stahl, Lynne. "Chronic Tomboys: Feminism, Survival, and Paranoia in Jodie Foster's Body of Work." *The Velvet Light Trap*, no. 77 (Spring 2016): 50–68.

Sterritt, David. "All in *The Game*." The Current (Criterion Collection), September 25, 2012.

Stimpson, Andrew. "20 Years On: Alien 3 Reassessed." *Quietus*, May 9, 2012.

Storius Magazine. "Fight Club Turns 20: Interview with the Film's Screenwriter Jim Uhls." Medium, October 7, 2019.

Svetkey, Benjamin. "How David Fincher Made 'Zodiac.'" *Entertainment Weekly*, February 23, 2007.

Szarvas, Réka. "Mad Housewife and Cool Girl: Gillian Flynn's Gone Girl as Feminist Metafiction." *Americana* XIV, no.2 (Fall 2018).

Tafoya, Scout. "The Unloved, Part 1: ALIEN 3." RogerEbert.com, December 1, 2013.

Tallerico, Brian. "Mindhunter Stakes Claim as Netflix's Best Drama." RogerEbert.com, August 16, 2019.

Taubin, Amy. "Chasing *Kane*: Amy Taubin on David Fincher's *Mank* (2020)." *Artforum*, December 3, 2020.

———. "Interview: David Fincher." *Film Comment*, January–February 2009.

———. "Interview: David Fincher." *Film Comment*, September 26, 2014.

———. "Se7en (1995): The Allure of Decay." Scraps from the Loft, April 18, 2017.

———. "Society Pages: Amy Taubin on The Social Network." *Artforum*, September 24, 2010.

Telaroli, Gina. "The Meaning of Money in The Game." The Current (Criterion Collection), October 7, 2020.

The Curious Birth of Benjamin Button. Directed by David Prior. Los Angeles: Dreamlogic Pictures, 2009.

"The Fincher Analyst." The Fincher Analyst. Accessed March 15, 2021.

"*The Game* Limited Edition [Blu-Ray]." London: Arrow Films, 2020.

The Making of 'Alien3.' Directed by Charles de Lauzirika. Los Angeles: 20th Century Fox Home Entertainment, 2003.

Tobias, Scott. "Fight Club at 20: The Prescience and Power of David Fincher's Drama." *Guardian*, October 15, 2019.

Tracy, Andrew. "11 Offenses of 2011." Reverse Shot (Museum of the Moving Image), January 6, 2012.

———. "F for Fake: Mank." *Cinema Scope*, April 30, 2021.

Travers, Peter. "Alien 3." *Rolling Stone*, September 9, 1992.

———. "Curious Case of Benjamin Button." *Rolling Stone*, December 25, 2008.

———. "'Gone Girl' Movie Review." *Rolling Stone*, September 23, 2014.

———. "Panic Room." *Rolling Stone*, March 29, 2002.

———. "The Social Network." *Rolling Stone*, October 15, 2010.

———. "Se7en." *Rolling Stone*, September 22, 1995.

———. "The Game." *Rolling Stone*, September 12, 1997.

Tyree, J. M. "Against the Clock: Slumdog Millionaire and The Curious Case of Benjamin Button." *Film Quarterly* 62, no. 4 (Summer 2009): 34–38.

Urbanek, Sydney. "What Happened Between Madonna and David Fincher?' Mononym Mythology, October 23, 2020.

VanDerWerff, Emily. "Gone Girl Is the Most Feminist Mainstream Movie in Years." Vox, October 6, 2014.

Vargas, Jose Antonio. "Mark Zuckerberg Opens Up." *The New Yorker*, September 20, 2010.

Ventura, Elbert. "The Curious Case of Benjamin Button." Reverse Shot (Museum of the Moving Image), December 23, 2008.

Vineyard, Jennifer. "*Gone Girl*'s Gillian Flynn on Cool Girls and David Fincher." Vulture, October 6, 2014.

Vishnevetsky, Ignatiy. "In the Process of the Investigation: David Fincher and 'The Girl with the Dragon Tattoo.'" Notebook (MUBI), December 13, 2011.

Watercutter, Angela. "'The Social Network' Was More Right Than Anyone Realized." *Wired*, February 5, 2019.

Weiner, Jonah. "David Fincher's Impossible Eye." *New York Times* magazine, November 19, 2020.

Weintraub, Steve "Frosty." "Julia Ormond Interview – THE CURIOUS CASE OF BENJAMIN BUTTON." Collider, January 5, 2009.

Westbrook, Caroline. "Panic Room Review." *Empire*, January 1, 2000.

Williams, David E. "*Seven*: Sins of a Serial Killer." *American Cinematographer*, June 1, 2017.

———. "Zodiac: Cold Case File." *American Cinematographer*, March 23, 2018.

Willmore, Alison. "Why The Social Network Feels Sharper Now Than It Did When It First Came Out." Vulture, June 17, 2020.

"Zodiac Killer." Biography, October 14, 2017. Updated December 14, 2020.

"Zodiac Movie vs. Zodiac Killer True Story - Real Robert Graysmith." History vs Hollywood. Accessed 11 May 2020.

FOR LITTLE WHITE LIES

Editor *David Jenkins*
Art Directors *Fabrizio Festa, Tertia Nash*
Designers *Olesia Lipskaia, Hannah Nightingale*
Head of Books *Clive Wilson*
Publisher *Vince Medeiros*

Research *Anna Swanson*
Transcription *Vikram Murthi*
Translation *Yoseob Shin*

FOR ABRAMS

Editor *Eric Klopfer*
Managing Editor *Mike Richards*
Design Manager *Diane Shaw*
Production Manager *Larry Pekarek*

COVER DESIGN BY
Fabrizio Festa/TCO London

ABOUT THE AUTHOR
Adam Nayman is a critic, lecturer and author who has written two other books for Abrams—*The Coen Brothers: This Book Really Ties the Films Together* and *Paul Thomas Anderson: Masterworks.* He lives in Toronto with his wife Tanya, their daughters Lea and Avery, and their cat River.

—

Library of Congress Control Number: 2021932419

ISBN: 978-1-4197-5341-1
eISBN: 978-1-64700-244-2

Printed and bound in the United States
10 9 8 7 6 5 4 3 2 1

ABRAMS The Art of Books
abramsbooks.com

195 Broadway
New York, NY 10007
abramsbooks.com